WOMEN

W9-CQA-521

Women who sell themselves to men, yet who retain a value money cannot buy . . . women who must submit to virtual slavery, yet who subtly assume power over their masters . . . women whose outward lives of idle elegance conceal inner lives of passionate perception and biting intelligence . . . women who hesitate on the threshold of freedom, torn between all they can be and all they have been told they are . . . women who discover that courage, daring, and authority do not belong to men alone . . .

These are among the women brought unforgettably to life by great writers the Western world has only recently come to know.

RICE BOWL WOMEN

Writings by and about the
Women of China and Japan

DOROTHY BLAIR SHIMER, until her retirement, taught Oriental literature in the Department of English at the University of Hawaii, and has had wide experience both traveling and sojourning in the Orient. She is a contributor of articles and reviews to literary journals in America and Asia, and was the editor of *The Mentor Book of Modern Asian Literature* as well as *Voices of Modern Asia.*

Women's Studies From MENTOR and SIGNET

(0451)

☐ **WOMAN IN SEXIST SOCIETY: Studies in Power and Powerlessness edited by Vivian Gornick and Barbara K. Moran.** Original work by anthropologists, sociologists, historians, literary critics, psychologists, artists, philosophers, and educators on every aspect of the women's liberation movement. "So full of new facts and moving insights, so reasoned, so free from rancor, so uniformly intelligent, that it makes for totally absorbing reading . . . the best try to date at undermining the conventional wisdom about women."— *Minneapolis Star.* (618831—$2.50)

☐ **THE EXPERIENCE OF THE AMERICAN WOMAN: 30 Stories edited by Barbara H. Solomon.** The American woman as she appears in American fiction from the first Victorian rebellion against conventional stereotypes to the most open manifestations of liberation today. Includes 30 stories by Kate Chopin, John Updike, Wright Morris, Jean Stafford, Tillie Olsen, Joyce Carol Oates, and others. (621158—$3.95)

☐ **DAUGHTERS & MOTHERS, MOTHERS & DAUGHTERS by Signe Hammer.** The first in-depth psychological study of the relationship between mothers and daughters examining the sex roles played by three generations of women. "Shows us how daughters do or do not free themselves emotionally from their mothers and thus shape their lives . . . a first. A must!"—Psychologist Lucy Freeman. (087216—$1.75)

☐ **A MARY WOLLSTONECRAFT READER edited and with an Introduction by Barbara H. Solomon and Paula S. Berggren.** This anthology of work by the great 18th century feminist, activist, and political philosopher includes excerpts from *A Vindication of the Rights of Men; A Vindication of the Rights of Women;* selections from her letters; the autobiographical *Mary, a Fiction;* the preface to her recently rediscovered pseudonymous work *The Female Reader;* and the complete text of *The Wrongs of Woman, or Maria.* Headnotes. Biographical data. Suggestions for further reading. Bibliography. Index. (621956—$3.95)

RICE BOWL WOMEN

*Writings by and about the
Women of China and Japan*

Edited with an Introduction and Notes,
by
Dorothy Blair Shimer

A MENTOR BOOK
NEW AMERICAN LIBRARY
TIMES MIRROR
New York and Scarborough, Ontario

Library of Congress Catalog Card Number: 81-85144

Acknowledgments

Tanka. From the Nippon Gakujutsu Shinkokai translation of *One
Thousanad Poems*, "The Manyoshu." Copyright 1965.

"The Story of Miss Li" by Po Hsing-Chien. Translated by Arthur
Waley. From *Anthology of Chinese Literature,* Volume 1, edited
by Cyril Birch. Reprinted by permission of Grove Press, Inc.
Copyright 1965 by Grove Press, Inc.

"The Story of Ts'ui Ying-ying" by Yüan Chen. Translated by
Arthur Waley. From *Anthology of Chinese Literature,* Volume
1, edited by Cyril Birch. Reprinted by permission of Grove
Press, Inc. Copyright 1965 by Grove Press, Inc.

"The Lady Who Was A Beggar," Anonymous. From *Stories from
a Ming Collection: Translations of Chinese Short Stories Published in the Seventeenth Century,* translated by Cyril Birch.
Reprinted by permission of Indiana University Press. Copyright
1958 by Cyril Birch.

"The Lady Knight-Errant" by P'u Sung Ling. From *Traditional
Chinese Stories: Themes and Variations,* edited by Ma and Lau.
Reprinted by permission of Columbia University Press. Copy-
right 1978 by Columbia University Press.

"Meng Xiangying Stands Up" by Zhao Shuli. From *Modern Chinese Stories* selected, edited, and translated by W.J.F. Jenner.
Reprinted by permission of Oxford University Press. Copyright
1970 Oxford University Press.

"Girl Rebel" by Adet and Anor Lin. Condensed from *Girl Rebel:
The Autobiography of Hsieh Pingying* (John Day Company).
Reprinted by permission of Harper & Row. Copyright 1940
Harper & Row.

"The Child-Bride" by Hsiao Hung. From *The Field of Life* and
Death and Tales of Hulan River, translated by Howard Goldblatt. Reprinted by permission of Indiana University Press.

"Slave's Mother" by Rou Shi. From *Modern Chinese Stories* selected, edited, and translated by W.J.F. Jenner. Reprinted by
permission of Oxford University Press. Copyright 1970 Oxford
University Press.

The following page constitutes an extension of the copyright page.

MENTOR TRADEMARK REG. U.S. PAT. OFF. AND FOREIGN COUNTRIES
REGISTERED TRADEMARK—MARCA REGISTRADA
HECHO EN WINNIPEG, CANADA

SIGNET, SIGNET CLASSICS, MENTOR, PLUME, MERIDIAN AND NAL BOOKS are published *in the United States* by
The New American Library, Inc.,
1633 Broadway, New York, New York 10019
in Canada by The New American Library of Canada Limited,
81 Mack Avenue, Scarborough, Ontario M1L 1M8

First Printing, April, 1982

2   3   4   5   6   7   8   9

Printed in Canada

Contents

JAPAN

Preface

The women of China and Japan—their hopes, dreams, disappointments, sufferings, and struggles for independence and recognition—are the subject of the stories and memoirs in this collection. Some were written anonymously—particularly the early Japanese selections. Some were written by women and a number by men. Together, they present valid and interesting insights into the lives of women of two closely associated cultures that have pursued very different courses, but whose early roots were intertwined.

I chose the title, *Rice Bowl Women* because rice is "the staff of life" for most of the peoples of Asia, and in the earliest mythologies of both China and Japan, rice plays a central role through imagery closely identified with the female world. In China, the Goddess of Mercy, Kuan Yin, is said to have fructified the young rice plants by enriching them with the milk from her breasts. Inari, Japan's God of Rice, is usually represented as a bearded man, but the deity is sometimes also depicted as a goddess whose crops are guarded by her fox messenger.

The rice bowl—whether full or reduced to a pitiful scattering of grains—has become the Asian symbol of traditional womanhood, of hospitality, security, and hope. Whether of simple baked clay or finest porcelain, the rice bowl remains as it has throughout history at the center of traditional households of every social level. To a modern woman attempting to break from binding tradition, the rice bowl may symbolize all that is restrictive and crippling from the past.

The tradition of the rice culture has given women distinct qualities that this anthology attempts to capture. The stories are from an eastern harvest that may bring a very different reaping from that of the West. As the contemporary Japanese poet Takamura Kotaro (1883-1956) wrote, this literature is not part of the West with its "physiology of wheatmeal and cheese and entrecotes", but rather,

> [It] is born at the farthest limits of the far east
> Bred on rice and malt and soya beans and the
> flesh of fish . . .

So this anthology is not intended as a work of scholarship. Selection has been subjective and not based solely on critical evaluation by scholars in the field. The background notes give information concerning customs and conditions but are not meant to be definitive. An entire book could be written about the women writers of Heian Japan, for instance, so dominant were they in the literary scene of their time. But this is not such a book.

Readers will note two different forms of spelling among the stories from China. I have carried over the romanization used by the several translators and have not attempted to resolve the differences between the present official usage and the Wade-Giles system in use from the mid-nineteenth century until 1978, when China's State Council adopted what is called *pinyin* as a standard for romanization. Under the new system, for example, Peking becomes Beijin, Mao Tse-tung becomes Mao Zedong, and Chou En-lai becomes Zhou Enlai. I assume these matters of style do not concern us here.

The names of all authors are given in the order customary in their homelands—that is, family name preceding given name.

Finally, I should like to express my appreciation to the University of Hawaii for the resources of its Asia collection; to Hawaii Loa College, Kaneohe, Hawaii, for opening its library to me "without let or hindrance"; to my husband, Elizabeth Erwin and Sue Kain, for helping to prepare the manuscript; and to the Community Church of Honolulu for generously providing duplicating facilities.

INTRODUCTION

Though, waiting for you to come,
I put your rice in the bowl
And stand outside by the gate,
You come not home, Arao!

from *The Manyōshu*

China has an extremely old culture, and her people have been blessed with a meticulous sense of history. It is best to say "sense" because fact is often liberally mixed with fiction, so that we must beware of being too ready to take historical records at face value. Nevertheless, China has been acclaimed for having the world's earliest and best preserved written annals.

The earliest surviving Chinese writing dates from about 1400 B.C. Early writers made their inscriptions on any material that lay at hand, progressing from tortoise shells and shoulder blades of oxen to strips of bamboo, then advancing to silk, and finally to paper. And the Chinese proved to be inveterate writers. Not only did they write, but they treasured what they had set down. In early eras when other cultures, such as those of India and Rome, were dependent upon memorized records, the Chinese were diligently etching, inscribing, and in later periods wielding their brushes to record fact and fancy. It is no wonder that China became the seminal influence for vast areas around her. The effects would be especially marked on her neighbor Japan.

1

The Chinese language itself—written and spoken—was to be of major importance in the development of Japanese culture. It has been to Japan what Latin was to Medieval Europe and what Sanskrit was to the subcontinent of India. For centuries in Japan, Chinese was thought to be the only worthy medium for all literature, except poetry, and it remained the means of written communication in court and government circles until comparatively recent times.

Today's spoken Japanese bears little resemblance to the dialects of China, but the calligraphies are still closely related. Japanese prose expression remained wedded to Chinese for centuries. However, the Japanese—to whom poetic expression has had a universal and deeply personal appeal—developed a distinctive language of poetry that deliberately excluded Chinese words, while at the same time retaining and further developing the Chinese poetic forms and elliptical expressions.

Certain basic philosophical concepts beloved of the Chinese have been shared by the Japanese. Since they are reflected in the writings that follow, some attention should be given to them here, especially as they pertain to the lives of the women of the two cultures.

The concept of two opposite but complementary, rather than opposing, forces whose interaction governs all life, is so old that its origin is lost in time. The Chinese believed that life arose from these reciprocating powers—the *yin* and the *yang*—and through them was motivated and developed.

A Chinese creation myth says, "In the beginning there was *Yang-yin*, the active and the passive, the male and the female. . . . The power that is *Yang*, the receptivity that is *Yin*, can never be added to, never taken away from: in these two principles is the All."[1]

Not only do these opposites create the dynamism on which life depends, but—as the accompanying illustration makes clear—each has within it the seed of the other. This is perhaps the most important part of the *yin-yang* concept. In accord with such belief, life assumes a serenity and staying power that explains much in China's literature and in her cultural and political history. If times are bad, we need but wait until

[1] Padraic Colum, *Myths of the World* (New York: Grosset and Dunlap, 1930), p. 237.

the seed of prosperity has fructified and we shall again experience well-being. If the nation is embroiled in war, we shall surely, in due time, know peace. Carried into our contemporary social sphere, we may see an interesting relationship to present-day thinking about the sexes: that the female possesses certain strengths of the male, and the male shares in the sensitivity and the "yieldingness" of the female.

The *yin-yang* principle continues to pervade Chinese life and thought. It is basic to *kung-fu* (the art of self-defense), tied into the medical practices of acupuncture, and finds a certain affinity with Marxist dialectical materialism. It may even be evident in the chef's or housewife's balance of foods in meal preparation.

The *yin-yang* concept had special appeal to the Japanese from the earliest times of interaction with China. As early as the *Nihongi* records of eighth-century Japan, this Chinese philosophy had been tied in with the purported origins of all things when "Heaven and Earth were not yet separated, and the *yin* and the *yang* not yet divided." By the Heian period, preoccupation with the *yin-yang* governed Japanese daily life. Room furnishings had to be placed to assure *yin-yang* balance, and food was prepared with similar concern. Diviners determined auspicious times for travel abroad when the "Five Elements" (wind, fire, earth, metal, water) would be in favorable relationship. A *yin-yang* department helped to assure that the government performed in proper balance.

From earliest times, family has been regarded as the cen-

tral unit of Chinese society—a family unit very different
from that of the West. When we speak of "family" in the
Chinese and Japanese context, we must set aside the limited
parent-child pattern that holds in most Western cultures. The
most important and cohesive of all social groupings in China,
India, Japan, and other Asian cultures is the extended family
in which several generations live together under one roof or
in one compound. Although today this structure is giving
way, especially in urban settings, a sense of inclusive family
remains strong.

The Chinese early refined the hierarchy of family, strictly
ordering relationships and their respective loyalties. According to Fung Yu-lan, a contemporary Chinese philosopher, there are now over a hundred terms used to define the
various family relationships. The sage Confucius (c. 551–479
B.C.), whose teachings became the basis of an ethical system
that was to dominate Chinese life for centuries, expounded at
great length on family relationships, respect for ancestors,
and reciprocity of ruler and subject. On the matter of family,
including respect for the ancestors, Confucius was explicit
and firm. He regarded all other relationships and loyalties as
stemming from those of the family. The ruler's love and
concern for his people must be as that of father for son. The
people's loyalty and respect for their ruler must be as that of
son for father. With these conditions recognized and adhered
to, all life would be well ordered.

The teachings of Confucius were long known in Japan and
in the sixteenth century they were given official standing by
the Tokugawa Shogunate. The divinely mandated rule of the
Emperor, as defined by Confucius, remained intact in Japan
until the Allied Occupation following World War II, though
it had begun to wane in China from the time of the establishment of the Ch'ing (Manchu) dynasty in the seventeenth
century.

But it was in family-life patterns that Confucianism was to
have its primary impact on the masses of the people in both
China and Japan. *The Analects* (a compendium of the sayings
and teachings of Confucius, dating from the first century
A.D.) has much to say about the relationship of father to son
and brother to brother. Although women may be subsumed

in occasional inclusive terms—such as "parents" or "ancestors"—their very absence from specific mention gives us a sense of the unimportance of women in Confucian thought.

The ancestors were to be revered through the carrying out of clearly defined rituals. Rites were to be led by the elder son, the other sons following in accordance with their age rank. Sons are even today of first importance in Confucian families, for it is upon them that the family's moral life depends. Among sons, as between child and parent, there is respect for status. Confucian tradition maintains remarkable vitality even in the face of direct assault from Communist leaders in China and the day-to-day erosion wrought by influences from the West in both China and Japan. In fact, so generally unsuccessful was the attack on Confucius carried out during the supremacy of Mao Tse-tung's ideology, that in recent years the Old Master has been restored to at least a modicum of respectability.

What of the place of women in the Confucian family? As may be inferred from what has been said concerning the importance of sons, daughters traditionally have been subjects more of sufferance than of joy. In early Chinese history, female infanticide was so prevalent that the philosopher-legalist Han Fei Tzu (d. 233 B.C.) was justified in writing:

> When a boy is born, the father and mother congratulate each other, but if a girl is born they put it to death. . . . The reason for this difference in treatment is that the parents are thinking of their later convenience, and calculating what will ultimately bring them profit.[2]

Ruth Benedict, noted American anthropologist, in 1944 was assigned by the U.S. Office of War Information to make a study of Japanese culture that would help Occupation forces to understand the nature of the people with whom they would be dealing. Even in the Japan of that time, Dr. Benedict found that "whatever one's age, one's position in the hierarchy depends on whether one is male or female. . . . The Japanese daughter of the family must get along as best she

---

[2] H. G. Creel, *Chinese Thought from Confucius to Mao Tse-tung* (New York: New American Library, 1953), p. 123.

can while the presents, the attentions, and the money for education go to her brothers."[3]

Nonetheless, daughters have been lucrative commodities. In earlier times, aristocratic families in both China and Japan found daughters valuable in forming profitable political and financial alliances. In early Japan families such as the Fujiwara achieved tremendous power by marrying their daughters into the imperial line. If first marriages could not be arranged, attractive girls could be placed as second or third wives or as concubines, who were an accepted part of the family unit. In China, progeny of such liaisons were regarded as children of the first wife and addressed her as "mother." In the lower classes, daughters could be sold as servants or as prostitutes. As some of the stories that follow will indicate, these practices are not entirely defunct today.

The arranged marriage remains even to the present time a part of the social pattern in most of Asia. A visitor to Japan in September and October will be aware of the flurry of activity during this marriage season, as *miai* parties are arranged by college professors, relatives, friends, or hired "go-betweens" on behalf of marriage-minded families. Although young people now have more opportunities to meet outside the home, especially on college campuses and in business situations, a majority still defer to family control in marital arrangements. Situations are managed so that young people have opportunity to meet and socialize to a certain extent before an agreement is formalized, and opposition on either side is generally respected. Under the present government in China, arranged marriage is officially a thing of the past. The marriage law of the People's Republic, adopted in 1950, includes these provisions:

> Article 1: The feudal marriage system based on arbitrary and compulsory arrangements and the supremacy of man over woman, and in disregard of the interests of children is abolished.
>
> The New-Democratic marriage system, which is based on the free choice of partners, on monogamy, on equal

---

[3] Ruth Benedict, *The Chrysanthemum and the Sword* (New York: World Publishing Co., 1967), p. 53.

rights for both sexes, and on the protection of the lawful interests of women and children, is put into effect.

Article 2: Bigamy, concubinage, child betrothal, interference in the remarriage of widows, and the exaction of money or gifts in connection with marriages, are prohibited.

Equal rights and responsibilities are then defined by the law, mutually agreed upon divorce is provided for, but then the State steps in to enforce some rather arbitrary determents:

No man or woman is allowed to marry in any of the following instances:

a) Where the man and woman are lineal relatives by blood or where the man and woman are brother and sister born of the same parents or where the man and woman are half-brother and half-sister. The question of prohibiting marriage between collateral relatives by blood (up to the fifth degree of relationship) is determined by custom.[4]

b) Where one party, because of certain physical defects, is sexually impotent.

c) Where one party is suffering from venereal disease, mental disorder, leprosy or any other disease which is regarded by medical science as rendering a person unfit for marriage.[5]

Lao-Tzu, an older contemporary of Confucius, emphasized a very different philosophy. It surfaces in some of the early Chinese stories in this collection that refer to Taoism, Taoist priests, and the way of life emphasized in the famous *Tao Te Ching*, or *Book of Lao Tzu*. Although no specific dating gives us this direction, it might well be that Lao Tzu's sayings were a response to the teachings of Confucius—actually a rebellion against them. For, where Confucius stresses order, duty, proper ritual, and strict adherence to the hierarchically structured family and society, Lao Tzu dwells on the *Tao*—"The Way"—a concept as deeply imbedded in Chinese thought, perhaps, as the idea of the *yin-yang*. Although the

---

[4] Probably refers to the customs of "minority nationalities" for whom "certain modifications" may be made.

[5] *The Marriage Law of the People's Republic of China* (Peking: Foreign Language Press, 1973), pp. 1-2.

Tao has the attributes of a supreme moral force, it cannot
be defined, nor can absolutes guide us in The Way. We must
come by it through the natural process of things. Further-
more, the *Tao Te Ching* is female-centered. The inactive,
the soft, the yielding, the empty—i.e., the female—are those
attributes that will overcome that which is hard, adamant,
full—i.e., male. The ambiguity that exists in living with these
teachings alongside the Confucian has never been resolved.
Indeed, we might suspect that the Chinese would see no reason to attempt to resolve the basic differences between the
strict order of the Confucian world and the "natural flow" of
the Taoist, because this is simply what life is. The opening of
the *Tao Te Ching* sums up the basic concepts:

> The way that can be told
> Is not the constant way;
> The name that can be named
> Is not the constant name.
> The nameless was the beginning of heaven and earth;
> The named was the mother of the myriad creatures . . .
> These two are the same
> But diverge in name as they issue forth.
> Being the same they are called mysteries,
> Mystery upon mystery—
> The gateway of the manifold secrets.[6]

Again and again emphasis is on the femaleness of things:

> The spirit of the valley never dies.
> This is called the mysterious female.
> The gateway of the mysterious female
> Is called the root of heaven and earth.
> Dimly visible, it seems as if it were there,
> Yet use will never drain it.[7]

Finally:

> Know the Male
> But keep to the role of the Female . . .

[6] *Lao Tzu: Tao Te Ching,* D. C. Lau, trans. (Baltimore, Md.: Penguin
Books, 1963), Book One, I, p. 57.
[7] *Ibid.,* Book One, VI, p. 62.

Know the white [i.e., male]
But keep to the role of the black [i.e., female]
And be a model to the empire. . . .[8]

Implicit here is a concept rooted in the *yin-yang*, a philosophy related to "The Middle Way," or what the Greeks called "moderation in all things." The Middle Way is the center course between extremes. The extremes in Chinese thought are the opposite forces of the *yin* and the *yang*. Although the *yin* represents the negative, dark, weak, retrogressive, female aspects of life, it does not by any means follow that the *yin* should be destroyed. On the contrary, the affirmation, the creativeness, the light, the male aspects of *yang* require the balancing nature of *yin*. The two are oppositions held in balance, necessary to each other, following corresponding, parallel, and nondiverging courses which nevertheless react and mutually influence and provide the dynamism for all life. The *I Ching* (*Book of Changes*) provides a formula for the production of all creatures: "A round of *Yin* and then a round of *Yang* equals the *Tao*."

The teachings of Taoism, that emphasized the importance of living in harmony with nature and following the natural flow of things, had special appeal to the Japanese ethos, while its teachings on the importance of the individual did not. The Taoist stress on silent, wordless communication would reach its apogee in the Zen school of Buddhism, now so important a part of Japanese culture. During the Heian period, Japanese imperial society found especially appealing the Taoist concept that frequent sexual intercourse with a variety of partners had therapeutic medical advantages. The teaching carried with it the idea that the woman, as well as the man, should realize satisfaction in the sex act.

A later influence that China would share with Japan was that of Buddhism. Buddhism entered China early in the first century A.D., brought in by missionaries from India and later by emissaries sent to India by Chinese emperors who had become interested in Indian religious thought. It was the popular Mahayana form of Buddhism that had special appeal for the Chinese, rather than the esoteric Theravada, which predominated in India, Sri Lanka, and Southeast Asia. China of-

[8] *Ibid.,* Book One, XXVIII, p. 85.

fered a fertile soil for Mahayana Buddhism, which set aside
scriptural learning for direct perception. Buddhahood was ac-
cessible to all, not just to a coterie of the intellectually elite.
Silent meditation, master with pupil, set the climate for
wordless transmission of thought from mind to mind. The
mind, deliberately emptied of thought, was open to sudden
enlightenment. We can recognize how simple the transition
would be from Taoism to Buddhism, given this wordless way.
In its combination of Buddhist and Taoist philosophies, the
Ch'an school emphasized enlightenment attained through
meditation in which the individual realized kinship with
other, nonhuman aspects of nature. The importance placed
on action without effort and teaching without words provided
a natural transition for the Chinese, who had long previous experience with Taoism's "natural way"—the "way of nature."
The Ch'an school of Buddhism would become the Zen of
Japan, which has entered so many aspects of Japanese life,
from flower arrangement to *haiku* poetry.

Certain generally shared concepts of Buddhism are evident
in many of the selections that follow and probably should be
defined here:

> *Nirvana*—Release from the wheel of rebirth, suffering,
> and ignorance; full enlightenment.
> *Karma*—Law of causality, of ethical consequences of
> one's acts in successive existences.
> *Dharma*—Norm of Buddhist conduct; law of righteous-
> ness; one's fate and one's duty, affected by *Karma*.
> *Enlightenment*—The final illumination or understanding.
> *Reincarnation*—Rebirth of the soul in successive bodies,
> affected by *Karma*.
> *Bodhisattva*—An enlightened being; one who refuses to
> attain *Nirvana* in order to help others along the way.

In so dwelling on the influences that have come to Japan
from China we run the danger of implying that Japan's culture is completely borrowed or that the various "borrowings"
from China have been totally unassimilated. Intermittently
Japanese rulers sent delegations to China (the first in A.D.
57) deliberately seeking out the richness of the Chinese heritage. Equally deliberately, however, the country was every so
often sealed off from outside contact, giving time for "Japon-

ization" of the new thoughts and ways, absorption into the thought and life patterns indigenous to the Japanese people.

The Tale of Genji (see pages 245–267) reflects the intense isolation of the early Heian period. When its author, Lady Murasaki, was born, circa A.D. 976, the country had been "sealed off" by government edict for almost a hundred years. There had been a similar move after the adoption of Buddhism as a state religion midway in the sixth century, and there would be a complete retreat from foreign contact after the growth of Christianity in the Nagasaki area late in the eighteenth century, not to be broken until Admiral Perry guided an American fleet into Nagasaki harbor in 1853.

The American demand that Japan open itself to navigation and trade followed on the heels of earlier efforts to establish economic ties with the reclusive islanders. From 1739 Russia had made recurring efforts to establish ties, and a British forced entry into the port of Nagasaki in 1808 had resulted in the shamed suicide of the port commissioner. During these periods, foreign influences were digested and acted upon by indigenous elements with the result that a distinctively "Japonized" life pattern emerged.

But the gods of Shinto had been with the people of Japan from the earliest time and every aspect of life had to come under the influence of this religion that was more than a religion; it was a prevailing life attitude. For a period after the introduction of Buddhism, "The Way of the Gods" was submerged, but gradually an accommodation was made between the two, as it would have to be made with any other influences from outside.

Of special interest here is the centrality of the female in Shinto thought. The Sun Goddess was chief deity of both nature and ancestors. It was she who guided the fortunes of both individual and nation. It was natural, then, that women should be well placed in Shinto leadership and that shrines scattered about the countryside should have women among the lay priesthood. Although the West is best acquainted with Shinto as the "state religion" of Japan that came to be closely associated with national chauvinism and militarism, this is a false skewing of its nature. To be sure, early in the nineteenth century Shinto experienced a revival that brought together Shinto mythology and Confucian ethics of the *bushidō* school ("Way of the Warrior") to form a nationally adopted state religion, but the animistic and nature-oriented early expression is that which most permeates Japanese life and thought.

A religion of no written precepts or creed, Shinto nevertheless has commanded adaptation from every formalized religion with which the Japanese have been involved. Buddhist temples give shelter to a host of unassuming Shinto shrines gathered about them, with the priests often serving both temple and shrines. A Christian or civil marriage will be followed by a Shinto ceremony presided over by a priest guiding the family in prayer and concluding with the young couple's drinking rice wine together. *Then* a marriage is truly sanctified.

A characteristically feminine observance of Shinto is typified in this fairly recent news item:

> About 200 kimono-clad young Japanese women visited a Shintō shrine in Tokyo's Shibuya district Saturday to honor the needle.
>
> They were observing Harikuyo, a custom dating back hundreds of years in which Japanese women express their gratitude to the needle for its hard work during the past year.
>
> While white-robed Shintō priests prayed, women silently stuck thousands of used needles, one by one, into a huge piece of bean curd . . . to give the tiny sewing tools a soft place to rest after their year's toil.
>
> After the needles were blessed the women carried them back to the school grounds. They will be buried there so that they may rest peacefully throughout eternity.[9]

Truly, Shinto permeates every aspect of life, finding a place for all elements, from the sewing needle to majestic Mount Fuji.

A final brief word should be given to the status of women in present-day Japan. With the adoption in 1947 of a constitution, based largely on American-oriented democratic design, came a bicameral legislature, recognition of the sovereignty of the people, establishment of a Supreme Court, provision for freedom in labor unionization, and democratization of the economic structure. Borrowed from the British was the limi-

---

[9] *The Honolulu Advertiser,* Hawaii, December 10, 1973.

tation of the power of the Emperor to that of a constitutional monarch. From the depths of the war-ravaged national ethos came a constitutionally mandated renunciation of war.

Included in the provision for the sovereignty of the people was the franchise for women. Since that time women have taken many roles outside the home that were previously closed to them. In the early exuberance accompanying their liberation an encouraging number of women were elected to local, prefectural, and national positions of leadership. There has been some drawing back since those early days, but women are more and more looking beyond the traditional roles, entering colleges and universities—many of them now coeducational—for professional training to take on new roles in society. Rural women of both China and Japan, as is true in most societies, continue much in the old patterns, tending the hearth, working the fields, nurturing the silk worm, filling the family's rice bowls. But all lives, in varying degrees, have been affected by the winds of change. Stories of the modern period give some sense of the tensions between old and new and of the courses women are pursuing to resolve those tensions—or, at the very least, to work out lives that will satisfy the demands of new times.

CHINA

T'ANG DYNASTY

618–905

The three-hundred-year span of the T'ang Dynasty, following a long period of social and political disunity, was marked by a refreshing sense of peace and prosperity, and a concentration on culture and the arts—especially poetry and painting. Prose fiction consisted of stories of the macabre and the occult, but reflections of real life situations and concerns began to emerge, and the T'ang era is now recognized as the birth period of the short story form in Chinese literature.

Buddhism and Taoism set the cultural norms, although Confucian precepts were sustained in the home and in the imperial bureaucracy, chiefly by means of the civil service examinations taken by young men seeking much-coveted government appointments that would determine future prestige and wealth. Although the examination system was egalitarian in that it permitted young men of any social level to contend, it was not open to women. Women, in general, received little formal instruction. Nevertheless, many were undoubtedly keen, and some may well have learned while their menfolk were instructed. One of the stories that follows tells of a former prostitute who coaches a young man for a successful examination competition.

Beauty in all its manifestations was the hallmark of the T'ang period—in the person, the home, nature, and every expression of the arts. Great works of art and architecture, as well as literature, enriched the lives of the people and honored the Buddha. Unfortunately, one beauty fetish of the time was to inflict daily agony on generations of Chinese

women. Emperor Li Hou-chu is said to have requested
a beautiful court dancer to make her already tiny feet
even smaller by binding them with silken ribbons so that
she might dance on a golden lotus. The Emperor was so enchanted by the results that it became court custom, and
thereafter girls of all wellborn families had their feet bound
at the age of three or four to achieve "three-inch golden
lotuses." It is difficult to appreciate the excruciating pain
caused by bending the toes back onto the sole of the foot and
then bandaging the foot tightly. But this agony was only the
prelude to a life-long crippling that would make it virtually
impossible for women to walk unassisted. The struggle
against one of society's cruelest forms of oppression has carried into the present century, as the excerpts from *Girl Rebel*
indicate. Not only the highborn suffered from this practice,
but poor working women as well. They could not afford to
have their feet bound for they had to bear their share of the
family's work, and not being "beautified," they were therefore
visibly bound to a lifetime of "ugliness" and social inferiority.

The T'ang stories that follow present an interesting mix of
Confucian/Taoist/Buddhist elements and cultural patterns—
expressed in an early use of the colloquial language that con-
tributes to their unusual sense of reality. Many of them are
dominated by strong, independent, "activist" women rarely
found in later periods.

"Red Thread Maiden," one of the best-known stories of
early China and the subject of a popular opera, inverts the
social structure and depicts a woman excelling in a male role,
explaining the phenomenon in terms of the Buddhist concept
of reincarnation.

"Story of Everlasting Sorrow" is another much-loved story,
the inspiration of many later poems, plays, dances, and
volumes of scholarly commentary. In an entertaining package
it combines concubinage, governmental corruption, and the
occult.

The custom of the civil service examinations is central in
"The Story of Miss Li." The protagonist is a prostitute who
first destroys a young scholar both socially and financially,
then rescues him and sees him through his civil service examinations with highest honors. The story is notable for its realism and its authentic revelation of customs of the times.

"The Story of Ts'ui Ying'ying" is another famous in early

Chinese literature. Central here is an independent young woman who first repels the advances of a young man, then passionately gives herself to him, but refuses marriage. Again, the civil service examination experience is central to this story of separated lovers. Note the judgment of the scholar Chang in this story that "any unique feminine creature ordered by providence will bring ruin to others if it does not wreck itself." Unique, nonsterotypical action on the part of a woman, it seems, will inevitably lead to catastrophe.

Red Thread Maiden

Yüan Chiao

According to Elizabeth Te-Chen Wang, translator and editor of *Ladies of the Tang*, this story is taken from a volume of short stories, *Kan Tse Yao*, by Yüan Chiao. However, a later collection, published in the Ming period, attributes the story to Yang Chü-yüan, a foremost poet of the early ninth century.

———

In the household of General Hsueh Sung, the military governor of Luchow, lived the maid Red Thread. Because Red Thread was well grounded in the classics as well as in letter writing, Hsueh appointed her as his personal secretary and put her in charge of his documents and correspondence. But he was particularly fond of her for another reason. She was good at music and could tell the emotional state of the player by listening to the tune of a musical instrument.

One day General Hsueh gave a feast for his staff members and the soldiers under his command. Red Thread was ordered to be present. While she was enjoying the musical performance, she noticed something wrong with the drummer.

"Something sad is on the drummer's mind," she remarked, "for the tune of the drum is sorrowful."

Hsueh Sung also understood music; he agreed with Red Thread and said, "I think so." He then summoned the drummer and questioned him.

The drummer was frightened. "My wife died last night," he murmured, with tears in his eyes. "Since I dare not ask for leave, I cannot control my grief when I beat the drum. Please forgive me if I have offended Your Excellency." Hsueh immediately gave him leave to go to the funeral.

It was during the period of Chih Teh, right after the rebellion led by An Lu-shan, and everything was not yet restored to order. Along the Yangtze and Yellow Rivers there still existed unrest and fighting, for the warlords did not trust one another and constantly made trouble. In addition to General Hsueh Sung, the most powerful and notable military governors were General Tien Cheng-tze of Weipo and General Ling-Hu Chang of Huachow.

Although the Emperor had put Hsueh Sung in charge of the newly organized Chaoyi Regiment with orders to set up his headquarters in Fuyang in order to control the whole of Shantung province, it was still doubtful whether there could be peaceful coexistence between the three rampant warlords. To pacify them the Emperor had arranged for the daughter of Hsuh Sung to wed the son of Tien Cheng-tze, and for Hsueh's son to marry the daughter of Ling-Hu Chang. Messengers and presents were sent back and forth, and there was superficial harmony among the three states.

Then Tien Cheng-tze fell ill with a kind of sickness caused by the bad weather. He felt worse during the summertime. "If I can change my office with Hsueh Sung and move to Shantung, where the weather is much cooler," he thought to himself, "I probably can cure my disease and live a few years longer." With this in mind, he conscripted three thousand soldiers, ten times braver than the ones he already had, and gave them special training. He paid them well and called them Outside Guards. Each night he ordered three hundred of them to take turns guarding his residence. A lucky date was chosen; he intended to move to Luchow by any means. This meant that an open conflict would occur between Weipo and Luchow.

When Hsueh Sung heard of the intention of General Tien,

he was surprised and worried, not because he did not want to have a fight with his kinsman, but because the troops he had were getting old and could not compete with the fresh soldiers of the Outside Guards. He did not know what to do except to worry all day long.

It was midnight. The gates of the headquarters were bolted. Hsueh Sung, cane in hand, was pacing agitatedly along the corridors of the courtyard. He had no other attendant besides Red Thread. "Why is it that Your Lordship has not slept or eaten well for the entire past month?" asked Red Thread. "Is it due to something from the neighboring state?"

"A big affair that concerns the safety of the whole country is something that you cannot understand," answered Hsueh Sung.

"Though I am a bondmaid, perhaps I know how to lift the burden from the mind of Your Lordship."

Hsueh Sung confided the whole story to her. "I inherited this command from my father and would like to keep it till the end of my life and bestow it on my son. If I lose this, I will lose everything."

"It is a simple matter and should not worry Your Lordship," said Red Thread. "Just let me go to Weipo to make a reconnaissance. I shall leave here at the first watch and come back by the third. Please prepare a good horse and a friendly letter and wait till my return."

"You mean you have a special skill that can enable you to venture on a trip to General Tien's region from such a distance at such an hour? Then you must be a supernatural being. I should have discovered that before. But what if you fail? Then he will send his troops here even sooner."

"I have never failed and I shall not fail this time."

Red Thread then went back to her own chamber and changed her costume. She wound her long hair into a knot and pinned it up with a golden hairpin made into the shape of a phoenix and covered her head with a red scarf. Donning an embroidered purple robe and a pair of black shoes, she hung around her waist a dagger that bore the sign of a dragon. On her forehead she wrote the name of the god Tai Yi to guard her from evil spirits. She saluted Hsueh Sung and at once disappeared.

Hsueh Sung walked into his room and, closing the door,

sat down in tense silence, with his back to the candlelight. He drank a dozen cups of wine, but felt neither drunk nor sleepy. As he was waiting in suspense, he heard the distant sound of the morning horn. A sudden breeze rustled by and a leaf fell from a dewy tree. Before he had time to wonder what it was, Red Thread was already standing in front of him. Hsueh Sung was in rapture.

"Was everything all right?" asked he.

"How dare I fail to carry out a mission for Your Lordship?"

"Did you do any killing?"

"No, I only took a golden box from beneath General Tien's pillow."

She gave the golden box to Hsueh Sung and then described her trip.

"About three quarters of an hour before midnight I arrived at General Tien's residence. I passed through several court-yards and finally reached his bedroom. His Outside Guards were sleeping in the corridors, snoring like thunder. Other soldiers were pacing in the courtyard so vigilant that a wisp of breeze would start them shooting. But I made no noise as I opened the door and approached General Tien's bed. When I lifted the bed curtains, I saw old General Tien sound asleep on a rhinoceros-horn pillow, with his chest uncovered. His hair was bound up in a piece of yellow silk. Beside his pillow there lay a sword with seven stars carved on it, and in front of the sword there lay a golden box containing the eight char-acters of his horoscope and the name of the god of the North Pole.

"How foolish he was to lie inside such a comfortable jade-like curtain, without any fear or concern! Never would he believe in his orchid-perfumed dream that his life rested in my hands. It would have been so easy for me to make sport of him by capturing him and then setting him free again, but I did not do that for fear that it might cause Your Lordship further trouble. I stood and gazed at him for a while until the candle gradually burnt out and the incense in the precious burner was almost extinguished.

"All of General Tien's bodyguards and servants were get-ting drowsy. Some rested their heads against the screens. Oth-ers leaned on their weapons and covered themselves with hand towels. I pulled the hairpin from one and touched the clothes of another, but they all slept like sick men or drunkards. Finally I took the golden box from beside General Tien's pillow and left the city of Wei by the west gate. After I had walked two hundred *li* away, I looked back and saw the bronze casement towering among the clouds above the Chang River, which runs eastward. It was beautiful to see the morning breeze beginning to stir the grass and flowers of the wild meadows and the declining moon half hidden by the tall trees.

"I was so glad to be back that I entirely forgot my worries and the fatigue of the strenuous trip. It makes me feel happy to be of a little service to you to repay some of your kindness. To show my gratitude to you is the main reason that I ran the risk of entering an enemy state, passing five or six cities, and completing a trip of about seven hundred *li* in three watches' time. I did this to lessen your grief, so I have no complaint."

Hsueh Sung hurriedly dispatched a messenger on the horse that he had prepared, giving him the letter that he had written. The letter was for Governor Tien, and it read:

"Last night a guest came from Your Lordship's headquarters and presented me with a golden box which he said he took from beneath your pillow. As your humble relative, how can I accept such a gift which is so precious and important to you? Therefore, I am sending it back with my best regards."

The messenger galloped as fast as he could. When he reached Weipo at daybreak, he found General Tien's headquarters in great confusion searching for the missing golden box. Everyone was under suspicion. The messenger hammered on the gate with his horsewhip and asked for the governor. Tien Cheng-tze immediately came out and, upon receiving the box, was terrified to think that someone could steal anything from beneath his pillow. The man who dared to do this must be of unsurpassable courage and skill, and could easily have cut his head off. He decided that he had better be loyal to General Hsueh from that time on, since the latter possessed such a magically endowed knight.

Governor Tien therefore invited the messenger to stay in his residence, treating him to a big feast and giving him many gifts. Next day, upon sending the messenger back, he presented to Governor Hsueh thirty thousand pieces of fine silk, two hundred good horses, and many other presents. He also wrote an exceedingly polite letter to Governor Hsueh:

"My life was at the mercy of a man from your state last night. As a relative, you have been very kind to me. How can I do anything that might cause you great concern? Please suspect me no more. The so-called Outside Guards were trained to deal with robbers and bandits only. Now I have discharged them and sent them back to their farms in order to show you my cooperation. From now on I shall be at your service. If you care to give any orders, I shall follow your carriage to carry them out; and if you ever come to my humble state, I shall stand by to watch your horse for you."

Thus the two governors were reconciled. Greetings were exchanged frequently, and the tension eased between the south and the north sides of the Yellow River.

A month or so later Red Thread asked for leave. "You were reared in my house," exclaimed Hsueh Sung. "Where can you go? Moreover, you have done me a great favor and I depend upon you for my safety. How can I let you go?"

But Red Thread told him:

"I was a man in my previous life, an herb doctor who wandered from village to village to cure people with prescriptions from the book of Shen Lung. One day I ran across a pregnant woman suffering from a kind of dropsy. I gave her some wine made of a certain kind of flower that caused her death and the death of her unborn twins. My mistake in killing three persons with one dose was reported to the king of the underworld, and as punishment I was reincarnated as a woman in this life. I was moreover punished by being born a lowbred maid with an ill star of ability to act like a burglar. It was fortunate that I was sold to your house. For nineteen years I have been so well treated that I have even tired of the soft dresses that you give me and the delicious food I have eaten day after day. You have been exceedingly kind to me. I was even honored by being appointed your personal secretary.

"Because our country has just survived the calamity of rebellion, I hated to see the warlords make trouble again and endanger the peace and safety of the whole nation. So I went to Weipo to give General Tien a warning. I did that to repay your kindness and to avoid a civil war which would no doubt destroy thousands of lives. My little deed of saving two states from destruction and warning the warlords of the cost of an

open conflict has made it possible for the military strategists
to set their minds at ease. As a woman, I feel that I have
done enough to redeem the crime I committed in my previous life, and now it is time for me to retreat from this world.
I hope to become a man again and live an immortal life."

"If you wish, I will give you a thousand ounces of gold
and buy you a hermit place on some high mountain," offered
Hsueh Sung.

"Thank you for your kind offer. But I do not know
whither I am going. I do not anticipate things that may happen in my next life."

Seeing it was futile to persuade her to stay, Hsueh Sung
gave her a big farewell party, with all of the high officers invited. In the midst of the elaborate food and the toasts,
Hsueh Sung asked Lung Chao-yang, a guest and also a poet,
to compose a poem for him to sing to Red Thread. The poem
became very famous. It runs as follows:

> *"From the orchid boat comes the sad*
> *water-chestnut song—*
> *Standing on the tall tower, everyone*
> *grieves over the parting.*
> *Like Fairy Lo flying to the clouds, you*
> *now leave,*
> *Boundless is the blue sky and the water*
> *runs on forever."*

Hsueh Sung felt the weight of great sadness after he had
sung the song. Red Thread wept. Because she did not want to
tarry any longer, she made an excuse that she was drunk and
must retire. She saluted the general and the guests and left.
No one ever saw her again.

—Translated by Elizabeth Te-chen Wang

Story of Everlasting Sorrow

Chen Hung

"Story of Everlasting Sorrow" is said to have been written by Chen Hung as an introduction to the poem, "Song of Everlasting Sorrow," by the famous T'ang poet Po Chu-i. The account may also be found in several adaptations for the stage.

During the middle of the Kai Yuan age of the Tang dynasty, there was peace and prosperity unusual in the history of China. Emperor Hsuantsung, who had reigned many years, had been worn out by the countless state affairs he had to attend to, which required him to get dressed before daybreak and always be late for his evening meal. Now that there was nothing serious for him to worry about, he put his prime minister in charge of everything and began to enjoy himself with music, games, and other amusements. He also desired to indulge in the company of women. His former favorites, Queen Yuanhsian and Concubine Wu, had passed away. Though there were still a thousand young girls in the royal palace, none was pretty enough to attract His Majesty. He was extremely unhappy.

It was October. Every year during this month Emperor Hsuantsung went to Huaching Palace for a brief vacation. All the royal concubines, ladies-in-waiting, and the wives of nobles and high officials were invited to be present. Wherever the royal carriage moved, there followed an array of ladies glittering with pearls, jade, and shining jewels.

Above all other favors and privileges they obtained from His Majesty, the ladies were given permission to enjoy the hot-spring baths in the palace. The Emperor himself enjoyed this kind of bath. The mist and steam of the hot water, caressing him like a warm spring breeze, touched him to the quick, and he felt his heart leap high, as if he were having a romance with a fairylike woman. He looked around, but found all those in his attendance only adornments of powder and rouge. Disappointed and disgusted, the Emperor ordered Kao Li-shih, a clever eunuch, to search secretly for a beautiful girl outside the inner court.

Kao Li-shih had heard of the beauty of the daughter of one Yang Hsuan-yen from Hunglung. At that time the girl was in the house of Prince Shou, but after Kao Li-shih had shown the prince the imperial edict, he was permitted to bring her to Hsuantsung.

Only fifteen, the girl was named Jade Bracelet Yang. She was exceptionally beautiful and intelligent. She had cloudlike black hair; a fair, flowerlike complexion; a finely molded figure; and above all, a charming and sweet disposition. The moment she was presented, Emperor Hsuantsung thought her the peer of Madam Li, the mistress of Emperor Wu of the Han dynasty, and became enamored of her. He ordered her to take a bath in his private warm spring before changing her dress. Delicate and shy, Jade Bracelet appeared so weak after bathing that she seemed not to have enough strength to support her silk-and-gauze dress. It was lovely to see her radiant face, with eyes sparkling like twinkling stars, as she cast her glances here and there. The Emperor was greatly enchanted and thought to himself that here was the girl worthy of his love. He instructed an actress to teach her to sing the "Rainbow Skirt and Feather Garment Song," and to his surprise, Jade Bracelet learned it quickly.

On the first night they were together, Emperor Hsuantsung bestowed on Jade Bracelet a hairpin and a jewelry box, both made of solid gold. He also gave orders that Jade Bracelet wear long golden earrings and a hair ornament made in the shape of a phoenix with dangling pearls which tinkled when she walked. She looked all the more beautiful with these jeweled adornments.

The next year, Jade Bracelet Yang was made *Kuei-fei*, the Royal Concubine, and was given the privilege of wearing and of using things that were half as precious as those of the queen. This elevated her position, and thenceforth she exerted herself even more in her make-up and manners to win com-

pletely the heart of His Majesty. Gifted with talent as well as
with beauty, she knew how to talk and to act in the exact
way that would please the Emperor. Her artful smile, her
graceful dancing and her charming singing voice made her
lord love her more and more each day.

The times continued to be peaceful. No wind of distur-
bance was heard within the nine seas. On the five high mountains, more images of Buddha were gilded with gold. In the
company of his beloved concubine, Emperor Hsuantsung enjoyed visiting Li Hill on snowy nights and rising early to welcome the bright dawn of the warm spring in Shangyang
Palace. Wherever the Emperor went, *Kuei-fei* was at his side;
together they rode in the same carriage and spent nights together in various resorts. Jade Bracelet became the only one
in the eyes of the Emperor. Though there were three *Fu-jen*,
nine *Pin*, twenty-seven *Shih-fu*,[1] eighty-one concubines, and a
great number of courtesans, singing girls, and actresses in the
inner court, the Emperor did not favor any of them with a
single glance. After *Kuei-fei* arrived, no other girl was summoned to attend to His Majesty for even a single night. It
was not only because *Kuei-fei* was of unsurpassable beauty,
but also because she was intelligent and an expert in coquetry
and flattery. The pleasing way in which she knew how to anticipate His Majesty's wishes was endearing beyond words.

Emperor Hsuantsung loved her so much that he made her
uncle, her brothers, and her cousins dukes and nobles and
bestowed on her sisters the title of *Kuo-fu-jen*, "ladies of the
state." The richness of the Yangs was second only to the royal
estate; their mansions, their carriages, their costumes, and
their other belongings were equal to those of the Princess
Tachang, elder sister of the Emperor, but they exercised more
power and influence through the imperial favor. Their actions
were not always according to law, but no one dared to say
anything. When they passed through the gate of the inner
court, even during forbidden hours, no one dared stop them.
All the officers in the capital looked at them with covetous
eyes. People made up a song which ran: "Do not feel unhappy
to beget a daughter, or happy to have a son. A son may not be
a duke, but a daughter can become a royal concubine. See

[1] Different ranks of royal concubines.

now how a girl may bring glory to your family." Thus the Yangs were admired and envied by the public.

Years flew by. Towards the end of the reign, Yang Kuo-chung, the elder brother of *Kuei-fei*, usurped the position of prime minister by dint of the Emperor's favor. He played with his influence and led the Emperor to neglect the affairs of state, thus weakening the nation. Dissatisfaction arose among military men as well as civilians.

General An Lu-shan, who hated Yang Kuo-chung, dispatched his troops to the capital with the demand to get rid of the "traitor." After a brief fight, the royal army was defeated and Tungkuan fell into the hands of the rebels. Emperor Hsuantsung had to evacuate his royal household from the capital. As the green feather-covered carriages moved south, guarded by retreating troops, they passed Mawei station outside Hsienyang. The soldiers were tired, and as they meditated on the cause of all the fighting, a desire for revenge began to burn in their hearts. With lances in hand, they refused to march farther.

When His Majesty inquired what was the matter, one officer kowtowed in front of the royal horse and reported that the public would like to have Chao Tsu[2] killed in order to punish the wrongdoer. Yang Kuo-chung, who was riding beside the Emperor, was forced to face the crowd and was immediately shot to death with arrows.

But the soldiers still were not satisfied. As they hesitated to move forward, the Emperor again inquired the reason. No one dared to answer at first. Then a certain officer with a strong sense of righteousness kowtowed to His Majesty and bravely stated that public resentment demanded the death of *Kuei-fei*. It was too much for Emperor Hsuantsung to grant. But what else could he do except to yield to the public to show his repentance for bringing his country to such a stage? However, he did not have enough courage to bear the sight of the death of his beloved concubine. Covering his face with his long sleeve in bitter grief, the Emperor ordered that *Kuei-fei*

---

[2] Chao Tsu, a supervisory officer of Emperor Chin (156 B.C.-143 B.C.), of the Han dynasty, suggested to the Emperor that he diminish the power of the seven feudal lords and thus precipitated a conflict. Upon the demand of the lords, Chao Tsu was later beheaded by the Emperor. The officer uses the name subtlely here to indicate Yang Kuo-chung.

be dragged out into the woods by the side of Mawei pavilion, where in a few seconds, with a few feet of silk sash, *Kuei-fei* hanged herself. It was the end of a world-renowned beauty.

After Emperor Hsuantsung had retreated to Chengtu in Szechuan province, his son, Emperor Shutsung, with the help of several loyal generals, suppressed the rebellion and mounted the throne in Lingwu. The next year, the new reign started with a proclamation of amnesty, and the old Emperor was asked to return to the capital. Emperor Shutsung gave his father the title of Grand Emperor and asked the latter to stay in the southern palace and enjoy his old age in the western inner court.

The old days were succeeded by new; everything had changed. The Grand Emperor found the end of his happiness and the beginning of his sorrow. During spring days and winter nights, when he saw water lilies blooming in the summer pond and forsaken leaves falling from the autumn trees, or when he heard the "Rainbow Skirt and Feather Garment Song" sung in harmony with jade flutes, he always felt so sad that he shed tears with his attendants. For three years he never could forget his beloved concubine and prayed he would have a chance to see her once again, even if only in his dreams. But the spirit of *Kuei-fei* did not appear.

Then it happened that a Taoist priest who had come from Szechuan heard of the sorrow of the Grand Emperor. He asked for an audience with Hsuantsung and recommended himself as one skilled in the mystic arts of Li Shao-chun and therefore able to summon the spirits of the dead.

The Grand Emperor was overjoyed. He asked the priest to do his best to get Jade Bracelet to appear before him. The priest exerted all his magical powers to summon the soul of *Kuei-fei*, but in vain. He then detached his own soul from his body and, by the method of controlling his breath, sent his soul flying to heaven and then to the underworld, but still he could find no trace of *Kuei-fei*, neither above the earth nor below it.

To make one more effort, he sent his spirit to the limits of the four directions and to the upper and the under spheres of the whole universe. When he reached the extreme east boundary of the heavenly sea, crossing Penghu, he saw many buildings and towers on the mountains inhabited by fairies. At the western foot of one hill was a grotto, with a house standing on the eastern side with doors closed. Upon seeing a sign, "Residence of Tai-chen, the Royal Concubine Jade," the priest took off his hairpin and tapped several times on the door. A pair of little girls answered the door and, before the priest had time to make any inquiry, went back again. Then a pretty maid clad in green came out and asked the priest why he had come. He told her that he was sent by the Tang Emperor with a special message to deliver personally to the royal concubine. "Goddess Jade is asleep," said the maid. "Please wait for a while."

It was just before dawn, with dark clouds floating endlessly like a boundless sea. Gradually the sun came out over the other side of the horizon and a dim light began shining on the towers and the grotto. The gates of the houses of this fairyland were still closed and there was a deep silence. The priest, clasping his hands, stood beside the gate and waited, holding his breath tensely. After a long while, the maid in green came out again and ushered him into the hall. "Goddess Jade will be here soon," she announced.

Presently the priest saw a lady wearing a golden crown in the shape of a water lily, a purple silk garment with a piece of jade hanging from the belt, and a pair of phoenixlike shoes. Seven or eight attendants stood by her. She was none other than Jade Bracelet Yang. The priest made a profound bow to show his respect.

"How is His Majesty?" the goddess inquired. She then went on to ask about things that happened after the fourteenth year of the Tien Pao era. There was a sad expression on her face. After finishing her inquiries, she ordered the green-clad maid to bring her the golden hairpin and the jewelry box that had been given to her in the early days by Hsuan-tsung, and broke each into two parts. Handing one part of each to the priest, she said, "Please convey my appreciation and greetings to His Majesty and tell him that I am sending back the old gifts in memory of our old love."

The priest promised that he would bring back the message and the broken ornaments, but he still lingered on instead of taking his leave. When Goddess Jade asked him what it was that he had on his mind, he bowed and said, "I would like to know one thing which is unknown to others, so that the Grand Emperor will believe that I really have seen you. Otherwise, the ornaments can be suspected as forgeries and I may be considered as dishonest as Hsin Huan-ping."

Goddess Jade was aghast. She stepped back a little and meditated deeply. After a few seconds, she revealed the following story:

"In the tenth year of the Tien Pao period, His Majesty took me to spend the summer in the Li Hill Palace. We were still there when the festival of the seventh night of the seventh month was celebrated. It was the night when the cowherd and the weaving maid have their annual reunion.[3] According to custom, the people of Shansi province set up a brocade tent, laying out fruits, nuts and drinks and burning incense in the courtyard so that the girls could kneel and beg from the weaving maid skill in needlework. The custom was thoroughly observed in the inner court. About midnight, after the royal guards were ordered to rest in the east and the west corridors, I alone attended His Majesty. We walked together to the courtyard. Shoulder to shoulder, we stood looking at the Milky Way and were deeply moved by the eternal love between the cowherd and the weaving maid. As we held each other's hands, we swore by the starlight that we would be husband and wife in every life. This secret oath is known only to His Majesty and me."

She was in tears as she continued. "Because of this love, I probably shall not be allowed to stay here very long and probably shall be banished once more to the human world. Bound by our mutual oath, His Majesty and I will become husband and wife again, only I do not know whether it is going to be in heaven or on earth. However, one thing is certain—we will be reunited soon."

After a brief pause, the goddess continued: "The Grand Emperor is not going to live long. So please tell His Majesty to take good care of himself and not to worry too much."

The Grand Emperor was heartbroken when the priest brought back the message and the token from the late *Kuei-*

---

[3] The seventh day of the seventh lunar month commemorates the legend of the divine weaving maid and the mortal cowherd. The cowherd married the weaving maid when she visited earth, but the Queen of Heaven, not wishing to lose the services of the weaving maid, separated the lovers in heaven by creating the Milky Way. Once every year, on Double Seven, the lovers are permitted to meet for a single night.

fei. Not long afterwards he fell ill and died in the southern palace in the fourth month of the same year.

In the eighth year of the Yuan Ho era of Emperor Hsien-tsung, Pai Chu-yi, then the mayor of Cheche, composed a long poem to narrate the event and asked me, a plain *hsiu-tsai*, to write the introduction. The poem is called "Song of Everlasting Sorrow," and it runs:

> *The Emperor Han, desiring beauty,*
> *Longing, till neglected the kingdom lies,*
> *Had searched through the passing years—*
> *Yet in vain the searching proved.*
>
> *There lived a maiden in the house of*
> *   Yang,*
> *Just entering the gate of womanhood;*
> *Living protected in the fragrant chamber*
> *Unseen by the eyes of wordly men.*

—Translated by Elizabeth Te-chen Wang

The Story of Miss Li

Po Hsing-Chien

Po Hsing-Chien (died 826) was the younger brother of the famous poet Po Chü-i (772–846), author of a poetic version of the "Everlasting Sorrow" story. "The Story of Miss Li," written about 795, was based on oral tradition and is judged by literary scholars to be one of the finest works in the world's early prose fiction. The Li romance was adapted for the stage in the Mongol (1260–1368) and Ming (1368–1644) dynasties. The story itself is marked by realism and may, in fact, have been inspired by a real-life situation.

Miss Li, ennobled with the title "Lady of Chien-kuo," was once a prostitute in Ch'ang-an. The devotion of her conduct was so remarkable that I have thought it worthwhile to record her story.

In the Tien-pao era [742–56] there was a certain nobleman, Governor of Ch'ang-chou and Lord of Jung-yang, whose name and surname I will omit. He was a man of great wealth and highly esteemed by all. He had passed his fiftieth year and had a son who was close on twenty, a boy who in literary talent outstripped all his companions. His father was proud of him and had great hopes of his future. "This," he would say, "is the 'thousand-league colt' of our family." When the time came for the lad to compete at the Provincial Examinations, his father gave him fine clothes and a handsome coach with richly caparisoned horses for the journey; and to provide for his expenses at the capital, he gave him a large sum of money, saying, "I am sure that your talent is such that you will succeed at the first attempt; but I am giving you resources for two years, so that you may pursue your career free from all anxiety." The young man also was quite confident and saw himself winning the first place as clearly as he saw the palm of his own hand.

Starting from P'i-ling he reached Ch'ang-an in a few weeks and took a house in the Pu-cheng quarter. One day he was coming back from a visit to the Eastern Market. He entered the city by the eastern gate of P'ing-k'ang and was going to visit a friend who lived in the southwestern part of the town. When he reached the Ming-k'o Bend, he saw a house on which the gate and courtyard were rather narrow; but the house itself was stately and stood well back from the road. One of the double doors was open, and at it stood a lady, attended by her maid-servant. She was of exquisite, bewitching beauty, such as the world has seldom produced.

When he saw her, the young man unconsciously reined in his horse and hesitated. Unable to leave the spot, he purposely let his whip fall to the ground and waited for his servant to pick it up, all the time staring at the lady in the doorway. She too was staring and met his gaze with a look that seemed to be an answer to his admiration. But in the end he went away without daring to speak to her.

But he could not put the thought of her out of his mind and secretly begged those of his friends who were most expert in the pleasures of Ch'ang-an to tell him what they knew of the girl. He learnt from them that the house belonged to a low and unprincipled woman named Li. When he asked what chance he had of winning the daughter, they answered, "The woman Li is possessed of considerable property, for her previous dealings have been with wealthy and aristocratic families from whom she has received enormous sums. Unless you are willing to spend several thousand pounds, the daughter will have nothing to do with you."

The young man answered: "All I care about is to win her. I do not mind if she costs a million pounds." The next day he set out in his best clothes, with many servants riding behind him, and knocked at the door of Mrs. Li's house. Immediately a page-boy drew the bolt. The young man asked, "Can you tell me whose house this is?" The boy did not answer, but ran back into the house and called out at the top of his voice, "Here is the gentleman who dropped his whip the other day!"

Miss Li was evidently very much pleased. He heard her saying, "Be sure not to let him go away. I am just going to do my hair and change my clothes; I will be back in a minute." The young man, in high spirits, followed the page-boy into the house. A white-haired old lady was going upstairs, whom he took to be the girl's mother. Bowing low the young man addressed her as follows: "I am told that you have a vacant plot of land, which you would be willing to let as a building site. Is this true?" The old lady answered, "I am afraid the site is too mean and confined; it would be quite unsuitable for a gentleman's house. I should not like to offer it to you." She then took him into the guest-room, which was a very handsome one, and asked him to be seated, saying, "I have a daughter who has little either of beauty or accomplishment, but she is fond of seeing strangers. I should like you to meet her."

So saying, she called for her daughter, who presently entered. Her eyes sparkled with such fire, her arms were so dazzling white and there was in her movements such an exquisite grace that the young man could only leap to his feet in confusion and did not dare raise his eyes. When their salutations were over, he began to make a few remarks about the weather; and realized as he did so that her beauty was of a kind he had never encountered before.

They sat down again. Tea was made and wine poured. The vessels used were spotlessly clean. He lingered till the day was almost over; the curfew-drum sounded its four beats. The old lady asked him if he lived far away. He answered untruthfully, "Several leagues beyond the Yen-p'ing Gate," hoping that they would ask him to stay. The old lady said, "The drum has sounded. You will have to go back at once, unless you mean to break the law."

The young man answered, "I was being so agreeably entertained that I did not notice how rapidly the day had fled. My house is a long way off and in the city I have no friends or relations. What am I to do?" Miss Li then interposed, saying, "If you can forgive the meanness of our poor home, what harm would there be in your spending the night with us?" He looked doubtfully at the girl's mother, but met with no discouragement.

Calling his servants, he gave them money and told them to buy provisions for the night. But the girl laughingly stopped him, saying, "That is not the way guests are entertained. Our humble house will provide for your wants tonight, if you are willing to partake of our simple fare and defer your bounty to another occasion." He tried to refuse, but in the end she would not allow him to, and they all moved to the western hall. The curtains, screens, blinds and couches were of dazzling splendour; whilst the toilet-boxes, rugs and pillows were of the utmost elegance. Candles were lighted and an excellent supper was served.

After supper the old lady retired, leaving the lovers engaged in the liveliest conversation, laughing and chattering completely at their ease.

After a while the young man said, "I passed your house the other day and you happened to be standing at the door. And after that, I could think of nothing but you; whether I lay down to rest or sat down to eat, I could not stop thinking of you." She laughed and answered, "It was just the same with me." He said, "You must know that I did not come today simply to look for a building site. I came hoping that you would fulfil my lifelong desire; but I was not sure how you would welcome me. What—"

He had not finished speaking when the old woman came back and asked what they were saying. When they told her, she laughed and said, "Has not Mencius written that 'the relationship between men and women is the groundwork of society'? When lovers are agreed, not even the mandate of a parent will deter them. But my daughter is of humble birth. Are you sure that she is fit to 'present pillow and mat' to a great man?"

He came down from the dais and, bowing low, begged that she would accept him as her slave. Henceforward the old lady regarded him as her son-in-law; they drank heavily together and finally parted. Next morning he had all his boxes and bags brought round to Mrs. Li's house and settled there permanently. From this time on he shut himself up with his mistress and none of his friends ever heard of him. He consorted only with actors and dancers and low people of that kind, passing the time in wild sports and wanton feasting. When his money was all spent, he sold his horses and menservants. In about a year his money, property, servants and horses were all gone.

For some time the old lady's manner towards him had been growing gradually colder, but his mistress remained as devoted as ever. One day she said to him, "We have been together a year, but I am still not with child. They say that the spirit of the Bamboo Grove answers a woman's prayers as surely as an echo. Let us go to his temple and offer a libation."

The young man, not suspecting any plot, was delighted to take her to the temple, and having pawned his coat to buy sweet wine for the libation he went with her and performed the ceremony of prayer. They stayed one night at the temple and came back next day. Whipping up their donkey, they soon arrived at the north gate of the Ping-k'ang quarter. At this point his mistress turned to him and said, "My aunt's house is in a turning just near here. How would it be if we were to go there and rest for a little?"

He drove on as she directed him, and they had not gone more than a hundred paces when he saw the entrance to a spacious carriage-drive. A servant who belonged to the place came out and stopped the cart, saying, "This is the entrance." The young man got down and was met by someone who came out and asked who they were. When told that it was Miss Li, he went back and announced her. Presently a married lady came out who seemed to be about forty. She greeted him, saying, "Has my niece arrived?" Miss Li then

got out of the cart and her aunt said to her, "Why have you
not been to see me for so long?" At which they looked at one
another and laughed. Then Miss Li introduced him to her
aunt and when that was over they all went into a side garden
near the Western Halberd Gate. In the middle of the garden
was a pagoda, and round it grew bamboos and trees of every
variety, while ponds and summerhouses added to its air of seclusion. He asked Miss Li if this were her aunt's estate; she
laughed, but did not answer and spoke of something else.

Tea of excellent quality was served; but when they had
been drinking it for a little while, a messenger came galloping up on a huge Fergana horse, saying that Miss Li's
mother had suddenly been taken very ill and had already lost
consciousness, so that they had better come back as quickly
as possible.

Miss Li said to her aunt: "I am very much upset. I think I
had better take the horse and ride on ahead. Then I will send
it back and you and my husband can come along later." The
young man was anxious to go with her, but the aunt and her
servants engaged him in conversation, flourishing their hands
in front of him and preventing him from leaving the garden.
The aunt said to him: "No doubt my sister is dead by this
time. You and I ought to discuss together what can be done
to help with the expenses of the burial. What is the use of
running off like that? Stay here and help me to make a plan
for the funeral and mourning ceremonies."

It grew late; but the messenger had not returned. The aunt
said: "I am surprised he has not come back with the horse.
You had better go there on foot as quickly as possible and
see what has happened. I will come on later."

The young man set out on foot for Mrs. Li's house. When
he got there he found the gate firmly bolted, locked and
sealed. Astounded, he questioned the neighbours, who told
him that the house had only been let to Mrs. Li, and that, the
lease having expired, the landlord had now resumed possession. The old lady, they said, had gone to live elsewhere.
They did not know her new address.

At first he thought of hurrying back to Hsüan-yang and
questioning the aunt; but he found it was too late to get
there. So he pawned some of his clothes, and with the
proceeds bought himself supper and a bed for the night. But
he was too angry and distressed to sleep, and did not once

close his eyes from dusk to dawn. Early in the morning he dragged himself away to the "aunt's house." He knocked on the door repeatedly, but it was breakfast-time and no one answered. At last, when he had shouted several times at the top of his voice, a footman walked majestically to the door. The young man nervously mentioned the aunt's name and asked whether she was at home. The footman replied: "No one of that name here." "But she lived here yesterday evening," the young man protested; "why are you trying to deceive me? If she does not live here, who *does* the house belong to?" The footman answered: "This is the residence of His Excellency Mr. Ts'ui. I believe that yesterday some persons hired a corner of the grounds. I understand that they wished to entertain a cousin who was coming from a distance. But they were gone before nightfall."

The young man, perplexed and puzzled to the point of madness, was absolutely at a loss what to do next. The best he could think of was to go to the quarters in Pu-cheng, where he had installed himself when he first arrived in Ch'ang-an. The landlord was sympathetic and offered to feed him. But the young man was too much upset to eat, and having fasted for three days fell seriously ill. He rapidly grew worse, and the landlord, fearing he would not recover, had him moved straight to the undertaker's shop. In a short time the whole of the undertaker's staff was collected round him, offering sympathy and bringing him food. Gradually he got better and was able to walk with a stick.

The undertaker now hired him by the day to hold up the curtains of fine cloth, by which he earned just enough to support himself. In a few months he grew quite strong again, but whenever he heard the mourners' doleful songs, would regret that he could not change places with the corpse, burst into violent fits of sobbing and shed streams of tears over which he lost all control; then he used to go home and imitate the mourners' performance.

Being a man of intelligence he very soon mastered the art and finally became the most expert mourner in Ch'ang-an. It happened that there were two undertakers at this time between whom there was a great rivalry. The undertaker of the east turned out magnificent hearses and biers, and in this respect his superiority could not be contested. But the mourners he provided were somewhat inferior. Hearing of our young man's skill, he offered a large sum for his services. The eastern undertaker's supporters, who were familiar with the repertoire of his company, secretly taught the young man several fresh tunes and showed him how to fit the words to them. The lessons went on for several weeks, without anyone being allowed to know of it. At the end of that time the two undertakers agreed to hold a competitive exhibition of their wares in T'ien-men Street. The loser was to forfeit fifty thousand cash to cover the cost of the refreshments provided. Before the exhibition an agreement was drawn up and duly signed by witnesses.

A crowd of several thousand people collected to watch the competition. The mayor of the quarter got wind of the proceedings and told the chief of police. The chief of police told the governor of the city. Very soon all the gentlemen of Ch'ang-an were hurrying to the spot and every house in the town was empty. The exhibition lasted from dawn till midday. Coaches, hearses and all kinds of funeral trappings were successively displayed, but the undertaker of the west could establish no superiority. Filled with shame, he set up a platform in the south corner of the square. Presently a man with a long beard came forward, carrying a hand-bell and attended by numerous assistants. He wagged his beard, raised his eyebrows, folded his arms across his chest and bowed. Then, mounting the platform, he sang the "Dirge of the White Horse." When it was over, confident of an easy victory, he glared round him, as if to imply that his opponents had all vanished. He was applauded on every side and was himself convinced that his talents were a unique product of the age and could not possibly be called into question.

After a while the undertaker of the east put together some benches in the north corner of the square, and a young man in a black hat came forward, attended by five assistants and carrying a bunch of hearse-plumes in his hand. It was the young man of our story.

He adjusted his clothes, looked timidly up and down, and then cleared his throat and began his tune with an air of great diffidence.

He sang the dirge, "Dew on the Garlic." His voice rose so shrill and clear that "its echoes shook the forest trees." Before he had finished the first verse, all who heard were sobbing and hiding their tears.

When the performance was over everyone made fun of the western undertaker, and he was so much put out that he immediately removed his exhibits and retired from the contest. The audience was amazed by the collapse of the western undertaker and could not imagine where his rival had procured such a remarkable singer.

It happened that the emperor had recently issued an order commanding the governors of outside provinces to confer with him in the capital at least once a year. At this time the young man's father, who was Governor of Ch'ang-chou, had recently arrived at the capital to make his report. Hearing of the competition, he and some of his colleagues discarded their official robes and insignia and slipped away to join the crowd. With them was an old servant, who was the husband of the young man's foster-nurse. Recognizing his foster-son's way of moving and speaking, he was on the point of accosting him, but not daring to do so he stood weeping silently. The father asked him why he was crying, and the servant replied, "Sir, the young man who is singing reminds me of your lost son." The father answered: "My son became the prey of robbers because I gave him too much money. This cannot be he." So saying he also began to weep, and leaving the crowd returned to his lodging.

But the old servant went about among the members of the troupe asking who it was who had just sung with such skill. They all told him it was the son of such a one; and when he asked the young man's own name, that too was unfamiliar for he was living under an alias. The old servant was so puzzled that he determined to put the matter to the test for himself. But when the young man saw his old friend walking towards him he winced, turned away his face and tried to hide in the crowd. The old man followed him and catching his sleeve said, "Surely it is you!" Then they embraced and wept. Presently they went back together to his father's lodging. But his father abused him, saying, "Your conduct has disgraced the family. How dare you show your face again?" He took him out of the house and led him to the ground between the Ch'ü-chiang Pond and the Apricot Gardens. Here he stripped him naked and thrashed him with his horse-whip, till the young man succumbed to the pain and collapsed. The father then left him and went away.

But the young man's singing-master had told some of his

friends to watch what happened to him. When they saw him stretched inanimate on the ground they came back and told the other members of the troupe.

The news occasioned universal lamentation, and two men were despatched with a reed mat to cover up the body. When they got there they found his heart still warm, and when they had held him in an upright posture for some time his breathing recommenced. So they carried him home between them and administered liquid food through a reed-pipe. Next morning he recovered consciousness; but after several months he was still unable to move his hands and feet. Moreover, the sores left by his thrashing festered in so disgusting a manner that his friends found him too troublesome, and one night deposited him in the middle of the road. However, the passers-by, harrowed by his condition, never failed to throw him scraps of food.

So copious was his diet that in three months he recovered sufficiently to hobble with the aid of a stick. Clad in a linen coat—which was knotted together in a hundred places so that it looked as tattered as a quail's tail—and carrying a broken saucer in his hand, he now went about the idle quarters of the town earning his living as a professional beggar.

Autumn had now turned to winter. He spent his nights in public lavatories and his days haunting the markets and booths.

One day when it was snowing hard, hunger and cold had driven him into the streets. His beggar's cry was full of woe and all who heard it were heart-rent. But the snow was so heavy that hardly a house had its outer door open, and the streets were empty.

When he reached the eastern gate of An-yi, about the seventh or eighth turning north of the Hsün-li Wall, there was a house with the double-doors partly open.

It was the house where Miss Li was then living, but the young man did not know.

He stood before the door, wailing loud and long.

Hunger and cold had given such a piteous accent to his cry that none could have listened unmoved.

Miss Li heard it from her room and at once said to her servant, "That is so-and-so. I know his voice." She flew to the door and was horrified to see her old lover standing before her so emaciated by hunger and disfigured by sores that he seemed scarcely human. "Can it be you?" she said. But the young man was so overcome by bewilderment and excitement that he could not speak, but only moved his lips noiselessly.

She threw her arms round his neck, then wrapped him in her own embroidered jacket and led him to the parlour. Here, with quavering voice, she reproached herself, saying, "It is my doing that you have been brought to this pass." And with these words she swooned.

Her mother came running up in great excitement, asking who had arrived. Miss Li, recovering herself, said who it was. The old woman cried out in rage, "Send him away! What did you bring him in here for?"

But Miss Li looked up at her defiantly and said, "Not so! This is the son of a noble house. Once he rode in grand coaches and wore golden trappings on his coat. But when he came to our house, he soon lost all he had; and then we plotted together and left him destitute. Our conduct has indeed been inhuman! We have ruined his career and robbed him even of his place in the category of human relationships. For the love of father and son is implanted by Heaven; yet we have hardened his father's heart, so that he beat him and left him on the ground.

"Everyone in the land knows that it is I who have reduced him to his present plight. The Court is full of his kinsmen. Some day one of them will come into power. Then an inquiry will be set on foot, and disaster will overtake us. And since we have flouted Heaven and defied the laws of humanity, neither spirits nor divinities will be on our side. Let us not wantonly incur a further retribution!

"I have lived as your daughter for twenty years. Reckoning what I have cost you in that time, I find it must be close on a thousand pieces of gold. You are now sixty, so that by the price of twenty more years' food and clothing I can buy my freedom. I intend to live separately with this young man. We will not go far away; I shall see to it that we are near enough to pay our respects to you both morning and evening."

The "mother" saw that she was not to be gainsaid and fell in with the arrangement. When she had paid her ransom, Miss Li had a hundred pieces of gold left over, and with them she rented a vacant room five doors away. Here she gave the young man a bath, changed his clothes, fed him with hot soup to relax his stomach, and later fattened him up with cheese and milk.

In a few weeks she began to place before him all the choicest delicacies of land and sea; and she clothed him with cap, shoes and stockings of the finest quality. In a short time he began gradually to put on flesh, and by the end of the year he had entirely recovered his former health.

One day Miss Li said to him, "Now your limbs are stout again and your will strong! Sometimes, when deeply pondering in silent sorrow, I wonder to myself how much you remember of your old literary studies?" He thought and answered, "Of ten parts I remember two or three."

Miss Li then ordered the carriage to be got ready and the young man followed her on horseback. When they reached the classical bookshop at the side-gate south of the Flagtower, she made him choose all the books he wanted, till she had laid out a hundred pieces of gold. Then she packed them in the cart and drove home. She now made him dismiss all other thoughts from his mind and apply himself only to study. All the evening he toiled at his books, with only Miss Li at his side, and they did not retire till midnight. If ever she found that he was too tired to work, she made him lay down his classics and write a poem or ode.

In two years he had thoroughly mastered his subjects and was admired by all the scholars of the realm. He said to Miss Li, "*Now*, surely, I am ready for the examiners!" But she would not let him compete and made him revise all he had learnt, to prepare for the "hundredth battle." At the end of the third year, she said, "Now you may go." He went in for the examination and passed at the first attempt. His reputation spread rapidly through the examination rooms and even older men, when they saw his compositions, were filled with admiration and respect, and sought his friendship.

But Miss Li would not let him make friends with them, saying, "Wait a little longer! Nowadays when a bachelor of arts has passed his examination, he thinks himself fit to hold the most advantageous posts at Court and to win a universal reputation. But your unfortunate conduct and disreputable past put you at a disadvantage beside your fellow-scholars. You must 'grind, temper and sharpen' your attainments, that you may secure a second victory. Then you will be able to match yourself against famous scholars and contend with the illustrious."

The young man accordingly increased his efforts and enhanced his value. That year it happened that the emperor had decreed a special examination for the selection of candidates of unusual merit from all parts of the empire. The young man competed, and came out top in the "censorial essay." He was offered the post of Army Inspector at Ch'eng-tu Fu. The officers who were to escort him were all previous friends.

When he was about to take up his post, Miss Li said to him, "Now that you are restored to your proper station in life, I will not be a burden to you. Let me go back and look after the old lady till she dies. You must ally yourself with some lady of noble lineage, who will be worthy to carry the sacrificial dishes in your Ancestral Hall. Do not injure your prospects by an unequal union. Good-bye, for now I must leave you."

The young man burst into tears and threatened to kill himself if she left him, but she obstinately refused to go with him. He begged her passionately not to desert him, and at last she consented to go with him across the river as far as Chien-men. "There," she said, "you must part with me." The young man consented and in a few weeks they reached Chien-men. Before he had started out again, a proclamation arrived announcing that the young man's father, who had been Governor of Ch'ang-chou, had been appointed Governor of Ch'eng-tu and Intendant of the Chien-nan Circuit. Next morning the father arrived, and the young man sent in his card and waited upon him at the posting-station. His father did not recognize him, but the card bore the names of the young man's father and grandfather, with their ranks and titles. When he read these he was astounded, and bidding his son mount the steps he caressed him and wept. After a while he said, "Now we two are father and son once more," and bade him tell his story. When he heard of the young man's adventures, he was amazed. Presently he asked, "And where is Miss Li?" His son replied, "She came with me as far as here, but now she is going back again."

"I cannot allow it," the father said. Next day he ordered a carriage for his son and sent him on to report himself at Ch'eng-tu; but he detained Miss Li at Chien-men, found her a suitable lodging and ordered a match-maker to perform the initial ceremonies for uniting the two families and to accomplish the six rites of welcome. The young man came back from Ch'eng-tu and they were duly married. In the years that followed their marriage, Miss Li showed herself a devoted wife and competent housekeeper, and was beloved by all her relations.

Some years later both the young man's parents died, and in his mourning observances he showed unusual piety. As a mark of divine favour, magic toadstools grew on the roof of his mourning-hut, each stem bearing three plants. The report of his virtue reached even the emperor's ears. Moreover a number of white swallows nested in the beams of his roof, an omen which so impressed the emperor that he raised his rank immediately.

When the three years of mourning were over, he was successively promoted to various distinguished posts and in the course of ten years was Governor of several provinces. Miss Li was given the fief of Chien-kuo, with the title "The Lady of Chien-kuo."

He had four sons who all held high rank. Even the least successful of them became Governor of T'ai-yüan, and his brothers all married into great families, so that his good fortune both in public and private life was without parallel.

How strange that we should find in the conduct of a prostitute a degree of constancy rarely equalled even by the heroines of history! Surely the story is one which cannot but provoke a sigh!

My great-uncle was Governor of Chin-chou; subsequently he joined the Ministry of Finance and became Inspector of Waterways, and finally Inspector of Roads. In all these three offices he had Miss Li's husband as his colleague, so that her story was well known to him in every particular. During the Cheng-yüan period [785–805] I was sitting one day with Li Kung-tso of Lung-hai, the writer; we fell to talking of wives who had distinguished themselves by remarkable conduct. I told him the story of Miss Li. He listened with rapt attention, and when it was over asked me to write it down for him. So I took up my brush, wetted the hairs and made this rough outline of the story.

—*Translated by Arthur Waley*

The Story of Ts'ui Ying-ying

Yüan Chen

Yüan Chen (779–831), like his contemporary Po Hsing-chien, was an innovator in imbuing the early story form with realism. His most famous story, "The Story of Ts'ui Ying-ying," is thought to have some autobiographical elements, which perhaps accounts for its special aura of immediacy. Yüan was also a highly regarded member of the coterie of poets gathered about Po Chü-i.

During the Cheng-yüan period [785–805] of the T'ang dynasty there lived a man called Chang. His nature was gentle and refined, and his person of great beauty. But his deeper feelings were absolutely held in restraint, and he would indulge in no license. Sometimes his friends took him to a party and he would try to join in their frolics; but when the rest were shouting and scuffling their hardest Chang only pretended to take his share. For he could never overcome his shyness. So it came about that though already twenty-three, he had not yet enjoyed a woman's beauty. To those who questioned him he answered, "It is not such as Master Teng-t'u who are true lovers of beauty, for they are merely profligates. I consider myself a lover of beauty, who happens never to have met with it. And I am of this opinion because I know that, in other things, whatever is beautiful casts its spell upon me; so that I cannot be devoid of feeling." His questioners only laughed.

About this time Chang went to Puchow. Some two miles east of the town there is a temple called the P'u-chiu-ssu, and here he took up his lodging. Now it happened that at this time the widow of a certain Ts'ui was returning to Ch'ang-an. She passed through Puchow on the way and stayed at the same temple.

This lady was born of the Cheng family and Chang's mother was also a Cheng. He unravelled their relationship and found that they were second-cousins.

This year General Hun Chan died at Puchow. There was a certain Colonel Ting Wen-ya who ill-treated his troops. The soldiers accordingly made Hun Chan's funeral the occasion of a mutiny, and began to plunder the town. The Ts'ui family had brought with them much valuable property and many slaves. Subjected to this sudden danger when far from home, they had no one from whom they could seek protection.

Now it happened that Chang had been friendly with the political party to which the commander at Puchow belonged. At his request a guard was sent to the temple and no disorder took place there. A few days afterwards the Civil Commissioner Tu Chio was ordered by the emperor to take over the command of the troops. The mutineers then laid down their arms.

The widow Cheng was very sensible of the service which Chang had rendered. She therefore provided dainties and invited him to a banquet in the middle hall. At table she turned to him and said, "I, your cousin, a lonely and widowed relict, had young ones in my care. If we had fallen into the hands of the soldiery, I could not have helped them. Therefore the lives of my little boy and young daughter were saved by your protection, and they owe you eternal gratitude. I will now cause them to kneel before you, their merciful cousin, that they may thank you for your favours." First she sent for her son, Huan-lang, who was about ten years old, a handsome and gentle child. Then she called to her daughter, Ying-ying: "Come and bow to your cousin. Your cousin saved your life." For a long while she would not come, saying that she was not well. The widow grew angry and cried, "Your cousin saved your life. But for his help, you would now be a prisoner. How can you treat him so rudely?"

At last the girl came in, dressed in everyday clothes, with a look of deep unhappiness on her face. She had not put on any ornaments. Her hair hung down in coils, the black of her two eyebrows joined, her cheeks were not rouged. But her features were of exquisite beauty and shone with an almost dazzling luster.

Chang bowed to her, amazed. She sat down by her mother's side and looked all the time towards her, turning from him with a fixed stare of aversion, as though she could not endure his presence.

He asked how old she was. The widow answered, "She was born in the year of the present emperor's reign that was a year of the Rat, and now it is the year of the Dragon in the period Cheng-yüan [800]. So she must be seventeen years old."

Chang tried to engage her in conversation, but she would not answer, and soon the dinner was over. He was passionately in love with her and wanted to tell her so, but could find no way.

Ying-ying had a maid-servant called Hung-niang, whom Chang sometimes met and greeted. Once he stopped her and was beginning to tell her of his love for her mistress, but she was frightened and ran away. Then Chang was sorry he had not kept silence.

Next day he met Hung-niang again, but was embarrassed and did not say what was in his mind. But this time the maid herself broached the subject and said to Chang, "Master, I dare not tell her what you told me, or even hint at it. But since your mother was a kinswoman of the Ts'ui, why do you not seek my mistress's hand on that plea?"

Chang said, "Since I was a child in arms, my nature has been averse to intimacy. Sometimes I have idled with wearers of silk and gauze, but my fancy was never once detained. I little thought that in the end I should be entrapped.

"Lately at the banquet I could scarcely contain myself; and since then, when I walk, I forget where I am going and when I eat, I forget to finish my meal, and do not know how to endure the hours from dawn to dusk.

"If we were to get married through a matchmaker and perform the ceremonies of Sending Presents and Asking Names, it would take many months, and by that time you would have to look for me 'in the dried-fish shop.' What is the use of giving me such advice as that?"

The maid replied, "My mistress clings steadfastly to her chastity, and even an equal could not trip her with lewd talk. Much less may she be won through the stratagems of a maid-servant. But she is skilled in composition, and often when she has made a poem or essay, she is restless and dissatisfied for a long while after. You must try to provoke her with a love-poem. There is no other way."

Chang was delighted and at once composed two Spring Poems to send her. Hung-niang took them away and came back the same evening with a coloured tablet, which she gave to Chang, saying, "This is from my mistress." It bore the title "The Bright Moon of the Fifteenth Night." The words ran:

> To wait for the moon I am sitting in the western parlour;
> To greet the wind, I have left the door ajar.
> When a flower's shadow stirred and brushed the wall,
> For a moment I thought it the shadow of a lover coming.

Chang could not doubt her meaning. That night was the fourth after the first decade of the second month. Beside the eastern wall of Ying-ying's apartments there grew an apricot-tree; by climbing it one could cross the wall. On the next night (which was the night of the full moon) Chang used the tree as a ladder and crossed the wall. He went straight to the western parlour and found the door ajar. Hung-niang lay asleep on the bed. He woke her, and she cried in a voice of astonishment, "Master Chang, what are you doing here?" Chang answered, half-truly: "Your mistress's letter invited me. Tell her I have come." Hung-niang soon returned, whispering, "She is coming, she is coming." Chang was both delighted and surprised, thinking that his salvation was indeed at hand.

At last Ying-ying entered.

Her dress was sober and correct, and her face was stern. She at once began to reprimand Chang, saying, "I am grateful for the service which you rendered to my family. You gave support to my dear mother when she was at a loss how to save her little boy and young daughter. How came you then to send me a wicked message by the hand of a low maid-servant? In protecting me from the license of others, you acted nobly. But now that you wish to make me a partner to your own licentious desires, you are asking me to accept one wrong in exchange for another.

"How was I to repel this advance? I would gladly have hidden your letter, but it would have been immoral to har-

bour a record of illicit proposals. Had I shown it to my
mother, I should ill have requited the debt we owe you. Were
I to entrust a message of refusal to a servant or concubine, I
feared it might not be truly delivered. I thought of writing a
letter to tell you what I felt; but I was afraid I might not be
able to make you understand. So I sent those trivial verses,
that I might be sure of your coming. I have no cause to be
ashamed of an irregularity which had no other object but the
preservation of my chastity."

With these words she vanished. Chang remained for a long
while petrified with astonishment. At last he climbed back
over the wall and went home in despair.

Several nights after this he was lying asleep near the verandah when someone suddenly woke him. He rose with a
startled sigh and found that Hung-niang was there, with bedclothes under her arm and a pillow in her hand. She shook
Chang, saying, "She is coming, she is coming. Why are you
asleep?" Then she arranged the bedclothes and pillow and
went away.

Chang sat up and rubbed his eyes. For a long while he
thought he must be dreaming. But he assumed a respectful
attitude and waited.

Suddenly Hung-niang came back, bringing her mistress
with her. Ying-ying, this time, was languid and flushed, yielding and wanton in her air, as though her strength could
scarcely support her limbs. Her former severity had utterly
disappeared.

That night was the eighth of the second decade. The crys-
tal beams of the sinking moon twinkled secretly across their
bed. Chang, in a strange exaltation, half-believed that a fairy
had come to him, and not a child of mortal men.

At last the temple bell sounded, dawn glimmered in the
sky and Hung-niang came back to fetch her mistress away.
Ying-ying turned on her side with a pretty cry, and followed
her maid to the door.

The whole night she had not spoken a word.

Chang rose when it was half-dark, still thinking that perhaps it had been a dream. But when it grew light, he saw her
powder on his arm and smelt her perfume in his clothes. A
tear she had shed still glittered on the mattress.

For more than ten days afterwards he did not see her
again. During this time he began to make a poem called

"Meeting a Fairy," in thirty couplets. It was not yet finished, when he chanced to meet Hung-niang in the road. He asked her to take the poem to Ying-ying.

After this Ying-ying let him come to her, and for a month or more he crept out at dawn and in at dusk, the two of them living together in that western parlour of which I spoke before.

Chang often asked her what her mother thought of him. Ying-ying said, "I know she would not oppose my will. So why should we not get married at once?"

Soon afterwards, Chang had to go to the capital. Before starting he tenderly informed her of his departure. She did not reproach him, but her face showed pitiable distress. On the night before he started, he was not able to see her.

After spending a few months in the west, Chang returned to Puchow and again lodged for several months in the same building as the Ts'ui family. He made many attempts to see Ying-ying alone, but she would not let him do so. Remembering that she was fond of calligraphy and verse, he frequently sent her his own compositions, but she scarcely glanced at them.

It was characteristic of her that when any situation was at its acutest point, she appeared quite unconscious of it. She talked glibly, but would seldom answer a question. She expected absolute devotion, but herself gave no encouragement.

Sometimes when she was in the depth of despair, she would affect all the while to be quite indifferent. It was rarely possible to know from her face whether she was pleased or sorry.

One night Chang came upon her unawares when she was playing on the zither, with a touch full of passion. But when she saw him coming, she stopped playing. This incident increased his infatuation.

Soon afterwards, it became time for him to compete in the Literary Examinations, and he was obliged once more to set out for the western capital.

The evening before his departure, he sat in deep despondency by Ying-ying's side, but did not try again to tell her of his love. Nor had he told her that he was going away, but she seemed to have guessed it, and with submissive face and gentle voice she said to him softly, "Those whom a man leads astray, he will in the end abandon. It must be so, and I will not reproach you. You deigned to corrupt me and now you deign to leave me. That is all. And your vows of 'faithfulness till death'—they too are cancelled. There is no need for you to grieve at this parting, but since I see you so sad and can give you no other comfort—you once praised my zither-playing; but I was bashful and would not play to you. Now I am bolder, and if you choose, I will play you a tune."

She took her harp and began the prelude to "Rainbow Skirts and Feather Jackets." But after a few bars the tune broke off into a wild and passionate dirge.

All who were present caught their breath; but in a moment she stopped playing, threw down her harp and, weeping bitterly, ran to her mother's room.

She did not come back.

Next morning Chang left. The following year he failed in his examinations and could not leave the capital. So, to unburden his heart, he wrote a letter to Ying-ying. She answered him somewhat in this fashion:

"I have read your letter and cherish it dearly. It has filled my heart half with sorrow, half with joy. You sent with it a box of garlands and five sticks of paste, that I may decorate my head and colour my lips.

"I thank you for your presents; but there is no one now to care how I look. Seeing those things only makes me think of you and grieve the more.

"You say that you are prospering in your career at the capital, and I am comforted by that news. But it makes me fear you will never come back again to one who is so distant and humble. But *that* is settled forever, and it is no use talking of it.

"Since last autumn I have lived in a dazed stupor. Amid the clamour of the daytime, I have sometimes forced myself to laugh and talk; but alone at night I have done nothing but weep. Or, if I have fallen asleep my dreams have always been full of the sorrows of parting. Often I dreamt that you came to me as you used to do, but always before the moment of our joy your phantom vanished from my side. Yet, though we are still bedfellows in my dreams, when I wake and think of it the time when we were together seems very far off. For since we parted, the old year has slipped away and a new year has begun. . . .

"Ch'ang-an is a city of pleasure, where there are many

snares to catch a young man's heart. How can I hope that you will not forget one so sequestered and insignificant as I? And indeed, if you were to be faithful, so worthless a creature could never requite you. But our vows of unending love—those *I* at least can fulfil.

"Because you are my cousin, I met you at the feast. Lured by a maid-servant, I visited you in private. A girl's heart is not in her own keeping. You 'tempted me by your ballads' and I could not bring myself to 'throw the shuttle' to repulse you.

"Then came the sharing of pillow and mat, the time of perfect loyalty and deepest tenderness. And I, being young and foolish, thought it would never end.

"Now, having 'seen my Prince,' I cannot love again; nor, branded by the shame of self-surrender, am I fit to perform the 'service of towel and comb,' to become your wife; and of the bitterness of the long celibacy which awaits me, what need is there to speak?

"The good man uses his heart; and if by chance his gaze has fallen on the humble and insignificant, till the day of his death he continues the affections of his life. The cynic cares nothing for people's feelings. He will discard the small to follow the great, look upon a former mistress merely as an accomplice in sin, and hold that the most solemn vows are made only to be broken. He will reverse all natural laws—as though Nature should suddenly let bone dissolve, while cinnabar resisted the fire. The dew that the wind has shaken from the tree still looks for kindness from the dust; and such, too, is the sum of *my* hopes and fears.

"As I write, I am shaken by sobs and cannot tell you all that is in my heart. My darling, I am sending you a jade ring that I used to play with when I was a child. I want you to wear it at your girdle, that you may become firm and flawless as this jade, and, in your affections, unbroken as the circuit of this ring.

"And with it I am sending a skein of thread and a tea-trough of flecked bamboo. There is no value in these few things. I send them only to remind you to keep your heart pure as jade and your affection unending as this round ring. The bamboo is mottled as if with tears, and the thread is tangled as the thoughts of those who are in sorrow. By these tokens I seek no more than that, knowing the truth, you may think kindly of me for ever.

"Our hearts are very near, but our bodies are far apart. There is no time fixed for our meeting; yet a secret longing can unite souls that are separated by a thousand miles.

"Protect yourself against the cold spring wind, eat well— look after yourself in all ways and do not worry too much about your worthless handmaid,

Ts'UI YING-YING."

Chang showed this letter to his friends and so the story became known to many who lived at that time. All who heard it were deeply moved; but Chang, to their disappointment, declared that he meant to break with Ying-ying. Yüan Chen, of Honan, who knew Chang well, asked him why he had made this decision.

Chang answered: "I have observed that in Nature whatever has perfect beauty is either itself liable to sudden transformations or else is the cause of them in others. If Ying-ying were to marry a rich gentleman and become his pet, she would forever be changing, as the clouds change to rain, or as the scaly dragon turns into the horned dragon. I, for one, could never keep pace with her transformations.

"Of old, Hsin of the Yin dynasty and Yu of the Chou dynasty ruled over kingdoms of many thousand chariots, and their strength was very great. Yet a single woman brought each to ruin, dissipating their hosts and leading these monarchs to the assassin's knife, so that to this day they are a laughingstock to all the world. I know that my constancy could not withstand such spells, and that is why I have curbed my passion."

At these words all who were present sighed deeply.

A few years afterwards Ying-ying married someone else and Chang also found a wife. Happening once to pass the house where Ying-ying was living, he called on her husband and asked to see her, saying he was her cousin. The husband sent for her, but she would not come. Chang's vexation showed itself in his face. Someone told Ying-ying of this and she secretly wrote the poem:

Since I have grown so lean, my face has lost its beauty.
I have tossed and turned so many times that I am too tired
    to leave my bed.

It is not that I mind the others seeing
　　How ugly I have grown;
It is *you* who have caused me to lose my beauty,
　　Yet it is *you* I am ashamed should see me!

Chang went away without meeting her, and a few days afterwards, when he was leaving the town, wrote a poem of final farewell, which said:

You cannot say that you are abandoned and deserted;
　　For you have found someone to love you.
Why do you not convert your broodings over the past
　　Into kindness to your present husband?

After that they never heard of one another again. Many of Chang's contemporaries praised the skill with which he extricated himself from this entanglement.

—Translated by Arthur Waley

MING DYNASTY

1368–1644

The Ming Dynasty was marked by stability, prosperity, and a sense of renewed national identity following the period of Mongol conquest and rule (1260–1368). Growing prosperity increased literacy and opened opportunities for achievement in the arts.

Both the short story and the episodic novel took on more finished forms. From early times, however, Chinese culture had revered poetry and had developed rigorous rules governing its writing and recitation. Prose was considered worthy only if it conformed to strict rules of structure and was a vehicle for the dissemination of moral—generally Confucian—precepts. Fictional prose was regarded as definitely unworthy and those who persisted in writing it (frequently highly regarded poets) usually preferred not to be associated with their "ignoble" works. Nevertheless, the *p'ing hua* type of fiction, which was written in the plainest of the vernacular tongues, may have been encouraged by the growing popularity of Ming drama, since both forms were especially appealing to the common people.

Although scholars of the period had begun to question the Confucian doctrinal authority and reverence of the classics, Confucian precepts were espoused by the government and Confucian rules of propriety continued to control home life and social customs.

The Lady Who Was a Beggar

Anonymous

"The Lady Who Was a Beggar" dramatically reveals the position of the woman in the family and in society—exploited as a marriage commodity, tenuously holding on to social position, subject to her husband's favor or disfavor.

It is not surprising that the story was written anonymously in an age that emphasized the superiority of poetic expression and brought forth a "golden period" in drama.

———

That side the wall, the branches—this side, the broken blossoms,
Fallen to earth, the playthings of every passing breeze.
The branches may be bare, but they will put out more flowers—
The flowers, once adrift, may never regain the trees.

This is the "Song of the Rejected Wife," by a poet of former times. It likens the position of a wife to that of the blossom on the branch: the branch may be stripped of its blossom, but it will bloom again in the spring; the flowers, once they have left the branch, can never hope to return. Ladies, if you will listen to me, then serve your husband to the extent of your powers, share with him joy and sorrow, and follow one to the end. Unless you wish to lay up repentance in store, do not scorn poverty and covet riches, do not let your affections wander.

Let me tell you now of a famous statesman of the Han dynasty whose wife, in the days before he had made his name, left him because "though she had eyes, she did not recognize Mount T'ai." In vain did she repent in later years. Who was this man, you ask, and where did he come from? Well, his name was Chu Mai-ch'en, he was styled Weng-tzu, and he came from the region of Hui-chi in the south-east. Of poor family, he had as yet found no opening, but lived, just himself and his wife, in a tumbledown cottage in a mean alley. Every day he would go into the hills and cut firewood to sell in the market-place for the few cash he needed to carry on existence. But he was addicted to study, and a book never left his hand. Though his back was bowed down under a weight of faggots, grasped in his hand would be a book. This he would read aloud, rolling the phrases round his mouth, chanting as he walked along.

The townspeople were used to him, they knew Mai-ch'en was here with his firewood as soon as they heard the sound of intoning. They all bought from him out of sympathy for a poor Confucian; moreoever, he never haggled but simply took whatever you wanted to give him, so that he never found his firewood difficult to sell. But there were always gangs of idlers and street-urchins ready to make fun of him as he came along, intoning the classics with a load of faggots on his shoulders.

Mai-ch'en never noticed them. But one day when his wife went out of doors to draw water, she felt humiliated by the sight of these children making fun of Mai-ch'en with his burden. When he came home with his earnings she began to upbraid him: "If you want to study, then leave off selling firewood, and if you want to sell firewood then leave studying to others. When a man gets to your age, and in his right senses, that he should act like that and let children make fun of him! It's a wonder you don't die of shame."

"I sell firewood to save us from penury," replied Mai-ch'en, "and I study to win wealth and esteem. There is no contradiction there. Let them laugh!"

But his wife laughed at this. "If it's wealth and esteem you're after, then don't sell any more firewood. Who ever heard of a woodcutter becoming a mandarin? And yet you talk all this nonsense."

"Wealth and poverty, fame and obscurity, each has its time," said Mai-ch'en. "A fortune-teller told me my rise would begin when I had passed fifty. They say you can't measure out the ocean with a gallon can—don't you try to measure my mind for me."

"Fortune-teller indeed!" said his wife. "He could see you were simple and deliberately made fun of you. You should pay no heed to him. By the time you're fifty you'll be past even carrying firewood. Death from starvation, that's what's in store for you, and then you talk about becoming a mandarin! Unless, of course, the King of Hades wants another judge in his court and is keeping the job vacant for you!"

"Chiang T'ai-kung was still a fisherman on the River Wei at the age of eighty," replied Mai-ch'en, "but when King Wen of Chou found him he took him into his chariot and honoured him as counsellor. Kung-sun Hung, a Chief Minister of the present dynasty, was still herding swine by the Eastern Ocean at the age of fifty-nine. He was turned sixty when fate presented him to the present Emperor, who made him a general and a marquis. If I begin when I am fifty I shall be some way behind Kan Lo, but in front of the two I have just mentioned. You must be patient and wait a while."

"There's no need to ransack all the histories," said his wife. "Your fisherman and swineherd were full of talent and learning. But you, with these useless books of yours, you'll still be the same at a hundred. What is there to hope for? I was unlucky enough to marry you, and now, what with the children following you about and poking fun at you, you've taken my good name away too. If you don't do as I say and throw those books away, I'm determined I won't stay with you. We'll each lead our own life, and then we shan't get in each other's way."

"I am forty-three this year," said Mai-ch'en. "In seven years' time I shall be fifty. The long wait is behind us, you have only to be patient for a little longer. If you desert me now in such a callous fashion you will surely regret it in years to come."

"The world's not short of woodcutters," his wife rejoined. "What shall I have to regret? If I remain with you another seven years it will be my corpse as well as yours that is found starved by the roadside. It will count as a good deed if you release me now, for you will have saved my life."

Mai-ch'en realized that his wife had set her heart on leaving him and wouldn't be gainsaid. So he said, with a sigh, "Very well, then I only hope that your next husband will be a better man than Chu Mai-ch'en."

"Whatever he's like he could hardly be worse," returned his wife, whereupon she made two obeisances and went joyfully out of the house and away without so much as looking back.

To relieve his distress, Chu Mai-ch'en inscribed four lines of verse on the wall of his cottage:

Marry a dog, follow a dog,
Marry a cock, follow a cock.
It was my wife deserted me,
Not I rejected her.

By the time Chu Mai-ch'en reached his fiftieth birthday the Han Emperor Wu-ti had issued his edict summoning men of worth to serve their country. Mai-ch'en went to the Western Capital, submitted his name and took his place among those awaiting appointment. Meanwhile his abilities were brought to the notice of the Emperor by a fellow-townsman, Yen Chu. Reflecting that Chu Mai-ch'en must have intimate knowledge of the people of his native place and of their condition, the Emperor appointed him Prefect of Hui-chi, and he rode off to take up his appointment.

Learning of the impending arrival of the New Prefect, the officials of Hui-chi mobilized great numbers of men to put the roads in order. Among these coolies was Chu Mai-ch'en's marital successor; and at this man's side, attending to his food, was Mai-ch'en's ex-wife, barefoot and with matted hair. When the woman heard the din of the approach of the new Prefect and his suite, she tried to get a glimpse of him—and saw her former husband, Chu Mai-ch'en.

Mai-ch'en also, from his carriage, caught sight of her and recognized his ex-wife. He summoned her and seated her in one of the carriages of his suite.

At the official residence, the woman did not know where to put herself for shame. She kotowed and poured out a confession of her faults. Mai-ch'en ordered her second husband to be summoned to his presence, and it did not take them long to bring him in. He grovelled on the floor, not daring to raise his eyes. Mai-ch'en burst out laughing: "A man like this—I don't see that he is much of an improvement on Chu Mai-ch'en?"

His ex-wife went on kotowing and confessing. She had eyes but no pupils and had not recognized his worth; she would wish to return as humble slave or concubine; as such she would serve him to the end of her days. Chu Mai-ch'en ordered a bucket of water to be brought and splashed on the floor. Then he told his wife: "If this spilt water can go back into the bucket, then you can come back to me. But in memory of our childhood betrothal, I grant you waste land from my demesne sufficient to support yourself and your husband."

When the woman left the residence with her second husband the passers-by pointed her out to each other: "That's the wife of the new Prefect!" Humiliated beyond measure, when she reached her piece of land she jumped in the nearby river and drowned herself.

There is a verse in evidence of all this:

> The general Han Hsin, starving, was looked after by a
>   washer-woman,
> But this poor scholar is deserted by his own good wife.
> Well aware that spilt water cannot be recovered
> She repents that in time past she would not let him study.

A second poem maintains that to despise poverty and esteem only wealth is a commonplace in this world, and not limited to such a woman as the wife of Chu Mai-ch'en:

> Using success or failure as the sole gauge of merit
> Who can discern the dragon lying hidden in the mud?
> Do not blame this woman for her lack of perception,
> More than one wife in this world has kicked over the
>   traces.

After this story of a wife rejecting her husband, let me tell one now about a husband rejecting his wife. It was equally a case of scorning the poor and adulating the rich, at the expense of justice and mercy alike, so that all that was gained in the end was a name among all and sundry for meanness and lack of feeling.

It is told that in the Shao-hsing reign-period of the Sung

dynasty [1131–1163], although Lin-an had been made the
capital city and was a wealthy and populous district, still the
great number of beggars had not diminished. Among them
was one who acted as their head. He was called the "tramp-
major," and looked after all the beggars. Whenever they
managed to beg something, the tramp-major would demand a
fee for the day. Then when it was raining or snow lay on the
ground, and there was nowhere to go to beg, the tramp-major
would boil up a drop of thin gruel and feed the whole beg-
gar-band. Their tattered robes and jackets were also in his
care. The result was that the whole crowd of the beggars
were careful to obey him, with bated breath like a lot of
slaves, and none of them dared offend him.

The tramp-major was thus provided with a regular income,
and as a rule he would lend out sums of money among the
beggars and extort a tidy interest. In this way, if he neither
gambled nor went whoring, he could build up a going
concern out of it. He depended on this for his livelihood, and
never for a moment thought of changing his profession.
There was only one drawback: a tramp-major did not have a
very good name. Though he acquired land by his efforts, and
his family had prospered for generations, still he was a boss
of the beggars and not to be compared with ordinary respect-
able people. No one would salute him with respect if he
showed himself out-of-doors, and so the only thing for him to
do was to shut his doors and play the great man in his own
home.

And yet, distinguishing the worthy from the base, we count
among the latter only prostitutes, actors, yamen-runners and
soldiers: we certainly do not include beggars. For what is
wrong with beggars is not that they are covered in sores, but
simply that they have no money. There have been men like
the minister Wu Tzu-hsü, of Ch'un-ch'iu times, who as a fugi-
tive from oppression played his pipes and begged his food in
the marketplace of Wu; or Cheng Yüan-ho of T'ang times
who sang the beggar's song of "Lien-hua lo," but later rose
to wealth and eminence and covered his bed with brocade.
These were great men, though beggars: clearly, we may hold
beggars in contempt, but we should not compare them with
the prostitutes and actors, the runners and soldiery.

Let us digress no longer, but tell now how in the city of
Hangchow there was once a tramp-major by the name of

Chin Lao-ta. In the course of seven generations his ancestors had developed the profession into a perfect family business, so that Chin Lao-ta ate well and dressed well, lived in a fine house and cultivated good land. His barns were well-stocked with grain and his purse with money, he made loans and kept servants; if not quite the wealthiest, he was certainly one of the rich. Being a man of social aspirations, he decided to relinquish this post of tramp-major into the hands of a relative, "Scabby" Chin, while he himself took his ease with what he had and mingled no more with the beggar band. But unfortunately, the neighbours were used to speaking of "the tramp-major's family," and the name persisted in spite of his efforts.

Chin Lao-ta was over fifty. He had lost his wife and had no son, but only a daughter whose name was Jade Slave. Jade Slave was beautiful, as we are told by a verse about her:

Pure to compare with jade,
Gracious to shame the flowers,
Given the adornments of the court
Here would be another Chang Li-hua.

Chin Lao-ta prized his daughter as a jewel, and taught her from an early age to read and write. By the age of fifteen she was adept in prose and verse, composing as fast as her hand could write. She was equally proficient in the womanly crafts, and in performing on the harp or flute: everything she did proclaimed her skill. Her beauty and talent inspired Chin Lao-ta to seek a husband for her among the scholar class. But the fact was that among families of name and rank it would be difficult to find anyone anxious to marry the girl— no one wanted a tramp-major's daughter. On the other hand, Lao-ta had no desire to cultivate a liaison with humble and unaspiring tradespeople. Thus, while her father hovered between high and low, the girl reached the age of seventeen without betrothal.

And then one day an old man of the neighbourhood came along with news of a student by the name of Mo Chi who lived below the T'ai-ping Bridge. This was an able youth of nineteen, full of learning, who remained unmarried only because he was an orphan and had no money. But he had graduated recently, and was hoping to marry some girl in whose family he could find a home.

"This youth would be just right for your daughter," said the neighbour. "Why not take him as your son-in-law?"

"Then do me the favour of acting as go-between," said Chin Lao-ta; and off went the old man on his errand, straight to the T'ai-ping Bridge.

There he sought out the graduate Mo Chi, to whom he said, "There is one thing I am obliged to tell you: the ancestors of Chin Lao-ta followed the profession of tramp-major. But this was long ago: and think, what a fine girl she is, this daughter of his—and what's more, what a prosperous and flourishing family! If it is not against the young gentleman's wishes, I will take it upon myself to arrange the whole thing at once."

Before giving his reply, Mo Chi turned the matter over in his mind: "I am not very well-off for food and clothes just now, and I am certainly not in a position to take a wife in the usual way. Why not make the best of it and marry into this family? It would be killing two birds with one stone; and I needn't take any notice of ridicule." Turning to the old man, he said, "Uncle, what you propose seems an admirable plan. But I am too poor to buy the usual presents. What do you suggest?"

"Provided only that you accept this match," replied the old man, "you will not even be called on to supply so much as the paper for the exchange of horoscopes. You may leave everything to me."

With this he returned to report to Chin Lao-ta. They selected an auspicious day, and the Chin family even provided clothes for Mo Chi to wear at the wedding.

When Mo Chi had entered the family and the ceremony was over, he found that Jade Slave's beauty and talents exceeded his wildest hopes. And this perfect wife was his without the outlay of a single copper! He had food and clothes in abundance, and indeed everything he could wish. Even the ridicule he had feared from his friends was withheld, for all were willing to make allowances for Mo Chi's penniless condition.

When their marriage had lasted a month Chin Lao-ta prepared a generous banquet at which his son-in-law could feast his graduate friends and thus enhance the dignity of the house. The drinking went on for a week: but what was not foreseen was the offence which all this gave to the kinsman "Scabby" Chin. Nor was Scabby without justification.

"You're a tramp-major just as much as I am," said he in his heart, "the only thing is that you've been one for a few generations longer and have got some money in your pocket. But if it comes to ancestors, aren't yours the very same as mine? When my niece Jade Slave gets married I expect to be invited to drink a toast—here's a load of guests drinking for a week on end to celebrate the first month, but not so much as a one-inch by three-inch invitation-card do I receive. What is this son-in-law of yours—he's a graduate, I know, but is he a President of a Board or a Prime Minister as well? Aren't I the girl's own uncle, and entitled to a stool at your party? Very well," he concluded, "if they're so ready to ignore my existence, I'll go and stir them up a bit and see how that pleases them."

Thereupon he called together fifty or sixty of his beggars, and took the lot of them along to Chin Lao-ta's house. What a sight—

Hats bursting into flower, shirts tied up in knots,
A rag of old matting or a strip of worn rug, a bamboo stick and a rough chipped bowl.
Shouting "Father!", shouting "Mother!", shouting "Bene-factor!", what a commotion before the gate!
Writhing snakes, yapping dogs, chattering apes and mon-keys, what sly cunning they all display!
Beating clappers, singing "Yang Hua", the clamour deafens the ear;
Clattering tiles, faces white with chalk, the sight offends the eye.
A troop of rowdies banded together, not Chung K'uei him-self could contain them.

When Chin Lao-ta heard the noise they made he opened the gate to look out, whereupon the whole crowd of beggars, with Scabby at their head, surged inside and threw the house into commotion. Scabby himself hurried to a seat, snatched the choicest of the meats and wines and began to stuff him-self, calling meanwhile for the happy couple to come and make their obeisances before their uncle.

So terrified were the assembled graduates that they gave up

at once and fled the scene, Mo Chi joining in their retreat. Chin Lao-ta was at his wits' end, and pleaded repeatedly, "My son-in-law is the host today, this is no affair of mine. Come another day when I will buy in some wine specially for you and we will have a chat together."

He distributed money among the beggar band, and brought out two jars of fine wine and some live chickens and geese, inviting the beggars to have a banquet of their own over at Scabby's house; but it was late at night before they ceased their rioting and took their leave, and Jade Slave wept in her room from shame and rage.

That night Mo Chi stayed at the house of a friend, returning only when morning came. At the sight of his son-in-law, Chin Lao-ta felt keenly the disgrace of what had happened, and his face filled with shame. Naturally enough, Mo Chi on his part was strongly displeased; but no one was anxious to say a word. Truly,

When a mute tastes the bitterness of cork-tree wood
He must swallow his disgust with his medicine.

Let us rather tell how Jade Slave, conscious of her family's disrepute and anxious that her husband should make his own name for himself, exhorted him to labour at his books. She grudged neither the cost of the works, classical and recent, which she bought for his use, nor the expense of engaging tutors for learned discussion with him. She provided funds also for the entertaining that would widen her husband's circle of acquaintances. As a result, Mo Chi's learning and reputation made daily advances.

He gained his master's degree at the age of twenty-two, and ultimately his doctorate, and at last the day came when he left the great reception for successful candidates and, black hat, doctor's robes and all, rode back to his father-in-law's house. But as he entered his own ward of the city a crowd of urchins pressed about him, pointing and calling— "Look at the tramp-major's son-in-law! He's an official now!"

From his elevated position Mo Chi heard them, but it was beneath his dignity to do anything about it. He simply had to put up with it; but his correct observance of etiquette on greeting his father-in-law concealed a burning indignation. "I always knew that I should attain these honours," he said to himself, "yet I feared that no noble or distinguished family would take me in as a son-in-law, and so I married the daughter of a tramp-major. Without question, it is a life-long stain. My sons and daughters will still have a tramp-major for their grandfather, and I shall be passed from one man to the next as a laughing stock! But the thing is done now. What is more, my wife is wise and virtuous, it would be impossible for me to divorce her on any of the seven counts:[1] 'Marry in haste, repent at leisure'—it's a true saying after all!"

His mind seethed with such thoughts, and he was miserable all day long. Jade Slave often questioned him, but received no reply and remained in ignorance of the cause of his displeasure. But what an absurd figure, this Mo Chi! Conscious only of his present eminence, he has forgotten the days of his poverty. His wife's assistance in money and effort are one with the snows of yesteryear, so crooked are the workings of his mind.

Before long, Mo Chi presented himself for appointment and received the post of Census Officer at Wu-wei-chün. His father-in-law provided wine to feast his departure, and this time awe of the new official deterred the beggar band from breaking up the party.

It so happened that the whole journey from Hangchow to Wu-wei-chün was by water, and Mo Chi took his wife with him, boarded a junk and proceeded to his post. After several days their voyage brought them to the eddies and whirlpools below the Coloured Stone Cliff, and they tied up to the northern bank. That night the moon shone bright as day. Mo Chi, unable to sleep, rose and dressed and sat in the prow enjoying the moonlight. There was no one about; and as he sat there brooding on his relationship with a tramp-major an evil notion came into his head. The only way for him to be rid of life-long disgrace was for his wife to die and a new one to take her place. A plan formed in his mind. He entered the cabin and inveigled Jade Slave into getting up to see the moon in its glory.

Jade Slave was already asleep, but Mo Chi repeatedly urged her to get up, and she did not like to contravene his

---

[1] A wife could be put aside for failing to give birth to a son, for adultery, disobedience to her husband's parents, for nagging, stealing, jealousy, or for contracting an evil disease.

wishes. She put on her gown and crossed over to the doorway, where she raised her head to look at the moon. Standing thus, she was taken unawares by Mo Chi, who dragged her out on the prow and pushed her into the river.

Softly he then woke the boatmen and ordered them to get under way at once—extra speed would be handsomely rewarded. The boatmen, puzzled but ignorant, seized pole and flourished oar. Mo Chi waited until the junk had covered three good miles before he moored again and told them that his wife had fallen in the river while gazing at the moon, and that no effort would have availed to save her. With this, he rewarded the boatmen with three ounces of silver to buy wine. The boatmen caught his meaning, but none dared open his mouth. The silly maidservants who had accompanied Jade Slave on board accepted that their mistress had really fallen in the river. They wept for a little while and then left off, and we will say no more of them. There is a verse in evidence of all this:

> The name of tramp-major pleases him ill;
> Hardened by pride he casts off his mate.
> The ties of Heaven are not easily broken;
> All he gains is an evil name.

But don't you agree that "there is such a thing as coincidence"? It so happened that the newly-appointed Transport Commissioner for Western Huai, Hsü Te-hou, was also on his way to his post; and his junk moored across from the Coloured Stone Cliff just when Mo Chi's boat had disappeared from view. It was the very spot where Mo Chi had pushed his wife into the water. Hsü Te-hou and his lady had opened their window to enjoy the moonlight, and had not yet retired but were taking their ease over a cup of wine. Suddenly they became aware of someone sobbing on the river bank. It was a woman, from the sound, and her distress could not be ignored.

At once Hsü ordered his boatmen to investigate. It proved indeed to be a woman, alone, sitting on the bank. Hsü made them summon her aboard, and questioned her about herself. The woman was none other than Jade Slave, Madam Chin, the wife of the Census Officer at Wu-wei-chün. What had happened was that when she found herself in the water her

wits all but left her, and she gave herself up for dead. But
suddenly she felt something in the river which held up her
feet, while the waves washed her close to the bank. Jade
Slave struggled ashore; but when she opened her eyes, there
was only the empty expanse of the river, and no sign of the
Census Officer's junk. It was then that she realized what had
happened: "My husband, grown rich, has forgotten his days
of hardship. It was his deliberate plan to drown his true wife
to pave the way for a more advantageous marriage. And
now, though I have my life, where am I to turn for support?"

Bitter reflections of this kind brought forth piteous weeping, and confronted by Hsü's questioning she could hold nothing back, but told the whole story from beginning to end.
When she had finished she wept without ceasing. Hsü and his
wife in their turn were moved to tears, and Hsü Te-hou tried
to comfort her: "You must not grieve so; but if you will
agree to become my adopted daughter, we will see what
provision can be made."

Hsü had his wife produce a complete change of clothing
for the girl and settle her down to rest in the stern cabin. He
told his servants to treat her with the respect due to his
daughter, and prohibited the boatmen from disclosing anything of the affair. Before long he reached his place of office
in Western Huai. Now it so happened that among the places
under his jurisdiction was Wu-wei-chün. He was therefore
the superior officer of Mo Chi, who duly appeared with his
fellows to greet the new Commissioner. Observing the Census
Officer, Hsü sighed that so promising a youth should be capable of so callous an action.

Hsü Te-hou allowed several months to pass, and then he
addressed the following words to his staff: "I have a daughter
of marriageable age, and possessing both talent and beauty. I
am seeking a man fit to be her husband, whom I could take
into my family. Does any of you know of such a man?"

All his staff had heard of Mo Chi's bereavement early in
life, and all hastened to commend his outstanding ability and
to profess his suitability as a son-in-law for the Commissioner. Hsü agreed: "I myself have had this man in mind for
some time. But one who has graduated at such a youthful age
must cherish high ambitions: I am not at all sure that he
would be prepared to enter my family."

"He is of humble origin," the others replied. "It would be

the happiest of fates for him to secure your interest, to 'cling as the creeper to the tree of jade'—there can be no doubt of his willingness."

"Since you consider it practicable," said Hsü, "I should like you to approach the Census Officer. But to discover how he reacts, say that this plan is of your own making: it might hinder matters if you disclose my interest."

They accepted the commission and made their approach to Mo Chi, requesting that they should act as go-betweens. Now to rise in society was precisely Mo Chi's intention; moreover, a matrimonial alliance with one's superior officer was not a thing to be had for the asking. Delighted, he replied, "I must rely entirely on you to accomplish this; nor shall I be slow in the material expression of my gratitude."

"You may leave it to us," they said; and thereupon they reported back to Hsü.

But Hsü demurred: "The Census Officer may be willing to marry her," said he, "but the fact is that my wife and I have doted on our daughter and have brought her up to expect the tenderest consideration. It is for this reason that we wish her to remain in her own home after marriage. But I suspect that the Census Officer, in the impatience of youth, might prove insufficiently tolerant; and if the slightest discord should arise it would be most painful to my wife and myself. He must be prepared to be patient in all things, before I can accept him into my family."

They bore these words to Mo Chi, who accepted every condition.

The Census Officer's present circumstances were very different from those of his student days. He signified acceptance of the betrothal by sending fine silks and gold ornaments on the most ample scale. An auspicious date was selected, and Mo Chi itched in his very bones as he awaited the day when he should become the son-in-law of the Transport Commissioner.

But let us rather tell how Hsü Te-hou gave his wife instructions to prepare Jade Slave for her marriage. "Your step-father," Mrs Hsü said to her, "moved by pity for you in your widowhood, wishes to invite a young man who has gained his doctorate to become your husband and enter our family. You must not refuse him."

But Jade Slave replied, "Though of humble family, I am

aware of the rules of conduct. When Mo Chi became my
husband I vowed to remain faithful to him all my life. However cruel and lawless he may have been, however shamefully
he may have rejected the companion of his poverty, I shall
fulfill my obligations. On no account will I forsake the true
virtue of womanhood by remarrying."

With these words her tears fell like rain. Mrs Hsü, convinced of her sincerity, decided to tell her the truth, and said,
"The young graduate of whom my husband spoke is none
other than Mo Chi himself. Appalled by his mean action, and
anxious to see you reunited with him, my husband passed
you off as his own daughter, and told the members of his
staff that he was seeking a son-in-law who would enter our
family. He made them approach Mo Chi, who was delighted
by the proposal. He is to come to us this very night; but
when he enters your room, this is what you must do to get
your own back. . . ."

As she disclosed her plan, Jade Slave dried her tears. She
remade her face and changed her costume, and made
preparations for the coming ceremony.

With evening there duly appeared the Census Officer Mo
Chi, all complete with mandarin's hat and girdle: he was
dressed in red brocade and had gold ornaments in his cap,
under him was a fine steed with decorated saddle and before
him marched two bands of drummers and musicians. His colleagues were there in force to see him married, and the whole
procession was cheered the length of the route. Indeed,

> To the roll and clang of music the white steed advances,
> But what a curious person, this fine upstanding groom:
> Delighted with his change of families, beggar for man of
>   rank,
> For memories of the Coloured Stone Cliff his glad heart has
>   no room.

That night the official residence of the Transport Commissioner was festooned with flowers and carpeted, and to the
playing of pipe and drum all awaited the arrival of the bridegroom. As the Census Officer rode up to the gate and dismounted, Hsü Te-hou came out to receive him, and then the
accompanying junior officers took their leave. Mo Chi walked
straight through to the private apartments, where the bride

was brought out to him, veiled in red and supported by a maidservant on either side. From beyond the threshold the master of ceremonies took them through the ritual. The happy pair made obeisances to heaven and earth and to the parents of the bride; and when the ceremonial observances were over, they were escorted into the nuptial chamber for the wedding feast. By this time Mo Chi was in a state of indescribable bliss, his soul somewhere above the clouds. Head erect, triumphant, he entered the nuptial chamber.

But no sooner had he passed the doorway than from positions of concealment on either side there suddenly emerged seven or eight young maids and old nannies, each one armed with a light or heavy bamboo. Mercilessly they began to beat him. Off came his silk hat; blows fell like rain on his shoulders; he yelled perpetually, but try as he might he could not get out of the way.

Under the beating the Census Officer collapsed, to lie in a terrified heap on the floor, calling on his parents-in-law to save him. Then he heard, from within the room itself, a gentle command issued in the softest of voices: "Beat him no more, our hard-hearted young gentleman, but bring him before me."

At last the beating stopped, and the maids and nannies, tugging at his ears and dragging at his arms like the six senses tormenting Amida Buddha in the parable, hauled him, his feet barely touching the ground, before the presence of the bride. "What is the nature of my offence?" the Census Officer was mumbling; but when he opened his eyes, there above him, correct and upright in the brilliance of the candle-light, was seated the bride—who was none other than his former wife, Jade Slave, Madam Chin.

Now Mo Chi's mind reeled, and he bawled, "It's a ghost! It's a ghost!" All began to laugh, until Hsü Te-hou came in from outside and addressed him: "Do not be alarmed, my boy: this is no ghost, but my adopted daughter, who came to me below the Coloured Stone Cliff."

Mo Chi's heart ceased its pounding. He fell to his knees and folded his hands in supplication. "I, Mo Chi, confess my crime," he said. "I only beg your forgiveness."

"This is no affair of mine," replied Hsü, "unless my daughter has something to say. . . ."

Jade Slave spat in Mo Chi's face and cursed him: "Cruel

wretch! Did you never think of the words of Sung Hung? 'Do
not exclude from your mind the friends of your poverty, nor
from your house the wife of your youth.' It was empty-
handed that you first came into my family, and thanks to our
money that you were able to study and enter society, to make
your name and enjoy your present good fortune. For my
part, I looked forward to the day when I should share in your
glory. But you—forgetful of the favours you had received,
oblivious of our early love, you repaid good with evil and
threw me into the river to drown. Heaven took pity on me
and sent me a saviour, whose adopted daughter I became.
But if I had ended my days on the river-bed, and you had
taken a new wife—how could your heart have been so callous? And now, how can I so demean myself as to rejoin
you?"

Her speech ended in tears and loud wails, and "Cruel,
cruel!" she continued to cry. Mo Chi's whole face expressed
his shame. He could find no words, but pleaded for forgiveness by kotowing before her. Hsü Te-hou, satisfied with
her demonstration of anger, raised Mo Chi to his feet and admonished Jade Slave in the following words: "Calm your anger, my child. Your husband has now repented his crime, and
we may be sure that he will never again treat you ill. Although in fact your marriage took place some years ago, so
far as my family is concerned you are newly-wed; in all
things, therefore, show consideration to me, and let an end be
made here and now to recriminations." Turning to Mo Chi,
he said, "My son, your crime is upon your own head, lay no
blame on others. Tonight I ask you only to show tolerance. I
will send your mother-in-law to make peace between you."

He left the room, and shortly his wife came in to them.
Much mediation was required from her before the two were
finally brought into accord.

On the following day Hsü Te-hou gave a banquet for his
new son-in-law, during which he returned all the betrothal
gifts, the fine silks and gold ornaments, saying to Mo Chi,
"One bride may not receive two sets of presents. You took
such things as these to the Chin family on the previous occasion, I cannot accept them all over again now." Mo Chi lowered his head and said nothing, and Hsü went on: "I
believe it was your dislike of the lowly status of your father-
in-law which put an end to your love and almost to your

marriage. What do you think now of my own position? I am only afraid that the rank I hold may still be too low for your aspirations."

Mo Chi's face flushed crimson, and he was obliged to retire a few steps and acknowledge his errors. There is a verse to bear witness:

> *Full of fond hopes of bettering himself by marriage,*
> *Amazed to discover his bride to be his wife;*
> *A beating, a cursing, an overwhelming shame:*
> *Was it really worth it for a change of in-laws?*

From this time on, Mo Chi and Jade Slave lived together twice as amicably as before. Hsü Te-hou and his wife treated Jade Slave as their own daughter and Mo Chi as their proper son-in-law, and Jade Slave behaved towards them exactly as though they were her own parents. Even the heart of Mo Chi was touched, so that he received Chin Lao-ta, the tramp-major, into his official residence and cared for him to the end of his days. And when in the fullness of time Hsü Te-hou and his wife died, Jade Slave, Madam Chin, wore the heaviest mourning of coarse linen for each of them in recompense for their kindness to her; and generations of descendants of Mo and of Hsü regarded each other as cousins and never failed in friendship. A verse concludes:

> *Sung Hung remained faithful and was praised for his virtue;*
> *Huang Yün divorced his wife and was reviled for lack of*
>   *feeling.*
> *Observe the case of Mo Chi, remarrying his wife:*
> *A marriage is predestined: no objection can prevail.*

—*Translated by Cyril Birch*

CH'ING DYNASTY

1644–1912

The Ch'ing Dynasty, though dominated by a foreign political power—the Manchu—witnessed significant achievement in all the literary arts. Some writers of the period were subservient to the governmental and cultural strictures set by the alien rulers; others, however, used their talents for purposes of resistance. Drama and fiction, both most dearly loved by the masses of the people, were the chief vehicles for independent expression. Characters were, in general, represented as free agents, often given to unconventional and erratic behavior. Favorite plots involved the horrible, the macabre, the miraculous.

"The Lady Knight-Errant" combines a number of these favorite Ch'ing elements. A sullen, reserved young woman and her old mother, apparently rootless, settle down in a small village. The substance of the plot has to do with how the daughter gives her love to the young man next door but refuses marriage, bears his child and gives it up, lives on alone in the house after her mother's death, and finally reveals her strongly "masculine" motivation before leaving the village on her lonely and self-sufficient way.

The Lady Knight-Errant

P'u Sung Ling

P'u Sung Ling (1640–1715) was one of the leading writers of his time, although he was repeatedly unsuccessful in his attempts to pass the governmental literary examinations. In addition to writing short stories in the classical style, he wrote poetry and anonymously authored a lengthy novel in the dialect of Shantung Province—a revolutionary undertaking in a time when only rigorously classical prose was considered acceptable. His characters are noted for their realism, even in the often improbable situations in which he and his readers delighted.

Realistic in fact was the woman warrior, for there appears to be historical evidence that women actually served on the field of battle. A Chinese reference, *The Dictionary of Famous People*, cites the warrior career of one Mu-lan, a "filial daughter" who in "ancient days" dressed as a man and substituted for her father in twelve years of frontier fighting. There is some reason to believe that she lived under the Wei, sometime between A.D. 386 and 557. The *Dictionary* also gives sketchy information of other women warriors of the same period and later.

———

There was once a young man by the name of Ku, born of a poor family in Chin-ling.[1] He was talented and skilled in a variety of arts and crafts. However, since he could not bear to leave his aging mother, he made a simple living by selling calligraphy and paintings. He was single even at the age of twenty-five.

———

[1] Modern Nanking, in the present Kiangsu Province.

Opposite to where he lived was an empty house. One day, an old woman and a young girl came by to rent the place, but since there was no man in their family, Ku did not feel that it was appropriate for him to make a courtesy call.

One day when he returned home he saw the young girl coming out of his mother's room. She was about eighteen or nineteen, and of rare beauty and gracefulness. She made no attempt to hide when she saw Ku. There was an air of awe-inspiring composure about her. Ku went inside and questioned his mother. Mrs. Ku said, "That is the girl across the street. She came to borrow my scissors and ruler. She told me that only her mother lived with her. She doesn't seem to come from a poor family. When I asked why she isn't married, she said that she has to take care of her aged mother. I shall pay her mother a visit tomorrow, and sound her out. If they don't ask for too much, perhaps you can take care of her mother for her."

The next day, she went over to the young girl's house. She found the mother hard of hearing, and when she looked around the house, there did not seem to be enough food there for the following day. She asked the old woman how they managed to get by, and the latter replied that they depended solely on the young girl's needlework. Finally, Mrs. Ku brought up the question of a possible marriage between the two families. The old woman seemed agreeable and turned around to seek the opinion of her daughter. Though the girl did not say anything, she was apparently not too happy about it. So Mrs. Ku returned home.

Later, as she thought about the girl's reaction, she said to her son, "Do you think we've been turned down because we're too poor? What a strange girl! So quiet and so straight-faced. Just as the saying goes. 'As beautiful as the peach and pear blossoms, but cold as the frost and snow.'" Mother and son exchanged their views on the matter for a good while and then ended their discussion with a sigh.

One day, Ku was at his studio when a young man came to buy paintings. He looked handsome enough, but his manner was rather frivolous. Ku asked where he came from, and the young man replied that he came from the neighboring village. From then on, he came over every two or three days, and became fairly close to Ku. Later, they started to tease and joke with each other; and when Ku embraced the young man, he made no more than a show of refusing. Thus they carried on a secretive relationship which was to become more intimate by the day.

One day, as the girl happened to pass by, the young man gazed at her for a while and asked Ku who she was. Ku told him what he knew about her and the young man said, "What a beautiful and fearsome girl she is!"

Later, when Ku went inside, his mother said, "The young girl just came over to borrow some rice. She said that they haven't eaten for one whole day. This girl is devoted to her mother; what a pity that she should be in such circumstances. We should try to help her."

Ku agreed with what his mother said, and carried a peck of rice over to the girl's house, conveying his mother's goodwill. The girl accepted the rice but did not say a word of thanks to him.

After that, she often went over to Ku's house, helping with his mother's sewing and other needlework. She took care of all the household chores like a housewife. So Ku held her in even higher esteem. Whenever he had some delicacies, he would bring a portion over to her mother. The girl never thanked him. Once, when Ku's mother got an abscess on her private parts which caused her to cry out day and night in pain, the girl frequently stayed by her bedside, looking after her, washing the wound, and applying medicine to it three or four times a day. Mrs. Ku felt uneasy, but the girl did not seem to mind the task at all. Ku's mother sighed and said to her, "Ah, where can I find a daughter-in-law such as you to see me through the end of my days?" As she said that, her voice was choked with tears.

"Your son is devoted to you," the girl comforted her, "so you're much better off than my mother, who has only a helpless girl to look after her."

"But surely even a devoted son can't do bedside chores like these! Anyhow, I'm old and could die any day. What I'm worried about is an heir for the family."

As she spoke, Ku came in. Mrs. Ku wept and said, "I'm grateful for all that this young lady has done for us. Don't you forget to repay her kindness."

Ku bowed deeply, but the girl said, "You were kind to my mother and I didn't thank you, so why should you thank me now?"

Ku's respect and love for her grew deeper; yet she remained just as cold and aloof to him as before.

One day, Ku had his gaze fixed on the girl as she walked out the door. Suddenly she turned and smiled bewitchingly at Ku. Ku was overjoyed and followed her to her house. When he flirted with her, she did not rebuke him, so they went to bed happily and made love. Afterward, she cautioned Ku, "I hope you understand that this is a one-time thing." Ku returned home without saying anything.

The next day, he approached the girl again, but she flatly refused him and left. However, she went to Ku's place as frequently as before and met him quite often; but she did not give him the slightest encouragement. Any effort on his part to exchange pleasantries with her was met with unyielding sternness.

One day, when they had a moment to themselves, she abruptly asked Ku, "Who is that young man you were talking to the other day?" Ku told her and she said, "He has taken liberties with me several times. Seeing that you're quite close to him, I didn't want to mention it earlier. But please tell him this time: if he doesn't mend his ways, he won't live to see another day."

Ku relayed her message to the young man when he came in the evening, adding, "You must be careful. Don't offend her again!"

"If she's so chaste," the young man said, "how come the two of you are on such good terms?" Ku protested his innocence, but the young man retorted, "If there is nothing between the two of you, then why would she tell you improper things like these?" Ku could not answer, whereupon the young man said, "Well, tell her this for me, too. Tell her, don't be so self-righteous and try to put up such a chaste appearance; otherwise, I shall certainly spread this whole thing far and wide!"

Ku was extremely angry and his face showed it, so the young man left.

One night, when Ku was sitting alone at home, the girl came in unexpectedly and greeted him with a smile. "It seems that our love hasn't ended yet."

Ku was overwhelmed with joy and held the girl tightly in his arms. Suddenly they heard footsteps and both jumped up.

as pushed open and the young man walked in. Ku asked him, "What are you doing here?"

The young man laughed. "I've come to watch the show of some virtuous and chaste people!" Then he looked at the girl and said, "You can't blame anyone now, can you?"

The girl scowled and flushed with anger. Without a word, she pulled up her topcoat and took out a shiny foot-long dagger from a leather bag, the sight of which frightened the young man so much that he immediately took to his heels. The girl gave chase, but there was no one in sight outside. She flung the dagger into the air; it rose with a loud twang and was as bright as a rainbow. Then something fell to the ground with a loud thud. Ku hurried to look at it by candlelight. It was a white fox with a severed head. Ku was terrified.

"This is your Boy Charmer!" the girl told him. "I've spared him time and again, only he didn't seem to care enough for his life."

As she was replacing the dagger in the leather bag, Ku pulled her toward the house, but she said, "I don't feel like it anymore. Your Boy Charmer has spoiled the game. Wait until tomorrow night." And she left immediately without looking back.

The next evening, the girl came as promised and they spent the night together. When Ku asked her about her magic, she said, "This is something you shouldn't know about. Also, keep what you saw last night to yourself; otherwise it will bring you only trouble."

Ku then brought up the subject of marriage again, and in reply she said, "I sleep with you in the same bed, and I do all the housework here; what am I if not a wife to you? Since we live like husband and wife already, why talk about marriage?"

"Is it because I'm poor?"

"If you're poor, I'm not any better off. It's only because I feel for you in your poverty that I'm here with you tonight."

Before she left, she reminded Ku again, "Meetings such as this can't be repeated too often. If I can come, I will; but if I cannot, it's no use forcing me."

Afterward, whenever they ran into each other and Ku wanted to talk privately with her, she avoided him. Yet she kept doing all the housework and needlework in Ku's house, as before.

Several months later, the girl's mother died. Ku exhausted all his resources to help the girl bury her. From then on, the girl lived alone. Ku thought that he could take advantage of the situation, so one day he climbed over the wall and called to her from outside the window. When there was no answer, he looked through the doorway and found the house empty. He suspected that the girl had gone out to meet someone else. He returned at night but again the girl was not there. He left his jade pendant by the window and departed.

The next day, they met in his mother's room. When Ku came out, the girl followed him out and said, "You seem to have doubts about me, am I right? Everyone has his own secrets that can't be shared with others. How can I make you believe me? Anyway, there is something urgent which I must discuss with you right now." Ku asked her what it was, and she said, "I'm already eight months pregnant and I'm afraid that the child might come any time. Since I have no legitimate position in your family, I can only give you a child; I can't raise it for you. You can tell your mother secretly to look for a wet-nurse, under the pretext that she herself wants to adopt a child. Don't tell anyone that the child is mine."

Ku agreed and relayed her wish to his mother. She smiled and said, "What a strange girl! She refused to marry you and yet she has no qualms at carrying on an affair with you!"

She carried out the girl's plan happily and waited for her delivery.

More than a month had passed, and when the girl failed to show up for several days in a row, Mrs. Ku became suspicious and went over to have a look. The door was tightly shut and all was quiet inside. She knocked for a long time before the girl came out, with her hair all disheveled and her face soiled. She opened the door for Ku's mother and closed it immediately. Inside her room, Mrs. Ku found a baby crying on the bed. The old woman was surprised and asked, "When was he born?"

"Three days ago," she replied.

Mrs. Ku unwrapped the baby and found it to be a chubby boy with a wide forehead. Overjoyed, she said, "You have given me a grandson, but what is a single girl like you going to do all alone in the world?"

"This is my secret, and I'm afraid I can't explain it to you," the girl replied. "You can carry the baby home at night when there is no one around."

The old lady returned and told her son, and both of them were puzzled. They went over and took the baby home at night.

Several nights later, the girl suddenly came over around midnight, carrying a leather bag in her hand. She smiled and said, "I've accomplished my goal. It's time for me to say good-bye."

Ku immediately pressed her for a reason, to which she answered, "I've always remembered your kindness in helping me to support my mother. I once told you that our bedding together was a one-time affair because one should not repay one's debt in bed. But since you're so poor and could not afford to get married, I tried to give you an heir. I was hoping to bear you a boy by taking you just once, but unfortunately my period came as usual afterward so I had to break my rules and do it again. Now that I have repaid your kindness, my wish is fulfilled and I have no regrets."

"What is inside that bag?"

"The head of my enemy."

Ku picked it up and looked inside. He saw a bearded head, all smashed and smeared with blood. Though frightened out of his wits, he managed to get the story from the girl, who finally took him into her confidence. "I've never mentioned it to you before because I was afraid that you might let the secret out inadvertently. Now that my work is finished, I can tell you about it freely. I'm originally from Chekiang Province. My father was a prefect. He was falsely charged and killed by his enemy, and our house was confiscated. I took my mother away and we lived quietly for three whole years under concealed identities. The reason why I waited so long before avenging my father was that my mother was still alive. And after my mother died, I was held up by my pregnancy. Remember the night you came by and I was out? Well, I went out to better acquaint myself with the ways in and out of the enemy's house. I didn't want to take chances." As she was leaving, she said these parting words to Ku: "Please take good care of my son. You yourself will not be blessed with long life, but this son of yours can bring fame and great honor to your family. Since it's so late, I don't want to wake your mother. Good-bye!"

Grief-stricken, Ku was about to ask her where she was going when, quick as a lightning flash, the girl disappeared. Ku sighed and stood there petrified for a long time.

He told his mother everything the next morning, but they could do no more than express their sorrow and admiration for her.

Three years later, just as was predicted by the girl, Ku died a premature death. His son later became a *chin-shih* at the age of eighteen, and he took care of his grandmother throughout her old age.

—*Translated by Lorraine S. Y. Lieu, Ma Yau-Woon, and Joseph S. M. Lau*

MODERN PERIOD

1912 to the present

It is in the writings of the modern era that we get a sense of the traumatic impact of Western values and mores on traditional Chinese life. Although China had experienced some East-West interchange since the time of Marco Polo in the thirteenth century, and subsequent development of trade routes along which treasured silks and porcelains found their way to an eagerly receptive Europe, it was not until the nineteenth and twentieth centuries that the masses of the people began to feel the disruptive influences of Western culture, accompanied by industrialization and urbanization.

There is now a rich mother lode of contemporary fiction well translated in America and England, as well as officially issued from the Foreign Language Press in Peking and from publishers on Taiwan. With the increasing accessibility of Chinese literature in English translation, the literary road between China and the West has become a busy two-way street.

The stories about women of the modern period given here are remarkable for the revelation of the diverse reactions of Chinese women to their peculiar life situations. Some are traditionalists who continue to submit unquestioningly to injustice. Others, having felt the influence of new ways, struggle briefly and give up. Still others—notably few—fight for and achieve their liberation from the stultifying bonds of custom.

One of the most notable differences between early writings and the stories of contemporary times is that the latter are prosaically down-to-earth. Gone are the fanciful stories of the highborn and powerful, of mystical and implausible situations, replaced by the actual concerns of actual people—increasingly those of the lower classes.

Since the Chinese are an innately literary people, it is not surprising that revolution in literary expression should have gone hand-in-glove with social and political revolution. As early as 1895, Sun Yat-sen (1860–1925), a product of American schools, had spoken out against the long and decadent rule of the Manchu conquerors from the north who had been in political control of China since the seventeenth century. Final overthrow did not come until 1912, following a year of violent struggle. Under Sun's leadership a government was established that sought to wed traditional Confucian ethics with a Western form of representative government.

In the meantime, the tocsin for change in literary expression was sounded in far-off America by Hu Shih (1891–1962), an internationally respected scholar, statesman, historian, author, lecturer, and writer. His "Dream and Poetry," written in the vernacular *pei-hua*, touched the heartstrings of his countrymen with its claim that poetry is "all ordinary experience," "all ordinary images," "all ordinary words." Though not claiming to be a poet, Hu's collection of verses, *Book of Experiments*, demonstrated a literary form in touch with new times and with appeal to the masses of the people. Its publication in 1911 began what was to be recognized as a true literary revolution. Later (1917), an essay—"A Preliminary Discussion of Literary Reform"—summed up his philosophy and demonstrated the fitness of using new literary means for a new time. The main thesis of his essay emphasized the practical application of literary expression in a medium that could reach all the people, not just the highly educated elite. "The literary revolution we are promoting aims merely at the creation of a Chinese literature of national speech," he declared. "Only when there is such a literature can there be a national speech of literary quality. And only when there is a national speech of literary quality can our national speech be considered a real national speech." Pa Chin's novel *Family* (1931) admirably points up the strong linkage between the literary revolution and the social.

"The Curse of the Blood-Glow," an excerpt from *Family*, pictures a twentieth-century birth in which adherence to centuries-old customs results in the inhuman suffering and ultimate death of the young mother. In "Meng Xiangyin Stands

Up," a young bride proves to be intractable in her relationship with her younger husband and his overbearing mother. Eventually, Meng Xiangyin develops into a "heroine of the New Order."

"Girl Rebel" presents excerpts from an autobiographical novel by a young woman who breaks the shackles of a custom-bound past to become a leader in her country's struggle for political independence and woman's struggle for freedom. "The Child-Bride" also comes from a volume of reminiscences by a contemporary woman writer. This frank and objective account of the custom of selling a girl child into early marriage, and one possible result, amounts to a devastating condemnation of a social pattern that had gone generally unchallenged from early times.

"The Moon on a Frosty Morning" depicts a wife and her mother-in-law joined in dedication to the hard work of the commune, rejecting the husband/son who abandoned them for the good life. Here women are depicted as the strong village leaders, in sharp contrast to the women in such stories as "Slave's Mother," which has to do with the selling of a woman into a second marriage against her will. The sale, initiated by the woman's first husband, leads to her unhappy aging and estrangement from her son.

"The Elder Mrs. King" depicts the cruelty exerted by an entire family against an older wife who has brought them property and wealth. Her response to the final insult is to take her own life.

The Curse of the Blood-Glow

Pa Chin

Pa Chin is the pen name for Li Fei-kan (1904–   ), one of modern China's most prolific and admired writers. Although he has written in practically every literary genre, from political tracts to romantic dramas, his chief reputation has been as a novelist of social reform. In addition to two trilogies— *Turbulent Stream* and *Love*—Pa Chin has written several other novels and scores of short stories. The first book of the trilogy *Turbulent Stream* is the novel *Family*, from which the story of the Blood-Glow is taken.

An anarchist from his student days, Pa Chin ran into hard times with both the Kuomintang and the Communist governments. During the first years of the Chinese People's Republic, he realized considerable fame. But after speaking out too frankly during the quickly-aborted "Hundred Flowers Period" of 1956–57 when Mao Tse-tung called for freedom of thought and expression, his home was vandalized, and his internationally-famous library of anarchist literature destroyed. In 1968, Pa Chin was publicly denounced as a traitor, first kept under house arrest, and then "sent to labor for re-education." He was among a considerable number of intellectuals who were later accepted back into the mainstream of China's life.

Pa Chin's *Family* presents in fictional form a picture of old China and the forces that are rising to destroy it. Women suffer their special agonies. Arranged marriages, foot-binding, submission to men and to elders, are all becoming increasingly hard to accept.

The struggles, hopes, and aspirations of the Kao family are rooted in the reality of the China of the day. While parents and grandparents remain bound to the Confucian classics, the young people read such magazines as *New Youth*, one of the most influential periodicals of the New Culture Movement that was inspired by Hu Shih's call for the use of the spoken language as a literary medium. They read and dream about the strange life of the West. They are ripe for change and freedom.

———

It was almost time for Jui-chueh to give birth, and Mistress Chen and other women of the family were deeply disturbed. At first they only discussed the matter privately. Then, one day, with stern visage, Mistress Chen talked to Ke-ming and his brothers about "the curse of the blood-glow."

There was a superstition that if, while the body of one of the elder generation was still in the house, a birth should take place at home, the glow of the blood emitted by the mother would attack the corpse and cause it to spurt large quantities of blood. The only means by which this could be prevented was for the pregnant woman to leave the compound and move outside the city.

Nor was that enough. The big city gates weren't strong enough to keep the blood-glow from returning—she had to move across a bridge.

Even that was not necessarily fool-proof. The coffin had to be covered with a layer of bricks and earth. Only thus could it be protected from "the curse of the blood-glow."

Madam Shen of the Fifth Household was the first to approve of these preventive measures; Madam Wang of the Fourth Household quickly seconded her. Ke-an and Ke-ting agreed next, followed finally by Ke-ming and Madam Chou. Of the elder generation only Madam Chang of the Third Household expressed no opinion. In any event, it was decided to act according to Mistress Chen's recommendation, and the elders wanted Chueh-hsin to move his wife out immediately. They said the interests of the Venerable Master Kao should transcend all.

Although the decision struck Chueh-hsin like a bolt from the blue, he accepted it meekly. He had never disagreed with anyone in his life, no matter how unfairly they may have treated him. He preferred to swallow his tears, suppress his anger and bitterness; he would bear anything—rather than oppose a person directly. Nor did it ever occur to him to wonder whether this forbearance might not be harmful to others.

Jui-chueh made no complaint when he informed her. She expressed her unwillingness in tears. But it was no use. She hadn't the strength to protect herself. Chueh-hsin hadn't the strength to protect her either. She could only submit.

"You know I don't believe in this, but what can I do?" Chueh-hsin helplessly spread his hands. "They all say it's better to be on the safe side."

"I'm not blaming you. I blame only my unhappy destiny," Jui-chueh sobbed. "My mother isn't even in town to look after me. But I can't let you get the reputation of being unfilial. Even if you were willing, I wouldn't agree."

"Jui, forgive me, I'm too weak. I can't even protect my own wife. These years we've been together . . . you know what I've been suffering."

"You shouldn't . . . talk like that," Jui-chueh said, wiping her eyes with her handkerchief. "I know . . . what you've been through. You've . . . suffered enough. You're so good to me. I'm very grateful. . . ."

"Grateful? You're going to give birth any day now, and I'm sending you to a lonely place outside the city where there are no conveniences and you'll be all alone. I'm letting you down. What other man would let his wife be treated so badly? And you still say you're grateful!" Chueh-hsin wept miserably.

Jui-chueh stilled her crying, rose quietly and walked out. Soon she returned, holding little Hai-chen by the hand and followed by the nursemaid.

Leading the child to the softly weeping Chueh-hsin, she instructed him to call his *"Tieh-tieh,"* to take his father's hand and tell him not to cry.

Chueh-hsin embraced the little boy and gazed at him with loving eyes. He kissed the child's cheek several times, then put him down and returned him to Jui-chueh. "There's no hope for me," he said hoarsely. "But rear Hai-chen well. I don't want him to be like me when he grows up!" Chueh-hsin left the room, wiping his eyes with his hand.

"Where are you going?" Jui-chueh called after him in concern.

"Outside the city to look for a house." He turned around

to face her, and his eyes again were blinded by tears. After wrenching these words out, he hastily walked away.

That day Chueh-hsin returned very late. Finding a house was not easy, but in the end he had succeeded. It was a little place in a small compound, ill-lighted, with damp walls and an earthen floor. The rent was cheap enough, but that wasn't the reason Chueh-hsin took it. He had been concerned with only two things—"outside the city" and "across a bridge." Such matters as comfort and convenience were secondary.

Before Jui-chueh moved, Mistress Chen and a few other ladies of the family went to inspect the house. They could find no objections.

Chueh-hsin insisted on doing all the packing for Jui-chueh. He made her sit in a chair and supervise. Before putting anything in the suitcase, he would hold it up and say, "What about this?" and she would smile and nod her head, whether she really wanted it or not. When the packing was done Chueh-hsin declared proudly, "You see, I know exactly what you like."

Jui-chueh smiled. "You do indeed. The next time I go on a trip I'll be sure to ask you to pack for me again." She hadn't intended to make the last remark, but it slipped out.

"Next time? Of course I'll go with you next time. Where will you be going?"

"I was thinking of visiting my mother. But we'll go together, naturally. I won't leave you again."

Chueh-hsin changed colour, and he hastily dropped his head. Then he raised it again and said with a forced laugh, "Yes, we'll go together."

They were fooling each other and they knew it. Though they smiled, they wanted to cry. But they masked their true feelings behind a cheerful countenance. Neither was willing to give way to tears in the presence of the other.

The girls, Shu-hua and Shu-ying, came in, then Chueh-min and Chueh-hui. They could see only the pleasant expressions on the faces of Chueh-hsin and Jui-chueh, and could not guess the turmoil that was in their hearts.

Chueh-hui couldn't keep silent. "Big Brother, are you really going to let Sister-in-law go?" he demanded. Although he had heard something about this, at first, he had thought people were joking. But when he had come home, a few minutes before, he had met Yuan Cheng, Chueh-hsin's middle-aged servant, at the gate to the inner courtyard. The man had greeted him affectionately, and Chueh-hui stopped to chat with him.

"Third Young Master, do you think it's a good idea for Mistress Jui-chueh to move outside the city?" Yuan Cheng had asked with a frown, his thin face darker than usual.

Chueh-hui was startled. "Of course not. But I don't believe she'll really go."

"Third Young Master, you don't know. First Young Master has ordered me and Sister Chang to look after her. They've already called in a mason to make a false tomb for the old man's coffin. I don't think she ought to go, Third Young Master. Even if she must, it ought to be to some place decent. Only rich people have all these rules and customs. Why doesn't First Young Master speak up? We servants don't understand much, but we think her life is more important than all these rules. Why don't you talk to First Young Master, and Madam Chou?"

There were tears in Yuan Cheng's eyes. "We ought to think of the Young Mistress. Everyone in the compound wishes her well! If anything should go wrong. . . ." Yuan Cheng couldn't continue.

"All right. I'll speak to First Young Master immediately. Don't worry. Nothing's going to happen to the Young Mistress," Chueh-hui had said, agitated, but determined.

"Thank you, Third Young Master. But please don't let anyone know I told you," Yuan Cheng said in a low voice. He turned and went into the gate house.

Chueh-hui had immediately sought out Chueh-hsin. Although the appearance of the room already proved the truth of Yuan Cheng's words, Chueh-hui demanded to know whether Big Brother was sending Jui-chueh away.

Chueh-hsin looked at him vaguely, then silently nodded his head.

"Are you crazy? Surely you don't believe in all this superstitious rot!"

"What difference does it make what I believe?" cried Chueh-hsin, wringing his hands. "That's what they all want. . . ."

"I say you should fight back," said Chueh-hui angrily, his eyes gleaming with hatred. He didn't look at Chueh-hsin.

"This is the last act of their farce." His gaze was fixed outside the window.

"Third Brother is right," said Chueh-min. "Don't send Sister-in-law away. Go and explain your reasons in detail. They'll understand. They're reasonable people."

"Reasonable?" echoed Chueh-hsin fretfully. "Even Third Uncle who studied law in a Japanese university was forced to agree. What chance have I? I couldn't bear it if I became known as unfilial. I have to do what they want. It's just hard on your Sister-in-law. . . ."

"What's hard about it? It will be much quieter outside the city. . . . I'll have people to look after me and keep me company," said Jui-chueh with a forced smile. "I'm sure it'll be very comfortable."

"You've given in again, Big Brother! Why do you always give in? Don't you realize how much harm you do?" Chueh-hui demanded hotly. "Your weakness nearly wrecked the happiness of Chueh-min and Chin. Luckily, Second Brother had the courage to resist. That's why he won."

Chueh-min couldn't repress a smile of satisfaction. He agreed with Chueh-hui. His happiness had been won through victory in battle.

"Certainly, you've triumphed." Chueh-hsin suppressed his anger. He seemed to be ridiculing himself. "You resist everything, you have contempt for everything, and you've won. But your victory has deepened my defeat. They heap upon me all their resentment against you. They hate me, curse me behind my back. You can resist, go away. But can I run away from home like Second Brother? There are many things you don't know. How much abuse I had to put up with on account of Second Brother. The trouble I had over Third Brother working on that magazine and mixing with those new friends. I took it all, without a word. I kept my bitterness inside me. No one knew. It's all very well for you to talk about resistance, struggle. But who can I say those fine-sounding words to?"

Gradually his anger abated. An unbearable oppression seemed to be crushing him. He hurried to his bed and lay down, hiding his face with his hands.

This crumpled Jui-chueh's last line of defence. Dropping her false smile, she buried her head on the table and wept. Shu-hua and Shu-ying, their own voices tearful, tried to comfort her. Chueh-min regretted he had spoken so hastily. He had been too harsh with Big Brother. He tried to think of something to say to make amends.

Chueh-hui was different. There was too much hatred in his heart for him to find room for sympathy for his Big Brother. He could see a lake before him, and a coffin . . . Ming-feng and Mei. . . . And now . . . this . . . and what it would bring. These thoughts made him burn with rage.

Like his two older brothers, Chueh-hui had enjoyed the loving care of a devoted mother. After she died, he tried to carry out her teachings—love and help others, respect your elders, be good to your inferiors. But what a spectacle his elder generation was making of itself today! How the dark forces in the family that destroyed love were growing! The life of the girl he had adored had been uselessly snuffed out. Another girl had been driven to her grave. And he had not been able to save them. Sympathy, he was bereft of sympathy—even for his brother. In his heart there were only curses.

"One girl has already died because of you," he said to Chueh-hsin coldly. "I should think that would be enough." He strode from the room.

Outside, he met the nursemaid bringing in little Hai-chen. The child hailed him, laughing, and he returned the salutation. He was miserable.

Back in his own room, Chueh-hui was overcome with a loneliness, the like of which he had never felt before. His eyes grew damp. The world was such a tragic place. So many tears. So much suffering. People lived only to destroy themselves, or to destroy others. Destruction was inevitable, no matter how they struggled. Chueh-hui could see plainly the fate that lay ahead for his Big Brother, but he was helpless to save him. And this fate was not only Big Brother's, but the destiny of many, many others.

"Why is there so much misery in the world?" he asked himself. His mind was filled with pictures of innumerable unhappy events.

No matter what happens, I must go my own road, even if it means trampling over their dead bodies. Chueh-hui seemed to be hemmed in by bitterness, with no way out, and he encouraged himself with these words.

Then he left the compound. He went to the magazine office, to join his new friends.

Temporarily suppressing his unhappiness, Chueh-hsin accompanied Jui-chueh to her new abode. Madam Chou, Shu-hua and Shu-ying went with them. There were also the man servant, Yuan Cheng and Sister Chang, the stout maid, who would stay with Jui-chueh. Chueh-min and Chin came out a bit later in the day.

Jui-chueh didn't like the place. It was the first time she and Chueh-hsin would be separated since their marriage. She would have to live without him in this damp gloomy house for over a month. She tried to think of something to console herself, but she could not. Everyone was busy arranging furniture, and she wept behind their backs. But when anyone spoke to her she managed to look cheerful. This made the people concerned about her feel somewhat reassured.

It was soon time for the others to return to the city.

"Must you all go? Can't Chin and Shu-hua stay a little longer?" Jui-chueh pleaded.

"It's getting late. They'll be closing the city gates. I'll come and see you again tomorrow," said Chin with a smile.

"City gates." Jui-chueh repeated the phrase as if she had not understood it. Actually she knew very well that tonight she would be separated from Chueh-hsin not only by distance but by a series of ponderous gates. Between dusk tonight and dawn tomorrow even if she died out here, he wouldn't know, he wouldn't be able to reach her. She was like a criminal, exiled in a distant land. This time she couldn't control her tears; they welled from her eyes.

"It's so lonely here. I'm afraid. . . ."

"Don't worry, Sister-in-law," said Shu-hua. "I'll move out tomorrow."

"I will too. I'll speak to Ma about it," added Shu-ying emotionally.

"Be patient, Jui. You'll get used to it in a day or so," said Chueh-hsin. "The two servants staying with you are very reliable. There's nothing to be afraid of. Tomorrow the girls will move out to keep you company. I'll try and find time too. Be patient. The month will pass quickly." Though he tried hard to appear confident, Chueh-hsin felt more like embracing Jui-chueh and weeping with her.

Madam Chou gave some final instructions, the others added a few words, then they all departed. Jui-chueh saw them to the compound gate and watched them get into their sedan-chairs.

Chueh-hsin had already entered his conveyance. Suddenly he got out again to ask whether she wanted him to bring her anything from home. Jui-chueh said she had everything she needed.

"Bring Hai-chen out tomorrow. I miss him terribly," she said. "Take good care of him," she directed, and she added, "Whatever you do, don't let my mother hear about this. She'll worry."

"I wrote to her two days ago. I didn't tell you. I knew you wouldn't let me write her," replied Chueh-hsin.

"Why did you do it? If my mother knew I was———" Jui-chueh stopped herself abruptly. She was afraid of hurting him.

"I had to let her know. If she can come to Chengtu, she'll be able to help look after you." Chueh-hsin swallowed his pain. He didn't dare think of Jui-chueh's unfinished sentence.

The two looked at each other as if they had nothing to say. But their hearts were filled with unspoken words.

"I'm going now. You get some rest." Again Chueh-hsin walked to his sedan-chair. He turned his head to gaze at her several times.

"Come early tomorrow," Jui-chueh called from the gate. She waved her hand until his sedan-chair disappeared around a bend in the road. Then, supporting her heavy abdomen, she went into the house.

She wanted to take some things out of her luggage, but her limbs were powerless. Her nerves were tense too. Wearily making an effort, she walked over and sat down on the edge of the bed. Suddenly, she thought she felt the child move in her womb; she seemed to hear it cry. In hysterical anger, she beat her abdomen with her hand weakly. "You've ruined me!" she exclaimed. She wept softly until Sister Chang, the maid, hearing her, came hurrying in to soothe her.

The following morning, Chueh-hsin indeed came early, and he brought Hai-chen with him. Shu-hua moved out, as promised. Shu-ying came too, but she had not been able to obtain her mother's consent to live outside the city. Later, Chin also arrived. For a while, the little compound was very gay, with chatter and happy laughter.

The hours passed quickly. Again it was time to part. Hai-chen burst into tears; he wanted to remain with his mother. Of course, this was not possible. After much persuasion, Jui-chueh managed to cajole a smile from him again. He agreed to go home with his father.

Once more Jui-chueh saw Chueh-hsin to the gate. "Come again early tomorrow," she said. Tears glistened in her eyes.

"I'm afraid I can't come tomorrow. Masons are coming to build a simulated tomb for *Yeh-yeh*. The family wants me to supervise," Chueh-hsin said morosely. Noticing her tears, he said quickly, "But I'll definitely find time to come out. You mustn't get upset so easily, Jui. Take care of your health. If you should get sick. . . ." Chueh-hsin swallowed the rest. He was afraid of weeping himself.

"I don't know what's wrong with me," said Jui-chueh slowly with a mournful smile, her eyes fixed upon his face. She patted Hai-chen's cheek. "Each time you leave, I'm afraid I'm never going to see you again. I'm scared. I don't know why." She rubbed her eyes.

"You shouldn't be. We live so near each other, and I come to see you every day. And now Shu-hua is staying with you." Chueh-hsin forced a smile. He didn't dare let himself think.

"Isn't that the temple?" Jui-chueh suddenly pointed at a tile-roofed building far off to the right. "I hear that's where Cousin Mei's coffin is. I must go and see her one of these days."

Chueh-hsin turned pale. He hastily looked away. A terrifying thought possessed him. He took her warm soft hand and pressed it, as if afraid that someone would snatch her from him. "You mustn't go, Jui!" he exhorted. Jui-chueh was impressed with the gravity of his tone, though she couldn't understand why he should be so set against her going.

But he said no more. Dropping her hand abruptly, after Hai-chen again said goodbye to "Mama," Chueh-hsin strode to his sedan-chair. As the two carriers raised the conveyance to their shoulders, Hai-chen leaned out of the window and called, "Mama! Mama!"

On returning home, Chueh-hsin went to the family hall, where the old man's body was lying in its coffin. He met Mistress Chen, who was coming out.

"How is Jui-chueh? Well, I hope," she greeted him, smiling.

"Not bad, thank you." Chueh-hsin forced an answering smile.

"Will she be giving birth soon?"

"It will still be a couple of days, I'm afraid."

"Don't forget, Young Master. You mustn't enter the delivery room!" Mistress Chen's voice suddenly became hard. She walked away.

Chueh-hsin had been given this warning several times before. But today, hearing a person like Mistress Chen issue it in such a tone made him speechless with rage. He stared after her retreating figure. When little Hai-chen, whom he was holding by the hand, raised his head and called *"Tieh-tieh,"* Chueh-hsin didn't hear him.

Four days later, Chueh-hsin paid his usual visit to Jui-chueh. Because he had been delayed by some business at home, he didn't arrive until past three in the afternoon.

Calling Jui-chueh by name as he entered the courtyard, he hurried to her room. But before he could set foot across the threshold, he was stopped by the stout maid, Sister Chang.

"You can't go in, First Young Master," she said severely.

He understood, and meekly withdrew to the little garden outside Jui-chueh's window. The door closed. Inside, he heard footsteps and the voice of a woman he didn't know.

Chueh-hsin gazed distractedly at the grass and flowers in the small garden. He couldn't tell whether he was happy or sad, angry or satisfied. It seemed to him he felt all these emotions at the same time. It seemed to him that he had been in a similar state of mind several years before, though only to a very slight extent. Actually it had been quite different.

How he had suffered through her struggles then, how happy and grateful he had been when she presented him with the precious gift of their first child. He had been by her side when she won through to victory; his tension had relaxed, his worry had turned to joy. When the midwife handed him the infant, he had kissed its adorable little red face. He had vowed in his heart that he would love the child and make every sacrifice for him; his whole life was deposited in the body of that infant. He had gone to the bedside of his wife and looked at her pale weary face with a love and gratitude beyond words. She had gazed back at him, triumphant, loving; then she had looked at the baby.

"I feel fine now," she had said to Chueh-hsin, happily. "Isn't he a darling? You must decide on a name for him, quickly!" Her face shone with the radiance of a mother's bliss.

Today, she was again lying in bed. She had begun to moan. There were hurrying footsteps in the room and low serious voices. All that was the same. But now she was in this rustic place. They were separated by a door. He couldn't see her, encourage her, comfort her, share her pain. Today, again he waited. But there was no joy or satisfaction—only fear, shame and regret. In his mind there was just one thought—I have injured her.

"Young Mistress, how are you feeling?" he heard Sister Chang ask.

There was a long silence. Then an agonized cry pierced his ears. He trembled, gritted his teeth, clenched his fists. Can that be her? he wondered. She had never uttered a sound like that before. But who else could it be? It must be her: It must be my Jui.

Again those terrible screams. Cries hardly human. Footsteps, voices. The rattle of crockery and cries blended together. Chueh-hsin covered his ears with his hands. It can't be her. It can't be my Jui. She could never scream like that. Nearly frantic with worry, he tried to look through the window, but the blinds were closed. He could only hear things; he couldn't see. Disappointed, he turned away.

"Be patient, Young Mistress. You'll be all right in a little while," said the unknown woman.

"It won't be long now," urged Shu-hua. "Just be patient."

Gradually, the cries subsided into low moans.

The door suddenly opened and Sister Chang hurried out. She went into another room, then hastened back to Jui's room. Chueh-hsin stared in through the half-opened door. He hesitated, wondering whether to go in. By the time he made up his mind, the door was closed in his face. He pushed it a few times, but inside there was no response. As he dejectedly turned to leave, from the room came a terrible cry. He pushed the door hard and pounded it with his fists.

"Who's there?" shouted Sister Chang.

"Let me in!" There was fear in voice, and pain and anger.

No one answered. The door remained shut. His wife continued to scream.

"Let me in, I say!" He furiously pounded the door.

"You can't come in, First Young Master. Madam Chou, Elder Master Ke-ming, Mistress Chen—they all left strict instructions. . . ." Sister Chang shouted through the door.

Chueh-hsin's courage ebbed away. He remembered what they had told him. Silently, he stood before the door. He had nothing more to say.

"Is that you, Chueh-hsin?" It was Jui-chueh's agonized voice. "Why don't you come in? Sister Chang, let the First Young Master in! Oh, the pain . . . the pain. . . ."

A chill ran up Chueh-hsin's spine. "I'm coming, Jui, I'm coming! Open this door immediately! She needs me! Let me in!" he yelled, beating a wild tattoo on the door with his fists.

"Hsin, it hurts! . . . Where are you? Why don't you let him in? Oh!"

"I'll protect you, Jui! I'll never leave you! Let me in! Can't you see how she's suffering? Have you no pity!" He heard a violent thrashing about.

Then the cries in the room stopped. A dead silence followed. That awful stillness was suddenly pierced by the bright clear wail of a new-born babe.

A stone seemed to drop from Chueh-hsin's heart. "Thank Heaven, thank Earth!" he breathed. Her pain was probably over now. Fear and suffering left him. Again he felt an indescribable joy; his eyes filled with tears. "I'll love and cherish her more than ever," he said to himself. "And I'll love our second child." He smiled with tears running down his cheeks.

"Sister-in-law!" Shu-hua's terrified exclamation smashed him like a blow. "Her hands are cold!"

"Young Mistress!" cried Sister Chang.

Their cries were a mournful dirge. Besides the midwife, they were the only other persons in the room.

Chueh-hsin knew that disaster had struck. He didn't dare to think. He went on beating against the door and yelling. No one paid any attention. The door stood implacable. It wouldn't let him rescue her, or even see her for the last time. It cut off all hope. In the room, women wept.

"Jui, I'm calling you. Can you hear me?" An insane shout, embodying all his love, was wrenched from the depths of his heart. A cry to bring her back from another world, to restore life not only to her but himself. For he knew what sort of an existence he would lead without her.

But death had come.

Footsteps approached the door. He thought it was going to be opened. But no, the midwife stood with the baby in her arms and spoke to him through a crack. "Congratulations, First Young Master. It's a boy."

He heard her start to walk away, and then the dreadful words, "Unfortunately, the baby has no mother."

The announcement went through Chueh-hsin's heart like a knife. He had none of the father's love for his infant. The child was his enemy, an enemy who had stolen Jui-chueh's life.

Gripped by hatred and grief, he pounded savagely on the door. He had wanted to kneel at his wife's bedside and beg forgiveness for his wrongs. But it was too late. The stubborn door barred their final love, their last farewell. It would not even let him weep before her.

Suddenly it dawned upon him. The door had no power. What had taken his wife away was something else. It was the entire social system, with its moral code, its superstitions. He had borne them for years while they stole his youth, his happiness, his future, the two women he had loved most in the world. They were too heavy a burden; he wanted to shake them off; he struggled. Then, all at once, he knew it was impossible. He was powerless, a weakling. Slumping to his knees before the door, he burst into bitter tears. He wept for her; he wept for himself. His weeping mingled with the sobs inside the room. But how different the two sounds were!

Two sedan-chairs halted outside the compound gate and Chueh-hsin's stepmother Madam Chou and another woman entered. Madam Chou heard the weeping as she came in the gate. Her expression changed. She said to the other woman agitatedly, "We're too late!" They hurried into the house.

"What are you doing?" Madam Chou, surprised, asked Chueh-hsin when she saw him still kneeling outside the door.

Chueh-hsin quickly rose. Spreading wide his hands, he sobbed, "Jui, Jui!" He recognized the other woman and greeted her shamefacedly, then again began to cry aloud. At the same time, wails came from the infant inside.

Not speaking, the woman dabbed her eyes with her handkerchief.

The door finally opened. Madam Chou said, "Please go in, Mrs. Li. Our family is not allowed in the confinement chamber."

Mrs. Li entered, and her penetrating voice was added to the other sounds of grief.

"Jui, why couldn't you wait? Ma came from so far to see you. If you have anything to tell me, speak! Come back, Jui. Couldn't you have waited one more day? You died a cruel death, my poor little girl! Deserted in this lonely place. They drove you out and left you all alone. If I had only come back earlier, you'd still be alive. My poor child. Why did I let you marry into that family? Your Ma destroyed you."

Madam Chou and Chueh-hsin heard it all clearly. Every word was like a needle, piercing deep into their hearts.

"Big Brother, I can't live in this family any longer! I'm leaving!"

Chueh-hsin had been sitting alone in his room at dusk, when Chueh-hui burst in on him. He had been gazing at the photograph he and Jui-chueh had taken when they got married. Although he couldn't see very plainly in the dim light, her every feature was etched upon his heart. Her full pretty face, her lovely big eyes, her shy smile, the faint dimples in her cheeks—they all seemed to come alive in the photograph. He had been staring at it tearfully when Chueh-hui's exclamation brought him back to reality. He turned to see his Third Brother looking at him with flashing eyes.

"You're leaving?" Chueh-hsin asked, startled. "Where are you going?"

"Shanghai, Peking—any place, as long as it's away from here!"

Chueh-hsin made no reply. His heart ached. He massaged his chest.

"I'm leaving. I don't care what they say, I'm leaving!" Chueh-hui jammed his hands into his pockets and heatedly paced the floor. He didn't know that each step fell like a heavy tread on Chueh-hsin's heart.

"Second Brother?" Chueh-hsin wrenched out the question.

"Sometimes he says he's going, sometimes he says he's not. I don't think he'd give up Sister Chin and go off by himself," Chueh-hui replied irritably. Then he added with determination, "Anyhow, I intend to leave."

"Yes, you can leave if you want to. You can go to Shanghai, to Peking, any place you like!" Chueh-hsin said almost sobbing.

Chueh-hui remained silent. He understood what his Big Brother meant.

"But what about me? Where can I go?" Chueh-hsin suddenly buried his head and wept.

Chueh-hui continued to pace the floor, from time to time shooting unhappy glances at his brother.

"You mustn't go," Chueh-hsin pleaded. He stopped crying and removed his hands from his face. "No matter what happens, you mustn't go."

Chueh-hui halted and stood looking at his Big Brother with a distressed expression.

"They won't allow you to leave. They'll never let you go!" Chueh-hsin said in a loud argumentative tone.

"I know they don't want me to go." Chueh-hui laughed contemptuously. "But I'm going to leave just to show them!"

"How can you? They have many arguments you won't be able to deny. *Yeh-yeh*'s body is still in the house; there hasn't been any memorial service yet; he still hasn't been buried. . . ." Chueh-hsin seemed to be speaking for "them" at this point.

"What's all that got to do with me? How can they stop me? They won't dare to kill me—like they killed Sister-in-law!"

—Translated by Sidney Shapiro and Lu Kuang-huan

Meng Xiangying Stands Up

A True Story

Chao Shu-li

Chao Shu-li (ca. 1903–ca. 1966) was a worker in the anti-Japanese struggle of the 1930s following a varied career that included teaching, journalism, and working as an entertainer as well as writing novels and short stories. "Meng Xiangying Stands Up" is said to be based on the involvement of actual village women in politics and in the freedom movement. One of Chao's most notable works is a short novel, *The Changes in Li Village*, published in 1945, which contrasts life in a village under pre-Communist and Communist governments. After recognition as a writer who exemplified Maoist literary norms, Chao later fell into disfavor and is thought to have died in 1966 or shortly thereafter.

---

1 *The Old Rules and New Reasons*

By the Qingzhang river in the south-east corner of Shexian county lies the village of Xiyaokou. Niu is the most common surname. A mile to the west, in the village of Dingyan, the predominant name is Meng. The Nius and the Mengs are both large clans, and they have intermarried for generations. In the old days, when you could not call women by their personal names, you can imagine how difficult it was to find a particular woman who had one of these surnames because there were so many women known as "Mrs. Niu from the Meng family" or "Mrs. Meng from the Niu family." Meng Xiangying, who came from Dingyan and had married into Xiyaokou, was herself a "Mrs. Niu from the Meng family."

Do not imagine that just because the two clans have inter-married for generations every couple is very happy. Indeed, many are the reverse. This is wild hill-country: as they used to say in the old days, "the mountains are high and the em-peror is far away," which could be brought up to date as "the mountains are high and the government is far away"—it is some fifteen miles to the district government office. For this reason the customs here have not changed much since the last years of the Qing dynasty. For women the old rule still holds good that as a daughter-in-law you have to put up with beating and abuse, but that once you become a mother-in-law yourself you can beat and curse your daughter-in-law. If you don't you're failing to put up a good show of being a mother-in-law. The old rule for men in handling their wives is, "a wife you've married is like a horse you've bought—you can ride them or flog them as you like." Any man who does not beat his wife is only proving that he is afraid of her.

Apart from following all the usual rules, Meng Xiangying's mother-in-law has a distinction of her own—a sharp tongue. When she was young she used to have a lot of friends outside the home, and though her husband did not approve he was scared of quarrelling with her because she could beat him whether it was an argument or a slanging match. If her own husband was intimidated by her, what chance could her daughter-in-law have?

The old village rules and her mother-in-law's sharp tongue ought to have been enough to put paid to Meng Xiangying, and on top of this there were things in Meng Xiangying's own background to make her position even worse. In the first place, she had nobody in her own family to protect her. Her parents had died when she was eight, leaving her with only a twelve-year-old sister and a baby brother. Later on her sister had also married into Xiyaokou, but because her sister's in-laws and her own were on bad terms her sister could not even come to her wedding, with the result that she had to see her-self off in the bridal sedan chair. With a family like this be-hind her, there was nobody to speak up for her when she was beaten. Secondly, her own family was destitute. Thirdly, be-cause she had lost her mother so young she had not learnt to sew well. Fourthly, she had natural feet. In this area women with natural feet are thought as odd as women with bound feet where natural ones are usual. And lastly, since she had been running the home from when she was a child she was not prepared to let her mother-in-law put upon her as she pleased. To the mother-in-law these were all reasons why she deserved to be beaten and cursed.

2 *She Could Not Even Cry*

Someone who has been cruelly wronged but has no way of protesting cannot usually help weeping, but Meng Xiangying did not have much chance of doing even that. Had her parents still been alive, she could have gone to cry in their house, but with only a ten-year-old brother there it was not merely difficult for her to go and cry on his shoulder, she had to go on looking after him when she did cry. Had she got on well with her husband she could have turned to him for a weep at night when her mother-in-law mistreated her; but as he was the one who generally gave her the beatings she suffered on his mother's orders, it would only have been asking for a second dose if she had gone crying to him.

Meng Xiangying did have one or two people to whom she could take her troubles. Her sister was a close neighbour, and she could cry whenever they met. There was also Changzhen, a young wife in the family next door who had to put up with the same sort of beating and abuse from her mother-in-law as Meng Xiangying did from hers; the two of them could weep on each other's shoulders. Apart from this she could cry by herself when she hung home-made paper out to dry on the wall. It was by the paper-drying wall that she cried the most, and the lapels of her cotton tunic would become soaked right through as she wiped the tears away with it.

Finding another chance to cry once caused some trouble. She had harnessed the donkey to the roller to grind some millet, and she burst into tears as she scooped the grain into place. An uncle of her husband's happened to meet her and ask her why. Unfortunately her mother-in-law turned up just as he was making some critical remarks about her. Realizing that he had been overheard, he took advantage of his position as her husband's brother to criticize the mother-in-law to her face. For fear that he would expose the faults of her own youth, she did not try to rebut him directly. All she could do was to change the subject.

The mother-in-law had long been against Meng Xiangying

talking with outsiders, particularly with other young married women. In her own experience, when young wives got together it was always to compare the faults of their mothers-in-law; so whenever she found out that Meng Xiangying had been talking to the women in the neighbouring houses she would discover some wrongdoing for which to beat and curse her. Although it was to a man that Meng Xiangying had been talking this time, her mother-in-law had heard herself being criticized with her own ears. "The so-and-so," she thought, "she must be spreading the dirt about me outside every day. I'll have to teach her a lesson." According to the old custom, when a mother-in-law wanted to find fault with her daughter-in-law she was as thorough as a donkey going round and round the rolling millstone: she did not miss a step. As it happened Meng Xiangying had carelessly smashed a brush-handle with the roller that day, so her mother-in-law used this as a pretext for abusing Meng Xiangying's parents. It became so unpleasant that Meng Xiangying could hold herself back no longer.

"Stop that, mother. I'll bind it up for you."

"Bind up your mother's ———," replied her mother-in-law.

"My sister will lend me a new one to replace it."

"Replace your mother's ———."

Mending it would not do, replacing it would not do, and on top of that she had to hear all this abuse of her mother. Meng Xiangying was now so furious that she had the courage to say, "My own mother has been dead for many years. You're my mother now. You're swearing at yourself, mother."

"——— your mother."

"Mother!"

"——— your mother."

"Mother! Mother! Mother!"

Mother-in-law stopped swearing. As she had met her match in her daughter-in-law, swearing gave her no pleasure. "The so-and-so's got an even sharper tongue than I have," she thought. "I'll have to think of some other way to deal with her." Later on she did indeed change her methods.

3 *She Could Not Die*

One day Meng Xiangying asked her mother-in-law for some cloth with which to patch her husband's clothes, and the mother-in-law told her to ask the father-in-law for it. According to the old rules she should not have had to ask him for patching cloth, and when Meng Xiangying argued the point with her mother-in-law, leaving her without a leg to stand on, the mother-in-law started abusing her again. The mother-in-law, realizing that she could not possibly win against Meng Xiangying who was in the right and prepared to argue, hurried to the fields to call her son.

"Meini" (this was Meng Xiangying's husband's name), "come back at once. I can't do anything with that young madam of yours. She wants to eat me alive."

As she could not control the young madam, Meini had to come back and flaunt his authority as young master. The moment he arrived he grabbed a stick and went for Meng Xiangying—according to the old rules there was no need for him to bother to ask why. But Meini did not have much authority himself, being a lad of only sixteen, and a year younger than his wife, and Meng Xiangying snatched the stick back from him.

This caused real trouble. By the old rules, when a man beat his wife she was expected to take a few blows and then run away, after which somebody else would take the stick from him and that would be the end of the matter. But Meng Xiangying had not simply refused to be beaten and to run away, she had actually disarmed him, making him feel thoroughly humiliated. In his rage he picked up a sickle and hacked a bloody wound on Meng Xiangying's forehead, from which the blood kept gushing out even after they had been pulled apart.

The people who broke up the fight seemed to think that Meini had done wrong. Nearly everyone said that if he had to hit her, he should have done so anywhere but on the head: They were only saying that he had hit her in the wrong place. Nobody asked why he had hit her. By the old rules there was no need to ask why a man had hit his wife.

After the fight everyone dispersed as though it were no business of theirs. The only person not to take so casual an attitude was Meng Xiangying herself. If her head had been cut open when she was completely in the right, and nobody was going to say a fair word for her, then it seemed that there was nothing to stop her husband from hitting her whenever he wanted to. Was this to go on for ever? The more she thought about it the more hopeless it seemed. Finally she decided on suicide and swallowed some opium.

As she did not swallow enough she did not die but started retching violently. When her relations discovered this they poured some dirty water, in which combs had been cleaned, down her throat, which made her bring it all up.

"If you like swallowing opium that's fine," her mother-in-law said. "I've got a whole jar of it. I hope you can swallow the lot." Meng Xiangying would have been glad to, but her mother-in-law did not produce it.

Another time, when Meng Xiangying came back after dark from working in the fields, her mother-in-law would not let her eat and her husband refused to allow her indoors. The yard gate was shut, as were the doors of her mother-in-law's and husband's rooms. She was left standing by herself in the yard. Changzhen, the young married woman who lived nearby, came to see her, as did her sister. They whispered a few words to her from the other side of the yard gates, which she dared not open. Changzhen and her sister were crying quietly on one side of the gates, while Meng Xiangying cried quietly on the other. Later she sat under the eaves and cried herself to sleep. When she woke up her mother-in-law and husband were both still sound asleep, the yard was quiet, the sky was bright with stars, and her clothes were soaking wet.

She had nothing to eat the next morning or at noon either, so, reckoning that she could not go on living, she went back to her room while her husband was taking his siesta in his mother's room and hanged herself.

Her neighbour Changzhen came to see her again, and when she heard that Meng Xiangying's in-laws and husband were fast asleep she thought this would be a good chance to talk. Changzhen got such a fright when she went into the room and found her hanging from the rafters that she screamed and ran out. The shouting that ensued brought a lot of people to the rescue, including Xiangying's sister, who held the body in her arms and sobbed.

After a lot of effort had been made to revive her, Xiangying opened her eyes. She saw that she was in the arms of her sister, who by now seemed to be made of tears.

Both her attempts to kill herself had failed. She had to go on suffering.

4 How She Became a Village Cadre

In 1942 a worker came from the Fifth Sub-region to Xiyaokou. When he asked them to choose a leader for the Women's National Salvation Association the villagers suggested Meng Xiangying. "She can talk," they said, "and that means she can keep a firm grip on what is right." But nobody had the courage to discuss the proposal with her mother-in-law. "I'll go myself," said the worker, but he met with some opposition. "She won't do," said Meng Xiangying's mother-in-law. "She's a failed suicide. She couldn't cope." No matter what arguments he used, they were met with "she couldn't cope." Why did Meng Xiangying's mother-in-law refuse so obstinately to let her become leader? This was something to do with Notquite Niu. (He is a former enemy agent who has come over to our side, and they call him Notquite because he has not yet reformed properly.)

When the troops of Zhu Huaibing[1], that expert trouble-maker, were stationed in this area, Notquite Niu was a big man in the village. Later, after Zhu Huaibing fell and the local security chief went over to the enemy, Notquite Niu made contact with him a couple of times in enemy territory. Then, when the Fortieth Army[2] was stationed in Linxian county, Notquite Niu got on good terms with them too. He certainly knew how to run with the hare and hunt with the hounds. He was very close to Meng Xiangying's in-laws. When Meng Xiangying's father-in-law Niu Mingshi ran into debt over his papermaking and had to make his land over to someone else as security, leaving himself none, Notquite rented him an acre. Notquite's wife had been as sociable as Meng Xiangying's mother-in-law when younger, and through introducing friends to each other the two women had themselves been friends for a long time. As Notquite Niu was an important man and Niu Mingshi's landlord, and as the two

---

[1] A Kuomintang commander.
[2] Kuomintang.

wives were such old friends as well, the two families were on very close terms. Although Niu Mingshi kept only three-tenths of the grain he harvested and had to give the remaining seven-tenths to Notquite, he and his wife still felt honoured at being on good terms with such an important man.

After the fall of Zhu Huaibing this area came, in name at least, under the control of our Shansi-Hopei-Shantung-Honan Border Region; but in fact, because "the mountains are high and the government far away," most of the local people could be swayed by what Notquite Niu and his friends said. Every few days Notquite would announce that the Japanese or the Fortieth Army were coming at any moment; and whichever it was, he always said the Eighth Route Army was no good. Meng Xiangying's father-in-law was only half convinced by this; after all, there had been no sale for his home-made paper after the beginning of the Anti-Japanese War until the Eighth Route Army came. They encouraged the revival of papermaking, and arranged for the paper to be bought by the government, which had started everyone making it again. Niu Mingshi had himself made a lot of money by making paper, and had taken less then two years to redeem the land he had made over to someone else as security for a loan. He could see that the people who had been coming to buy paper for the past two years were all from the Eighth Route Army, so he knew that they were really far from being "no good." But when he heard Notquite's stories he would start to change his mind again: so important a man, after all, must know what he was talking about. While Meng Xiangying's father-in-law was half-convinced by Notquite, but at the same time doubtful too, her mother-in-law became the faithful disciple of Notquite's wife. It made no difference to the mother-in-law who bought their paper, or how the land had been redeemed—she followed one leader: Notquite's wife. When Notquite's wife said the Fortieth Army would be coming soon, she expected it the next day or the day after. When Notquite's wife said the Fortieth Army would shoot all the present village cadres, she thought the right thing to do was to tell all the cadres' families to get the coffins ready. As you can imagine, such a mother-in-law could not possibly approve of Meng Xiangying becoming the leader of the Women's Association.

The worker, a young man, lost his patience when all his arguments were met with "she couldn't cope" by Meng Xiangying's mother-in-law. "If she can't," he shouted, "then you'll have to." To his surprise this did the trick. Meng Xiangying's mother-in-law had always thought that being a village cadre was dangerous because sooner or later you were bound to get shot by the Fortieth Army. The reason why she did not want Meng Xiangying to be one was not so much out of love for her as that she was afraid of being in trouble herself as a cadre's relation. This was why, after all her refusals, the worker's suggestion that she should do it herself threw her into a panic. She would get into less trouble by having her daughter-in-law as a cadre than by being one herself. So she became much more amenable: "It's none of my business, none at all. If she can cope, let her."

The worker had won. From then on Meng Xiangying headed the Women's Association.

5 Uncontrollable

As a village cadre she had to go to meetings. Meng Xiangying would say to her mother-in-law, "Mother, I'm going to a meeting," and off she would go. Mother-in-law was astonished at the idea of a young woman going to a meeting, but she could not stop Meng Xiangying for fear that the worker would make her take the job on herself. Although she felt that the Eighth Route Army was "no good," she reckoned that her own capacity was even smaller; if she resisted openly, then unless the Fortieth Army came to her rescue early the next morning there was nothing to stop the worker taking her to the district government office at noon.

Meng Xiangying's mother-in-law had mixed feelings about women taking part in meetings. She would have liked to go along and have a look, but decided she had better not; if she did, the Fortieth Army would say when they came that she had gone to meetings organized by the "Eighth Route faction." The next day her curiosity made her go along to find out what a lot of young women together talked about at a meeting. Her investigations shocked her. The women wanted emancipation; they were against being beaten and sworn at by their mothers-in-law and husbands; they were for ending foot-binding; they wanted to gather firewood, fetch water, and till the fields; they wanted to do the same work and eat the same food as the men; they wanted to go to winter school. In her view this was rebellion. If mothers-in-law and husbands could not beat young wives, who would? Surely someone had to beat them. Her second daughter-in-law, Meng Xiangying (her older son and his wife were farmers in Xiangyuan), had feet that she would not allow her mother-in-law to bind small enough no matter how she was beaten and cursed; surely she did not have the nerve to demand that they be allowed to grow still. Would women who gathered firewood and fetched water still be women? She was uncontrollable enough while illiterate, but if she learned to read and write she'd be even more high and mighty. What was the world coming to?

Meng Xiangying was not particularly bothered by her mother-in-law's worries. With the worker's help her job ran smoothly. She went to a lot of meetings and frequently attended winter school. When a young wife was beaten by her mother-in-law or bullied by her husband she told Meng Xiangying, who told the worker. Then there would be meetings, criticism, and struggle.

The harder Meng Xiangying worked at her job, the more information on her the mother-in-law gathered. "I can't control the so-and-so," she said to Meini, now that she could neither beat nor swear at her. "She tells everything to that worker. What are we to do about her?" Meini had no solution. He sucked in his breath, and his mother sucked in hers.

When Meng Xiangying came back from gathering firewood her mother-in-law pulled a face and muttered, "Disgraceful." When Meng Xiangying carried some water in, her mother-in-law pulled a face and muttered, "Disgraceful."

To promote the unbinding of feet, the worker told Meng Xiangying to be the first to unbind, and she was. Mother-in-law pursed her lips, and her glare followed Meng Xiangying's feet around.

The young women in the village were not like Meng Xiangying's mother-in-law. When they saw Meng Xiangying gather firewood, some of them went along to gather it with her. When they saw her fetch water, some went to fetch water with her. When they saw that she had unbound her feet, some unbound theirs. Not all the husbands were like

Meini. Many of them were progressive. One said, "A woman with natural feet can work as well as a man." Another was of the opinion that if women fetched firewood and water men had to waste less time on these odd jobs. A third view was, "Notquite Niu is always saying that the Eighth Route Army is no good, but I think the things they stand for are all fine."

No matter what everyone else thought, Meng Xiangying's mother-in-law was developing a stronger and stronger dislike for her. Now that she could not beat or swear at her there was no way of working off her resentment, so she decided to have a conference with Notquite Niu's wife. One day, on her way to the fields, she saw Notquite's wife ahead of her. "Wait for me," she shouted, but instead of waiting Notquite's wife went faster. The mother-in-law ran after Notquite's wife to catch her up, only to be told:

"Our two families are going to be seeing less of each other. Don't think your second daughter-in-law is very fashionable with her unbound feet. When the Fortieth Army comes they're sure to say she's an Eighth Route Army wife. If your family has connections with the Eighth Route Army, we're not going to get into trouble on your account."

These few words turned Meng Xiangying's mother-in-law numb with horror from her head to the soles of her feet. Resentment had been building up inside her for days, but she had never imagined that the situation could be so terribly dangerous that even this conversation was impossible. She went straight to Meini to see if he had any ideas, but he had not. The two of them sat there sucking in their breath as before.

6 *She Can't Even Be Sold*

Once, when the villagers were going to Taicang Hamlet for a struggle meeting against the enemy agent Ren Erhai, Notquite Niu and his friends said to them, "Off you go then. The Fortieth Army thinks the world of Ren Erhai, so if you're in the struggle against him watch out for your head. The Fortieth Army will settle the score with you the moment they come." Remarks like these terrified Meng Xiangying's parents-in-law and husband. Although none of them dared to try and dissuade her directly, they all turned pale. "This time we're in for real trouble," whispered the mother to her son. "Real trouble," he whispered back.

The strange expressions they wore worried even Meng Xiangying. When she spoke to the other young women about it some of them said it might be best to stay away. Unable to make up her mind, she asked the worker if it would be all right not to go. "It's not compulsory," he said, "but if the masses are going, the cadres should too." Meng Xiangying had no answer to that, so she decided to go. She wondered if she could avoid having to say anything.

In Taicang Hamlet she saw a crowd, even bigger than one for the opera, filling the square. Far more people wanted to speak than could get a word in, and Ren Erhai hung his head, not daring to look anyone in the face. Her attitude changed at once. She did not believe that so many people could all be unconcerned about being shot: obviously there would be no trouble. Before long she was leading the Xiyaokou villagers in shouting slogans against Ren Erhai.

After this struggle meeting she became bolder, no longer believing the enemy agent's rumours about a change of regime, and working with more enthusiasm than ever. Her mother-in-law was just the opposite. No sooner was Meng Xiangying back from the meeting than Notquite and his friends were saying, "Sooner or later she's for it." In cold fear her mother-in-law racked her brains until she found what seemed to be the ideal way of dealing with Meng Xiangying.

One day the mother-in-law said to Meini's aunt, "After two bad harvests there's no food in the house. Meini had better take his wife to his brother's in Xiangyuan." It was true that there was nothing to eat in the house, and Meng Xiangying would have been delighted to be separated from her mother-in-law, but now that she had started work in the village she had to carry on with it. That evening her mother-in-law had another talk with Meini's aunt while Meng Xiangying was at the literacy class for women. As the oil for the class's lamps was kept at her home Meng Xiangying came back to fetch it, and she overheard a snippet of their conversation.

"She should be taken to Xiangyuan and sold," her mother-in-law was saying. "Our Meini's young. There'll be no trouble getting him another wife."

"Aren't you afraid she'll report it to the Eighth Route Army there?" asked the aunt.

"No. Xiangyuan is occupied by the Japanese."

This was enough to tell Meng Xiangying what her mother-in-law's brilliant scheme was, and she lost no time in telling the worker. "As she hasn't told you directly," he said, "don't question her about it. Just say that you are too busy here and can't go."

As she would not go there was nothing her mother-in-law could do about it. Her plan had come to nothing.

7 *The Heroine Emerges*

That summer Pang Bingxun and Sun Dianying went over to the Japanese with the Fortieth and New Fifth Armies, after which the Eighth Route Army smashed them in Linxian. When all the Notquite Nius heard that several thousand men of the Fortieth and New Fifth Armies had crossed the Zhang river and were heading north, they were just getting ready to spread the news when they learnt of their capture by the Eighth Route Army in a Japanese strongpoint. Instead they kept quiet. But the fact was plain to see, and they could not suppress news of the victory. As soon as the village cadres heard the news they were delighted, and they gave it a great deal of publicity. From then on there was a general change of view. Even the people who had previously believed Notquite's talk about a change of regime now realized that it was his regime which had collapsed. In these much happier circumstances Meng Xiangying's work naturally went more smoothly than ever.

Unfortunately that autumn brought the worst of a string of disastrous harvests. No rain fell throughout the summer, and the crops were so dry you could almost have lit them like matches. The ears of millet that autumn were like gong-mallets with things like wax tapers a mere inch long on them. The maize did not even reach the height of a man's thigh, and half an acre yielded scarcely enough to fill a small basket. Then there were weeks on end of rain and dull days in the autumn, so that not a grain of millet was harvested. The weeds grew taller than the crops.

The government urged everyone to gather wild plants to eat during the famine. When the village cadres discussed this,

Meng Xiangying was put in charge of organizing the women. Everyone in the village was depressed by the bad harvest, and some were even saying, "We can't possibly survive after all these years of getting no crops in, so why should we bother gathering a few handfuls of leaves?" Meng Xiangying went to every house to encourage the women. "We won't die, but we'll have to eat if we're not to," was the sort of argument she used. Another was, "It won't be any good trying to gather wild plants once autumn's over." A third was, "A mixture of wild plants and grain husks is better than husks alone."

Besides talking, she took some of the keener women to make a start at the work. It now appeared that when some of the families without any food had said they would rather be left to die in peace they were only giving vent to bad tempers, because when they saw the courtyards of Meng Xiangying and her helpers filled with wild plants they went out gathering too. Meng Xiangying organized the women into four teams that went separately into the mountains every day. Within a week all the edible leaves had been stripped from the trees on the mountains nearby and were drying in the women's courtyards. When the area round their village was exhausted, they went to other villages; and when there was nothing left west of the river, they went east of the river. They went on until the autumn winds blew all the leaves from the trees. By then the twenty or so women had gathered some forty tons of leaves.

When they had finished gathering leaves they heard that a local herb could be sold for a dollar a pound, so Meng Xiangying now organized the women to collect it. Organizing this was easier because the huge piles of wild food that every family had meant that nobody was thinking now in terms of dying of starvation. Everyone was reminded of Meng Xiangying whenever they saw the leaves, so that no sooner did she mention organizing the women to gather the herb than everyone in the women's families said, "Go with her. That girl knows what she's doing." They gathered over ten tons of the herb, which brought in more than 20,000 dollars.

8 *Dividing the Household*

It has been said that because Meng Xiangying could work to beat the famine, her mother-in-law and husband turned over a new leaf. On careful inquiry this turns out to be quite wrong.

Mother-in-law had no objection to eating the wild leaves Meng Xiangying brought back, but she disapproved of her going out to gather them. "She's luring a gang of young women to go out." "Going out" originally had two meanings. There used to be a vicious kind of coal-mine boss who would buy workmen "to the death" (which meant that if the man did anything wrong he could be beaten to death) and keep them locked up at the bottom of the pit, only letting them out to see the sunlight once every five or ten days. This was called "going out." The other kind of going out was when a prisoner was let out from his cell into the prison yard. Being locked up again in his cell was called "being put away." Meng Xiangying's mother-in-law was not totally against her going out, as was proved by the way Meng Xiangying used to go to the fields for harvesting and thinning seedlings when she was first married. The mother-in-law's idea was that she should be the one to decide when Meng Xiangying went out and when she was put away. According to the old rules, if a young wife went out of the house on her mother-in-law's orders she had to be back within the time set. If she asked to be allowed out, it was up to the mother-in-law to give or refuse permission; and even if permission was given, the daughter-in-law still had to have a careful look at her mother-in-law's expression before she went. She could be beaten, scolded, or given no food if she was late back. By the old rules it was unthinkable that Meng Xiangying should organize all the women in the village. This was why her mother-in-law felt that she could not possibly be allowed to go out like this.

Several other mothers-in-law shared such ideas. Notquite Niu's wife used this chance to spread a rumour that eating wild plants was no remedy, with the result that some of the older women would not let their daughters-in-law go. Meng Xiangying had to call the women to a special meeting to look into the matter before the rumour could be quashed.

After the tree leaves and the herbs had been gathered Meng Xiangying summed up her achievements and her mother-in-law did the same. Instead of adding up how many wild plants and herbs Meng Xiangying had gathered, the mother-in-law's summary was that she was less and less like what a daughter-in-law should be. In her view, a daughter-in-law should be like this: her hair should be combed as straight as a broom handle and her feet should be as small as lotus-leaf cakes; she should make tea, cook, husk millet, mill flour, offer soup and hot water, sweep the floor, and wipe the table clean. From the moment when she started the day by emptying the chamber-pots till she set the bedding out at night she should be at her mother-in-law's beck and call, without wandering off for a single moment. She should hide whenever she saw a stranger, so that outsiders would never know you had a daughter-in-law unless you told them yourself. This was how she felt daughters-in-law should be, even though she had not always lived up to it in her own youth. She felt that Meng Xiangying was getting further and further from being a model daughter-in-law: she wore her hair in a bun; her feet were getting bigger every day; she climbed mountains all the time; and, as if it were not enough for her to go rushing around her own village, she went off three or more miles away at times. Instead of discussing things with her mother-in-law and keeping some of them from the worker, she told him everything. As the mother-in-law made this summary she thought gloomily, "What am I to do? I can't beat her, I can't swear at her, I can't control her, and I can't sell her. She won't regard herself as a member of the family much longer. Anyone would think the worker her own father." After many sleepless nights she finally thought of a solution: to divide the household.

She asked Notquite Niu to be the witness to the division. It was a fair one—if it had not been, Meng Xiangying would probably not have agreed to it. Meng Xiangying and her husband took two-thirds of an acre of level land and the same amount of sloping land, but they did not get any grain. "It's all been eaten," her mother-in-law said, "because we harvested so little." After the division the husband went back to his mother's house to eat and sleep, which left Meng Xiangying free to go her own way by herself.

9 *Meng Xiangying's Influence Spreads Beyond the Village*

After the division, in which all the food she got was less than three pounds of turnips, she had nothing to eat but the wild plants. As she had no grain at the New Year, she borrowed nearly three pounds of millet, seven of wheat, and one of salt.

As the district government office is some fifteen miles away they could not oversee work there, and, besides, local cadres were very hard to find. The district Women's Association found it most unreasonable that someone as good as Meng Xiangying was both at working herself and at organizing others to beat famine should be driven from home and left to go hungry. Besides, it hindered work throughout the district. They asked higher authority for permission to issue her with some grain to help her out, and kept her there to organize some of the Women's Association work at the district level.

Meng Xiangying has been a most successful district cadre this year.

In the first month of the lunar calendar she was chosen as a labour heroine, and she came to the Fifth Sub-region's Labour Heroes' conference. As she was passing through Taicang Hamlet on her way back, the head of the Women's Association there asked her what lessons she had learnt about how to organize women. "When there's trouble, explain the rights and wrongs," said Meng Xiangying. "Lead by doing the work yourself, and set a good example." She went on to talk at length about organizing the women to unbind their feet, gather firewood, carry water, collect leaves, and pick herbs. Following her example the head of the Taicang Women's Association led the women of her village in digging a canal over a mile long and clearing two and a half acres of waste land.

On the fifteenth of the second month Meng Xiangying did some campaigning at the temple fair in Baishan Village (some thirteen miles from Xiyaokou). The women from many villages all thought her methods were good. This year the women in the seventh district of Shexian county have worked very hard at food production, and of the very many labour heroines many became heroines as a result of her influence.

Her own achievements have been even more remarkable. In the spring she organized the women to hoe 93 acres of wheat and dig two acres of level land as well as seven and a half of hillside. In the struggle against locusts that summer they cut over ten tons of grass for burning to smoke them out. There is no need for me to go into her other achievements—harvesting wheat, loosening the soil, raking with branches, stripping the twigs of the paper-mulberry tree, and gathering wild plants to eat—because it has all been reported in the press.

10 *Some Questions*

Why are Meng Xiangying's mother-in-law and husband still on such bad terms with her? Is it because she walks too steadily now that her feet are a natural size? Is it because she does so much work that there is not enough left for them to do? Is it because she has loosened the soil too far? Is it because she has taken all the edible leaves from the trees?

Her mother-in-law has never made any such announcement.

I have not written about Notquite Niu or Meng Xiangying's mother-in-law and husband very respectfully. Am I giving them no chance to change in future?

Meng Xiangying is only twenty-two this year. Another chapter can be written at the Labour Heroes' conference every year, so we'll see who has changed for the better and who for the worse.

—Translated by W. J. F. Jenner

Girl Rebel

Hsieh Pingying

Hsieh Pingying (c. 1907–) was one of the foremost student activists of the early Chinese revolution. Introducing her novel, *Girl Rebel*, Lin Yutang writes that Hsieh Pingying was typical of the young intellectuals who joined the Revolution partly in patriotic idealism and partly to liberate themselves from stultifying home traditions. During the freedom struggle, he says, their energetic participation was encouraged; later, many were charged with Communism and imprisoned. But it was really their protest against the old ways that condemned them, he says, not their political activism. Hsieh herself was jailed two or more times. According to Lin, the revolutionist girls were especially set upon, facing "a stigma at home and official persecution abroad." In summary, he writes: "Miss Hsieh's story is the story of Young China in the convulsions of an age of social upheaval."

We might also see Hsieh Pingying as being in the tradition of the prototypical woman warrior of early times as depicted by P'u Sung Ling in "The Lady Knight-Errant" (pages 77–84).

My Childhood

The new autumn seemed even hotter than the summer. Though it was night, and a little breeze blew in from the paper window, I was sweating all through as my grandmother held me to her bosom. That day my mother had beaten me with a leather strap. My skin was bruised and Grandmother said that my face was pitifully white in the silver moonlight. I was six years old. Grandmother's nickname for me was "Phoenix Precious."

Suddenly I shivered and cried out.

"My Precious," said Grandmother, as she tenderly patted me, "don't cry again. If you waken Mother she will beat you again."

"I am not afraid of being beaten. Why doesn't she beat me to death?" I spoke loudly, as if I wanted Mother to know; and in the next room Mother heard and was angry, but did not speak.

"Precious, don't be naughty after this," said Grandmother. "Because of you, your mother went through much torture. Remember when you got a penny in your throat, and you could not get it out or swallow it down, and for the whole day you were like a dead child, with your eyes turned white and saliva running out of your mouth. Your mother was so frightened that she went twenty miles up the mountain to call a doctor. She spoke like an insane person and kneeled down and said, 'If anyone can save my child, I will give him my life if he wants it.' Then, when you swallowed the copper down, she was afraid that it would suck your blood, and that you might not live. So she sent men specially to Paoching to buy ten pounds of *tseku* herbs and every day she looked through your waste to see if the penny had come out. Another time, because you wanted to play with a pigeon's nest, you fell down from the roof; your face was hurt, your whole body was icy cold; you lost all consciousness. Tears ran down from your mother's eyes, and she hurried to get a doctor. Then, kneeling before the Buddha, she prayed, 'Spirit, if my Phoenix Precious has any bad luck, give it to me. I will go through it for her, but give her health, happiness, and let me have all her bad luck!' These things you must still remember."

I stopped crying and quietly listened to Grandmother telling her stories about me.

"Oh! My heart and liver!" she sighed, and went on again. "You are much too naughty; I don't know where you came from. Even in the first month your mother conceived you, no matter what she ate, she threw it all up again. Even a mouthful of water and a pea she had to throw up. Every day she had a headache and a stomachache. When she reached the last two or three months she suffered until she almost wanted to commit suicide. But she thought of the sons and daughter she had to care for, and changed her mind.

"Then came the critical time when you were going to enter the world. Two days before, she said that she had a stomachache; she could not get up and did not want to eat, not even to take water. She rolled on her bed in pain for two whole days. Your head suddenly came out, and I thought your birth was to be soon. I had a bellyful of hope, and I waited anxiously. But after a day and a night, that little hairy head was still in the same place. Your mother's energy was giving out. Your father was not at home, and I watched her alone and did not dare to move away for one instant. But there seemed nothing to do about it. After a long struggle, I told Sixth Grand-Auntie to call a midwife. Ah, talking about a midwife really makes people angry! Your mother had given birth to four children before, and never needed a midwife. Every time it was over in an hour. But who would have thought that this time after a day and a night, you would not come out? The midwife came to look and shook her head and said:

" 'There is no hope. You had better prepare the last rites.'

"She could say a thing like that! Sixth Grand-Auntie urged

the midwife to get the child out and cried, 'Anyway, you must save the mother, even if you have to sacrifice the child.'

"I was so worried that I didn't know what to do. But your mother had more presence of mind and she mumbled, half weeping, 'Mother, hurry to the Holy Ruler of the South Sacred Mountain and burn incense! If a boy comes, then when he is sixteen, he will go and burn incense to give thanks. If it is a girl, when she is twenty, I will take her myself and burn incense.' "

According to the superstition in our village, people who have difficult labor in the family go to offer the "Blood Basin Incense" to the Holy Ruler of Nanyo. At the time of giving thanks for answer to the prayer, the child must wear a red jacket and red trousers and a red turban on his head.

"So I listened to her," my grandmother said, "and went and knelt before the god and promised to burn 'Blood Basin Incense' in thanks for answer to the prayer. And so at dawn you came out with a cry. Your voice was so big that you woke the whole courtyard. Your eyes were as bright as two lanterns. The eyeballs turned very quickly, and your hands and feet never stopped moving. Sixth Grand-Auntie sighed and said, 'Pity it is a girl. If it were a boy, surely he would be a high official. Look at those lovely eyes!'

" 'Boys and girls are the same,' your mother said, very much annoyed.

"So you must know that your mother loves you, even though she went through a lot of suffering for you. Precious, from now on, you must think of your mother's sufferings and her love!"

Grandma thought I was asleep, but I was still wide awake, listening quietly. In my mind, I acted out Mother's giving birth to me. But at the same time I carved deeply the memory of Mother's beating me for the first time with a leather strap. I suspected that what Grandmother had told as Sixth Grand-Auntie's remarks were really her own, but because I loved her so much, I did not say so to her.

Ah! Mother really loved me, but why did she beat me so hard? Is not a child a person too? Can she never have her own way? Must she obey every word a grown-up says? These questions went round and round in my head.

Yes, I was a naughty child. I often made Mother angry. Mother could control any man, even all the men and women

in the village, old and young. But she could not control me
when I was naughty. This was what angered Mother most.
Sometimes, when she was exasperated she would say to Father, "Take her away! Let her leave me forever! This is not
like my own child." Or she would say, "Let's marry her off
early, to save us trouble."

At the age of three I was engaged to the son of one of my
father's friends. Who would have guessed that a little child,
lying on her mother's soft breast, already had her future
settled for her? . . .

The tomboy child must begin to prepare for wifehood.

The First Cry of Pain

Mother heard outside much gossip about me, saying that I
was so big and had not yet bound my feet, and that in future
surely no mother-in-law would want me. Besides, although a
girl of eight, I was still often with the boys, making clay Buddhas and throwing stones. I even organized a group of the
village children to play at being soldiers, with myself as the
"commander," which was most improper for a girl. The gossips said that, according to ancient rules, boys and girls after
four years old should not eat at the same table, and that
Mother, being an educated woman, ought to know this rule.

To be fair, Mother loved me very much. Our country tradition was such that when a girl had unbound feet, not only
no one would marry her, but everyone who saw her would
say, "Is your mother dead? A pair of fanlike big feet like
that! How disgraceful!" Mother felt that her own feet were
too short and inconvenient for walking. Sister's feet had been
bound by Mother herself, and they were like a pair of red
peppers. Though she thought they were pretty, after two steps
Sister had to lean on the wall, almost like a cripple. So
Mother had decided to bind my feet later to avoid breaking
the bones as she did in Sister's case. But when I was ten years
old she thought that if she did not begin, the bones would
grow too much and it would be impossible to hope for small
feet.

When Mother was making me a little pair of pointed red
shoes, to hang before the incense container of the Goddess
of Mercy, I did not understand what she was trying to do.

"Precious," she said, "today I am going to bind your feet. Come and worship the Goddess of Mercy, and she will grant you a pair of very small feet, like the Spirit herself."

Mother took an incense stick in her hand and lighted it and burned paper money, and waited for me to kneel down.

I watched her from across the room and dared not approach. Two big tears suddenly rolled down my face, and my heart began to feel the taste of fear and pain. I said, "Mother, I don't want to have my feet bound."

"Come quick, come quick! The Buddha will protect you," she said, and came over and seizing me made me kneel down.

Ah! she had prepared it all—pointed shoes embroidered with twin plum blossoms, and a long strip of blue cloth, three inches wide. I saw and shivered. I took the shoes up and looked at them carefully; they were made with dark red satin with a thin sole and were very pretty. I did not know when Mother had made them, for I had never seen her embroider them.

"Mother, binding feet is too painful. I shan't be able to walk. Don't do this to me," I begged her with tears of fear.

"Binding your feet is out of love for you; not binding them would be really doing you harm. You must think, how can a big-foot maiden be married off?"

She had taken a mouthful of holy water and sprayed it on my feet, and was already putting red ashes between my toes. I roared with pain. "Mother, I can't stand it! I'd rather not marry than have bound feet!"

"Such a little thing!" she said. "I haven't begun yet, and you are already crying about pain. So I shall bind them all the tighter." She began winding the cloth around one foot, while I kicked furiously. I threw the shoes to the floor and snatched at the cloth again and again. Mother angrily called to my sister-in-law to hold my arms. My left leg was squeezed under her knees while she bound my right foot. I was like a criminal being dragged to the execution ground. I cried and shouted wildly, and the neighbors gathered to see the show. Sixth Grand-Auntie came in and said, "Darling, don't cry. When you are through with footbinding, I will carry you on my back to see the monkey show."

The others all stared at me and laughed, and none of them

sympathized with me or was moved by my crying. They were all allied to Mother; they were all on the side of my executioner!

By the time both my feet were squeezed inside the red shoes, my whole body was numb. Mother helped me down to walk; but I felt as if my bones were cracking. Suddenly with a moan I fell on the floor. . . .

After that I could only sit beside the fireplace and spin, or walk about slowly in the house. I was like one wearing fetters and could not go freely. No longer could I see the lovely flowers and the green grass and the lively fish and crabs.

On the birthday of the Flower Spirit, while I was asleep Mother drilled a hole in each of my ears. I woke in pain from my dream, but she had already put two red silk threads through them.

"Good! Now I have done two of your three big affairs," Mother said happily. Her idea of the three big affairs for a girl were:

1. Binding the feet,
2. Drilling the ears,
3. Marrying off.

"Yes, the remaining affair of killing me hasn't been done yet," I answered angrily and got a great scolding again.

The year Sister was married off Mother borrowed money to buy her trousseau. She told the trousseau maker to make sixteen sets of silk bedding, thirty-six wooden cases of furniture, eight trunks of dresses, shoes, and stockings. All were embroidered with flowers. Sister embroidered them from the time she was eight until eighteen. She never went out of the door but stayed in the little house all day, from six in the morning till six in the evening, and she spun at night. She was so tired that she could hardly breathe, but she dared not complain to Mother at all, and only sighed secretly.

Mother wished me to embroider as much as Sister had, so that they could carry the trousseau proudly to my future mother-in-law's home, but I said, "I don't want anything, I only want to study."

"Oh!" she cried, "this is really turning the sky and earth upside down! Studying is your brother's business. You were born for the embroidery room. What is the use of a girl's studying? There are no degrees for girls." . . .

The years pass at home and at school, which Elder Brother has insisted she be allowed to attend. In school, Hsieh Pingying indulges in forbidden dreams of a love marriage. But finally she puts aside her "dreams of romance" for military service.

Farewell to Romance

We learned to sing the song *Fight On:*

"Be quick to train, be quick to drill.
  Pioneers of the people.
  Down with feudal society!
  Farewell to dreams of romance!
  Complete the social revolution,
  Great womankind!"

When we sang the line "Farewell to dreams of romance!" we all lifted our voices and sang high, as if to warn ourselves and others that during the revolution there was to be no romance.

The spring came, warm and intoxicating, and planted the seeds of love in the hearts of many young boys and girls. But it also sprayed the dew of blood on the young bodies of boy and girl soldiers. The call to "fight on" had waked young people from their dreams. They came out of the pink palace of romance, going to the social front which was covered with corpses and reeked with the smell of blood. They gave up their idea of love, and substituted for it the love of the masses suffering under suppression, the love of the poor, the love of their comrades.

Although there were some boy and girl students who fell in love, the first condition was whether the lover had the same revolutionary point of view and was willing to sacrifice all for the revolution. Their love was "the revolutionary love of comrades."

One would think that girls who had suffered under the oppression of the family system and who were now like birds let out of a cage, would need very much the solace of love and romance. On the contrary, they did not regard love as something extraordinary or important. Their only immediate desire was the revolution. They had staked all their happiness and their future on a revolutionary career. Everybody realized that unless the old family system was overthrown, there would never be a day when girls would be free. Man must create a permanent happiness, the happiness of the entire society; love is only a personal affair, certainly not as important as eating rice. To those who are willing to devote their lives to the people and who have a firm faith in their social mission, love is only a little game for the rich sons and daughters of the leisure class. Such were our ideas and our attitude toward love.

One morning during the second month of probation, I received from the officer of the day a thick envelope. It was from the one whose image was always before me. It was such a thick letter it weighed on my palm like a piece of lead. The students all smiled and thought that it was a love letter, for at that time I often wrote articles in the school paper, and boys would write me love letters. When I saw the handwriting on the envelope, it was as if I had been struck by lightning. My whole body was numb and my whole heart shaken. After a great struggle I waited until the class ended; then I went quietly to a corner of the drill ground and opened the letter.

What was this? The paper was smeared with bloodstains and the handwriting was hasty. I did not have the courage to read the letter and immediately put it into my pocket. If I had opened this letter two months before, how precious it would have been to me! But now, alas! My life was already given to the people. My thoughts were changed. I wanted to throw away this love that might make me lose courage.

I wished that I could tear the letter up and throw it into the wastepaper basket, or burn it and let it leave no trace in the world. But I did not have the courage to burn it. So at last, I opened and read the sad and loving pages. . . . He wished me to accept his love; he was willing to fight with me at the front, willing to give his life to the people. This was the last page of his letter, and on it there were six words written in blood—*"symbols of the tide of blood."*

When I read, "the tide of blood," I remembered what I had written in my diary of that first love. Just a little while, yes, just a little while, and then I heard the bugle call for assembly. I ran to stand in line.

"Whose love letter was it?" Shuyung softly whispered into my ear.

I shook my head, and almost shed tears. "It isn't a love letter," I said.

But Shuyung was my good friend. If there was anything to tell, we told each other. That night I showed her this letter of blood and tears. She read it and sighed, "Oh, it is a pity that he is not our comrade. . . ."

I had heard from others that his ideas were quite the opposite of ours. What more could I say?

Driven by both reason and emotion, I wrote him a short letter to tell him to come immediately to Wuhan and take active part in the work. But one month, then two months passed, and there was no answer. I knew that his letter had been written in the mood of a moment, and that his fundamental ideas had not changed. I could not love someone who was not my comrade. He was my enemy and I had to treat him with cruelty. In such times, those who agree with us in thought are our friends and those who differ from us are our enemies.

It was all over. Gone was the dream of my first love. I had to forget the lovely image in my heart!

Farewell to you from now on! . . .

Hsieh Pingyin's letters record her work among village women who experience the restricted lives of tradition.

Dear Fuyuan:

I swear I won't fool you any more. You see how my "diary" has fooled so many people. It was interrupted once, and now I have stopped again for five days. Perhaps you will ask me why. I can simply tell you this: first, we have been constantly moving about, and when we arrived at a place I was too tired to write. And I have been ill. My eyes were so sore that I was compelled to lie down for two entire days. Luckily, I am well now.

I have decided not to keep a diary any more, but to write as I please. But where shall I keep it? As I have already told, I have lost everything except myself and my first-aid kit. The only way is to send it to you after writing as I did with some of the diary.

I sent you an unfinished letter from Puchi—which I hope you have already received. That morning we started at six. Oh, the serene beauty of that calm starlit sky, the waning moon and the wafts of morning air, mingled with the sound of the brook—how we all slept in that quiet beautiful dawn! I still remember that before we started, I was lying on the fine sand on which we were encamped and scribbling a few lines to you against my knees, but I forget what I wrote. Oh, Fuyuan, I have forgotten all those fine expressions; instead there are in me only hot, boiling, revolutionary and militant feelings. I can no longer write elegant essays and sentimental poems. I have already told you that, if I expect to resume my old literary life, I must wait until the revolution is over.

The singing birds and the flowers along the way are a delight, for I had not seen them for half a year. But I must not digress. I will tell you some important news. I actually rode horseback for over twenty *li*. Moreover, I rode on the major's horse, which is known to be skittish. At a village about six *li* from Kiayu my mare and some cavalry horses got into a race. Taking a fancy to her, the horses came launching a general attack on me! One of my comrades got so frightened that she fell with all her equipment. It scared the wits and even the mother's milk out of me. Many fellow cadets turned their heads to look at me and smiled. Of course I could only cry to them, "What, ho! I am not a bit afraid! Not a bit!" And really I was not afraid of death. But if I should fall and lose a leg or otherwise get disabled, wouldn't that be frightful? Well, Fuyuan, again I have talked too much.

I arrived at Kiayu first and alone. In order to look for living quarters, I had to ride about the streets, back and forth. "Ah, here comes a girl soldier!" "The girl soldiers have arrived!" "A girl officer on horseback!" Such cries turned whole crowds of women folk out to see me. As I was surrounded by the crowd, I could only whip the horse and hurry on. I was truly afraid of a fall, as I had never ridden before in my life. You can imagine the embarrassment I was in.

When I arrived at the church I dismounted. As I was informed we were going to be put up in a foreign house, I guessed that this must be the place. A crowd of over a hundred had followed me to the church. Some addressed me as "old general," some as "lady teacher," some as "lady officer," and one boy called me "lady generalissimo." I was sweating all over and my face was burning hot, and I did not know what to do. I realized that I had become an old curio—or rather a new monstrosity. Both men and women stared at me from head to foot, and I believe they even counted the numbers of my hair. An old woman said: "I have lived eighty years without seeing a short-haired, big-footed, uniformed female devil like you. Ha! ha!" We all joined in her laughter.

Another woman of over forty came and offered me tea, for which I was truly thankful. Besides, she said something which was painful—yet really not painful—to me. She said, "If such a blithe young girl should die on the battlefield, what will her parents feel at home?" I said calmly, "Madam, I am ready to die for the revolution and the people. As for the parents, of course we are sorry to leave them but . . ." Some nodded assent, others made signs to the woman as if to reproach her for mentioning the topic. Still another group of old people were saying in their minds, "Poor, ignorant child!"

We stayed in the Roman Catholic church. Here were old, tall trees, soft, green meadows, and springs and whistling pines and chirping birds, and—well, I need not go through the long list of good things. I would call it the Peach Paradise—but no, how can the Peach Paradise compare with this place?

After a good night's rest and recovery after a hard day's work, we are today to start again. Although I am reluctant to leave this place, my heart leaps at the idea of going to the country, to the farmers. As the revolutionary army is the army of farmers and workers, and as we want close contact between the army and the farmers, we want to go to the people happily.

And so I am gone, really gone to see the humble farmer folks. The poor farmers, how they have been frightened by the soldiers of H———! They ran away at the sight of us.

This is my hardest and at the same time my happiest day since our start on the expedition. Although we sleep on the ground on straw like pigs in the sty, although our clothing is soiled with animal excrescence, although we smell what we never smelled before in our lives, and see what we never saw before, we are supremely happy, for we are having such joyous talks with the farmers. All the six girl cadets wish very much to talk with them, but the farmers understand only the Hupeh and Hunan dialects. Four of them were so disappointed and angry with themselves that they have gone to bed.

The bound feet here are insufferable. The small ones measure only two inches, and even the big ones are only four inches at best. Once I was sitting in a meadow writing letters. A company of women came and talked with me. So I laid down my pen and began to talk to them on the evils of foot-binding. One well-to-do, middle-aged woman who had a three-inch "golden lotus" said to me: "Your feet are so big. Won't your husband get into your shoes sometimes by mistake?" The soldiers, officers, and peasants who were standing by broke into laughter. They laughed so that even a brave little girl like myself began to blush. . . .

Hsieh Pingying reluctantly concludes her service in the Liberation Army (1927) and returns home to the old ways, intent on breaking an engagement arranged for her.

Interned by My Mother

Two thin little sedan-chair carriers carried me step by step nearer to the home which I had left two years ago. My heart was feeling heavier and heavier.

"We are nearly there, Aunt Ming," Hsiang shouted to me from her sedan chair.

I did not want to meet people whom I knew, and hid my head between my shoulders.

We passed the tea pavilion, and half a mile beyond stood the large, newly built house that was my home. Looking at the new house for the first time, I heard a faint sorrowful voice whispering in my ear, "This is the prison you are going into!"

But I was not afraid; I had made up my mind to come back, and I believed I should be able to break out of this prison even though it was so strongly built.

Home again! My mother, sister, sisters-in-law, and many children came to receive me. Their faces were beaming; they held my hands tightly. The children pulled at my dress and said, "Remember me, Auntie?" My white-haired grandmother was so glad that tears stood in her eyes.

"You are much thinner, dear," she said. "You must have suffered much."

Mother was wiping her eyes with her sleeves, and Sister's eyes were moist. But little Yunpao pulled my hand and asked,

"Did you bring me a doll, Auntie?"

I went into the main hall, and there I saw all kinds of furniture painted red and green, shining, glittering. I knew these were part of my dowry, and I felt sorry for Mother for wasting so much money.

After lunch they took me through the new house. The rooms were big and high and sunny, though quite old-fashioned. There was plenty of light and the good country air of the village. Mother said the original plan had been to make two main houses and two annexes; but when they finished the main houses, they had already spent three thousand dollars. The bricks, the stones, the wooden beams could not have been stronger. I was sure this home would remain intact after three thousand years—if no imperialist came to bomb it. I did not feel much concerned about it because I did not intend to stay in this little town. I should not have felt like living here if it were as spacious and magnificent as a cathedral.

"See what your mother has done for you!" said Mother. "During the two months they were painting the furniture I hardly slept. On windy days I was afraid the dust might stick to the golden foil, and I came and covered up the pieces with oilcloth. In the daytime I was afraid the children or the sparrows might dirty them. And then I had to watch the workers every day, or it might not have been finished in two years. Now they are all painted, all thirty of them. The bedding, even the mosquito nets, all are ready. We were just waiting for you to come home to make the dresses." She said it all in one breath, but I did not answer a single word. I bent my head, and she thought it was girlish shyness, and continued happily:

"It is really the Buddha who sent you back. After I learned that you had become a soldier, I washed my face every morning with tears, worrying that you might be in danger. I prayed and burned much incense for you. When I heard that you were fighting I fainted three times. I was unconscious for fully an hour! The Hsiao family was anxious too, and constantly sent people to inquire about you. They thought they would not have the luck of having you as their bride. Now, thank Heaven, you have come home safe and sound."

I did not know how to begin all I wanted to say. It was better not to say anything about the engagement before Father came back. Mother was a stubborn woman, and it was no use talking to her. I passed two days like a dumb person. But in the village news spread faster than by the radio. The Hsiao family knew I was home. Chulin, the uncle of my fiancé, wrote a letter to our family asking for the wedding date. Elder Brother showed me the letter.

"How are you going to answer?" he asked.

"Ask them to wait till Father comes."

But how was I to settle the problem? The wedding date could not be put off too long. If I did not hurry to break the engagement it might be too late.

It so happened that Father returned that very night. After reading the letter he came with Mother to ask me what I thought would be a suitable date.

"Father, I have come home especially to settle this matter," I began. "You must remember the letter I wrote you. I cannot possibly live with Hsiaoming. We are not even fond of each other; indeed, we feel absolutely nothing toward each other. His ideas, his interests, differ altogether from mine. I cannot understand his character, I just do not understand him. How can I be his wife?"

"You don't want to live with him? Do you mean to say you wish to break the engagement?" Father shouted and banged on the table.

"Yes, I have come back to break it off," I replied calmly.

Mother shouted, angrily, "You can't break the engagement unless you leave this house and never come back. Now that you are here, do you suppose you are going to escape from marriage by running away? No matter what you do, you can't escape." She raised her hand as if to strike me. Father left the room puffing with anger, and I could not go on, and went to my bedroom and wrote a five-thousand-word letter explaining why I did not want to be married.

The next day, to my surprise, Father did not seem to be a bit touched by my words, but, with a severe countenance, started berating me.

"Your reasons for breaking the engagement are evident in your letter. First, no love, second, difference in ideas. Let me answer you: As to your first reason, love exists only between husband and wife. Love begins after marriage, and not before. You are not married to him yet, so of course you don't love him. As to your second reason, the question of 'ideas' comes up only between revolutionary comrades, not between husbands and wives. If you two are united, you will make a 'husband-sing-wife-accompany' sort of happy couple, and you will give birth to sons for the ancestors. Then you will be a model of the 'clever wife and wise mother.' You are not going with him to join the revolution. Why should you need the same ideas?"

"Father," I replied, "love after marriage is your philosophy, a strange symptom of the old society. Nowadays man and woman become husband and wife through different stages of emotion. First they know each other as friends and the affection of friends develops into true love. And when love reaches its highest point, they unite and become companions for life. That is what marriage means. As to having the same ideas or beliefs, that is even more important. Two persons whose ideas differ could never be friends. How much more should this be true of marriage which should be the basis of happiness for a lifetime! If their ideas are different and each goes his own way, love will not last. Modern marriage differs entirely from that of the older times. The purpose then was simply to make a happy family. Today when two persons are married, they don't strive only for selfish happiness. The chief thing is that they must work together for society. They are sincere friends and faithful comrades, as well as husband and wife. Hsiaoming's ideas are utterly different from mine. The first fundamental for a marriage with me is lacking."

"Hunh!" my father exclaimed. "Ideas? What need has a woman of such dangerous revolutionary ideas? Of course, you have had several years of education and you will be allowed to be a primary school teacher after marriage. I don't think he will object to that."

"Don't argue with her any more!" Mother burst out. "She is not even human! We are her parents. How dare she oppose us?" Turning to me, she went on, "When we sent you to school, we were hoping that you might learn social manners and a sense of honor. We did not expect you to turn out to be a beast. You don't even care for your parents! This engagement was made when you were still suckling at my breast. Are you so shameless as to break it and ruin your parents' name and disgrace your ancestors?"

She quoted an old verse: " 'A good husband and a good wife are predestined.' No matter what kind of person you are engaged to, you've got to marry him. Besides, the Hsiao family has a large property and a good name; Hsiaoming is a good young man. He is not blind or crippled. You know it is said that 'a thread of romantic destiny can unite a husband and wife a thousand miles apart.' Marriage is something already settled in your previous incarnation. How can you oppose it?"

I listened without a word, without even a sneer, for I knew before she spoke all that she was going to say.

"I realize," said Father, "that in these times we cannot force you to 'follow a cock if you are married to the cock, and follow a dog if you are married to the dog.' But Hsiaoming is a nice fellow; you can marry him in any case. Read his letter to your third brother. It is clearly written and well-worded." At this I almost laughed. As a matter of fact, Hsiaoming could not write an ordinary, clear letter. I remembered that a certain teacher in the primary school had said, "What difference there is between you and your fiancé! Your work in school is at the top, and his, I am afraid, is at the bottom." Later I had several letters from him, and his ability was really as the teacher had said. How could I be married to a man with such a simple and vacuous mind?

Mother was scolding again, saying that she had not thought I would disappoint her thus after sending me to school for so many years. She said she was not going to let any of the daughters of Elder Brother and Third Brother go to school any more. I was worried for the children, who were now in the fourth grade. After this, they would certainly never go to school again. Would it be my fault or that of society?

Absorbed thus in my own thoughts, I suddenly heard Father renew his curses. "What kind of witch house is the school! Every girl comes out of it bewitched and demands the breaking of the engagement her parents have settled! She has to break it, however good it is."

"Of course," I said. "How can parents know what kind of husband or wife their child should have? Marriage is a great part of life. Everyone has to choose for herself if marriage is to be successful!"

I knew these words would provoke them more than ever, but if I did not say them, my head would burst!

"Outrageous! A young girl picking a husband for herself!" Mother cried. "The Hsiao family has high standing. Hsiaoming's third uncle was once a member of the provincial assembly and very well known. The Hsiaos have all studied in the cities. And I have received so many presents from the family! Last year your fiancé even came to congratulate me on my birthday. Now you are creating this scandal. How can I ever face them? The proverb says, 'A good horse will never turn round to feed on past pasture; a good girl will never marry twice.' Do you remember the story in the *Book of Heroines?*"

Father interrupted. "Do you think she reads the *Book of Heroines* any more? She reads only new novels of free love, newspaper stories about how a girl committed suicide because she could not have freedom in marriage, and how a boy broke with his family because he hated the old conventions. She is affected by all this and is turning against her parents, against the conventions!"

"The old conventions were set by the sages thousands of years ago." Mother's tone became more and more severe. "And you, a girl, dare to defy them! Don't you know how chastity-monuments were built? Even girls of twelve know the importance of chastity. And I am afraid your group, who talk about freedom, won't pass a New Year with a husband even if you marry twenty-four times a year!"

I realized that it was completely useless to argue with her. The only way was to fight it out, not to give in until I had broken the engagement.

She went on, "The Hsiaos own a lot of property and you can earn money too. You will set up a home and build a fortune. You will become rich with land and fields! You will have a very comfortable life!"

These words hurt me deeply; I considered them insulting. She belittled my sense of honor. Fundamentally she did not understand what kind of person her daughter was. She thought I feared poverty and worshiped wealth and was trying to tempt me.

"Don't talk of these things," I cried with visible annoyance. "I'd rather marry a poor man I love than a rich man!"

"What do you want then?" Mother banged on the table.

"She wants to break the engagement," Father answered for me.

"What will she do if she can't break it?"

"In her letter she said she would commit suicide!"

"All right! Let her do it! I have brought her up and sent

her to school in vain. Perhaps I owed her a debt in the previous incarnation, and I am asked to repay it now!"

Mother burst into tears and struck her head against the wall. Afraid that she might be hurt, Father went to her and held her, and my sister and sister-in-law went to her too, and while they were thus occupied, I slipped away and went outside to walk.

The sun was warm, but my heart was sad and cold.

I saw a man in a long white gown approaching and recognized him as my eldest brother. He asked me what I was doing out there alone, and I told him the whole melodrama that had just been enacted. He paused and knitted his eyebrows and said, "You ought not to have come home. Now that you are at home, I think . . ."

"What are you thinking?" I interrupted. "Do you want me to sacrifice myself and marry Hsiaoming?"

"I—that's what I mean," he said slowly.

"No, I cannot; I will fight to the end!" . . .

After a series of marriage rejections, Hsieh Pingying ultimately submits to her mother's wishes and is wed.

The Fourth Escape

What I did then, I did not because I was afraid of society, still less for the curiosity of it, but merely on account of Mother. I saw that it was really getting too hard for her; I was willing to give her temporary comfort. I realized that in revolution the aim is to reach the ultimate goal, and the way you take is of minor importance.

So I really became a bride! As I look back now, it is no longer the painful, humiliating surrender I used to think it; it seems only comical.

I curse the primitiveness of the village, for there was no photographer there. If I had a picture of myself as the bride with that heavy headdress, that red veil, and that fancy sedan chair, how interesting it would be now!

That day I adorned myself with a sky-blue jacket and a black silk skirt; the costume looked worse than what I wore as a student. I had a pair of red embroidered shoes, which were to be worn only on the wedding day and not a day more, for such was the custom of our village. It was said that the shoes would stamp out all misfortunes. People would fight later to put on these "lucky shoes" for luck's sake.

My hair cost Mother much worry. It was not long enough to cover my forehead, even after I had let it grow for half a year. Hsiang's mother was the one invited to "open my face" by removing the hair with a twirl of thread. She combed my hair and put oil on it and made it shiny. Then she began to draw my eyebrows and opened the rouge and powder boxes.

"These are not necessary. Let me keep my natural face," I said seriously, and impolitely pushed her hand away.

"Everybody goes through this on her wedding day," said Mrs. Tu; "it is customary. Besides, when I put a little rouge and powder on such a pretty bride, people will think you are a fairy from Heaven. Ha-ha!"

I knew she was being sarcastic, for when I was in the army my skin had turned brown, and my cheeks had some freckles. She wanted to put powder on to see me like the Goddess of the Moon on the stage. It was too much, and I obstinately refused. Mother was considerate this time and said:

"All right, let her have her natural face."

I put on the cumbersome headdress and the bright red veil; now my whole head was covered and I could see only through the red silk. Everything looked disturbingly red. Mrs. Tu led me through the halls as if I were a blind person. I first paid my respects to Heaven and Earth, then to my ancestors, then said my farewells to my parents and other relatives.

Ordinarily when a bride gets into the sedan chair with red and swollen eyes, she is considered a filial and affectionate daughter. With my hatred for this feudalistic home, which I was leaving with no regrets, I had no reason to weep. Yet not knowing why, at the instant I stepped into the chair and heard my sister and sisters-in-law sobbing, I found myself crying bitterly and I continued until the chair was carried for ten *li*. I think now that I wept for the decline of the old family influence and for my mother who was not to see her daughter again, rather than over my own fate.

The chair was carried by four men. The door was locked, and inside the chair was curtained and lined with red silk.

From our village to the Hsiao home was about thirty *li*, with many villages and hills on the way. There were about eighty people carrying my trousseau for display, and with the chair carriers and the band the procession had about one hundred and fifty people and was festive with the playing of drums and horns. Inside the chair I lifted my veil and took out the little mirror that hung on a chain around my neck to take a look at myself, the clown of the show. It was really ridiculous. Embroidered shoes had taken the place of the straw sandals I wore as a soldier. My hand instead of holding a gun now wore a golden ring and bracelets. Two ancient coins weighing over a pound hung on my chest—they said these old coins would drive evil spirits away. They were so heavy that I was forced to bend my neck forward.

Whenever we passed through a village, people would set off firecrackers and demand to see the bride. The women were most disgusting; to be allowed to see the bride was not enough but they lifted my face and made all sorts of remarks. Often I thought of boxing their ears, but I was afraid to make more trouble by upsetting the whole procession. So I only said, "All right, look at me, but please don't touch me!"

"What a ferocious bride!" they would say.

The rhythmic old music of the band was rather entertaining; but other thoughts began to crowd into my mind. Why hadn't I managed to get a gun? I could have fired it now and everybody would flee for their lives and I could walk away. I might jump up on the table in the middle of the marriage ceremony and make a speech, giving vent to all the troubles in my breast.

The hardest time probably would be tonight. If he should be unreasonable or brutal, unhappy things would happen tonight! If he becomes unreasonable and obstinate, I thought, I will not endure it. A girl's chastity must not be sacrificed to a man she does not love. I will not make such useless sacrifice. I will resist. I will gamble with my life but not yield.

Escape would be more difficult hereafter, but I must watch for an opportunity at any time. If I use my intelligence, I thought, and have will power and courage, I shall reach my goal one day. If I had courage I could not possibly fail. Thus when everyone thought I had surrendered to the old conventions, I was planning my fourth escape.

When the sedan chair reached the gate of the Hsiao family, the noise of firecrackers became louder and more constant. With all my effort to be calm, my heart beat fast.

A woman wearing a new dress came and helped me out, and we went into Hua Tsu's house to rest for a while before the moment when they should let off more firecrackers and shout, "The ceremony begins!"

Hua Tsu was the daughter of the matchmaker. She used to go to Tatung Girls' School and I liked her very much, and began talking to her, to the surprise of everyone there. They said, "After all, a bride who has been a soldier is different. See how dignified and at ease she looks, not a bit shy."

I tried not to offend them or to make my father uncomfortable, but stayed as still as a statue for them to move around. Once, when I should have made "three kneelings and nine kowtows," I made three bows instead, but otherwise I performed the whole program according to the custom.

Hsiaoming's father boasted happily to his friends, "After all, one who has studied has more sense. She does not oppose the old wedding ceremony."

With all the merrymaking, night finally came and the bridal chamber was filled with the guests who had come to "tease the bride" as was customary. No woman was present, but two little girls came in with the crowd. Half of the group were relatives and half were Hsiaoming's schoolmates. At first I acted as dumb as a piece of wood while they made silly jokes. But when they began to be disgusting, I gave them a lecture, and finally it no longer seemed funny and they went away a few at a time, until by midnight they were all gone. Hsiaoming drove the last guests out of the room with a forced smile.

I turned down the wick in the lamp to make the room dim and seated myself near the fire which was going out, pondering over Hsiaoming's melancholy expression.

He came back through the door very quietly, almost like a ghost. I was staring at the fire with my head bent almost touching my knees. He put more coal into the stove and came to sit beside me.

"I am sorry to have you go through all this today," he said. "Don't feel too badly about it. One is really helpless with such an obstinate family." His voice was sad and almost trembling. At that moment I began to feel sorry for him.

"Whatever play excites the audience is worth performing," I replied.

"Do you consider what we performed today a tragedy or a comedy?" he asked.

"From your side it is a tragedy, but from mine a comedy."

"What do you mean? Are you still thinking of running away?"

"I am sorry," I said. "Let's talk it over plainly and calmly. Let's decide upon the end of this marionette show."

Ten minutes passed before a word was said; then I gave him a long discourse on the difficulties of a marriage without love. He nodded sympathetically, but when I finished he said resolutely:

"Perhaps the reason you have no love for me is because I did not join you in the northern expedition. But I have loved you since I was a child. I could hardly bear to part with you. No matter how cruel and cool you are to me, I shall always love you."

"Love is not to be forced," I said. "You cannot force two people without love into a marriage, nor can you force apart two people who are in love. You are free to love me, and I also free not to love you. I cannot prevent you from loving me, just as you cannot persuade me to love you. For our future it is better that we end this marriage sensibly. You will marry your ideal wife, and she will help you to make a good home; and I shall marry my ideal lover and live happily. This will be best for both of us as individuals, and for the country too. Please do not be stubborn and ruin our future lives."

We talked the whole night. Some women were outside the door trying to hear us, but we spoke in a Changsha dialect which they were not able to understand.

There was no sleep the second night either, for we continued our discussion.

His mother told him that he was foolish to spend the precious time just talking. "Since she has come to us in a red chair, she is a member of the Hsiao family, dead or alive. You are her husband. Do whatever you like. Does she dare to disobey? Only a dead cat will allow a mouse to pass by his mouth."

To be fair, Hsiaoming was a good man; he was not boorish and he did not insist. He understood my character, my thoughts, and my determination, knowing that the matter would become more serious and the solution still farther off were he to use force or threats.

But he said, "Ming, why are you so cruel? I am not a gangster or a beast, I won't eat you up or harm you! Believe me, I will carefully guard your reputation and your future. Can't you give me just a little love? I will accept it even if it comes out of pity for me, even if it should be pretended, even if it should be temporary!" Tears rolled down his face, but though I pitied him, I had resolved not to be moved by his tears.

"Love is not to be given away for pity's sake," I said. "Nor can it be a pretense. You will be my good friend, but I cannot possibly give you more than friendship. I cannot give up my ideals; I cannot be your wife. If you wish to have the happiness of a family life, please end this marriage as soon as possible and marry another woman!"

He shed more tears. I handed him a handkerchief, and after wiping away his tears he returned it to me. It was a tragedy and beyond my power to turn it into a comedy.

"If we had called off the wedding before," he agreed, "it would not have mattered so much. Now we have gone through the ceremony, and everyone is celebrating it. Your father is still here. If we have a divorce now, how am I going to face all these people? And my parents would never consent. How could they face other people after having a daughter-in-law who ran away right after the wedding? And it would injure your parents' name and your own. Let us give it a trial; let us live together until it really is impossible."

Hearing all this, I began to feel a certain intense dislike for him. The "prestige" and "face" he was talking about were the last gasps of that ancient system which he was trying to maintain. I decided all of a sudden not to argue any more. If I could reach my final goal, there was no harm playing a little politics. So I answered, "All right, let us leave it as it is for the present. We will find a way out."

On the third day, my father was leaving and, knowing that we had not slept for the last two days, yet pretending not to know, he came to my room and said:

"Don't create any more trouble. Live and be content. I shall arrange for you to teach in Tatung Girls' School next year."

Then he turned to Hsiaoming and said, "You know you have a better temper than she has. Yield a bit."

After my father went, I fell to weeping aloud. Even now I still do not understand why I was so emotional. Perhaps I was afraid that I might not be able to see my father again.

To be honest about it, Father really loved me; he was not like Mother, so stubborn and unreasonable. . . . At last, I fell asleep sobbing.

That night I could really stand it no longer. I laid out the green quilt and went to bed with my dress on, leaving the red quilts for Hsiaoming. I was as cautious as a detective watching his every movement. Somewhat to my surprise he was considerate and respected my freedom and there was no "violation." I was grateful to him, though I thought he was doing only what he should. But his kindness had a purpose too. He knew that I had suffered much for the past six months because of my three attempts to escape, and that to force me against my wishes might result in a tragic ending.

According to the custom of the village, the bride and groom were to return together to the bride's family after the third day of marriage. We went and stayed at home for two days. Mother did not know at all that I was still a virgin.

When we returned to the Hsiao family again, it was the time of the Chinese New Year. We were invited out to almost every meal and were busy all day. Hsiaoming was treating me gently; he had self-confidence and thought that if he gave in a little I would belong to him in time.

Two telegrams came from Changsha, asking him to go back to his work in a highway company. His mother wanted never to let him go, but he knew that he would only suffer at home. Why not go away and let me go to him some day? This was his foolish dream, but it shows the trouble he took to win me over.

On the night of his departure, he told me, "I respect your freedom. I, too, am under the control of the family and was forced to come home to go through this comedy. Now you can go anywhere you like. But I shall always love you."

I wanted to go with him, but his mother would not permit it fearing I would run away on the journey. I knew that by yielding I could gain more, so I decided to stay at home, and be a filial daughter-in-law.

It was not as easy as I thought it would be. When he went, he made his mother responsible for watching me very closely. That old mistress looked very kind, but in fact she was no kinder than my mother. On the ground of comforting me in my loneliness, she hired a little maid to sleep with me. When I could not go to sleep and wanted to open the door and look at the moonlight, I found the door locked. I tasted again the experience of family imprisonment.

Even though the Hsiaos were rich, they hired only one man servant and no maids, just as in my own family. Therefore, all the housework had to be done by ourselves. Luckily I had done housework when I was small, so I did not find it hard.

I changed my way of living completely and tried to learn the ways of country folk. I helped feed the pigs and the hens, sweep the floor, wipe the furniture; I failed only in building a fire, even after a few hard attempts. Old Mistress did not scold me. Sometimes when she saw me starting to wash the dishes, she would say:

"You never did this in school. Don't bother. You are still a bride, and no one will dare say anything even if you don't do a thing."

A short week passed peacefully. The go-between came to chat with the old mistress every day and she often raised her voice and said proudly, "I told you so. Brides always yield after they are married. Look, she knows how to read and how to fight, and can do housework besides. How much incense you must have burned before Buddha in your previous life that you get such a good daughter-in-law!"

"It is all due to you. We never thought that she could manage a household," the old mistress would say.

One morning during breakfast suddenly we heard shouting: "Oh! Oh! The bandits are coming! Hurry! Run!"

When we went out many people were running toward the hill, shouting and crying, the men carrying beddings and trunks, the women carrying children. I put my diary book into my pocket and ran with them. The old mistress and my sister-in-law had bound feet and they moved one step forward and two backwards! I held Old Mistress with my right hand and a child with my left and with great difficulty, we reached the thick bamboo forest and stopped at a farm. We could see the bandits in the village, thirty or forty of them.

"All your dowry will be taken. Oh, we didn't bring away a thing!" Old Mistress was so excited that she shivered. I comforted her and said, "The proverb says, 'As long as there is a mountain, don't worry that there will be no fuel.' If we all escape, losing the things doesn't matter."

She worried about her sick husband and the third daughter-in-law, who was soon to give birth.

Ten minutes after the bandits had left I ran down the hill. Old Mistress thought that I would take this chance to run away, so she hurried down too, and found me cooking for the sick.

She praised me before her husband, "Mingkang is really very good. She knew that I was worried about you and Third Daughter-in-law, so she came down regardless of danger. She is really a thoughtful and kind person."

From then on I had a good reputation in the Hsiao family. From big to small, they all liked me and trusted me and lost the fear of my going to extremes. The door was not locked any more, and the little maid did not have to stay with me. I knew that now was my time to run away.

While I was worrying how to do it, a letter came from my father. It enclosed a letter from the principal of Tatung Girls' School asking me to go to teach the sixth grade. I was so happy that every cell of my body was tense. I at once went to my parents-in-law and told them.

"It is very near home and I can come often to look after you two old people. I shall get $240 a year and I can save at least $120 a year and buy more food for you. So I come specially to ask you old people, if I may have your permission to go."

"What do you say?" said Old Mistress. "Will Hsiaoming object?"

"How can he?" said my father-in-law. "Teaching is a good thing. It is Mingkang's mother school, and today her father sent a man specially to deliver the letter. How can we object?"

They consented without suspicion. I did not know what words to use to thank them.

It was a bright spring morning when I finished packing. The children came and looked at me with their bright eyes, and asked, "Auntie, when are you coming back?" Naughty Huats'u came with her hair uncombed and said something I did not like: "Auntie, you wouldn't run away and not come back, would you?"

"Silly!" I cried. "I'll come back twice a month."

Old Mistress did not hear us; she was busy cooking eggs and frying peas for me to eat on the way.

"Good-by, Mother!" I said as I jumped into the sedan chair, using my kindest voice. I saw her wiping her eyes with her sleeves.

"Poor Old Mistress, you will never see your nominal daughter-in-law again!" I thought. I felt the sorrow of departure a little, but in five minutes I had the smile of bright hope on my face.

I arrived at school too soon. It was not open yet, and there were no students there, only the two servants. Before that empty house I shed happy tears.

I learned from the servants that the principal would arrive the next day. I thought it would be best to leave that very night, for if he came back it would be difficult. We were schoolmates, and he wanted me to teach the graduating class. If I should leave before the end of the term, I would not be doing the right thing toward him.

And besides, if I ran away after school began, he would send someone after me or would at least have to let the Hsiao family know.

I did not hesitate. I went to find two strong sedan-chair carriers. Taking advantage of the moonlight, I started from the mountain of tin mines, going by the narrow roads to Changsha.

This last escape was successful. I was not afraid at all this time, and as I went leisurely along the river bank under the willow trees, I hummed a tune I made.

> Good-by my native village!
> My lovely village
> With your green mountains
> And gurgling brooks,
> With prune and peach trees like a
>   painting
> And drooping willows like silken threads—
> My village,
> That once shook my soul
> And buried the gift of my youth,
> But now leaves in my heart only a bloody
>   stain.
> The monster shadow of feudal society
> Would devour the flickering star
> And envelop all in darkness.

But rebellion undaunted will triumph.
Good-by forever, my ancient village!

*From here on Hsieh Pingying's life will be her own, given as
she wishes to the national independence movement.*

—*Translated by Adet and Anor Lin*

The Child-Bride

Hsiao Hung

Hsiao Hung (1911–1941) was taken as a writing name by
Chang Nai-ying, daughter of a wealthy landlord family of
China's northeasternmost province of Heilunkiang. It is her
own family that Hsiao Hung uses as the basis for the portray-
als given in chapters three through five of her autobiographical novel, *Tales of Hulan River* (1940). "The Child Bride"
is the last chapter in this group. Howard Goldblatt, an editor
of her works, calls this story "the author's most powerful in-
dictment of the cruel and dehumanizing effects of traditional
society." He calls an *idée fixe* Hsia Hung's depiction of
"young women whose lives . . . are all sacrificed in the
name of traditional morality and wisdom." Well it might be,
since she herself either experienced or observed such situations at first hand.

Although undoubtedly politically biased, Hsiao Hung con-
veys authenticity and immediacy in her writings. The writer
herself suffered under a cold and dictatorial father, sought
comfort with a loving grandfather, suffered more than she
enjoyed two common-law marriages, lost two children in
birth, and knew abandonment and rejection. Continuing poor
health led to her death in Hong Kong shortly after the

Japanese occupation during the Battle of the Pacific at the outset of World War II.

Except for the time I spent playing in our rear garden, accompanied by Granddad, I was left to my own devices to find amusement. Sometimes all by myself I pitched a makeshift tent beneath the eaves, then after playing for a while I would fall asleep there.

We had removable windows in our house that, when taken down, would stand up only if they were propped up against a wall, making a nice little lean-to. This I called my "little chamber." I often took naps there in my little chamber.

Our entire compound was covered with mugwort, over which swarms of dragonflies flew, attracted by the fragrance of the red smartweed flowers. I amused myself by catching dragonflies until I grew tired of it, after which I lay down in the mugwort and went to sleep.

Clumps of wild berries grew among the mugwort, looking like mountain grapes, and delicious to eat. I foraged for wild berries to eat among the mugwort, and when I grew weary of that I lay down beside the wild-berry bushes and went to sleep. The dense mugwort served as a kind of mattress for me as I lay atop it, and I also enjoyed the shade the tall grass offered.

One day just before suppertime, as the sun was setting in the west, I lay dreaming on my bed of mugwort. I must not have been sleeping all that soundly, for I seemed to hear a great many people talking somewhere nearby. They were chatting and laughing with real gusto, but I couldn't quite make out just what was happening. I could only sense that they were standing off in the southwest corner, either inside the compound or just beyond it—whether it was inside the compound or not, I simply couldn't tell—and out there somewhere there was quite a bit of excitement. I lay there half awake for a while, and the noise eventually died out; most likely I had fallen asleep again.

After I woke up I went into the house, where I was given the news by our old cook: "The Hu family's child-bride arrived, and you weren't even aware of it; hurry up and eat so you can go have a look at her!" . . .

The moment Granddad put his rice bowl down, I began dragging him along with me over to the southwest corner of the wall without even letting him light up his pipe. As we hurried along, I experienced feelings of regret every time I saw someone coming back from watching all the fun. Why had I had to wait for Granddad anyway? Couldn't I have run over there by myself a long time ago? The recollection that I had heard some excitement coming from over here while I was lying in the mugwort added to my displeasure. Really, the more I thought about it, the stronger my regrets grew. This affair had already taken up half the afternoon, and I just knew that the good part was over, and that I was too late. Coming now was a waste of time—there was nothing more to be seen. Why hadn't I rushed over to take a look the second I heard all that talking and laughing while I was lying in the grass? My regrets grew so strong that I was getting mad at myself, and just as I had feared, when we drew up next to old Hu's window, there wasn't a sound coming from inside. I was so mad I nearly cried.

When we actually walked in the door, it wasn't at all as I had been led to expect. Mother, Third Granny Chou, and several people I didn't know were all there, and everything was contrary to what I had imagined; there was nothing worth seeing here. Where was the child-bride? I couldn't spot her anywhere until the others pointed and nodded, then I saw her. This was no bride, it was just a young girl! I lost all interest the moment I saw her, and I started pulling Granddad toward the door.

"Let's go home, Grandpa."

The next morning I saw her when she came out to draw some water to wash up. Her long black hair was combed into a thick braid; unlike most young girls, whose braids hung down to about their waists, hers came down almost to her knees. Her complexion was dark and she had a hearty laugh.

After the people in the compound had all taken a look at the child-bride of old Hu's family they agreed that apparently there was nothing wrong with her, except that she seemed a little too proud-spirited and didn't look or act much like a child-bride.

Third Granny Chou said: "She hasn't the least bit of shyness when she's with people."

Old Mrs. Yang from the next compound agreed: "She isn't even a tiny bit shy. Her very first day at her mother-in-law's house she ate three bowls of rice!"

Then Third Granny Chou said: "Gracious! I've never seen the likes of it. Even if she weren't a child-bride, but someone who came to the house already married to the boy, she'd still have to get to know what the people are like her first couple of days in the home. Gracious! She's such a big girl, she must be well into her teens!"

"I hear she's fourteen!"

"How could a fourteen-year-old be that tall? She must be lying about her age!"

"Not necessarily. Some people develop early."

"But how are they going to handle their sleeping arrangements?"

"You've got a good point there, since there are three generations of family and only three small *k'angs*."[1]

This last response to Third Granny Chou came from old Mrs. Yang, as she leaned over the top of the wall.

As for my family, Mother was also of the opinion that the girl was not at all like a child-bride should be.

Our old cook said: "I've never seen the likes of her, with such a proud bearing and eyes that look right at you."

To which Second Uncle Yu added: "What's this world coming to when a child-bride doesn't look anything like a child-bride ought to?"

Only Granddad had nothing to say on the subject, so I asked him: "What do you think of that child-bride?"

"She's quite all right," he said.

So I felt she was quite all right too.

Every day she led their horse to the well to drink, and I saw her on many of these occasions. No one properly introduced us, but she smiled when she saw me, and I smiled back and asked her how old she was.

"Twelve," she replied.

I told her she must be wrong: "You're fourteen—everybody says so."

"They think I'm too tall," she said, "and they're afraid people will laugh if they know I'm only twelve, so they told me to say I'm fourteen."

---

[1] Sleeping platforms.

I couldn't figure out how being very tall would cause people to laugh.

"Why don't you come over and play in the grass with me?" I asked her.

"No," she said, "they won't allow it."

Before many days had passed, the people in that family began to beat the child-bride. They beat her so severely that her cries could be heard far away, and since none of the other families in the entire compound had any children, cries or shouts were seldom heard there.

As a result, this became *the* topic of conversation throughout the neighborhood. The consensus was that she had deserved a beating right from the start, for whoever heard of a child-bride with no trace of shyness, one who sat up straight as a rod wherever she was, and who walked with a brisk, carefree step!

Her mother-in-law, having led the family horse up to the well to drink one day, said to Third Granny Chou: "We've got to be harsh with her from the outset. You mark my words, I'm going to have to beat her when I go back to the house; this little child-bride of ours is really a handful! I've never seen the likes of her. If I pinch her on the thigh, she turns around and bites me, or else she says she's going home to her mother."

From then on the sounds of crying filled our compound daily; loud, bitter cries accompanied by shouts.

Granddad went over to old Hu's house several times to try to dissuade them from beating her, since she was just a young girl who didn't know much, and if there were problems in her behavior, he recommended trying to educate her. But as time went on the beatings grew even more severe, day and night, and even when I woke up in the middle of the night to recite my poems[2] with Granddad I could hear the sounds of crying and shouting coming from the southwest corner of the compound.

"That's the child-bride crying, isn't it?" I would ask Granddad.

[2] Granddad is hearing her recite from the classical *Book of Odes*, "The 300."

To keep me from being frightened, he would answer: "No, it's someone outside the compound."

"What could they be crying about in the middle of the night?" I would ask him.

"Don't concern yourself about that," he would say, "but just keep reciting your poems."

I got up very early, and just as I was reciting, "I slept in spring, not conscious of the dawn," the crying sounds from the southwest corner started in again. This continued for the longest time, and only when winter arrived did the sounds of her crying finally come to an end.

The sounds of weeping had been replaced by those of the sorceress, who came to the southwest corner every night to do her dance. The staccato beats of a drum resounded in the air, as the sorceress first chanted a line, and was then answered by her assistant. Since it was nighttime, the words they sang came through loud and clear, and I soon memorized every line.

There were things like: "Little spirit flower," and "May the Genie let her 'come forth.'" Just about every day the sorceress chanted these kinds of things.

Right after I got up in the mornings I started to mimic her chants: "Little spirit flower, may the Genie let her 'come forth. . . .'" Then I went *bong-bong, bang-bang,* imitating the sounds of the drumbeat.

"Little spirit flower" meant the young girl; the "Genie" was supposed to be a fox spirit; to "come forth" meant to become a sorceress.

The sorceress performed her dances for nearly the whole winter, until she finally succeeded in causing the child-bride to fall ill. The child-bride soon had an unhealthy look about her, but even though her complexion was no longer as dark as it had been when she first arrived that summer, she retained her hearty laugh.

When Granddad took me over with him to visit her family, the child-bride even came over and filled his pipe for him. When she looked at me she smiled, but on the sly, as though she were afraid her mother-in-law would see her. She didn't speak to me.

She still wore her hair in a thick braid, but her mother-in-law told us she was ill and that the sorceress had been engaged to drive the evil spirits away. As Granddad was leaving their house, the mother-in-law walked out with him, saying in a low voice: "I'm afraid this child-bride isn't going to make it; she's being claimed by a genie who is determined to have her 'come forth.' "

Granddad would have liked to ask them to move, but here in Hulan there is a custom that the time for moving in the spring is March and in the autumn, September. Once March or September has passed, it is no longer the time for moving.

Each time we were startled out of our sleep in the middle of the night by the sorceress' dance, Granddad would say: "I'm going to ask them to move next March."

I heard him say this on any number of occasions. Whenever I imitated the shouts and cries of the sorceress and chanted "Little spirit flower," Granddad said the same thing—he'd ask them to move next March.

But during the interim the commotion emanating from the southwest corner of our compound grew in intensity. They invited one sorceress and quite a few assistants, and the beat of drums resounded the day long. It was said that if they allowed the little child-bride to "come forth," her life would be in peril, so they invited many assistants in order to wrest her from the sorceress' clutches. . . .

The child-bride grew more seriously ill with each passing day, and according to her family, she often sat bolt upright as she slept during the night. The sight of another person threw a terrible fright into her, and her eyes were invariably brimming with tears. It seemed inevitable that this child-bride was fated to "come forth," and if she were not allowed to do so, there seemed little hope that she would ever be well again.

Once the news of her plight began spreading throughout the area, all of the people living nearby came forth with their suggestions; how, they said, could we not come to the rescue of someone at death's door? Some believed that she should simply be allowed to "come forth," and let that be the end of it. Others were of the opposite opinion, for if someone of such tender years were to "come forth," what hope was there for her ever living a normal life?

Her mother-in-law adamantly refused to let her "come forth": "Now don't any of you get the wrong idea that I'm opposed to letting her 'come forth' only because of the money I spent when I arranged for the engagement. Like the rest of you, I feel that if someone so young were to 'come forth,' she would never be able to live a normal life."

Everyone promptly agreed that it would be best not to allow her to "come forth," so they turned their collective energies to finding the right prescription or engaging the right sorceress, each extolling the virtues of his own plan.

Finally there came a soothsayer.

This soothsayer told them he had come unhesitatingly from the countryside a great distance away as soon as the news reached him that old Hu's family had recently brought a child-bride into their home, one who had fallen ill shortly after her arrival and remained so even after being seen by many eminent physicians and mystics. He had made the trip into town expressly to have a look for himself, for if he could perform some service that might spare her life, then the trip would have been worth making. Everyone was quite moved by this speech of his. He was invited into the house, where he was asked to sit on the grandmother's *k'ang*, was given tea, and offered a pipeful of tobacco.

The wife of the elder grandson was the first to approach him: "This younger sister of ours is actually only twelve years old, but since she is so tall, she tells everyone she is fourteen. She's a cheerful, sociable girl who up to now was never sick a day in her life. But ever since she came to our house she has grown thinner and paler every day. Recently she lost her appetite for food and drink, and she even sleeps with her eyes open, as she is easily startled. We've given her every imaginable remedy and have burned incense of every kind for her benefit, but nothing has worked. . . ."

Before she had finished, the girl's mother-in-law interrupted her: "I've never abused her all the time she's been in my home. Where else will you find another family that has not abused its child-bride by giving her beatings and tongue-lashings all day long? Now I may have beaten her a little, but just to get her started off on the right foot, and I only did that for a little over a month. Maybe I beat her pretty severely sometimes, but how was I expected to make a well-mannered girl out of her without being severe once in a while? Believe me, I didn't enjoy beating her so hard, what with all her screaming and carrying on. But I was doing it for her own good, because if I didn't beat her hard, she'd never be good for anything.

"There were a few times when I strung her up from the rafters and had her uncle give her a few hard lashes with a leather whip, and since he got a little carried away, she usually passed out. But it only lasted for about the time it takes to smoke a pipeful, and then we always managed to revive her by dousing her face with cold water. We did give her some pretty severe beatings that turned her body all black and blue and occasionally drew some blood, but we always broke open some eggs right away and rubbed the egg whites on the spots. The swellings, which were never too bad, always went down in ten days or a couple of weeks.

"This child is such a stubborn one; the moment I began to beat her she threatened to return to her home. So I asked her: 'Just where do you think your home is? What is this, if not your home?' But she refused to give in. She said she wanted to go to her *own* home. And this made me madder than ever. You know how people are when they get mad—nothing else seems to matter—so I took a red-hot flatiron and branded the soles of her feet. Maybe I beat her soul right out of her body, or maybe I just scared it away—I don't know which—but from then on, whenever she said she wanted to go home, instead of beating her, all I had to do was threaten to chain her up if she even tried, and she would start screaming with fright. When the Great Genie saw this he said she should be allowed to 'come forth.'

"It costs a lot of money to bring a girl into a family as a child-bride. Figure it out for yourself: the engagement was arranged when she was eight years old, at which time we had to hand over eight ounces of silver. After that there was the money we spent for her trousseau, and finally we had all the expenses of bringing her here by train from far-off Liao-yang. Then once she got here, it was a steady series of exorcists, incense, and one potion after another. If she had gotten better as time went on, then everything would have been fine, but nothing seemed to work. Who knows eventually . . . what the outcome will be . . . ?"

The soothsayer, who had come unhesitatingly from so far away, was a most proper and serious man who showed the signs of much travel. He wore a long blue gown under a short lined coat, while on his head he wore a cap with earflaps. He was a man whom others treated with the respect due a master the moment they saw him.

Accordingly, the grandmother said: "Please draw a lot quickly for my second grandson's child-bride and tell us what her fate will be."

The soothsayer could tell at first glance that this family was a sincere and honest one, so he removed his leather cap with the earflaps. The moment he took off his cap everyone could see that his hair was combed into a topknot and that he was wearing Taoist headwear. They knew at once that this was no ordinary run-of-the-mill individual. Before anyone could even utter the questions they wanted to ask, he volunteered the information that he was a Taoist priest from such-and-such a mountain, and that he had come down to make a pilgrimage to the sacred Mount T'ai in Shantung. But how could he have foreseen that midway on his journey he would have to cut his trip short for lack of traveling expenses? He had drifted to the Hulan River area where he had been for no less than half a year.

Someone asked him why, if he was a Taoist, he wasn't wearing Taoist garb.

"There's something you people ought to know," he replied. "Each of the 360 trades in this world of ours has its share of miseries. The police around here are really fierce; the minute they see someone dressed as a Taoist, they start in with a detailed interrogation, and since they are disbelievers of the Taoist creed who won't listen to reason, they are all too ready to take one of us into custody."

This man had an alias—the Wayfaring Immortal—and people far and near knew of whom you were speaking when you mentioned his name. Whatever the disease or discomfort, whether the signs were good or evil, life and death was settled for all time with the drawing of one of his lots. He told them that he had learned his divining powers from the head priest of the Taoists himself, Chang T'ien-shih.

He did not have many divining lots—four in all—which he took out of the pocket of his gown one at a time. The first lot he brought forth was wrapped in red paper, as was the second; in fact, all four were wrapped in red paper. He informed everyone that there were no words written on his divining lots, nor were there any images; inside each there was only a packet of medicinal powder—one red, one green,

toward the big vat to discover that the young child-bride had vanished. She had collapsed inside the big vat.

At that moment the crowd witnessing the excitement yelled in panic, thinking that the girl had died, and they rushed forward to rescue her, while those of a more compassionate nature began to weep.

A few moments earlier, when the young child-bride was clearly still alive and begging for help, not a single person had gone to rescue her from the hot water. But now that she was oblivious to everything and no longer seeking help, a few people decided to come to her aid. She was dragged out of the big vat and doused with some cold water. A moment before, when she had lost consciousness, the crowd watching all the excitement had been moved to unbelievable compassion. Even the woman who had been shouting, "Use hot water! Pour hot water over her!" was pained by the turn of events. How could she not be pained? Here was a sprightly young child whose life had suddenly come to an end.

The young child-bride was laid out on the *k'ang*, her whole body as hot as cinders. A neighbor woman reached out and touched her body, then another woman did the same. They both exclaimed: "Gracious, her body's as hot as cinders!"

Someone said that the water had been too hot, while someone else said that they should not have poured it over her head, and that anyone would lose consciousness in such scalding water.

While this discussion was going on, the mother-in-law rushed over and covered the girl with the tattered coat, exclaiming: "Doesn't this girl have any modesty at all, lying there without a stitch of clothing on!"

Originally, the young child-bride had fought having her clothing taken off out of a sense of modesty, but she had been stripped on the orders of her mother-in-law. Now here she was, oblivious to everything, with no feelings at all, and her mother-in-law was acting in her best interests.

The sorceress beat some tattoos on her drum, as the assistant spoke several times to her, and the onlookers cast glances among themselves. None could say how this episode would end, whether the young child-bride was dead or alive; but whatever the outcome, they knew they had not wasted their time in coming. They had seen some eye-opening incidents, and they were a little wiser in the ways of the world—that alone made it all worthwhile.

As some of the onlookers were beginning to feel weary, they asked others whether or not the final act of these rites had drawn to a close, adding that they were ready to go home and go to bed. Seeing that the situation would turn sour if the crowd broke up, the sorceress gathered her energies to make sure she kept her audience. She beat a violent tattoo on her drum and sprayed several mouthfuls of wine into the child-bride's face. Then she extracted a silver needle from her waistband, with which she pricked the girl's fingertip. Before long the young child-bride came to.

The sorceress then informed the people that three baths were required—there were still two to go. This comment injected new life into the crowd: the weary were given a second wind, renewed vigor came to those wanting to go home to bed. No fewer than thirty people were gathered there to watch the excitement; a new sparkle in their eyes, they were a hundred times more spirited than before. Let's see what happens! If she lost consciousness after one bathing, what will happen when she takes a second? The possible results of yet a third bath were completely beyond their imagination. As a result, great mysteries crowded the minds of the onlookers.

As anticipated, the moment the young child-bride was carried out to the large vat and dumped into the scalding water, her eerie screams began anew. All the time she was shouting she was holding on to the rim of the vat, trying desperately to pull herself out. Meanwhile, as some people continued to douse her with water, others pushed her head down, keeping her under control until once again she passed out and collapsed in the vat.

As she was fished out this time, she was spurting water from her mouth. Just as before, among the onlookers there was no one of conscience who was not moved to sympathize with the plight of this young girl. Women from neighboring families came forward to do whatever they could to aid her. They crowded around to see whether or not she was still alive. If there was still a spark of life, then they need not worry about rescuing her. But if she was breathing her last, then they must hurriedly douse her with cool water. If there was still life in her, she would come around of her own, but if her life was ebbing away, then they would have to do something quickly in order to bring her to. If they didn't they would surely lose her.

The young child-bride was bathed three times that evening in scalding water, and each time she passed out. The commotion lasted until very late at night, when finally the crowd dispersed and the sorceress returned home to go to bed. The onlookers, too, returned to their homes to retire.

On this winter night the moon and stars filled the sky, ice and snow covered the ground. Snow swirled and gathered at the base of the wall, winds beat against the window sills. Chickens were asleep in their roosts, dogs slumbered in their dens, and pigs holed up in their pens. All of Hulan River was asleep.

There were only the distant sounds of a barking dog, perhaps in White Flag Village, or possibly a wild dog in the willow grove on the southern bank of the Hulan River. Whatever the case, the sound was coming from a great distance away and belonged to those affairs that occurred outside the town of Hulan River. The whole town of Hulan River was fast asleep.

There was no longer any hint of the dancing and drumbeating of the sorceress from the previous evening, and it was as though the shouts and cries of the young child-bride had never happened, for not a single trace of all of this remained. Every household was pitch dark, its occupants all sound asleep. The child-bride's mother-in-law snored as she slept.

Since the third watch had already been struck, the fourth watch was nearly upon them.

The young child-bride slept as though in a trance the whole day following, as well as the day after and the day af-
pletely closed; a small slit remained, through which the
ter that. Her eyes were neither completely open nor com-
whites of her eyes were visible.

When members of her family saw how she lay there, they all said that she had undergone a great struggle, but that her true soul still had a grip on her body; if that was the case, then she would recover. This was the opinion not just of her family, but of the neighbors as well. As a result, not only did they feel no anxiety over her condition—neither eating nor drinking, and always in a sort of half-consciousness—but on the contrary, they felt it was something over which they should rejoice. She lay in a stupor for four or five days, which were four or five happy days for her family; when she had lain there for six or seven days, they were six or seven happy days for her family. During this period not a single potion was used, and not a single type of herbal medication was put to the test.

But after six or seven days had passed she remained in a coma, neither eating nor drinking, and giving no indication at all that she was on the road to recovery. The sorceress was called back, but this time she said nothing about effecting a cure; she said it had now reached the point where there was no alternative but for the girl to "come forth," to become a sorceress herself.

The family then decided to apply the true methods of exorcism, so they went to the ornaments shop; there they had a paper image of her made, which they dressed in cotton clothing made especially for it (the cotton clothes were to make the image even more lifelike). Cosmetics were applied to the face and a colorful hankie attached to its hand; the result was a delight to behold—dressed completely in colorful clothes, it looked just like a maiden of seventeen or eighteen years. The image was carried by people down to the big pit on the south bank of the river where it was burned.

This procedure is called burning a "proxy doll," and according to legend, when this "proxy doll" is burned, it takes the place of someone's real body, sparing that person's life.

On the day the "proxy doll" was burned, the child-bride's mother-in-law showed proof of her devotion by engaging a few musicians, who filed in behind the people hired to carry the image; the procession made its way to the big southern pit to the accompaniment of the musicians' tooting and clanging. It would have been accurate to call the procession a boisterous affair, with the trumpets blaring the same tune over and over again. But it would have been no less accurate to call it a mournful affair, for with the paper figure going in front and three or four musicians bringing up the rear, it looked like something between a funeral procession and a temple excursion.

There weren't many people who came out onto the street to watch all the commotion, since the weather was so cold. A few folks did stick out their heads or venture out to take a look, but when they saw there wasn't much worth seeing they closed up their gates and went back inside. Therefore the paper figure was burned in the big pit in a mournful ceremony with little fanfare.

The child-bride's mother-in-law experienced pangs of regret as she burned the figure, for had she known beforehand that there weren't going to be many people looking on, she could have dispensed with dressing the figure in real clothing. She felt like going down into the pit to retrieve the clothing, but it was already too late, so she just stood there watching it burn. She had spent a total of more than a thousand coppers for that set of clothes, and as she watched it burn, it was as though she were watching more than a thousand coppers go up in smoke. There was both regret and anger in her heart. She had by then completely forgotten that this was a "proxy doll" for her prospective daughter-in-law. Her original plan had been to intone a prayerful chant during the ceremony, but it slipped her mind completely until she was on her way back home, at which time it occurred to her that she had probably burned the "proxy doll" for nothing. Whether or not it would prove effective was now anybody's guess!

Later we heard that the child-bride's braid had fallen off one night as she slept. It had simply fallen off beside her pillow, and no one was quite sure how that could have happened.

The mother-in-law was firmly convinced that the child-bride was some kind of demon, and the detached braid was kept around and shown to everyone who dropped by. It was obvious to anyone who saw it that it had been snipped off with scissors, but the mother-in-law insisted that such was not the case. She stuck to her story that it had simply fallen off by itself one night while the girl slept.

Eventually, as this curious news made the rounds throughout the neighborhood and outlying areas, not only were the members of her family unwilling to have a demon among them, even others in the same compound felt that it was a terrible situation. At night, while closing their doors and windows, the people commented: "The Hu family's child-bride is a demon for sure!"

The cook at our house was a real gossip, who was forever

telling Granddad one thing or another about the Hu family's child-bride. Now there was something new to report: the girl's braid had fallen off.

"No it didn't," I retorted. "Someone cut it off with a pair of scissors."

But as far as the old cook was concerned, I was too young, and to ridicule me, he stopped me by putting his finger over my mouth and saying: "What do you know? That young child-bride is a demon!"

"No she isn't. I asked her in secret how her hair had fallen off, and she had a grin on her face when she said she didn't know!"

"A nice child like that," Granddad interjected, "and they're going to kill her."

A few days later the old cook reported: "The Hu family is going to arrange a divorce; they're going to divorce away that little demon."

Granddad didn't hold the people in the Hu family in very high esteem. "Come March I'm going to have them move," he said. "First they nearly kill someone else's child, then they just abandon her."

Before March rolled around, however, that dark-complexioned young child-bride with the hearty laugh died. Early one morning the elder son of the Hu family—the carter with the sickly face and big eyes—came to our house. When he saw Granddad he brought his hands together in front of his chest and bowed deeply.

Granddad asked him what had happened.

"We would like you to donate a small plot of ground to bury our young child-bride."

"When did she die?" Granddad asked.

"I was out with my cart and didn't get home till daybreak," he replied. "They say she died during the night."

Granddad agreed to his request, telling him to bury her on a piece of ground on the outskirts of town.

—Translated by Howard Goldblatt

Slave's Mother

Jou Shi

Jou Shi was adopted as a pseudonym by Chao P'ing-fu (1901–1931), a member of the League of Left-Wing Writers and of the Communist Party. Jou's writings were vehicles for protest against what he viewed as socio-economic oppression. As "Slave's Mother" indicates, he was deeply concerned about the wretched condition of women, who had been the chief—and usually silent—sufferers throughout China's social history. In 1931, Jou was secretly executed by the Kuomintang as a Communist conspirator.

The Kuomintang—literally, "national people's party"—was founded by Sun Yat-sen in 1912 and became the Chinese Nationalist party that ruled China from 1928 to 1949, when it was defeated by Communist armies in the civil war and driven to Taiwan, where it was headed by General Chiang K'ai-shek.

———

Her husband was a leather merchant. He bought wild-animal skins from the village hunters and oxhides to sell in the big city. Sometimes he did a little farming too, helping transplant rice seedlings in the spring. He could plant so straight a row that if five others were working in a paddy-field with him they put him at the end of the line as marker. But things were always against him; his debts piled up over the years. It was probably because everything had gone so badly that he had taken to opium, drink, and gambling, which had finally turned him into a cruel and loutish fellow, poorer than ever and no longer able even to raise a small loan to tide them over.

His destitution brought with it a disease that turned him a withered yellow-brown all over: his face went the colour of a little bronze drum, and even the whites of his eyes turned brown. People said that he had the yellow liver sickness, and the children called him Yellow Fatty.

One day he said to his wife, "There's nothing for it. If we go on this way we'll even be selling our little cooking pots before long. Looks as though you'll have to provide the solution. No use your staying and starving with me."

"Me?" his wife asked dully. She was sitting behind the stove holding her baby boy, now just three years old, as she fed him at her breast.

"Yes, you." Her husband's voice was weak with sickness. "I've pledged you."

"What?" His wife almost fainted. There was a moment of silence in the room before he continued, gasping for breath, "Wolf Wang came here three days ago and went on and on demanding that money back. When he went I followed him as far as the Two Acre Pond. I wanted to do myself in. I sat under the tree you can jump into the pond from and thought and thought, but I hadn't got the strength to jump. Besides, an owl was hooting in my ear, and it made me so scared I came home. On the way back I met Mrs. Shen who asked me why I was out so late. I told her everything and asked her to borrow some money for me or some clothes or jewellery from a girl that I could pawn to keep Wolf Wang's wolf-eyes from glaring around the house every day.

"She said, 'Why are you keeping your wife at home? Look how sick you are yourself.' I couldn't say anything, just looked at the ground, but she went on, 'You've only got one son, and you couldn't spare him. But what about your wife?' I thought she was going to tell me to sell you—'Even though you are married there's no other option when you're hard up. Why keep her at home?'

"Then she said straight out, 'There's a gentleman of fifty who has no son and wants to marry a second wife. His first wife won't agree, and will only let him hire one for three or four years. He's asked me to look out for a suitable woman. She must be about thirty and have had two or three children. She should be quiet, well-behaved, hard-working, and willing to obey the first wife. The gentleman's wife told me that if these conditions were met they'd pay eighty or a hundred dol-

a fat face and calculating eyes came out to meet her. This must be the first wife, the woman thought. She stole an embarrassed glance at her and could say nothing. The older woman helped her up the steps in a very friendly way as a man with a long, thin face came out of the house. He took a good look at his new second wife and said, his face heaped with smiles, "You've come very early. Your clothes are wet."

Ignoring his remark, the older woman asked her, "Is there anything else in the chair?"

"No," the new wife said.

Some women who lived nearby were peering in through the main gate. They went indoors.

She did not know where she was. All she was thinking about was her old home and how she could not bear to leave Chunbao. It was clearly true that she should be glad about the three years now beginning. Both the new family and the new husband she had been hired to were better than her old ones. The soft-spoken scholar was indeed a good and kind man, and even the senior wife was far better than she had expected her to be. She was so considerate and she told her all about her thirty years with her husband from their splendid wedding right down to the present. She had given birth to a baby fifteen or sixteen years previously who was, she said, such a pretty and clever little boy, but he had died of smallpox before he was ten months old. She had never had another child. She had thought her husband ought, well, to take a concubine, but she never made it clear whether he did not because he loved her, or because he had never found the right girl. This state of affairs had gone on right up to the present. Talking about it made her, straightforward as she was, jealous, sad, happy, then depressed. Finally the older woman spoke her hopes out straight although her face was red:

"You've had several children, so of course you must know more about *that* than I do."

With these words she left her.

That evening the scholar told her all sorts of things about the family, though in fact it was nothing more than boasting and trying to win her favour. She was sitting beside a long table, a redwood one the like of which was not to be found in her old home. As she looked at it in a daze the scholar sat down on the other side of it and asked, "What's your name?"

She stood up without answering or smiling and walked over to the bed. He followed her over and asked with a titter:

"Feeling shy? Missing your husband? I'm your husband now." He laughed very quietly and tugged at her sleeve. "Cheer up. You're missing your baby, aren't you? Still. . . ."

Instead of finishing what he was saying he tittered again and took off his long gown.

She could hear the senior wife scolding someone in a loud voice outside. She could not make out at first who was at the receiving end: was it the kitchen maid or was she scolding her? At any rate, it was for her benefit that the older woman was losing her temper. The scholar, now in bed, said:

"Come to bed. She's always going on like that. She used to be very fond of one of the labourers, but ever since he got too friendly with Mrs. Huang in the kitchen she's been going for her all the time."

The days passed. Her old home gradually dimmed in her memory, as her present situation slowly became more real and familiar to her. All the same, Chunbao's howls still echoed in her ears and she occasionally saw him in her dreams, although he became increasingly indistinct as her present life grew more complicated every day. She now knew that the senior wife was suspicious, and that for all her show of generosity to her she was so jealous that she watched the scholar's every move as closely as a spy. If ever the scholar met the new wife first and talked to her, the senior wife would suspect that he was giving her something special and call him to her own room to give him a piece of her mind. "Have you been bewitched by that fox-spirit?" "You ought to have more sense of dignity." These were the sort of remarks that the new wife heard her make more than once. From then on she would scurry away if ever she saw him coming in when the older woman was not with her. When the senior wife was there the new wife had to give way to her which was only natural, but if anyone else noticed the new wife giving way, the senior wife would lose her temper with her and say that she was deliberately making everyone think that she was cruel. Later on menial household tasks were heaped upon her as if she were a servant girl. She tried to be clever and wash the clothes that the older woman had changed out of, but the senior wife said:

"You needn't wash my clothes. You can tell Mrs. Huang to wash yours too. Dear sister," she continued, "would you mind having a look at the pigsty? Why are those two pigs squealing? Perhaps they're hungry. Mrs. Huang never gives them enough to eat."

Eight months had passed, and that winter her tastes began to change. She wanted to eat fresh noodles and sweet potatoes instead of rice, but after two meals she was tired of them. Then she wanted to eat ravioli soup, but too much of it made her feel sick. Next she wanted pumpkin and plums although they were summer things that could not be had then. The scholar realized what these changes foretold. He smiled all day, eagerly fetching any of the things she wanted that he could find. He went out himself to buy her some tangerines and sent someone else to buy oranges. He walked up and down the verandah reciting something to himself that nobody could make out, and when he saw her milling flour for the New Year holiday with Mrs. Huang he told her to rest although she had only done a few pounds: "Take a rest. Let the hired hand do it—after all, everyone eats the New Year cakes."

Sometimes when everyone else was talking in the evening he would take a lamp and start reading the *Book of Songs*:

> *Qua qua cries the osprey*
> *On the island in the river.*
> *The beautiful maiden*
> *Is a fine match for the gentleman.*

"Sir, you're not taking the official exams," said the hired hand once, "so why read that?"

"He rubbed his beardless cheek and said happily, "Do you know about the joys of life? About 'the candlelit night in the bridal chamber, one's name on the list of successful candidates'? Do you know what those two lines mean? They are the two most happy things on earth. I've passed through that stage, and now I've got something to be even happier about."

Everyone except his two wives burst out laughing.

All this made the older wife look extremely cross. She had

been pleased when she first heard that the new wife was pregnant, but when she saw what a fuss the scholar was making of her she resented her own failure to have another child. In the third month of the new year the other woman stayed in bed for three days because she was feeling ill and had a headache. The scholar wanted her to rest, and when he kept asking her what she wanted, the senior wife really lost her temper. She said that the new wife was just pretending to be delicate and nagged at her throughout the three days. She started by mocking her unkindly, saying that since coming to the scholar's house she had grown high and mighty and was putting on a concubine's airs with her backaches and headaches. She was quite sure she had not been so spoilt in her own house and probably had to go round begging for food like a pregnant bitch, right up to the moment of birth. But now she was putting on her fine and fancy manners because the old fool—this was how the older woman referred to her husband—was making such a fuss over her.

"Everyone has had sons," she once said to Mrs. Huang in the kitchen. "I was pregnant myself for over nine months and I just don't believe it can make you feel that ill. Besides, this son isn't here yet. He's still on the king of Hell's register—how can we be sure that it won't be a monster? She'd better wait until the brat is born before being so high and mighty and putting on those airs in front of me. She's showing off a bit too early."

That evening the woman had gone to bed before supper, and when she heard all this sarcasm and abuse she began to sob quietly. The scholar, who was sitting fully dressed in bed, shook and sweated with fury when he heard it. He wanted to button his clothes up, get up, and go and hit her. He wanted to grab her by the hair and lay into her until he had worked off his fury. But for some reason he could not summon up the strength as he was trembling down to his finger-tips and his arms felt limp.

"Oh dear," he said with a low sigh, "I've been too good to her. I've never hit her once in thirty years of marriage. I've never even flicked my finger-nail at her. That's why she's as difficult as an empress today."

He rolled over to the other side of the bed where the new wife was and whispered in her ear:

"Don't cry, don't cry. Let her yap away. She's like a doctored hen—she can't bear to see anyone else hatch an egg. If you can produce a boy this time I'll give you two jewels—a green jade ring and a white one."

Before he could finish he was unable to bear any longer the jeering laughter of his senior wife that he heard through the door, so he undressed quickly, buried his head in the quilt, and moved towards her breasts.

"I've got a white jade one. . . ."

Her belly swelled day by day until it was the size of a bushel measure. The older wife finally hired a midwife and even started making baby clothes in brightly patterned cotton when other people were there to see her.

The sixth month of the old calendar,[2] when the heat of summer was at its greatest, passed in hope. Autumn began and cool breezes started to blow through the country town. One day, when everyone's hope was at its highest pitch, the atmosphere in the house was thrown into confusion. The scholar was extremely anxious. He paced up and down the yard with an almanac in his hands reading it out as if he wanted to learn it by heart. "*Wu-chen, jia-xu,* the year *ren-yin*"[3] was what he kept repeating lightly to himself. Sometimes he cast an impatient glance at the room with closed windows from which came the low groans of a woman in labour; otherwise he looked up at the sun masked by cloud. He went to the door of the room and asked Mrs. Huang who was standing outside:

"What's happening now?"

Mrs. Huang nodded continuously and said nothing. Then she breathed out and replied:

"It'll be born any minute now, any minute now."

He picked up his almanac and started walking up and down the verandah once more.

This went on until, as the evening mist began to gather and lamps were lit in the room like wild flowers in spring, a baby boy was born. While the baby bawled inside the room the scholar sat in a corner, almost weeping with happiness. Nobody in the house was interested in eating supper, and as they

[2] About July.
[3] The scholar was working out the time and date of the baby's birth in terms of the traditional calendar.

sat at the unappetizing meal the senior wife said to the servants:

"We won't let on that he's a boy yet so as to keep bad luck away from the little brat. If anyone asks, you are to say that it's a girl."

They all smiled and nodded.

A month later the baby's soft, little white face was reflecting the autumn sunlight as the young wife suckled him, surrounded by the neighbouring women. Some were praising the baby's nose, some his mouth, and some his ears. Others praised his mother, saying that she looked fairer and stronger than before. The senior wife and the baby's grandmother were giving instructions, protecting it, and saying, "That's enough for now. Don't make him cry."

The scholar racked his brains for a suitable name for the child but could not think of one. The senior wife thought he should choose one from the words "long life, wealth, and glory" or "happiness, office, longevity, and blessings." "Longevity" or some other words with the same meaning would be best, like Qixi or Pengzu. The scholar thought them too common and did not agree: they were names that anyone might have. He leafed through the *Book of Changes* and the *Book of History* and searched high and low, but after a fortnight and then a month he still had not found a suitable one. In his view it had to be a name that would bring the child luck while also meaning that he had been given a son in his old age. One day he was holding his three-month-old son while looking through a book for a name for him. With his spectacles on his nose he carried the book over to the lamplight. The baby's mother was sitting silently on the other side of the room with her mind far away when suddenly she opened her mouth and said:

"I think we should call him Qiubao."[4] All the eyes in the room turned towards her as everyone listened to what she had to say next. "He was born in the autumn, wasn't he? So he's an autumn treasure. Let's call him Qiubao."

"Yes," the scholar said immediately, "I've put a great deal of thought into it. I'm over fifty, in the autumn of my life, and the child was indeed born in the autumn. Autumn is the

[4] Literally "Autumn Treasure."

time when everything comes to maturity. Qiubao is an excellent name. And it's in the *Book of History*, isn't it? 'And there will be an autumn.' I'm having my autumn now."

Then he praised the child's mother, saying that study was useless and intelligence was inborn. All this made the woman feel awkward, just sitting there. With her head bowed and a sad smile she said, holding back her tears, "It was only because I was missing Chunbao."

Qiubao grew every day into a child who was charmingly inseparable from his mother. He had extraordinarily large eyes that gazed tirelessly at strangers and could recognize his mother at a distance with a single glance. He clung to her all day, and although his father loved him even more than she did, the child did not like him. The scholar's wife pretended to love the child as if he were her own, but the boy's big eyes saw her as a stranger and looked at her with tireless curiosity, clinging more closely to his mother. But the day when his mother would be leaving this house was drawing nearer. The jaws of spring bit the tail of winter and the feet of summer were always close behind spring. This put a problem in the front of everyone's mind: the three years would soon be up for the child's mother.

Because he was so fond of his son the scholar suggested to his wife that they should pay out another hundred dollars and buy her for good. But his wife's reply was:

"If you're going to buy her you'd better poison me first."

The scholar snorted angrily and said nothing for a long time. Finally he forced a smile and said, "Just think of that poor child without his mother."

"Don't I count as his mother?" asked the senior wife tartly, with a cold smile.

There were two conflicting feelings clashing in the mind of the child's mother. On the one hand the words "three years" were always in her brain, and three years would pass easily even though she was now living like a servant in the scholar's house. Besides, the Chunbao of her imagination was as lively and adorable as the Qiubao in front of her, and although she could not bear to part with Qiubao it would be even worse to lose Chunbao. On the other hand she would like to stay in this house for good because, she thought, Chunbao's father was not fated to live long and his disease would carry him off to a very distant place in a few years. So she asked her second husband to bring Chunbao here, too, so that she could have him with her.

Once she was sitting exhausted on the verandah in the early summer sunlight that has such an amazing power to make you so drowsy that you start imagining things. Qiubao was asleep in her arms, her nipple in his mouth, and she somehow felt that Chunbao was standing beside her. She stretched out her hand to take hold of him, wanting to say something to the two brothers, but there was nothing beside her after all.

In the doorway further away from her stood the older wife, staring at her with her kind face but evil eyes. The woman realized with vague regret that she should escape as soon as she could; the older woman was watching her like a spy. Then the child in her arms cried, and she could only cope with the senior wife by inventing things to do even when she was not really busy.

Later the scholar changed his plan. He now wanted to send for Mrs. Shen to ask the former husband of Qiubao's mother if he would agree to continue the arrangement for another three years for another thirty dollars—or at most fifty dollars. "When Qiubao is five," he said to his senior wife, "he'll be able to leave his mother."

His wife, while telling her Buddhist beads and reciting "I dedicate myself to Amitabha Buddha," replied:

"She has her elder son at home. You ought to let her go back to her original husband."

"Just imagine poor Qiubao without his mother at two," continued the scholar, his head lowered.

The older woman put down her beads and said, "I can bring him up, I can look after him. Do you think I'd try to kill him?"

At this last remark the scholar started to walk away, but the older wife went on behind him:

"That child was born for my good as well. Quibao is mine. If we have no descendants it will be your family that dies out, but remember that I depend on your family. You've really been taken with her. You've gone so senile you can't think straight any longer. You're so eager to have her with you— how much longer do you think you're going to live? I'm certainly not going to share a place with her in the ancestral temple."

She apparently had more cruel and biting things to say, but the scholar was by now out of earshot.

That summer a boil appeared on the child's head and he ran a slight fever. The senior wife went everywhere to consult goddesses and ask for Buddha-medicine to smear on the baby's boil or pour down his throat. The child's mother did not think it was a very serious illness and was not happy to see the young creature cry himself into a terrible state, so she would tip the medicine away discreetly when he had drunk only a few mouthfuls of it. This made the senior wife sigh aloud and say to the scholar:

"Just look! She doesn't care in the least about his illness. She even says he's not really losing weight. Only love that comes from the heart is genuine; superficial affection is false."

All the woman could do was wipe away her tears in secret. The scholar said nothing.

At the time of Qiubao's first birthday the family laid on a noisy banquet in his honour that lasted all day. Thirty or forty guests came, bringing clothes, noodles, silver lions to hang round his neck, or gilded figures of the god of longevity to pin on his hat. All these presents arrived in the guests' sleeves. They wished him great success and long life. The host's face gleamed and shone as if the colour of the sunset were reflected on his cheeks.

But just when the feasting was about to begin, that evening, a visitor came into their courtyard in the dim light of dusk. Everyone looked closely at him. He was a destitute-looking countryman with patched clothes and long hair, and under his arm he carried a bundle wrapped in paper. The host greeted him with some astonishment and asked who he was. His mumbled reply confused the host at first before it came to him in a flash that this was the leather merchant.

"Why, have you brought a present too?" the host asked quietly. "You really didn't have to."

The visitor looked all around him before answering:

"I . . . I wanted to. I've come to wish the baby long life. . . ."

Leaving his remark apparently unfinished he started to open the paper parcel that was under his arm. With trembling fingers he untied several layers of paper and took out the four characters for "Longevity like Southern Mountains." They were made of silver-plated copper and each was about one inch square.

The scholar's wife came over and examined him closely. She seemed rather angry, but the scholar invited him to join the feast. The other guests all whispered to each other.

Two hours of eating and drinking had put everyone in high spirits. They were playing guess-fingers, the drinking game, and competing in the downing of large bowls of rice wine. The house seemed to shake with the din. Only the leather merchant was sitting there quietly although he too had drunk a couple of cupfuls, and the other guests were ignoring him. When the general excitement had died down the guests hastily swallowed a bowl of rice, exchanged polite remarks and went away in the light of two or three lanterns at a time.

The leather merchant went on eating to the very end, only leaving the table when the servants came to clear up the soup bowls. He went to a dark corner of the verandah where he met his hired-out wife.

"Why did you come?" she asked in a very sad voice.

"It wasn't because I wanted to; I had no alternative."

"But why did you have to come in this state?"

"How do you think I got the money to buy the presents? I had to rush around all morning pleading with people to lend it to me, then I had to go into town to buy them. That made me tired, hungry, and late."

"How's Chunbao?" the woman asked.

Her husband paused before replying.

"It's about him that I've come."

"About Chunbao?" She sounded alarmed.

"Ever since last summer," her husband slowly replied, "he's been getting terribly thin. He became ill during the autumn. I hadn't the money to pay a doctor or buy medicine for him, so now he's worse than ever. If we can't find some way of helping him he may die any hour." After a moment's silence he continued, "I've come to borrow some money from you."

The woman felt as if several cats were clawing and biting her inside and chewing up her heart. She longed to weep, but today was the day on which everyone had come to wish Qiubao well, so how could she follow their good wishes with sobs? She gulped back her tears and said to her husband:

"I haven't any money either. They only give me twenty cents a month for pocket-money, and I don't have the use of any of that because I have to spend it all on the baby. What are we to do?"

After a silence the woman asked, "Who's looking after Chunbao now?"

"I left him at a neighbour's. I must go back this evening, so I'd better be off."

As he spoke he wiped away his tears. The woman said, sobbing, "Wait a moment. I'll go and see if I can borrow some money from him." She went away.

One evening three days later the scholar asked her, "What happened to that green jade ring I gave you?"

"I gave it to my husband that night. He took it to pawn."

"But I lent you five dollars," said the scholar angrily.

"Five dollars wasn't enough."

"You always prefer your first husband and son," continued the scholar with a sigh, "no matter how good I am to you. I was wanting to keep you for another couple of years, but now I think you'd better go next spring."

The woman sat there impassively, not even weeping.

A few days later he said to her, "That ring was very valuable. When I gave it to you I meant to pass it on to Qiubao. I'd never have imagined you would pawn it. It's a good thing *she* doesn't know about it—if she did the row would last three months."

The woman became thinner every day. There was a dullness in her eyes, and her ears were filled with mocking and abusive voices. Chunbao's illness was preying constantly on her mind and she was always on the look-out for a friend from her own village or a visitor who was going there to bring her the news she longed to hear—"Chunbao is better." But there was never any news. She wanted to borrow two dollars to send him some sweets by a visitor who was passing that way, but no such visitor came. She used to stand holding Qiubao beside the main road that passed near the main gate looking at the way home. This made the scholar's senior wife feel most uncomfortable.

"She doesn't want to stay here," she kept saying to him. "She's longing to go flying back there as soon as she can."

Some nights she would cry out as she lay sleeping with

Qiubao in her arms, which frightened him and made him howl.

"Why did you do that? Why?" the scholar asked as if he were interrogating her.

She patted Qiubao, humming and not replying.

"Did you shout because you dreamt that your first son had died?" he continued. "You woke me up."

"No, no," she hastily objected. "I thought I saw a grave-mound in front of me."

The scholar said nothing else, but gloomy images kept coming up before her eyes and she wanted to walk towards the grave.

At the end of the winter the birds that were about to leave were twittering in front of her window all the time. First she weaned the child and then she had a Taoist priest perform the appropriate ceremonial. The separation, the eternal separation, of mother and child had been decided on.

Earlier that day Mrs. Huang had whispered to the scholar's senior wife, "Shall I arrange for a chair to take her back?"

The scholar's senior wife, who was telling her beads, said, "Let her walk. The chair would have to be paid for at that end and she hasn't any money. They say her real husband can't even afford to eat, so she shouldn't be extravagant. It's not far. I've walked ten or a dozen miles in my time, and her feet are bigger than mine. She'll do it in a few hours."

When the woman dressed Qiubao that morning tears streamed down her cheeks as the child called "Aunty, aunty"—the senior wife would only let him call his real mother "aunty" as she herself had to be called "mummy"—and she answered him through sobs. She was longing to say something to him like: "Good-bye, my darling son. Your mummy has always been good to you and you must be good to her in the future and forget about me."

But she could not bring herself to say it. Besides, she knew that a child of one and a half would not understand.

The scholar came up quietly behind her, put his hand under her arm with ten twenty-cent pieces. "Here, take it," he whispered, "it's two dollars." When she had finished doing up the child's buttons she put the coins in her bosom.

The senior wife came in again, and when she had watched the scholar go out she said to her: "Let me hold Qiubao so that he doesn't cry when you leave."

The woman said nothing, but Qiubao, most unwilling to leave her, kept hitting the senior wife in the face until she said angrily:

"You'd better go and have breakfast with him. Give him to me afterwards."

Mrs. Huang urged her as hard as she could to eat plenty. "You've been like this for a fortnight," she said. "You're even thinner than when you came. Look in the mirror and you'll see. Do eat a bowl of rice. You've got ten miles to walk today."

"You've been very good to me," the woman replied in a detached way.

The sun had now risen high and it was a beautiful day. Qiubao still did not want to leave his mother. When the senior wife snatched him cruelly away he kicked her in the belly with his little feet and pulled her hair with his little fists, howling at the top of his voice.

"Let me go after dinner," said the woman from behind.

The senior wife turned on her and said cruelly: "Pack your bundle and go. It'll be the same whenever you do it."

The child's howls grew fainter in her ears.

As she packed she could still hear him crying. Mrs. Huang stood beside her trying to console her but keeping an eye on what she put in the bundle. Finally she set off with her old bundle under her arm.

She could hear Qiubao crying as she went out through the main gate and could still hear him as she slowly walked the ten miles.

The road, under the warm sun, seemed as endless to her as the sky. As she walked beside a river she longed to rest her feeble feet and jump into the water. It was so clear she could see herself in it. But after sitting on the bank for a while she had to start moving her shadow in the same direction once more.

The sun was past its height when an old countryman told her in a village that she had five more miles to go.

"Uncle," she said to him, "please could you arrange a sedan chair for me. I can't walk any further."

"Are you ill?" the old man asked.

"Yes."

She was now sitting in a cool shelter at the edge of the village.

"Have you come from the village?"

After a moment's silence she replied, "I'm going there. This morning I thought I could do it on foot."

The old man was understanding enough to ask no more questions before going to find two chair porters and a chair. Because this was the rice transplanting time no hood could be spared for it.

At what seemed to be about three or four in the afternoon an uncovered chair was carried down a narrow, dirty village street. In the chair lay a middle-aged woman with a face as shrivelled as a dried-up cabbage leaf. Her eyes were half shut with exhaustion and her breathing was weak. The people in the street all gazed at her with astonishment and pity, and a crowd of children followed the chair shouting and yelling. It was as if something strange had arrived in the silent village.

Chunbao was one of the children following the chair. He was shouting as if he were driving a pig, but when the chair turned into the lane leading to his own home he stretched out his hands in amazement. Then it reached his front gate. He stood stock still, leaning on a pillar some way away from it. The other children stood timidly on either side of the chair. As the woman stepped out her eyes were too blurred to recognize as her own Chunbao the six-year-old boy in ragged clothes and with matted hair who was no taller than he had been three years ago. Then suddenly she started crying and called "Chunbao."

The children were startled. Chunbao was so frightened that he went indoors to hide in his father's room.

The woman sat in the murky room for a very long time. Neither she nor her husband spoke. As night fell his drooping head straightened up and he said: "Cook us a meal."

She had to get up. After walking round the room she said weakly to her husband:

"The rice jar is empty."

Her husband laughed bitterly. "You really have been living with the gentry. The rice is in that cigarette tin."

That evening her husband said to her son:

"Go and sleep with your mother, Chunbao."

But Chunbao started to cry in the alcove. His mother went up to him, calling him by his name, but when she tried to caress him he dodged away from her.

"I'll hit you for forgetting her as fast as that," said her husband to him. She lay with her eyes wide open on a dirty and narrow plank bed with Chunbao lying beside her like a stranger. In her numbed brain a fat and lovable Qiubao was fidgeting beside her, but when she put out her hands to hug him he turned out to be Chunbao. Chunbao, now asleep, turned over. His mother hugged him tight, and as he snored lightly he lay his head on her chest, stroking her breasts with his hands.

The long night, as cold and lonely as death, dragged interminably on and on.

—Translated by W. J. F. Jenner and Gladys Yang

The Moon on a Frosty Morning

Fang Shumin

Fang Shumin is one of a number of younger authors of whom very little is known. It is assumed he is of Hopei province, since it was there that his short story collection, *Lanterns in the Snow,* was published in 1964. "The Moon on a Frosty Morning" first appeared in that volume. The assertive and competent woman pictured here as a leader in her village offers interesting contrast to "Slave's Mother."

Cassia had just fed her one-year-old baby and was covering her head with a towel to go to the fields, when her four-year-old son Shigour said to his granny, "Why are you making shoes for my father? He's away."

"I'm not making them for that spineless father of yours." She rubbed the awl against her hair and thrust it hard and angrily through the sole of the shoe. "I'm making them for your mother."

"But her feet are too small for those shoes," Shigour protested solemnly.

"Out of the way, brat." With Shigour driven away the old lady handed her daughter-in-law the black canvas shoes for which she had just finished making the sole.

"Oh well," she said, smiling till her eyes creased right up, "you can't blame the boy. You've been so busy these last few months rushing all over the place through mud and water. No wonder these great boots aren't proper women's shoes. Try them on."

Cassia tried on the new shoes and found that they fitted perfectly. Even she could not help laughing. Then she tucked a sickle in her belt and hurried off to the threshing-ground.

The threshing-ground lay to the north of Bean Hamlet, as the village was called. It was bigger than last year, and heaped within new fencing in the middle of it were two huge mounds of bright red sorghum that had yet to be milled; the corn-cobs stacked in frames built of sorghum stalks gleamed in the autumn sun like a golden palace, and the piles of late millet were pushing at the fence round the threshing-floor, making it lean like an overhanging cliff.

The rich fragrance of grain drifted across the threshing-floor. Although it was now late autumn and the light north-west wind blowing across the fields was reminding everyone that the cold season had begun, Cassia felt only warmth at the sight of the fine harvest on the floor as she cut off the sorghum tops with her sickle.

Eyes sparkled as people returning to other counties from market passed the threshing-floor. They sighed with admiration and said, "What a good harvest they've had in this team."

"Indeed," somebody agreed awkwardly. "Looks even better than the Cherry Orchard Team we passed earlier."

"A fat lot you know. They left the famous Cherry Orchard Team behind months ago."

"Which team is this then?" asked the ill-informed man with another sigh.

"Bean Hamlet."

"At last. So this is the famous 'poor Bean Hamlet'," a voice said with a hoarse chuckle. "The paupers have managed a decent harvest this year—like a blind man catching an eel."

This last remark stung Cassia as she worked. There was an explosion in her head as she flung a bundle of sorghum tops to the ground, flicked her short, untidy hair back and shot a furious glare at the hoarse, middle-aged man. He blushed in fear and embarrassment. She softened her expression, suddenly realizing that she had no reason to lose her temper like an eighteen-year-old. A woman of thirty-two should be more tolerant; besides, she was deputy work-team leader. She waved to the men in the road and smiled at them. "Are you thirsty, friends? Take a rest on the threshing-floor."

"No thanks," one of them replied. "Looks like a good harvest you've had this year."

"It certainly is," she shouted happily, stepping back with her strong legs. An old man in a little felt hat jumped off his grey donkey and croaked, "Hey, comrade. Come here, comrade."

A cheeky youth beside him who was grinning all over his face grabbed him and whispered: "You're asking for trouble, you shameless old devil. You're not on comrade terms with her."

When Cassia heard this she ran to the fence and said to the old man, "Never mind that nonsense, uncle. You go ahead and call me 'comrade' as bold as you please. What do you want to say?"

The old man shifted the pouch-sack on his shoulder before relaxing and letting himself reply. "I came through here on the way to market during the floods in July, and the oceans of water covering the fields made me think that you'd been washed out again. After two bad years running I was sure you'd be going hungry again this year. I'd never have dreamed you could get this good a harvest."

Cassia waved her sickle and laughed, her eyebrows raised. "You can't have been to market since then. You may have seen the floods, but you didn't see how we fought against them."

The old man now apparently understood everything. He took off his hat, nodded, jumped back on his donkey, and rode away. Cassia smiled as she watched them go off towards the Grand Canal ferry. The full evening sun cast a golden light over her tanned face. The boundless plain beyond the village and the fields of green wheat shoots that covered it gave her a feeling of expanse and excitement. At the same time she was a little depressed. She had wanted badly to tell those strangers who did not know the story how their village had fought against the flood. But she must put all such ideas out of her head. Anyone would think that Bean Hamlet was not tough enough. As she gazed into the distance deep in thought she saw a trail of yellow dust rising from the road behind the brick-kiln. She knew it came from a rider and trembled as she realized that it must be Big Wu galloping at that speed. Just then she heard some women on the threshing-floor crying out, "It's Big Wu." "It's him, it's Big Wu." Unable to think of anything else she dropped her sickle and ran after the other women and the children towards the road. Shielding her eyes with her right hand she made out a chestnut horse pounding through the dust, and the bare-chested man astride it was indeed Big Wu, the team leader.

"Big Wu." She was waving and shouting.

The chestnut horse carried its rider to the fence. The tall rider, a man in his forties, dismounted with a leap into a cloud of dust and put his hand on the horse's back.

"Have you been impatient waiting for me to come back? Come and take a look at our horse."

Cassia was the first to reach it. "It's a fine sturdy beast," she said.

"It's kicking," shouted Big Wu, deliberately frightening the women and children so that they scattered like chickens. Cassia alone stepped forward and grabbed it by the mane. When it shook its head violently, she pinched its nostrils shut and forced its mouth open.

"Be quiet, you devil." It whinnied, pawed the ground, and then calmed down. "What did you want to make it do that for?" she said to Big Wu, adding, "Tell me quickly, how old is it?"

"Six. It's a strong one all right."

As she kneaded the horse's back she could not hold back her praises. "And such a glossy coat. What breed is it?" "It's Mongolian—from beyond the Great Wall." "Good." Then she anxiously asked, "Have we bought her yet?" "I paid on the nail and I've got the papers to prove it." "Good." Cassia tugged at the reins as she said, "Yesterday Tiedan and I built the stable, and last night Grandpa Baishun was chosen as stock-keeper. He's so pleased he's spent the morning cooking and rolling feed. I'll take him along to be watered and fed.

the determined way her eyebrows were raised, could only smile. It would have been a waste of time to say anything more.

She was a long time settling in the new horse with Grandpa Baishun before going home. As it was the end of the lunar month there was not even a sliver of moon above the trees. She felt her way into the courtyard and grimly remembered to wedge the gates shut by sticking a pole hard against them. In the house she heard her mother-in-law ask sleepily from the darkness, "Is that you back? Shall I light the lamp?"

"No," Cassia replied quickly. "Are the children asleep? Why are you still awake?"

"I rocked them to sleep. Why did you have to make such a noise shutting the gates? We haven't used the date-wood pole for months, so why shut the gates with it tonight?"

"I thought the wind would blow them open."

"Fool," the old woman went on, "idiot. Didn't you notice that the wind had dropped ages ago?"

Cassia did not want to tell her mother-in-law that Waizi was coming that night in case the news gave her a seizure and killed her. She climbed on to the *kang*, but no matter which way she lay she could not get to sleep. She gritted her teeth and hardened her heart, longing to hear him trying to force the gates while she lay there on the *kang* and would not get up to open them. He could freeze—he had asked for it. As she lay there her heart would start to pound at the slightest sound from the yard, but as she waited she heard no loud noise to follow.

An evening in July flashed before her eyes. That night when, with one cloud-burst following another, she had waded home from a team meeting through the floods, her feet heavy with mud, supporting herself with difficulty on the vegetable-garden fence. Just as she and her mother-in-law had been looking for a big spade in the shed they had heard squelching footsteps in the yard. She had opened the door and said, "Oh, you're back."

The stocky Waizi had come in and was wiping the mud off his feet while she lit the lamp and asked him, "Where've you been? We shouted ourselves hoarse trying to get you to the team meeting."

"I went to Cherry Orchard," he had said.

"What a thing to do," she had replied, flaring up. "You just don't care about the team's crops. Big Wu's been elected team leader and he'll be a good one. He's taken men and women from our village down to the river bend as fast as they can go to drain the water out. But you had time to go and visit the children's granny. What do you mean by it at a time like this?"

"You want to know what I was doing?" said Waizi with a laugh. "I was negotiating. It's all settled. Tomorrow the whole family moves to Cherry Orchard."

Cassia had been stunned. "What? What did you say?"

"What's the point of thinking about nothing but work all the time? Can't you see that this poverty-ridden hollow has been a frog pond for two years running? Even the team's donkey has starved to death. Now this year's rains have drowned us again. There's nothing to stay for. The sooner we find some dry land the better."

Cassia had realized at once what he was thinking. "Frightened of starving?" she had said. "Want to sneak off, don't you?"

Waizi had tilted his head to one side and replied, "Say what you like as long as you understand that tomorrow we're shutting the place up and going, bedding and all."

"Who's going?" she had asked.

"All of us," he had said.

At this she had flared up and shouted furiously, "You can clear off by yourself. You may have it all nicely worked out, but nobody's going with you."

The stocky Waizi had rushed forward and grabbed her. "Stay where you are. Where are you going with that spade?"

"Get away from me," Cassia had said, breaking away from him. "I'm going to drain off the water and guard the dike with Big Wu. This is a crisis. I've got no time to waste talking to you." Waizi had raised his hand, but Cassia had moved her spade instantly to parry it, screaming "Don't touch me. If you lay a finger on me you'll get a dose of this." With their quarrel the room had felt as hot as a kiln; gongs were being beaten outside to tell everyone to go to the dike at once, the boy was crying, and the adults were shouting at each other. It had been too much for the old woman, who released a torrent of abuse on him: "Worthless wretch, evil son, get the hell out of here and eat and drink as well as you can."

When Cassia had come back the next day from her work at the river she had tried to win him round, but he was so set in his twisted ideas that when she had finished he just replied, "The flood waters are here to stay. This dump won't ever get rich. Are you coming with me or aren't you?"

"No," Cassia had said, steeling herself, "I won't go."

"If you're not coming that's your lookout. Mother and Shigour are coming with me."

The old lady had jabbed her finger at his nose and said, "You're not going to take even a hair of any of us, not one hair."

Red-faced and hoarse, Waizi had issued his last warning: "Very well then; don't come if you don't want to. But don't expect me to be nice to you when you come begging from me in the autumn."

This had made the old lady angrier than ever: "If that's how you're going to talk to us you'd better clear out at once. Go off and hatch your plans, my fine lad. There may not be much flesh on us but our bones are hard, really hard."

Waizi had wrapped up his bedding and gone, his pipe between his teeth.

His last superior glance at them was deeply etched on Cassia's mind. The thought of it still made her almost burst with indignation; she gave an involuntary and contemptuous snort. This woke her mother-in-law, who rolled over and asked:

"Are you cold?"

"No, mother, I'm boiling hot."

She tried as hard as she could to calm herself down as she lay there in the dark, her eyes wide open, struggling to drive away the image that flickered in front of them. But it hovered there more clearly than ever. She imagined him coming back and apologizing to her. She would tell him straight out that what he'd done had been completely wrong, and it had all been because he had not had confidence in the group and the people's commune. . . . She fell into a doze. When she woke again a little later there was still no sound from the courtyard. "He hasn't come back," she thought. The crescent moon setting in the south-west was filtering its light through the window, and she could hear the first cock-crow of the morning. She could stay in bed no longer. The old lady leant over to her and said:

"Why are you tossing and turning so?"

"Keep your voice down, mother." Cassia sat up smartly and felt for her clothes. "I've got to get up early to take the tax grain in."

"You'll be frozen right through this early in the morning," the old lady said, "so mind you wear a jacket over your green tunic. I finished the soles of your new shoes last night and put them by your pillow. Have you found them?"

"I've put them on," Cassia replied.

"It'll be a long, cold journey, so wait till I've boiled you some noodles and egg."

"No thanks." Cassia got down from the *kang.* "I must be on my way before the third cock-crow. I can get something to eat on my way through Zimu township."

She groped lightly for her child's head, kissed his lips, and went out. She felt the cold in the courtyard at once, pulling her warm hands straight away from the frozen window-sill and sucking in her breath. There had been a frost that night, the first since last winter, and the young crows perched in the locust tree in the yard were cheeping miserably. Some dead leaves, covered in white, were drifting to the ground. She looked up again at the golden crescent of the moon in the south-western sky and at the stars shimmering in the cold air, overcome with a warm feeling of pity. It had been the height of summer when Waizi left wearing only a thin shirt and trousers. He would choose the cold season to come back, the pig-headed fool. Well, if he wanted to come back he'd have to change his way of thinking.

She regretted her anger of the previous night. He hadn't come back, so she need not have blocked the gates so securely. She went over and worked the heavy date-wood pole loose. As she stepped through the gates all her courage could not stop her from gasping with fright: there was somebody squatting in the shadows outside.

"Who's that?" she called.

The man did not look up. He stayed there with his arms clasping his shoulders and his head buried in them.

There was no need to ask any questions. The faint moonlight was bright enough for her to see that it was Waizi.

—Translated by W. J. F. Jenner and Gladys Yang

The Elder Mrs. King

Pai Hsien-yung

Pai Hsien-yung (1937–   ) went to Taiwan in 1952 from his birthplace in Kwangsi province, China. After studying engineering for a period at Taiwan University, he changed to English literature, taking a degree in that subject in 1961. In addition to his writing of novels and short stories, he has served on the editorial staff of the periodical *Modern Literature*, published in Taipei. *Jade Love*, a short novel, has been published in English in *New Chinese Writing*.

Related in the first person by a young boy, this story has as its focal point the elderly matriarch of a family whose wealth had established her husband's high status in society but who—in violation to the Confucian tradition of veneration of the elderly—is literally hounded to death by all.

———————

I remember the year when we won the war, the Second World War. My parents were still in Nanking, and I, accompanied by my amah, Swen Sao, went to live in Hungjao county, just outside of Shanghai. Most of the people living there were farmers, but there were also some merchants who commuted to and fro from Shanghai. Whatever they were, they were all well-to-do people who did not have to worry about their living, with more than enough rice to eat. This was because the earth there was very rich; when spring came and the rapeseed flower was at full bloom you could see a whole expanse of yellow—in truth, "an earthfull of gold."

Among the residents of Hungjao, our neighbors, the Kings, were the wealthiest. Swen Sao told me this. She said that if they did not have hundreds of *mou* of rice fields, they could not possibly live the way they did. Swen Sao was very good at the social amenities, and we had only settled down there a few days when she was already on the very best of terms with everyone in the King household. When she took me over and just walked in unannounced, even the police dog that was supposed to be watching the gate did not make a sound.

The King residence was very large, an old-fashioned rambling place with two courtyards. In the large front court were many elm trees, and not far from the entrance was a spacious hall that could hold more than twelve banquet tables. The square "eight-fairy"[1] tables, with tops inlaid with gray veined marble. In summer this was cool and soothing to the touch. On the walls hung ancient paintings and calligraphic scrolls; the tea tables scattered around displayed multi-colored pots of shrubs and beautiful antiques. Sometimes I could not refrain from touching them, and then Swen Sao would hiss at me through clenched teeth.

"Brother Yung, my little ancestor, I will bow to you, but please don't touch or disturb anything in any way. If you break any of their things, we certainly cannot afford to replace them!"

We used to go there very often, so we became very familiar with their family affairs. There were two brothers in the King family. Because the elder Mr. King was often in Shanghai, all the household and farm affairs were managed by the younger Mr. King.

However, everyone in the household was subject to the pleasure of the younger Mrs. King, even the younger Mr. King himself. The younger Mrs. King was a most capable housewife, sharp-tongued and hard-hearted. Because she had the wholehearted trust of the elder Mr. King, everyone in the family, even the lazy good-for-nothing bond maid, Ah-hung, would jump at her slightest cough and did not dare to stop work for a minute.

But this strong-willed lady was eager to solicit Swen Sao's goodwill, most probably because Swen Sao's needlework was so much above the ordinary. Every other day or so she would send over someone to ask Swen Sao to go over and help her

---

[1] A square table that can seat eight people. There are eight fairies in old Chinese legends.

embroider something. The younger Mrs. King was also especially nice to me on account of her precious son, Little Tiger. Little Tiger and I struck it off from the very start; we were both around ten years old and, although we had just known each other a few days, it seemed as if we had been friends since childhood. Little Tiger was a born troublemaker, and he told me everything. He said he wasn't afraid of his father: his father was good-natured but not of much use. On mentioning his mother he stuck out his tongue, looking stealthily around, but didn't dare say a word. Speaking of his uncle he stuck out his thumb, exclaiming: "Huh! He is one of the very best!" I agreed. Even till this day I cannot forget the elder Mr. King's tall and manly figure, his neat black mustache and his light and carefree manner. The thing I remember most clearly about him is the bright red tie that he wore—he was the only man who wore a tie in that whole town. Little Tiger told me that he was already forty years old but I could not believe him to be more than thirty-five.

As a matter of course, the elder Mrs. King should be Little Tiger's Aunt. But when I asked him about it he sneered, "To hell with her! What kind of an aunt is she? Just call her 'old hag' and you've said it!"

It was very strange indeed: everybody in the King family called the elder Mrs. King "the old hag" behind her back. Little Tiger called her this, the younger Mrs. King called her this, and even when Ah-hung took food into the elder Mrs. King's room she would grumble in a nasty way: "This awful old hag! Why should someone with such a sour-looking face tell us what to do!"

The elder Mrs. King seldom left her room. Sometimes I saw her sneaking into the sitting room to get a glass of tea. If the younger Mrs. King happened to be sitting there, the older woman would immediately withdraw in frightened haste. Even at mealtime, the elder Mrs. King never sat down at the table. Only after the younger Mrs. King and the others had finished eating would Ah-hung dump some of the left-over rice and vegetables into a dish to take to her room.

But what surprised me most was that when the elder Mr. King came back from Shanghai, he paid her no attention at all. They stayed in separate rooms—his, very spacious with handsome furniture bought from Shanghai while hers was a small room with only one window, dim and musty and way at the back, as far as possible from the entrance. I did not go to her room very often, since the younger Mrs. King had told me not to do so. Once she saw me just as I reached the door and pulled me away. She took me by the hand and, pointing at the door, said in a low voice, "Yung brother, don't ever bother Old Hag. She is just a cheap woman, understand?" I really didn't "understand" at all about the elder Mrs. King being a "cheap woman," but when the younger Mrs. King looked at me so penetratingly, I was scared into nodding my head vigorously.

"Old Hag is really the most hateful old thing," Little Tiger said to me one day as we were sitting under an elm tree in the front court eating baked sweet potatoes.

"Why?" I asked, between big bites of sweet potato, because I thought even if the elder Mrs. King was hateful, she couldn't be "the most hateful."

"Hah!" Little Tiger rolled his eyes. "My mother told me so. My mother said Old Hag is not a good woman, not fit to sit with us at meals! Why say anything more? Just looking at that face of hers, I couldn't even swallow my rice!"

I could only agree with this statement of his, for the elder Mrs. King's appearance was really not very pleasing. Little Tiger said that she was already fifty-three years old, thirteen years older than his uncle, but looking at the white strands among the short hair on the top of her head, I thought she was much older. Short and fat with bound feet, she waddled from side to side when she walked. Little Tiger said she looked like a big mother duck, and I felt that he was right. Worst of all, her face was all wrinkled up and she only had a few hairs left in her brows, but every day she would smear on a thick layer of cream and draw a pair of curving eyebrows. Sometimes she didn't draw them too well so that one was higher and the other was lower, really unpleasant to see. Little Tiger then compared her to the clown at the Peiping opera and I had to agree.

"Pooh! Old Hag is really no match for my uncle!" Little Tiger spat out the sweet potato skin and swung his feet as he said this.

"Uh!" I grunted, and immediately the elder Mr. King's suave mustache and the elder Mrs. King's pair of false eyebrows appeared together before my eyes.

"My uncle doesn't like to talk to her. Sometimes Old Hag

goes running to him nagging about this or that and he will just brush her off, cursing her and calling her an old . . ." Little Tiger thought awhile, then clapped his hands, shouting: "old bitch. Ha! . . . Ha! That's right, an old bitch. You should see Old Hag's face then! Really something to look at!"

"Isn't she very unhappy then?" I asked, firmly believing that she must have looked even uglier than usual at that moment.

"Who cares if she is happy or unhappy? Anyway, my uncle often curses her." Little Tiger raised his head and took a fierce bite at his sweet potato, seemingly very proud of the fact.

"I guess she must cry very often, mustn't she?" I had heard her crying several times and again before my eyes was the picture of her waddling along, stealthily dabbing at her tears.

"Old Hag not only cries, she also swears at people in secret. One day as I walked past her window she was muttering away about how heartless my uncle was, how mean and sharp-tongued my mother was. I ran to tell my mother and she immediately tiptoed softly, softly to the door of Old Hag——" As he reached this part of his tale, Little Tiger lowered his voice to a whisper, glaring as he hunched up his shoulder. From his expression I could almost see the younger Mrs. King's sharp eyes and hard look as she stole up to the door of the elder Mrs. King, just like a female cat about to pounce on a frightened mouse.

"Oh," I couldn't repress a shudder at the thought and unconsciously I clutched the front of my jacket.

"Ma kicked the door open, jumped in and grabbed Old Hag's hair. Then she beat her up. Old Hag squealed like a dying pig and fainted dead away."

"Ai-ya!" I loosened my clutching hands and my sweet potato rolled onto the ground.

Little Tiger saw my shock and was even more exultant. He spat for emphasis. "Then my father came running and poured two bowls of ginger water down her throat before she woke up. After this scare, Old Hag was in bed for half a month before she could get up again. It was really funny!"

As we came to know the King family, Swen Sao became good friends with the elder Mrs. King, but this relationship was very secret. She always picked out the times when the younger Mrs. King was scolding the servants in the kitchen or playing mahjong in the sitting room to slip into the elder Mrs. King's room. Sometimes they would talk for a very long time, and when Swen Sao came out, her eyes would be red-rimmed and her cheeks would be all puffed out, a sure sign that she had heard of something unfair.

"Swen Sao, who do you think is the best person in the King family?" I asked her once as we left the King family after a visit.

"The elder Mrs. King, of course!" she answered, without even thinking it over.

"But Little Tiger told me that Old Hag is the most hateful old thing!" I remembered all that he had told me that day.

"Nonsense!" Swen Sao's plump cheeks began to swell again. "Those people have really sinned against the heavens, all ganging up to ill-treat her. Ai! you don't know how pitiful a life the elder Mrs. King has had!"

"How is she pitiful?" I asked with curiosity. I also felt that she was pitiful, but without knowing why I thought so.

"Children shouldn't ask about this, about that." I never could stand this from her, so I started using all my tricks to pester her into giving in to me. Finally she consented to tell me about it after dinner, but she insisted that I swear never to tell anybody, because she said if it reached the ears of the younger Mrs. King, it would be really bad for the elder Mrs. King.

After dinner, I took a small bamboo stool and went into the garden with Swen Sao to cool off. She again told me that I should never repeat a word of what she was going to tell me. It was only after I closed my eyes and swore to her that she began her story:

"The elder Mrs. King had been married before to a very wealthy family. The house the King family is living in now and most of their land all belonged to her first husband. She had some soft living in those early days, but unfortunately her first husband had tuberculosis when he married her. After a few years when she was only thirty years old, he died, leaving her childless and all alone. Naturally when a woman is all alone there are always people who are only too ready to take advantage of her." Swen Sao's cheeks started to puff up again in righteous indignation.

"First, there were her husband's rascally relatives, who all came running to try to get something for themselves. And they did manage to get away with quite a lot of land. Then, by some unkind fate, she met the present elder Mr. King. At that time the elder Mr. King was only a young fellow around twenty. He had just returned from school in Shanghai, where he hadn't learned anything but a suave manner and an oily tongue. I have heard from others that the elder Mr. King is an outright scoundrel who has quite some influence with the underworld there in the Hsu Chia Hwei part of Shanghai."

"The elder Mr. King doesn't seem to be a bad man," I protested. The picture of the elder Mr. King with his mustache and red tie came into my mind.

"Huh! Do all bad men have a sign carved on their faces?" Swen Sao's fat jowls were swollen up like two little balls. "Just because he doesn't look like a bad man the elder Mrs. King fell for his tricks. At that time he lived opposite her house and would drop over every day, loitering around until he had trapped her. She told me that when they were first married he was wonderful to her. It was only after he had gotten hold of all her jewelry and the deeds to her land and house that he changed into an entirely different person. He either cursed her or beat her up and never had a single good word for her. What is worse is that when the younger Mrs. King moved in with them she took over her position in the family and helped the elder Mr. King mistreat her. Ai! the poor thing doesn't even have someone in the family to whom she can unburden herself."

"Didn't you say she had a gang of rascally relatives?"

"Ai-ya-ya! Don't mention those rascals! All that the elder Mr. King needs to do is to spend some money and their mouths are stopped up. And since Mr. King knows quite a lot of small-time gangsters in Shanghai, who wants to make trouble?"

"Those old servants who used to work for her, how can they just stand by and do nothing?" When I was over there I seldom saw these servants talking to the elder Mrs. King and, even when they did, they would scuttle away if they caught sight of the younger Mrs. King in the distance.

"Those heartless creatures! Why, they try to breathe out of the same nostril as the younger Mrs. King. Even those who have a heart would not dare say anything for fear of losing their rice bowls. Ai! I really feel sorry for her!" Swen Sao sighed. The two little balls had receded, but her eyes began to redden. When I saw the pity in Swen Sao's face I began to feel that although the false eyebrows and the waddling bound feet of the elder Mrs. King were in truth disagreeable to look at, they were also very pitiful.

During the months that we were the Kings' neighbors, Little Tiger would tell me something about the elder Mrs. King almost every day. His uncle had brought a sing-song girl home for dinner and Old Hag had wanted to make a jealous scene but had been beaten up instead. When Old Hag had tried to pour some tea, she had broken his mother's tea pot and been roundly cursed until she hid in her room and didn't dare show her face. Then Ah-hung had forgotten to take her supper into her room and Old Hag had wanted to scold her but Ah-hung was so rude to her that she broke into tears. All told, whoever else in the King household the elder Mrs. King had a run-in with, it was always the elder Mrs. King who suffered.

One winter morning when Swen Sao and I were sitting by the door enjoying the sun, there suddenly was a great outcry from the courtyard of the King family, a woman's piercing scream and then the voice of a man swearing. I grabbed Swen Sao and ran toward their house. At the gate we met Little Tiger grinning and clapping his hands to welcome us. He hastily pulled me after him as he ran toward the courtyard. "Brother Yung, hurry up, hurry up! Or you'll miss the good show. Uncle and Ma are really giving it to Old Hag over there in the courtyard."

We ran into the courtyard and saw the whole King family gathered there. The elder Mr. King and the younger Mrs. King were busy with the elder Mrs. King, one pulling at her and the other pushing from behind, while the poor woman held on to the round post of the balcony for dear life. She looked worse than usual. Her white hair was in a mess, falling all over her face, the back of her dress had been torn, and through the big hole, I could see her white undershirt and a splotch of fresh blood on it. She struggled and sobbed wildly. "Oh Lao Tien! all of you, how can you be so heartless. Ai-yah! Ai-yah! You take my house and want me to get out. Elder King . . . Elder King . . . I was blind to have married you! You heartless creature without a conscience; the heavens will not let you get away with it . . . Ai-yah! Ai-yah! Younger mistress, I'm not afraid of you! Even if I die here today you won't drag me out of this gate!"

The elder Mr. King's red tie was messed up, although his mustache was still as neat as ever. His usual suave manner was replaced by an expression of ruthlessness. The younger Mrs. King's eyes were even sharper than ever, and she helped Mr. King by using the most malicious and venomous words in her vocabulary as they struggled. Then, when they still could not budge the woman she tried to wrench her fingers away from the post. The elder Mrs. King stood it for a while, then suddenly bit the hand that was trying to pry her fingers loose. The younger Mrs. King let out a scream and at the same time Swen Sao, who was standing behind me with puffed cheeks, muttered under her breath, "A good bite! A good bite!"

"Ai! This old shrew bit me! Elder brother, make way, let me deal with her!" She pushed the elder Mr. King out of her way and, snatching a handful of the elder Mrs. King's hair, she dragged her into the middle of the courtyard. The elder Mrs. King wailed loudly as she was pulled along, her two little feet tottering unsteadily. When they reached the middle of the courtyard, the younger Mrs. King pushed her down on to the ground and began to rain heavy blows on her face and head. At first the elder Mrs. King struggled to protect herself, but soon she became too weak even to cry out any more, and at last only her two little feet from which her shoes had already fallen off were still kicking; it was an ugly and painful sight.

Even then, the younger Mrs. King was not satisfied. Seeing a bucket full of duck feed standing near, she picked it up and emptied it over the prostrated older woman so that the wet grain fell all over her head and face. The elder Mrs. King could not move at all any more, but her husband just stood on the side with arms folded as if nothing was wrong. It was finally the younger Mr. King who pulled his wife away and helped the elder Mrs. King to return to her room. During this time, the little balls on Swen Sao's cheeks had puffed out I don't know how many times, and when she saw the elder Mrs. King staggering back to her room, the tears that she had held back for so long finally rolled down her face.

"Why does your uncle want to drive your aunt away?" I asked Little Tiger after this was over.

"Huh! Don't you know? My uncle wants to marry this sing-song girl from Shanghai, so he wants Old Hag out. My mother has already helped to move all the old bitch's things away but Old Hag herself refuses to leave. Really shameless!" Little Tiger answered nonchalantly.

That night Swen Sao stole in through the back door of the King house to see the elder Mrs. King, and when she returned her eyes were all swollen up. She said that as soon as she arrived the elder Mrs. King had caught hold of her hands and cried so hard she could hardly talk. Then she told Swen Sao that no matter what happened she would not let them drive her away and that Mr. King needn't think that she would let him bring a concubine into her house peacefully. Swen Sao said she really could not understand how people could be so cruel.

The news of the elder Mr. King's intended marriage spread quickly all through Hungjao town. Even in ordinary times the King family was famous for lavish spending, so everyone was eager to have a share in this grand affair. During those days the gate of the King's house was almost battered down by the stampede. The elder Mr. King was even more handsome than before. He was busy moving in load after load of new things from Shanghai. This delighted the country bumpkins, who had never seen such things in their lives and who never tired of looking at and touching everything.

The younger Mrs. King was also running around in circles. She had gathered all the best needlewomen in town to embroider a whole pile of curtains and pillow cases. Swen Sao was of course among those who were invited. She told me she did not want to go, but out of politeness, could not very well refuse. Everybody in the King family was smiling and trying to talk only about auspicious things and topics. Nobody had time to listen to the occasional fits of desolate sobbing in the elder Mrs. King's little back room. Occasionally Swen Sao told me to slip over to take her something to eat and I could see that she looked uglier than ever, and even more pitiable. But she insisted that she would rather die in her little back room than leave.

The marriage feast of the elder Mr. King was to be divided into three days. The first night the swarm of guests filled more than ninety tables laid out from the gate to the hall and into the garden. Every corner of the house was filled with people, and the noise was like the surge of the rising tide. That night the King house was all light and color. Bright red silk marriage curtains were hung on all the walls. Anywhere you looked, you saw wedding candles and lanterns, and in the main sitting room a pair of dragon-phoenix candles five feet tall burned with a high flame that lit up the character for happiness, big as a banquet table, that hung behind them, bathing it with a golden light. The garden was lit up bright as day, and an opera troupe on a specially-built platform filled the air with the noise of cymbals and drums. Half of the guests were crowded into the sitting room, waiting to see the bride, while the rest were in the garden watching the show.

The younger Mrs. King was the chief hostess that night, so she darted in and out among the crowds like a shuttlecock, followed by Little Tiger, dressed in a new padded jacket. Swen Sao was asked to help take charge of the tea and cigarettes, so she was also busy every minute. She again told me that she really didn't want to help, but there was no polite way to get out of it.

It was already past eight o'clock, but the bride and groom hadn't appeared to take their place at the table. When word got around that the bride was still dressing and would take quite a while yet, people all started to talk, the rising murmur of voices expressing their impatience at being kept waiting. Swen Sao came over to me at that moment, pulled me to a corner, took a plate of cakes from a cupboard and pressed it into my hands. "Yung brother, can you do a good deed for me?" she whispered. "I am really too busy to get away, so you take this plate of cakes to the elder Mrs. King. I know that with everyone so busy nobody will think of her tonight."

"But I want to see the bride!" I protested. My hands were full of colored streamers to throw at the bride and groom, and it was only after Swen Sao pleaded with me that I finally consented.

There were three corridors that connected with the elder Mrs. King's room, and I chose the one that had the least people in it. But half-way down I heard the sudden burst of firecrackers and a roar of laughter as the guests from the garden started to surge into the sitting room. "Just my luck! That must be the bride and groom coming out," I thought to myself, so I ran faster.

It was then in the middle of the twelfth month, and as I

ran from the warmth of the crowded room out into the cold
air, I could not repress a shudder. I drew my neck into the
protection of my collar. The lanterns along the corridor were
swaying in the chill breeze. Several had already gone out, and
the ground was littered with torn strips of red and green paper that swirled and swished with the wind. The further in I
ran the dimmer it became, and the sounds of people talking
and laughing became fainter also; it was quiet and lonely
with no one around.

Suddenly I was filled with an unknown fear, and even
though I had not as yet reached the door of her room, I
called out loudly: "Elder Mrs. King! Elder Mrs. King!"

There was no answer, and I guessed she was already
asleep, so I opened the door softly. A gust of cold wind followed me through the opened door, and the light on the table
sputtered, filling the room with swaying shadows. In the uncertain light I saw the elder Mrs. King lying on the bed.
"Elder Mrs. King," I called again, but still she did not answer. I tiptoed into the room, but as I approached her bed
and saw her face clearly my legs went rubbery with fear.
Crash! The plate in my hands fell to the floor. A cold chill
crept over my scalp, and I could not move a step. I wanted
to scream but something was clogging my throat.

The elder Mrs. King was lying flat on the bed, one small
bound foot dangling over the side while the bed covers were
all mussed up around her other leg. One hand clutched her
throat, while the other was clenched on her breast as if she
had exerted all her strength trying to tear open her dress. Her
eyes were rolled up, the whites staring fixedly at the ceiling,
and her wildly disordered hair had fallen over her forehead
and cheeks. Her lips were covered with white foam. On the
table by her bedside was a bottle. The smell of lysol was still
strong in the air.

Sudden fright had dazed me. I cannot remember how I escaped from that room. I only remember hazily that when I
ran into the sitting room, the groom was just coming out with
the bride and everyone was deluging them with the colored
confetti. As to how the guests started to surge towards the
elder Mrs. King's room and how the elder Mr. King and the
younger Mrs. King tried to stop them, I really have no clear
memory at all because when I returned home afterwards I
started to run a high fever. In a series of nightmares I always

saw the elder Mrs. King's little bound foot swinging back and forth.

Three days after her death they buried her, and after the burial nobody mentioned her name again. Everyone's attention was quickly riveted on to the new elder Mrs. King. This new Mrs. King was a young, pretty, generous and capable woman. She was quite a match for the younger Mrs. King, so that everybody hastened to call her "Elder Mrs. King." But after the arrival of this Mrs. King, Swen Sao and I never went to visit the King family again. Swen Sao, because she was sad, and I, because I was afraid.

From then on, every time I saw Little Tiger in front of the door I would avoid him. He seemed to be very angry with me, but I didn't care. One day I didn't get away in time and he grabbed hold of me, glaring at me.

"I haven't offended you! Why don't you come to my house any more?" he demanded.

"We are going to Shanghai. Does the new Elder Mrs. King like you?"

"Heh! you mean my elder aunt? She wouldn't dare not to! If it weren't for my mother she would still be hiding in Shanghai as a concubine. My mother said: bring her back here so that uncle won't go to Shanghai all the time——" Little Tiger talked so sure of himself, like a little grownup.

Then Swen Sao raised her voice inside the house.

"Brother Yung! If you're not going to do your homework, clear your books away; don't leave them around to annoy me."

I knew that Swen Sao was angry with Little Tiger, so I quickly ran inside, leaving him behind.

—Translated by Nancy Chang Ing

JAPAN

HEIAN PERIOD

794–1185

In many respects the Heian period in Japan is comparable to the T'ang Dynasty in China. T'ang influences can be seen in Japan today in the generously proportioned streets of the capital city (present-day Kyoto), in the ornate and colorful temples of the period such as those at Nara, and in the arts in general. All were patterned on the T'ang model. The Japanese Heian period, like the T'ang, was marked by a sense of unity, peace, and well-being (*Heian,* in fact, means "peace and tranquility"). As in the T'ang, the arts flourished and there was an emphasis in court circles on a refinement that bordered on affectation.

The two cultures shared the influences of Confucius on the social hierarchy and on family customs. And Buddhism, which had come to Japan from China in the sixth century, was another binding link. Although institutionalization and forms of worship were basically Chinese, the popular pilgrimages to holy shrines were deep in the Japanese setting—reverence for the beauties of nature being perhaps even stronger than for the Buddha and the multitude of gods of the Shinto shrines that clustered about the Buddhist temples. The pilgrimage for the highborn Heian woman—as for Chaucer's Wyf of Bathe—was a highly regarded worship experience, which emancipated women at the same time as it helped them gain merit. The practice was a blessed gift in a society that in other areas tended to restrict their lives.

Women of the nobility were especially fettered by custom, from the earliest years being confined to the women's quarters, their faces thereafter not to be exposed to the rude gazes of men. From puberty onward the woman's life passed in an imposed twilight state. Within her part of the house, blinds were drawn against the outside air and light. Within her rooms she sat with her attendants behind screens of state. Although she could receive male callers, she must talk with them unseen, the men forming their judgment of her attractiveness on the basis of glimpses of her robes, which were allowed to creep from below the screen, or a well-groomed hand, set off by several tiers of harmoniously tinted sleeves, arousing erotic dreams as it reached out to accept a love poem. To go abroad the lady must be taken in a clumsy ox-drawn cart or carried in a palanquin, blinds securely fastened against inquisitive male eyes. Compare this with the freedom in travel experienced by Lady Sarashina and Lady Nijō as they go from temple to temple in their later years. The temples offered quiet refuge for men and women of the court who sought a favorable environment for religious study or for writing. A major part of the epic novel *The Tale of Genji*, by Lady Murasaki Shikibu, was written in two quiet rooms behind the great shrine of the Ishiyama Temple on the outskirts of Kyoto.

It is difficult to understand the ambiguities of life for the women of Heian Japan without knowing the times. In the first place, extant literature deals almost exclusively with court circles and with the nobility. It is as though the rest of the populace did not exist. In fact, to the nobility the masses quite simply did *not* exist except as a support system for the one-tenth of one percent of the people who formed their circle. As Genji's friend To no Chujo says, when he ticks off the sorts of women to be found in the three classes of society: "As for the lower classes, they do not concern us."

Ladies of the nobility and of the court had a value as marriage commodities that lower class women did not enjoy. Laws of the time provided for female progeny to inherit and keep property, providing an economic base often surpassing that of their spouses; it forbade physical abuse. In some respects the woman had more value than her male counterpart; it was by way of female marital connection that the great Fujiwara family became the major power in the imperial court through a succession of generations. As the late noted Japanese scholar and translator Ivan Morris pointed

out, the Heian period is "the only one in Japanese history
when girls were more to be welcomed than boys."

Second, one must be aware of the ambiguity existing between the fact and the fiction of the elaborate provisions for
the protective seclusion of women. At the same time as aristocratic women were supposedly immured, they were often
embroiled in a succession of illicit love affairs. Observing the
niceties of society's game, a torrid physical relationship might
go on for its entire life with neither party seeing the other,
the lover arriving in the dark and leaving before dawn, blinds
and screens remaining enclosed throughout. Even the highest
born woman was not faulted, however, for engaging in a
variety of extramarital relationships, provided they were with
men of equal social standing. According to the mores of the
time, prolonged virginity was viewed as suspect. Indeed, a
too-old virgin might be regarded as being demonically
possessed and therefore a liability to her family.

In a society in which beauty was a fetish, how did men determine that the women for whom they vied were beautiful
or ugly? Round face, narrow eyes, plucked eyebrows, black-
ened teeth, and luxuriant hair were considered essential. In
terms of actual experience with the women, however, the hair
was most readily judged. In his first meeting with the child
Murasaki, what most impresses Prince Genji is her hair,
which was "thick and wavy [and] stood out fanwise about
her head." Some ladies of the court took great pride in hair
so long that it trailed several inches on the floor as they
walked. This could be seen from afar when a face was hidden from view. Its scented luxuriousness could be felt and its
perfume savored during a love tryst in which the lady herself
could not be seen. The hair might well speak for a totality of
beauty that would never be fully revealed.

Finally, to this complicated picture of women in the Heian
world one must add the remarkable achievements of Heian
women as writers. While men remained fettered by court
business, their literary efforts were largely in formalized verse
or in love poems to court ladies. Women, however, were pio-
neering in creating a new world of literary life. Blocked from
learning Chinese, their writing found wings in the *kana* free-
flowing script attuned to the native tongue. And they threw
themselves into the only outlet not restricted or proscribed by
the men in their lives. Their journals and novels were life

lines in otherwise uncreative and dependent lives. "Pillow-books"—informal collections of anecdotes, reminiscences, and gossip of court life—were another popular and completely feminine literary expression of the time. It is perhaps not to be wondered at that "during the period of about one hundred years that spans the world of Genji, almost every noteworthy author who wrote in Japanese was a woman," as Ivan Morris noted. *The Tale of Genji*, *The Pillow-Book of Sei Shōnagon*, and *The Bridge of Dreams*—excerpts from which follow—are imbued with a vitality, immediacy, validity, and enduring quality that lightened the lives of Heian ladies and illuminate an entrancing other world to a universe of readers today.

The Bamboo Cutter and the Moon Child

Anonymous

One of the earliest and most popular of the romances (*monogatari*) for which the Heian period is notable is the enchanting, ethereal tale of the bamboo cutter's daughter. Whereas girl children were considered liabilities in the lower classes of early times, this story reveals the delight a daughter can bring to a lonely couple. The competition for the hand of a desirable and marriageable young woman was a favorite theme in the literature of the period—as, indeed, in early Western literature from the time of Homer onward.

———

In ancient times a poor bamboo cutter named Takétori went one day into the mountain forests. While entering a stand of bamboo, he was startled by brilliant rays of light coming from a tree in the middle of the grove. He cut down the tree and was amazed to see a lovely creature, barely three inches tall, emerge from the shining bamboo.

"If I had not cut down the cane, you would never have gotten out," the old man announced. "By rights you belong to me." So he placed the tiny being in the palm of his hand and carried her home to his wife. The old woman put the child in a small box for safe keeping and, in the days that followed, she fed and cared for it without thought of weariness.

The fairy child was not to be the only blessing to come to the old bamboo cutter and his wife. Not long afterwards, Takétori cut down a second bamboo tree, discovering inside gold and all manner of precious gems. Once poor, the bamboo cutter suddenly found himself very rich, and soon his life was filled with an abundance of comforts and luxuries.

The fairy child grew quickly and it was not long before the box cradling her became too small. The old man and his wife released her in their newly built mansion, being very careful to keep the girl safely within doors. The fairy's beauty kept pace with her growth until it was without its match in all the world, and the glory radiating from her filled the house, lighting the dwelling even in the dark of night, so that if the old couple chanced to fall ill they soon forgot their aches and pains in its cheering rays; nor could anger or evil thoughts torment them while they gazed upon the fairy child.

During this time the old man and his wife gave the child a fitting name, calling her Kakuya Himé, or Graceful Bamboo, Night-Illuminating Princess.

As Kakuya Himé grew into womanhood, her loveliness flowered until the fame of it became known through the length and breadth of the land. All young men who chanced to look upon her beauty longed to win her as their bride, but even a passing glimpse was not to be had easily, for the maiden was closely sheltered in the inner apartments of the mansion. Because of this her suitors were in a lamentable state, scarcely sleeping for dwelling on the charms and loveliness they were not allowed to see. In time the young men of the region went to ruin, becoming unmindful of their duties and wasting their time foolishly—all from their love of Kakuya Himé.

Eventually, however, most of the young men tired of the futile pursuit until only five noble suitors stayed on, lingering about the mansion, hoping for an opportunity to show their love. These suitors were the feudal lords (daimyo): Ishidzukuri; Kuramochi; Abé no Mimuraji, second in rank only to the emperor himself; Otsu no Miyuki; and Lord Morotaka, of the province of Iso.

Finally one of their number succeeded in getting Takétori's attention. Throwing himself at the old man's feet with the utmost respect, he cried out imploringly, "I beg you, listen to my plea and give me your lovely daughter in marriage."

"The maiden is not my daughter," Takétori replied, "and I have no right to compel her obedience." So saying he went away.

Though month after month passed, still the five suitors remained outside the mansion, begging—whenever they found an opportunity—for Takétori to listen to their requests. But the old man always put them off, while the fairy maiden, undecided as to which among them was the noblest, would have none of them for a husband.

Seeing he could not stop their constant coming to his house, Takétori finally advised Kakuya Himé. "Although you are immortal," he began, "you have taken the form of a woman. While there is nothing wrong with you remaining a maiden during my lifetime, what will become of you when I die? Daily these five young men come to seek your hand. I beg that you fix your heart on one of them."

"I am not so beautiful that five suitors should come wooing me," Kakuya Himé answered modestly, "and if I become the bride of one without first proving his heart, I may regret my choice. I cannot marry without testing my future husband first."

"But all are men of rank and accomplishment. You could easily choose from among them now."

"It is not enough that they come here day after day. Each must show me some noble deed, some brilliant accomplishment, so that I can choose the man who excels for my husband. Please give this message to them."

At sunset that same evening the five lovers gathered before the mansion prepared to demonstrate their talents. One played the flute, a second danced, another was a gifted singer, still another was skilled in the art of whistling, while the last could use the fan as a harmonious accompaniment to music.

When all had finished, Takétori came to the gate. "Wel-

come to my humble dwelling," he greeted them. "I thank you
warmly for the fine entertainment. As I am more than sev-
enty years of age, I may die at any time—perhaps today, or
it may be tomorrow—so I have pleaded with my daughter to
choose a husband from among such a brilliant circle of
young men. But as you are all equally accomplished, my
daughter feels that any choice is impossible. I ask you, therefore, to grant her one more demand. Her words are these:
'He who fulfills my request shall claim me as a bride.' "

"Since she cannot judge from among us, the maiden's
words are reasonable," all cried eagerly as with one voice.
"We will do whatever she asks."

The old man then announced Kakuya Himé's test: "Let
Prince Ishidzukuri find the famous stone jar held in the hands
of the gods; let Prince Kuramochi travel the eastern seas in
search of Mt. Horai, where springs that priceless tree with
roots of silver, a trunk of gold, and boughs laden with lustrous white gems. Make it his task to bring me one of its
branches. Let Abé no Mimuraji find the red fire rat of China,
bringing back its glistening fur; let Otsu no Miyuki seek the
five-tinted jewel that sparkles in the dragon's head; while, as
for Morotaka, Lord of Iso, I ask that he return with the shell
which the swallow is said to own."

When he had first heard these requests, the old man was
quite distressed, and only reluctantly did he inform the young
men of the tasks laid upon them by Kakuya Himé. Yet none
of the noble lords showed even the slightest concern over the
mission given them. However, in their hearts there was irritation and all returned home full of resentment. Nonetheless,
all knew they would surely die from sheer despair should
they not be allowed to look upon the wondrous Kakuya
Himé, and each resolved that, even if obliged to journey to
distant India to fulfill her wishes, he would make the attempt.

It happened that the first suitor, Prince Ishidzukuri, was a
man given to deep-laid schemes. The more he pondered the
matter, the more clearly he saw that he might travel one
hundred times ten million miles and still not be certain of
finding the stone jar held by the gods. There was probably
only one of its kind in all the world. So he sent a message to
the maiden's home, falsely declaring that he was about to
start for India that very day in saerch of the jar. Instead
Prince Ishidzukuri traveled into the Yamato district and there

remained for three years. In a mountain temple he found a black jar suited to his purpose. Placing the jar in a brocade bag along with a branch laden with artificial blossoms, he returned with the gifts to Kakuya Himé's home. The maiden was very surprised, for she never believed that such a jar could be found. But a close examination of the jar revealed a poem inside which, in quaint meter, disclosed that the jar came from the forest temple of Mount Ogura in the Yamato region. Sure now of the fraud, the princess wrote a second poem, placed it in the jar, and ordered the jar returned to the prince. The prince returned to his house where he read Kakuya Himé's poem. With his trick exposed, he threw the jar out of the gate, swearing on holy vows to remain in seclusion until he could forget the maiden of his dreams.

Prince Kuramochi, the second suitor, being a very shrewd man, let it be known that he was setting out in search of Mt. Horai. Having deceived everyone as to his real intentions, he secretly returned home. Calling together six skilled carpenters, the prince ordered them to build a house in a secluded area with a furnace hidden by three arches of earth so that no one might see the smoke. As soon as the house was completed, the prince moved in, sending for artisans skilled in delicate work. These he commanded to fashion counterfeit gems of pure white to be fastened on a branch. So carefully was his order carried out that the jeweled branch, when finished, was the exact likeness of the one described by Kakuya Himé.

As soon as the branch was ready, the prince took a ship from Osaka—that he might deceive the maiden by returning from the sea—later landing at the place of his departure. Prince Kuramochi's retainers flocked to Osaka to welcome him. They escorted the prince, along with a chest covered with beautiful drapery and holding the supposed branch, to his residence. Before long news of Prince Kuramochi's treasure spread throughout the region, causing people everywhere to talk about the branch of gems rare as *udongé*, the fabled flower said to blossom but once in a thousand years.

Once she learned of Prince Kuramochi's return, Kakuya Himé was troubled, saying sorrowfully to herself: "I will have to yield to this prince," and even while these words were on her lips, a servant came with word that he was just then knocking at the gate.

"I have not held even life itself precious in my search for the jeweled branch," the prince said on greeting the old man. "Here, I give this treasure to you, asking only that you show it to your daughter."

Takétori immediately carried the branch of jeweled flowers along with a poem from the prince to the maiden. "Without a doubt," he said, "the noble prince has brought this branch all the way from Mt. Horai." When Kakuya Himé appeared reluctant to accept the offering, the old man asked, "What more can you want? He has even rushed to our home in traveling clothes. I beg you, agree to marry Prince Kuramochi."

As the maiden was too upset to reply, Takétori wrongly concluded that her silence meant consent, and he hurried to tell her waiting lover of the good news. While servants made preparations for the marriage feast, it occurred to the old man to ask the prince where he had come across the jeweled tree.

Prince Kuramochi replied, "The year before last, on the tenth day of the second month, I set sail on the great deep, not knowing my destination. We were blown along at the will of the wind, and I thought I would never live to return, but that while life lasted I would cross the seas in search of Mt. Horai. After we left the Sea of Japan, the waves at times rolled high enough to sink our ship, while fierce winds often drove us to unknown coasts inhabited by demons waiting to destroy us. Sometimes we roamed the seas not knowing in what direction we were going, and then again we lost everything and had to live off roots of sea grass or shellfish. I find it impossible to describe the fearful monsters which came upon us. And there were times beneath the skies of our journeyings when we fell sick and suffered terribly with no one to help.

"After we had wandered over the seas for the space of five hundred days, one day at the hour of the Hare—about dawn— I saw what looked like a small mountain rising from the waters. I quickly woke the ship's company. As we drew nearer, it seemed to grow wonderfully large, and from its beautiful outline, I knew it must be the object of my quest. It was like a miracle.

"For three days we sailed around the coast until we saw a woman looking like a goddess drawing water with a silver cup. Before she finished her work, we landed and went over to her. I asked the name of the mountain rising before us. She answered that it was called Mt. Horai.

"We rejoiced. But when I questioned this beautiful creature, she would say nothing else than her name, 'I am called Hakaruru,' then she suddenly vanished in the recesses of the mountain. As it looked impossible to scale the heights of the mountain, I contented myself with a walk around its base. I saw flowers unlike those anywhere else on earth, and streams—gold, silver and emerald in color, and spanned by jeweled bridges—flowing down from the mountain. I came across row upon row of trees, glittering with precious gems, but the branch of the tree I brought back was the poorest of all. Since the maiden ordered one like this—with jeweled fruit—I obeyed her command. Though the enchanting scenes of this mountain were beyond imagination, I grew uneasy and hurried back to my ship. After a voyage of four hundred days and more we finally returned to Japan. After landing at Osaka, I journeyed with all speed to the capital, and have even come here in traveling clothes still drenched with the salt spray of the sea."

The old man listened to the marvelous tale with compassion and admiration. At that moment, however, several artisans entered the courtyard and, bowing humbly, begged to be allowed to present a petition. "For more than a thousand days," stated their leader, "we have not spared our strength and skill in fashioning the jeweled branch. But so far we have received nothing in payment for our work. Give us our wages, we beg of you, so that we may feed our families at home."

The artisans presented a written scroll of their complaints to the shocked maiden, Kakuya Himé, whereupon Prince Kuramochi was so struck with shame that he lost his mind.

The fairy princess, on the other hand, seemed pleased. She called to her father. "I really thought this branch came from Mt. Horai. But since I have been deceived by so shallow a hoax, I ask you to return the gift at once."

The prince by this time was so chagrined that he could neither stand nor sit, but wandered about the courtyard until the sun had set, then, under cover of darkness, fled into the night.

With a light heart, Kakuya Himé called the petitioning artisans and gave each more than enough to compensate him for his work. But on their way home, the artisans were set upon by the retainers of Prince Kuramochi. Their money was taken from them and all were left half dead by the road. As to the prince—his knights and retainers searched the mountains for days, but he was never seen in that land again.

The third suitor, Abé no Mimuraji, held office as chief minister of state and was a man of great wealth and influence. To accomplish his task, Abé sent a messenger to a friend in China with a letter and a huge sum of money, commissioning the friend to obtain the skin of the famous fire rat. In due course, he received a reply declaring that the skin was not to be found in China. "However," his friend wrote, "if it is to be found in the world, someone is surely to bring it to China." Not long after, a courier arrived from China. A robe made from the desired fur had been brought as treasure in ancient times from India to China. The courier presented Abé with the robe, saying that it was to be returned if the price could not be paid. Abé happily gave the courier the required sum and, in gratitude, prostrated himself in respect towards the kingdom of China.

The box containing the skin was fashioned of a beautiful emerald tint, while the robe itself was a rich blue, the tip of each hair glistening in a glorious manner. It was a treasure of unrivaled beauty and, aside from its rarity, valuable for its color alone.

Attired in handsome dress, the noble suitor and his retainers arrived at Takétori's mansion, where they waited at the entrance until the old man came to greet them and receive the gift.

"Truly a beautiful fur robe," Kakuya Himé said when she first saw it, "but whether real or fake I do not know. Let the flames be the test!"

"Well spoken," answered her father.

"Such suspicion is groundless," Abé no Mimuraji objected, "but give it the test if you must." So they cast the robe into the flames where it immediately took fire and was consumed. At the sight of the burning fur, the noble's face took on the hue of leaves of grass. The amused Kakuya Himé then returned the emerald-tinted box to Abé no Mimuraji.

The fourth suitor, Otsu no Miyuki, devised a more straightforward plan for winning the maiden's hand. Calling together his warriors, he said: "In the dragon's head is a gem glittering with five colors. He who brings me this gem shall have

whatever his heart desires." Even though the warriors quickly
agreed, the nobleman laughed scornfully, chiding, "Since you
are part of my household, you have no choice but to agree.
Now set about with your task at once." After outfitting his
troops with vast stocks of silk, cotton, food and money, Otsu
no Miyuki ordered them to the port of Osaka. "Let no one
return until the five-colored jewel has been found," he said,
"and I vow to fast and pay homage to the gods in your absence."

While waiting for their ships at Osaka, the warriors
gathered to discuss the venture. All considered Otsu no
Miyuki to be haughty and selfish, and they decided that their
master should have led the quest himself. So they ended up
by dividing the supplies and money between themselves and
going their separate ways.

Lord Otsu meanwhile began building a magnificent mansion for the bride he was sure would soon be his. The mansion was fashioned bright with lacquer, red and golden and a
dozen other colors; its roof was suspended from vari-colored
strands of silken thread, while in the many apartments delicate paintings hung on rich brocades.

Once the mansion was completed, Lord Otsu watched anxiously each day for the coming of his warriors. But when a
year had gone by without their return, he disguised himself as
a commoner and, accompanied by two servants, started out
in search of his men. On reaching the port of Osaka, Lord
Otsu asked of news of the mission. But the seamen he questioned responded with laughter and scorn.

"Yours is the talk of fools. No one would ever go on such
a mission," they all answered.

In desperation, Lord Otsu finally said: "By the might of
my bow, were the dragon here I would kill him and take his
head. No, I will not wait for the return of those rascals. The
three of us will board ship and set out together."

That day Otsu hired a ship and sailed out into the sea. As
the ship approached a land far from the shores of Japan, a
storm arose. Soon the skies grew black and a mighty gale
arose, driving the ship off course. The gale blew as though it
would drive the ship beneath the sea, while angry waves beat
upon her and tossed her about as though she were caught in
a whirlpool, and so powerful were the flashes of lightning

that the crew expected momentarily that one of the great thunderbolts would strike and sink the ship.

"What will become of us?" the terrified Otsu asked the captain.

"I have sailed the oceans far and wide," replied the captain, "but never have I encountered perils like these. If we are not swallowed by the sea the thunder will strike us. And even if the gods favor us, the force of the gale may carry the ship far off to the southern oceans." Shedding a torrent of tears, the captain added, "We face disaster from following a merciless master like you."

"Why accuse me so bitterly?" cried out Lord Otsu. He was now dismally seasick. "One commits himself on the oceans to the care of the captain, as though he were putting his trust in the majesty of a lofty mountain."

"I am not a god," replied the captain, "and I can't control everything. A great gale is blowing, the waves are raging, and a thunderbolt is about to fall on our heads—all because you wanted to slay a dragon. I am sure this must be his work. I beg you—pray for our salvation."

Lord Otsu prayed, vowing a thousand times that he would give up his plan to steal even a single hair from the dragon's head. Before long there were signs that the gods had heard, for though the wind blew even more fiercely, the thunder had ceased and the flashes of lightning became less frequent. The wind proved favorable and in four days the ship managed to return to the coast of Japan.

Once back on land, Lord Otsu found himself exhausted and sick with cold, and his eyes had become so swollen that they looked like two large red plums. Soon all his warriors returned to him, saying: "Now you yourself know just how difficult it is to steal the jewel from the dragon's head."

"You are right," Lord Otsu agreed, "and I welcome you back into my service. Certainly the dragon belongs to the family of thunder gods, and he who seeks his jewel must come to an evil end. You were right in not going after it. This Kakuya Himé is nothing more than a fiend which tries to destroy men. I forbid anyone to go near her again."

And so crows and fish hawks carried away the strands of silken thread from the roof of the new mansion, while people jeered behind Lord Otsu's back, pointing at his still-swollen eyes.

"The gem from the dragon's head,"
  HAI! they said
"He brought back two red plums instead!"

Now the fifth suitor was Lord Morotaka of the province of Iso, whose task it was to secure the rare shell found in the swallow's nest. Lord Morotaka learned that a large number of swallows had built their nests on the roof of a certain government building, so he had a scaffolding erected, stationing twenty men there to watch the birds. However, the swallows became frightened at the sight of so many men and soon left the roof.

On the advice of a sage, Lord Morotaka dismissed all his servants but one, and with that servant he set out and searched day and night for the shell. It was a weary time of waiting, for Lord Morotaka had been told that the magic shell could be found only when the swallow deposits its eggs in the nest. Finally, one evening at sunset, Morotaka saw a swallow whirling about the top of her nest. Hurriedly, he raised his servant to the roof in a basket. But the servant frightened the bird and returned empty-handed, causing his master to fly into a rage: "You are too awkward," he cried. "I'll do it myself."

After Lord Morotaka was raised to the roof, he put his hand in the nest and, feeling something flat, grasped it tightly, then called out to the servant to lower him to the ground. The servant hurriedly seized the rope, making it snap, and plunging Morotaka into a large water jar that had been sacred to one of the gods. Recovering from the shock, Lord Morotaka found that he could not stand up. Despite his injuries, Morotaka was exalted at finding the treasure. Then the servant struck a light. In the glare of the flame, Lord Morotaka discovered that his treasure was not the rare shell, but a common rock. Lord Morotaka tried his best to hide the mishap from the people, but failed, and soon the story traveled throughout the land. What with his injuries and mental distress, the physical condition of Morotaka grew worse and, finally, he died from complications of sickness and humiliation.

The story of Kakuya Himé and her five suitors soon reached the ears of the emperor himself. The fascinated emperor ordered one of his courtiers to visit the maiden and report back on what manner of woman it was who forced men to suffer yet would not give her hand in marriage. The bamboo cutter's daughter refused the imperial representative an audience. At first the emperor was furious, but in time he decided her refusal was an indication of the maiden's wish to test him. Accordingly, one day while out hunting, the emperor took the opportunity of stopping at the bamboo cutter's mansion.

He peered into the house, where he saw a woman resplendent with light seated in a room. Sure that this could be none other than the fabled Kakuya Himé, he hurried in. The emperor took hold of the sleeve of her gown. Even though the startled maiden turned to hide her face, he caught a glimpse of its radiant loveliness. The emperor immediately demanded that she accompany him to the palace. But the maiden suddenly vanished. The emperor was grief-stricken, realizing then that Kakuya Himé was no mortal.

"Oh, Kakuya Himé, reappear. I beg you. Let me look upon your beauty once more, then I will return to my palace."

The emperor was overjoyed when the maiden again took human form. Words would be exhausted in depicting the raptures of the man as he gazed upon the maiden. After the courtiers had prepared a great feast of rejoicing, the emperor regretfully returned to his palace, leaving his heart in the mansion of the old bamboo cutter.

Three years passed. In the spring of the fourth year, servants noticed that Kakuya Himé was watching the moon with troubled eyes. One pleaded with her to stop, for it was clear that the maiden was becoming daily more saddened with its brightness. But Kakuya Himé would not stop staring up at the moon. The handmaidens then told the old bamboo cutter. He immediately asked the maiden why she was unhappy.

"I cannot tell you," she answered. "It is enough to say that my heart grows sad whenever I gaze upon the moon."

On moonless nights Kakuya Himé did not cry, but with the return of the moon, her grief was at once apparent. Then, as the fifteenth day of the eighth month drew near, Kakuya Himé grew so unhappy she no longer made even the slightest effort to hide her tears. Once more Takétori begged the maiden to tell him of the reason for her distress.

At last she agreed. "Long ago," she began, "I thought about telling you the truth. But I didn't want to hurt you." Tears filled the maiden's eyes. "I do not belong to your world. I am of the Moon world, and the time approaches when I shall have to return. On the fifteenth day of this month, messengers will descend to carry me home."

"Surely this is beyond all reason," the old man cried in wrath and anguish. "When you were no bigger than a ripe seed I found you in the hollow of a bamboo cane, and I have reared you with bone-breaking care. I will die if you are taken from me."

"It is not what I want. The lord of the Moon world commands it. And I must obey."

News of Kakuya Himé's plight soon reached the emperor, and he sent a page to the bamboo cutter's home. Excessive grief had doubled the old bamboo cutter's years: his beard had grown snow white, his body was bent and his eyes were red from constant weeping. Between tears and wails, Takétori asked the page to have the emperor send warriors so that, on the fifteenth day of the month, the celestial envoys might be taken captive.

On the dawn of the fifteenth day, the emperor dispatched a general with two thousand warriors. Half of these were stationed on a hill next to the mansion; the rest took up their positions on the roof of the house itself. Takétori ordered his many servants to arm themselves with bows and arrows and join in the defense. Kakuya Himé, meanwhile, was placed in a strong storehouse where serving women held her arms. Outside the door, the old bamboo cutter took up guard.

"If so much as a dewdrop descends from the heavens, destroy it," cried Takétori to the warriors, whereupon they all answered bravely. But Kakuya Himé said, "The bolted doors of a storehouse and two thousand warriors will not protect me. Bows and arrows are useless against heavenly armies. At their coming the stoutest of my defenders will lose courage."

"Let them beware," Takétori shouted in reply. "I will tear out their eyes, pull out their hair, rip off their clothing, and humiliate them before the people."

But Kakuya Himé answered, "It is best that none of the others should hear your boastful words. You have shown me much love and kindness and I long to be with you and my foster mother in your final years. I do not want to return to the Moon world, though sorrow never enters that land, and though all its subjects, fair of face and body, live in immortal youth."

"Don't trouble yourself," Takétori said boldly. "I'll have nothing to do with these heavenly messengers, however fair."

As nightfall deepened the moon became full, then grew ten times its normal size, so that the light from its rays filled the bamboo cutter's house. Finally the skies were filled by a host of mighty warriors riding atop great clouds. Soon they descended, where they stood rank upon rank five feet off the ground.

At the sight of them the maiden's defenders lost courage. Some later rallied and tried to give battle, but each found his hand too numb to take aim. There was one among them—a stalwart soul—who managed to shoot off all his arrows. But each missed its mark. And so all stood helpless, gazing like fools at the celestial array. So beautiful was the dress of the envoys from the moon that there is nothing on earth to which it could be compared, and the chariot brought to convey Kakuya Himé to her home was covered with a magnificent canopy.

One who seemed to be their leader started towards the door to the storehouse. Immediately Takétori staggered about like a man drunk with saké and, as a sleeper might fall, so he stumbled and fell to the ground.

"For some slight merit on your part," the leader said, "Kakuya Himé was permitted to bless your home. In years past she sinned in heaven. As the penalty for her sin she was exiled for a brief moment in eternity to your humble dwelling. The end of her punishment is at hand and your pleas are of no use. I order you to produce her at once."

Ignoring Takétori's protests, the celestial officer ordered the chariot brought and called out, "Come quickly!" At once the door to the storehouse flew open and some unseen, irresistible force pulled Kakuya Himé from the arms of the handmaidens. Going up to her heartbroken father, she said: "I do not want to return to the moon. But since I must, please look at me as I go."

"Take me with you," the old man pleaded, weeping. The maiden shook her head, handing him a note she had written to comfort him after she had gone.

A feather robe such as celestial beings wear was brought to Kakuya Himé as well as a cup holding the elixir of immortality. Though commanded to drink, the maiden only sipped from the cup, determined to leave enough elixir for the old man and the emperor. The celestial officer gave his reluctant consent, at the same time drawing the winged robe about the body of Kakuya Himé.

No sooner did the cloth of the immortals touch the maiden than the sadness in her heart vanished. No longer did she regret her departure from the world of man. She willingly mounted the chariot and, while the old man wailed and watched, the maiden and a thousand celestial warriors ascended into the skies.

When Kakuya Himé was gone the old bamboo cutter lost all interest in life. Not even the maiden's note would lighten his spirits, nor did he want to taste of the elixir of immortality. Before long, languishing in sickness and remorse, he lay down on his bed, never to rise again.

The general reported all these events to the emperor upon his return to the palace. He brought with him Kakuya Himé's note and the cup containing the wine of immortality. The emperor's heart was heavy. After long moments of suffering, the emperor called one of his advisors, questioning the sage as to which mountain in the empire rose nearest to the moon.

"In Surga province is a sounding mountain [volcano] which reaches far up into the skies. Surely that must be the highest and the mountain nearest to the moon," the advisor replied.

The emperor then commanded that the letter and the elixir of immortality be brought to the top of that mountain and cast in where it would be consumed by the flames . . .

    Because the *fushi* [elixir] was burned
Upon the crest of the great yama [mountain]
    It was thus called ever after
Fushi no Yama.
    And even to this day, it is said
Smoke rising from the still-burning elixir
    Can be seen ascending from the depths
Of the great sounding mountain
    And that mountain
Is Fujiyama.

—*Adapted by Gene Z. Hanrahan from a translation by F. B. Harris*

As I Crossed a Bridge of Dreams

Lady Sarashina

As I Crossed a Bridge of Dreams, selections from which follow, is one of the remarkable journals kept by court ladies of the Heian period. The unnamed woman of these dreamlike memoirs lived in the eleventh century. Translator Ivan Morris called her "Lady Sarashina," using the name the writer herself put on the book. Morris was able to provide some facts concerning her family: the father, Takasue no Musume, a court official who came of a respected literary family; the mother, of an obscure branch of the noted Fujiwara clan and sister of the "mother of Michitsune," author of the *Kagero Nikki*.

"Lady Sarashina" was born in 1008 in what is now known as Kyoto, spent three years in "the eastern wilds" of Japan where her father served as assistant governor ("the country so remote" with which she opens her diary), returning to live in the environs of the capital from the age of eleven on. At the advanced age of thirty-six she married and thereafter had three children, of whom little is written in her journal. Her predilection for intermittent pilgrimages gave her the substance for much of her most sensitive writing.

———

I was brought up in a part of the country so remote that it lies beyond the end of the Great East Road. What an uncouth creature I must have been in those days! Yet even shut away in the provinces I somehow came to hear that the world contained things known as Tales, and from that moment my greatest desire was to read them for myself. To idle away the time, my sister, my stepmother, and others in the household would tell me stories from the Tales, including episodes from Genji, the Shining Prince; but, since they had to depend on their memories, they could not possibly tell me all I wanted to know and their stories only made me more curious than ever. In my impatience I got a statue of the Healing Buddha built in my own size. When no one was watching, I would perform my ablutions and, stealing into the altar room, would prostrate myself and pray fervently, "Oh, please arrange things so that we may soon go to the Capital, where there are so many Tales, and please let me read them all."

On the third day of the Ninth Month, when I was twelve years old, we left our house and moved to a place called Imatachi in preparation for our journey to the Capital. . . .

Now that we had finally arrived [at the capital], I was desperately impatient to read some Tales. Though our household was still in confusion, I begged my stepmother to help me, and she wrote to our cousin, Lady Emon, who was a lady-in-waiting to the Princess in Sanjō Palace. Lady Emon, surprised and pleased by my request, sent me the lid of an inkbox containing an unusually fine collection of notebooks which, as she explained, had been passed on to her by Her Highness, the Princess. Overjoyed with this gift, I plunged into the Tales and read them day and night. I was eager for more. But who in the Capital was going to help this newcomer in such a quest?

My stepmother, who had served at Court before moving to the provinces, had been going through a difficult time and her marriage was no longer satisfactory. She now decided to leave, taking along her four-year-old child. "You have been very kind," she said to me. "I shall never forget it." Pointing to the great plum tree that grew close to the eaves of our house, she added as her parting words, "When this tree blooms again, I shall be back." After she left I yearned for her and wept silently day after day. And so the year drew to an end. . . .

During the spring there was a terrible epidemic, and my nurse, on whom I had gazed so tenderly in the moonlight at Matsusato Ford, died on the first day of the Third Month. I was crushed by grief and even lost my interest in Tales. All day long I shook with weeping; then I noticed how the eve-

ning sun threw its brilliant light on the scattering blooms of
the cherry tree, and I wrote the poem,

> *They will come back next Spring—those cherry blooms*
>   *that scatter from the tree.*
> *But how I yearn for her who left*
> *And never will return!*

Seeing that I had abandoned myself to grief, Mother did
her best to console me and managed to find some more Tales.
These had the expected effect and almost immediately my
spirits improved. I read some of the books about Lady
Murasaki and longed to see the later parts. Since I was still
new to the Capital and had no one to ask, it was impossible
to find what I wanted. I was burning with impatience and
curiosity, and in my prayers I used to say, "Let me see the
entire *Tale of Genji* from beginning to end!" When I went
with Mother to Uzumasa on a retreat, this was the one thing
I prayed for. If only I could find a complete copy which I
could start reading as soon as we got home! Yet my prayers
were all in vain.

I was feeling most dejected when one day I called on an
aunt of mine who had come up from the country. She received me affectionately and showed great interest in me.
"What a pretty girl you've grown up to be!" she said. As I
was leaving she asked, "What would you like as a present? I
am sure you don't want anything too practical. I'd like to
give you something you will really enjoy."

And so it was that she presented me with fifty-odd volumes
of *The Tale of Genji* in a special case, together with copies
of *Zai*, *Tōgimi*, *Serikawa*, *Shirara*, *Asanzu*, and many other
Tales. Oh, how happy I was when I came home with all these
books in a bag. In the past I had been able to have only an
occasional hurried look at fragments of *The Tale of Genji*,
and much of it had remained infuriatingly obscure. Now I
had it all in front of me and I could sit undisturbed behind
my curtain, bent comfortably forward as I took out the
books, one by one, and enjoyed them to my heart's content. I
wouldn't have changed places with the Empress herself.

Placing the lamp close to where I sat, I kept reading all
day long and as late as possible into the night. Soon I came
to know the names of all the characters in the book and I

could see them clearly in my mind's eye, which gave me the greatest satisfaction. One night I dreamt that a handsome priest appeared before me in a yellow surplice and ordered me to learn the fifth volume of the Lotus Sutra as soon as possible. I told no one about the dream, since I was much too busy with my Tales to spend any time learning sutras. I was not a very attractive girl at the time, but I fancied that, when I grew up, I would surely become a great beauty with long flowing hair like Yūgao, who was loved by the Shining Prince, or like Ukifune, who was wooed by the Captain of Uji. Oh, what futile conceits!

I lived forever in a dream world. Though I made occasional pilgrimages to temples, I could never bring myself to pray sincerely for what most people want. I know there are many who read the sutras and practise religious devotions from the age of about seventeen; but I had no interest in such things. The height of my aspirations was that a man of noble birth, perfect in both looks and manners, someone like Shining Genji in the Tale, would visit me just once a year in the mountain village where he would have hidden me like Lady Ukifune. There I should live my lonely existence, gazing at the blossoms and the Autumn leaves and the moon and the snow, and wait for an occasional splendid letter from him. This was all I wanted; and in time I came to believe that it would actually happen.

It occurred to me that my position in the world would greatly improve if Father received a proper appointment. I was hoping against hope when finally his new post was announced; but he was assigned to a very distant province.

"All these years," said Father, "I have been looking forward to the day—a day that I thought would come soon—when I would be appointed to one of the nearby provinces. Then I should have been able to look after you properly. I could have taken you along to my province and shown you the sea and the mountains and all the other beautiful sights. Above all, I should have made sure that you would get better treatment than the daughter of a mere provincial official. But you and I seem to have had bad karmas. To think that after all this waiting I should now have been sent to such a place! Many years ago when I took you to the East, I used to worry about you whenever I had the slightest illness. For, though you were just a little girl at the time, I knew what a difficult

life you would have if I died and left you there in the wilds
of Kazusa. The provinces are terrible places. I could have
managed if I had only had myself to think about, but it worried me to be accompanied by a large family and to know
that I was hemmed in by restrictions of every kind and could
not look after you as I wished. Now that you have grown up,
things are even more difficult. I may not be long for this
world and I can think of all too many examples of girls who
have lost their fathers and then gone to seed in the Capital.
Your plight will be worse still if I take you along to the East
and you turn into a mere country woman. On the other hand,
what will happen if you stay behind in the Capital, where we
have no relations or connexions to count on? Yet there is no
alternative. After all, I can hardly resign my post now that I
have finally received this appointment. I suppose I shall simply have to say a last farewell and leave you here. But I
know that you will have a hard time managing without me."

Thus he lamented day and night, making me so unhappy
that I could no longer even notice the beauty of the flowers
and the leaves. Soon I was in a really miserable state, but
there was nothing to be done about it.

It was on the thirteenth day of the Seventh Month that Father left for his province. During the five days before his departure he did not visit my room a single time, since our
meetings only made things worse. As a result, when the actual day came, we were even more upset than we would have
been otherwise.

"The time has come," said Father, raising the blind in my
room. We looked at each other and wept bitterly. Then he
left without another word. After he had gone, I lay there motionless, and my tears made everything turn dark.

Presently one of Father's servants, who had been ordered
to remain in the Capital but who had gone along part of the
way to see him off, returned carrying a pocket-paper with the
poem,

> *Fate is no friend of mine.*
> *Even this Autumn parting has been marred by haste.*

This was all Father had written, but I could not finish reading it. I had great difficulty in replying. Even at the best of
times I was not much good at poetry, and at a moment like

this I felt quite incapable of expressing myself. I believe I
jotted down something to the effect,

> *I never dreamt that such a thing could be—*
> *That you and I should part in this world even for a while.*

After Father left, we had fewer visitors than ever. I sat for-
lornly in my room, wondering exactly where he might be.
Since I knew the road to the East, I was able to follow him
lovingly in my mind, and from dawn till dusk I gazed sadly
at the ridges of the Eastern Hills. . . .

In the Tenth Month we moved back to the Capital. Mother
had now become a nun and, though she stayed in the same
house with Father and me, she lived separately from us. Father, who had more or less retired from the world, insisted
that I should be mistress of the house. I felt most helpless and
forlorn. One day a relation of ours, who had heard about my
condition, sent a message suggesting that I should give up this
idle, lonely life. In due course I was invited to attend Court,
but Father in his old-fashioned way thought that I would find
life there very trying and he persuaded me to remain at
home. Several people told him that he was mistaken.
"Nowadays no young woman hesitates to serve at Court,"
said one of them. "All sorts of good things happen to people
when they have taken service. Really, you should let her go
and see what happens." So it was that Father reluctantly gave
his consent.

My first period of service lasted exactly one night. When I
went to the Palace, I wore a dark crimson robe of glossed
silk over eight thin under robes of dark red. Having been totally absorbed in Tales, I knew scarcely anyone except the
people I used to visit in order to borrow books. Besides, I was
so used to staying with my old-fashioned parents at home,
gazing hour after hour at the Autumn moon or the Spring
blossoms, that when I arrived at Court I was in a sort of daze
and hardly knew what I was doing. So at dawn on the following day I returned home.

During my cloistered years I had often imagined that life
in the Palace would offer all sorts of pleasures which I never
encountered in my monotonous routine at home. As it turned
out, my first experience at Court suggested that I would feel

extremely awkward and unhappy in these new surroundings. Yet what could I do about it?

In the Twelfth Month I went to Court once more. I was given a room of my own, and this time I stayed in service for several days. When I was summoned to the Princess's apartments for night duty, I had to lie next to women I did not know and I could not sleep a wink. Overcome with nervousness and embarrassment, I wept secretly until dawn; then I returned to my room and spent all day in loving, anxious thoughts about Father, who was growing old and feeble and who depended on me so completely. I also thought of my poor nieces, who had lived with me ever since they lost their mother and who even used to sleep next to me, one on each side. As I sat in my room musing vacantly, I had the impression that an eavesdropper was standing outside peeping on me, which made me most uncomfortable.

When I returned home after about ten days, Father and Mother had lit a fire in the hearth and were waiting for me. Seeing me get out of the carriage, Father said, "When you were here, the house was full of visitors and attendants, but during the past days it has been completely silent and we have not seen a soul. It has been terribly sad and lonely. What will become of us if you stay at Court?" He burst into tears, and it was painful to see him in this state.

The next morning he said, "Now that you are back, the house is alive again. Look at all the people coming and going!" The expression on his face as he sat there brought tears to my eyes. I wondered why my presence in the house should make such a difference.

They say that even for a Saint it is difficult to dream of a previous incarnation. Yet in my confused and aimless state I had the following dream in the chapel of Kiyomizu Temple. A man, evidently the Intendant, appeared before me and said, "In a previous incarnation you were a priest in this temple. As a carver of many Buddhist images you accumulated great merit, and in your next incarnation you were born into a much better family than before. It was you who carved the sixteen-foot statue of the Buddha in the eastern wing of this chapel. In fact you were covering it with gold foil when you died."

"Dear me!" I said. "In that case I had better gild it now."

"No. Someone else finished the job after your death. And it is he who dedicated the image."

If I had followed up this dream by a series of pious visits to Kiyomizu, things might have turned out well for me, since it was here that I had worshipped in that earlier incarnation. In my usual feckless way, however, I never bothered to make any further pilgrimages to the temple.

On the twenty-fifth day of the Twelfth Month I was summoned to the Princess's Court for the Naming of the Buddhas, and I went to stay in her palace for just one night. There were some forty ladies in attendance, all wearing dark red robes of glossed silk over white under robes. I tried to make myself inconspicuous by staying behind the lady who had first introduced me at Court, and in that great throng of people no one got a clear view of me.

I set out for home before daybreak the next morning when the snow was coming down in scattered flakes. In the freezing dawn the moon was dimly reflected on the glossy sleeves of my dark red robe, and it seemed to me that the moon's face was wet with tears. These lines came to me,

Sadly I see the year is drawing to an end
And the night is giving way to dawn,
While moonbeams wanly shine upon my sleeves.

If, having once entered service, I had continued in regular attendance, I should in due course have grown accustomed to this new life. Despite all my family distractions I could then have been accepted as a regular member of the Court instead of being regarded as an eccentric. But for reasons of their own my parents soon decided that I should stay at home. . . .

Things now became rather hectic for me. I forgot all about my Tales and became much more conscientious. How could I have let all those years slip by, instead of practising my devotions and going on pilgrimages? I began to doubt whether any of my romantic fancies, even those that had seemed most plausible, had the slightest basis in fact. How could anyone as wonderful as Shining Genji or as beautiful as the girl whom Captain Kaoru[1] kept hidden in Uji really exist in this world of ours? Oh, what a fool I had been to believe such non-sense! . . .

Now that I was sincerely convinced of my errors and wanted to live a more serious life, I should have put my intentions into practice. This turned out to be impossible. I was told that no one at Court believed that I had actually retired to my home after my first period of service, and in the months that followed I was constantly being summoned to attend the Princess in her apartments. Since I was also ordered to bring my young nieces to Court, I was obliged to present them, and I myself had to make several appearances. But I had become far more modest in my desires and no longer had any great expectations.

Now that I was back in Court service—not through any wish of my own but because of my nieces—I could hardly be treated as a newcomer. On the other hand, I certainly did not qualify as one of those senior ladies-in-waiting who, from long experience at Court, go about with knowing looks on their faces and allow nothing to ruffle them. In consequence I was regarded rather scornfully as a sort of guest who came to Court for occasional visits. It was an awkward position. Yet, since I did not depend exclusively on my Court service, I was not particularly envious of the senior ladies; in fact I preferred my present situation, which allowed me to appear just when I was needed for service and to chat freely with other ladies-in-waiting when we were off duty. During ceremonies and other special occasions in the Palace I tried to keep to myself as much as possible; I liked to remain in the background and to get a general impression of what was happening rather than to become actively involved. . . .

Now I really began to regret having wasted so much time on my silly fancies, and I bitterly reproached myself for not having accompanied Mother and Father on their pilgrimages. My position had greatly improved, both in social standing and in material wealth, and I had also succeeded in rearing my little bud [her young son] exactly as I wished. The time had come, I told myself, to think about preparing my life in

---

[1] Prince Genji's adopted son and successor, hero of the last thirteen books of *The Tale of Genji*. It was the Lady Ukifune whom he established in remote Uji.

the world to come. Towards the end of the Eleventh Month I set out on a pilgrimage to Ishiyama. The country was beautiful under the heavy snow. When I reached Osaka Barrier, I remembered that the last time I had come this way it had also been Winter and that there had been a fierce wind. I wrote the poem,

> *There is no difference in their sounds—*
> *This wind that blows across the Barrier now*
> *And the one I heard so many years ago.*

In the Tenth Month of the following year I heard that the Sacred Purification for the Great Festival of Thanksgiving was to take place on the twenty-fifth day. Despite all the excitement I began to observe abstinence in preparation for a pilgrimage to Hase Temple and arranged to leave for Hase on the very day of the Purification ceremony. My brother was outraged. "This is a ceremony that you can witness only once in an Imperial reign," he said. "People are coming all the way from the country to see it. When there are so many days in the year, it is madness to choose precisely this one to to leave the Capital. You'll be the laughingstock for generations to come." My husband,[2] however, told me I should do exactly as I wished, and I was impressed by his understanding. . . .

Now that I was able to do exactly as I wished, I went on one distant pilgrimage after another. Some were delightful, some difficult, but I found great solace in them all being confident that they would bring me future benefit. No longer having any sorrows of my own, I concentrated on providing the best possible upbringing for my children[3] and waited impatiently for them to grow up. I also prayed for my husband's future, and I was confident that my prayers would be answered. . . .

What with one thing and another my life had been full of worries. My career at Court might have turned out well if

---

[2] This is her first reference to her husband. Somewhat later she refers to her marriage as "going badly," but husband and children are peripheral to the concerns of her diary.

[3] Lady Sarashina also had two other children who are only referred to in passing.

only I had settled down to my duties from the outset and persevered; but, since my attendance was always being interrupted, I never had a chance to get ahead. Now it was too late. I was past my prime[4] and realized that the time had come to abandon my youthful hopes. Besides I was rapidly losing my health and could no longer go on pilgrimages as I wished; soon I had to give up even the occasional retreat. I did not feel that I would live very long and was determined to do everything possible for my children during the years that remained. Their future was a constant source of concern.

My husband was due for an appointment and we waited for it anxiously. The announcement finally came in the Autumn, but it was not nearly as good as we had hoped and we were bitterly disappointed. I was told that his new province was nearer the Capital than the eastern districts that I knew so well from Father's time. So I resigned myself to the inevitable and made hasty preparations for my husband's departure. It was decided that he would leave the Capital about the tenth day of the Eighth Month, setting out from the house into which his daughter had recently moved. We had no way of knowing how things would turn out, and the last days were very lively, with lots of people gathered round us in high spirits.

When he left on the twenty-seventh, he was accompanied by our boy. The lad, dressed in a scarlet under robe of glossy silk, a hunting cloak of light purple with a green lining, and figured silk trousers also of light purple, set off carrying his sword. In front of him went his father, who wore bluish grey trousers of figured silk and a hunting cloak. They mounted their horses beside the covered gallery.

After all the commotion of their departure, I found time hanging heavily on my hands. Yet I did not feel quite as unhappy as I had been when I first heard about the appointment, for now I knew that his province was not too far away. On the following day the people who had accompanied my husband's procession on the first leg of his journey came back and reported that he had made a brilliant departure. One of them added, "This morning a huge human fire sprang up near the procession and moved towards the Capital." I took this to mean that the fire was for one of the men accompany-

---

[4] She was at this time about fifty years old.

ing my husband. How could I have guessed what the omen really meant?

During the months that followed I devoted myself to taking care of my children, and in the Fourth Month of the following year my husband returned to the Capital to spend the Summer and the Autumn at home.

On the twenty-fifth day of the Ninth Month he was taken ill, and on the fifth of the Tenth Month he faded away like a dream. Never have I known such sorrow. I remembered that, when Mother had dedicated a mirror at Hase Temple, the priest had dreamt about a weeping figure rolling on the floor. Such was my present state. There had been no happy person in the priest's dream; nor could I expect any happiness in my own life.

We cremated him on the evening of the twenty-third and he vanished with the smoke. My boy, whom I had seen off the previous Autumn when he had accompanied his father from the Capital, brilliantly attired and much praised by everyone, now wore a sad white tunic over his black robes. As I watched him walking along in tears beside the hearse, inexpressible thoughts flooded through me; it was as though I had moved straight into a dream. I felt that my husband was looking down at me in my wretchedness.

If only I had not given myself over to Tales and poems since my young days but had spent my time in religious devotions, I should have been spared this misery. After my first pilgrimage to Hase, when I had dreamt that someone threw an object before me and said that it was a branch of *sugi* bestowed from Inari as a special token, I should have gone directly on a pilgrimage to the Inari Shrines. Then things would not have turned out like this. The interpreter had explained that all those dreams about praying to the Heavenly Goddess meant that I would become an Imperial nurse, serve in the Imperial Palace, and receive the special favour of Their Majesties; but none of this had come true. Alas, the only thing that had turned out exactly as predicted was the sad image in the mirror. So I had wandered through life without realizing any of my hopes or accumulating any merit. . . .

—Translated by Ivan Morris

All About Women

Lady Murasaki

"All about Women" is an excerpt from the early-eleventh-century novel *The Tale of Genji*.

Kawabata Yasunari, in his lecture on acceptance of the Nobel prize in literature, referred to *The Tale of Genji* as "the highest pinnacle of Japanese literature. Even down to our day," he said, "there has not been a piece of fiction to compare with it."

It might be noted that at one time in the course of critical evaluation of *Genji*, certain scholars put forward the proposition that Japan's great epic must have been the work of a male writer. Fortunately, there are too many first-hand references to Lady Murasaki's work-in-process and her reading of passages to court friends for such pseudo-criticism to be taken seriously.

Recognized as the world's first novel, *The Tale of Genji* grew in stature as the years of its composition brought maturity and competence to its author. Lady Murasaki deals with hundreds of characters through a complex pattern of interrelationships and through several generations with unsurpassed skill and complete control. As time passes and characters come and go, we are aware of the ineluctable working out of *karma* through lifetimes and generations.

In the opening episode of the "Broom-Tree" (second) chapter of *The Tale of Genji* the "Shining Prince" Genji and his companions talk about various types of women and share their experiences and preferences for women who meet their definitions. The measurements given here are evident throughout the voluminous six-book masterpiece as women of the court and its environs come center stage for a time and then move on.

In preliminary action to this episode, Genji has been born to Kiritsubo, a court lady who emerges from relative obscurity to become the favorite of the Emperor. She is at once the object of bitter envy and harsh treatment by the other ladies of the court, especially the first wife of the Emperor, the Lady Kokiden. When the liaison produces a son so beautiful and so talented as to overshadow the son of Lady Kokiden, the heir apparent to the throne, the fate of Kiritsubo is determined and she pines away, victim of the unleashed hatred of the Empress and her ladies-in-waiting. But Genji grows in beauty and willfulness; no lady can resist him. *The Tale of Genji* carries the prince through picaresque adventures until his death in middle age when his son, the Emperor Royzen, follows as central interest.

Murasaki Shikibu lived from about 978 to about 1015. Most of what we know about her in a factual way comes from her episodic diary; something of her character, likes and dislikes, we read between the lines of her great novel. In Murasaki we have another literary figure of the great Fujiwara family, which also provided many of the empresses, court ladies, and high officials of government. Her father began as a student of literature, eventually finding his way into the upper echelons of government. As was usual at the time, the son was given a sound classical education based on a knowledge of Chinese language, literature, and history. What was unusual was that the daughter Murasaki was allowed to sit in on her brother's tutoring sessions. With obvious satisfaction she notes in her diary that she learned more readily than Nobunori and frequently was able to coach him in his studies, causing her father to say, "If only you were a boy how proud and happy I would be." Since it was considered unladylike for women to be educated in Chinese studies, Murasaki went to some lengths during her court years to hide the learning of which she was once so proud.

Sometime between the ages of sixteen and twenty-four Murasaki married a kinsman, Fujiwara no Nobutaka, who died a few years later. After his death, when she was about twenty-six, Murasaki entered the Kyoto court in the service of the Empress Akiko.

We are uncertain how the name of Murasaki Shikibu was given to the author of *Genji*. It is certainly not an authentic family name. The designation that comes down to us combines "lavender" or "wisteria" (*murasaki*) and the title of her father's court ministry (*shikibu shō*). That the author chooses to give the name Murasaki to a central character in *The Tale of Genji* adds further confusion.

Genji the Shining One . . . He knew that the bearer of such a name could not escape much scrutiny and jealous censure and that his lightest dallyings would be proclaimed to posterity. Fearing then lest he should appear to after ages as a mere good-for-nothing and trifler, and knowing that (so accursed is the blabbing of gossips' tongues) his most secret acts might come to light, he was obliged always to act with great prudence and to preserve at least the outward appearance of respectability. Thus nothing really romantic ever happened to him and Katano no Shosho[1] would have scoffed at his story.

While he was still a Captain of the Guard and was spending most of his time at the Palace, his infrequent visits to the Great Hall[2] were taken as a sign that some secret passion had made its imprint on his heart. But in reality the frivolous, commonplace, straight-ahead amours of his companions did not in the least interest him, and it was a curious trait in his character that when on rare occasions, despite all resistance, love did gain a hold upon him, it was always in the most improbable and hopeless entanglement that he became involved.

It was the season of the long rains. For many days there had not been a fine moment and the Court was keeping a strict fast. The people at the Great Hall were becoming very impatient of Genji's long residence at the Palace, but the young lords, who were Court pages, liked waiting upon Genji better than upon anyone else, always managing to put out his clothes and decorations in some marvellous new way. Among these brothers his greatest friend was the Equerry, To no Chujo, with whom above all other companions of his

---

[1] The hero of a lost popular romance. It is also referred to by Murasaki's contemporary Sei Shonagon in Chapter 145 of her *Makura no Soshi*.

[2] His father-in-law's house, where his wife Princess Aoi still continued to live.

playtime he found himself familiar and at ease. This lord too found the house which his father-in-law, the Minister of the Right, had been at pains to build for him, somewhat oppressive, while at his father's house he, like Genji, found the splendours somewhat dazzling, so that he ended by becoming Genji's constant companion at Court. They shared both studies and play and were inseparable companions on every sort of occasion, so that soon all formalities were dispensed with between them and the inmost secrets of their hearts freely exchanged.

It was on a night when the rain never ceased its dismal downpour. There were not many people about in the palace and Genji's rooms seemed even quieter than usual. He was sitting by the lamp, looking at various books and papers. Suddenly he began pulling some letters out of the drawers of a desk which stood near by. This aroused To no Chujo's curiosity. "Some of them I can show to you," said Genji, "but there are others which I had rather . . ." "It is just those which I want to see. Ordinary, commonplace letters are very much alike and I do not suppose that yours differ much from mine. What I want to see are passionate letters written in moments of resentment, letters hinting consent, letters written at dusk . . ."

He begged so eagerly that Genji let him examine the drawers. It was not indeed likely that he had put any very important or secret documents in the ordinary desk; he would have hidden them away much further from sight. So he felt sure that the letters in these drawers would be nothing to worry about. After turning over a few of them, "What an astonishing variety!" To no Chujo exclaimed and began guessing at the writers' names, and made one or two good hits. More often he was wrong and Genji, amused by his puzzled air, said very little but generally managed to lead him astray. At last he took the letters back, saying, "But you too must have a large collection. Show me some of yours, and my desk will open to you with better will." "I have none that you would care to see," said To no Chujo, and he continued: "I have at last discovered that there exists no woman of whom one can say, 'Here is perfection. This is indeed she.' There are many who have the superficial art of writing a good running hand, or if occasion requires of making a quick repartee. But there are few who will stand the ordeal of any

further test. Usually their minds are entirely occupied by admiration for their own accomplishments, and their abuse of
all rivals creates a most unpleasant impression. Some again
are adored by over-fond parents. These have been since childhood guarded behind lattice windows and no knowledge of
them is allowed to reach the outer-world, save that of their
excellence in some accomplishment or art; and this may
indeed sometimes arouse our interest. She is pretty and graceful and has not yet mixed at all with the world. Such a girl
by closely copying some model and applying herself with
great industry will often succeed in really mastering one of
the minor and ephemeral arts. Her friends are careful to say
nothing of her defects and to exaggerate her accomplishments, and while we cannot altogether trust their praise we
cannot believe that their judgment is entirely astray. But
when we take steps to test their statements we are invariably
disappointed."

He paused, seeming to be slightly ashamed of the cynical
tone which he had adopted, and added, "I know my experience is not large, but that is the conclusion I have come to so
far." Then Genji, smiling: "And are there any who lack even
one accomplishment?" "No doubt, but in such a case it is unlikely that anyone would be successfully decoyed. The number of those who have nothing to recommend them and of
those in whom nothing but good can be found is probably
equal. I divide women into three classes. Those of high rank
and birth are made such a fuss of and their weak points are
so completely concealed that we are certain to be told that
they are paragons. About those of the middle class everyone
is allowed to express his own opinion, and we shall have
much conflicting evidence to sift. As for the lower classes,
they do not concern us."

The completeness with which To no Chujo disposed of the
question amused Genji, who said, "It will not always be so
easy to know into which of the three classes a woman ought
to be put. For sometimes people of high rank sink to the
most abject positions; while others of common birth rise to be
high officers, wear self-important faces, redecorate the inside
of their houses and think themselves as good as anyone. How
are we to deal with such cases?"

At this moment they were joined by Hidari no Uma no
Kami and To Shikibu no Jo, who said they had also come to

the Palace to keep the fast. As both of them were great lovers and good talkers, To no Chujo handed over to them the decision of Genji's question, and in the discussion which followed many unflattering things were said. Uma no Kami spoke first. "However high a lady may rise, if she does not come of an adequate stock, the world will think very differently of her from what it would of one born to such honours; but if through adverse fortune a lady of highest rank finds herself in friendless misery, the noble breeding of her mind is soon forgotten and she becomes an object of contempt. I think then that taking all things into account, we must put such ladies too into the 'middle class.' But when we come to classify the daughters of Zuryo,[3] who are sent to labour at the affairs of distant provinces—they have such ups and downs that we may reasonably put them too into the middle class.

"Then there are Ministers of the third and fourth classes without Cabinet rank. These are generally thought less of even than the humdrum, ordinary officials. They are usually of quite good birth, but have much less responsibility than Ministers of State and consequently much greater peace of mind. Girls born into such households are brought up in complete security from want or deprivation of any kind, and indeed often amid surroundings of the utmost luxury and splendour. Many of them grow up into women whom it would be folly to despise; some have been admitted at Court, where they have enjoyed a quite unexpected success. And of this I could cite many, many instances."

"Their success has generally been due to their having a lot of money," said Genji smiling. "You should have known better than to say that," said To no Chujo, reproving him, and Uma no Kami went on: "There are some whose lineage and reputation are so high that it never occurs to one that their education could possibly be at fault; yet when we meet them, we find ourselves exclaiming in despair 'How can they have contrived to grow up like this?'

"No doubt the perfect woman in whom none of those essentials is lacking must somewhere exist and it would not startle me to find her. But she would certainly be beyond the reach of a humble person like myself, and for that reason I

---

[3] Provincial officials. Murasaki herself came of this class.

should like to put her in a category of her own and not to count her in our present classification.

"But suppose that behind some gateway overgrown with vine-weed, in a place where no one knows there is a house at all, there should be locked away some creature of unimagined beauty—with what excitement should we discover her! The complete surprise of it, the upsetting of all our wise theories and classifications, would be likely, I think, to lay a strange and sudden enchantment upon us. I imagine her father rather large and gruff; her brother, a surly, ill-looking fellow. Locked away in an utterly blank and uninteresting bedroom, she will be subject to odd flights of fancy, so that in her hands the arts that others learn as trivial accomplishments will seem strangely full of meaning and importance; or perhaps in some particular art she will thrill us by her delightful and unexpected mastery. Such a one may perhaps be beneath the attention of those of you who are of flawless lineage. But for my part I find it hard to banish her . . ." and here he looked at Shikibu no Jo, who wondered whether the description had been meant to apply to his own sisters, but said nothing. "If it is difficult to choose even out of the top class . . ." thought Genji, and began to doze.

He was dressed in a suit of soft white silk, with a rough cloak carelessly slung over his shoulders, with belt and fastenings untied. In the light of the lamp against which he was leaning he looked so lovely that one might have wished he were a girl; and they thought that even Uma no Kami's "perfect woman," whom he had placed in a category of her own, would not be worthy of such a prince as Genji.

The conversation went on. Many persons and things were discussed. Uma no Kami contended that perfection is equally difficult to find in other spheres. The sovereign is hard put to it to choose his ministers. But he at least has an easier task than the husband, for he does not entrust the affairs of his kingdom to one, two or three persons alone, but sets up a whole system of superiors and subordinates.

But when the mistress of a house is to be selected, a single individual must be found who will combine in her person many diverse qualities. It will not do to be too exacting. Let us be sure that the lady of our choice possesses certain tangible qualities which we admire; and if in other ways she falls short of our ideal, we must be patient and call to mind those qualities which first induced us to begin our courting.

But even here we must beware; for there are some who in the selfishness of youth and flawless beauty are determined that not a dust-flick shall fall upon them. In their letters they choose the most harmless topics, but yet contrive to colour the very texture of the written signs with a tenderness that vaguely disquiets us. But such a one, when we have at last secured a meeting, will speak so low that she can scarcely be heard, and the few faint sentences that she murmurs beneath her breath serve only to make her more mysterious than before. All this may seem to be the pretty shrinking of girlish modesty; but we may later find that what held her back was the very violence of her passions.

Or again, where all seems plain sailing, the perfect companion will turn out to be too impressionable and will upon the most inappropriate occasions display her affections in so ludicrous a way that we begin to wish ourselves rid of her.

Then there is the zealous housewife, who regardless of her appearance twists her hair behind her ears and devotes herself entirely to the details of our domestic welfare. The husband, in his comings and goings about the world, is certain to see and hear many things which he cannot discuss with strangers, but would gladly talk over with an intimate who could listen with sympathy and understanding, someone who could laugh with him or weep if need be. It often happens too that some political event will greatly perturb or amuse him, and he sits apart longing to tell someone about it. He suddenly laughs at some secret recollection or sighs audibly. But the wife only says lightly 'What is the matter?' and shows no interest.

This is apt to be very trying.

Uma no Kami considered several other cases. But he reached no definite conclusion and sighing deeply he continued: "We will then, as I have suggested, let birth and beauty go by the board. Let her be the simplest and most guileless of creatures so long as she is honest and of a peaceable disposition, that in the end we may not lack a place of trust. And if some other virtue chances to be hers we shall treasure it as a godsend. But if we discover in her some small defect, it shall not be too closely scrutinized. And we may be sure that if she is strong in the virtues of tolerance and amiability her outward appearance will not be beyond measure harsh.

"There are those who carry forbearance too far, and affecting not to notice wrongs which cry out for redress seem to be paragons of misused fidelity. But suddenly a time comes when such a one can restrain herself no longer, and leaving behind her a poem couched in pitiful language and calculated to rouse the most painful sentiments of remorse, she flies to some remote village in the mountains or some desolate seashore, and for a long while all trace of her is lost.

"When I was a boy the ladies-in-waiting used to tell me sad tales of this kind. I never doubted that the sentiments expressed in them were real, and I wept profusely. But now I am beginning to suspect that such sorrows are for the most part affectation. She has left behind her (this lady whom we are imagining) a husband who is probably still fond of her; she is making herself very unhappy, and by disappearing in this way is causing him unspeakable anxiety, perhaps only for the ridiculous purpose of putting his affection to the test. Then comes along some admiring friend crying 'What a heart! What depth of feeling!' She becomes more lugubrious than ever, and finally enters a nunnery. When she decided on this step she was perfectly sincere and had not the slightest intention of ever returning to the world. Then some female friend hears of it and 'Poor thing' she cries; 'in what an agony of mind must she have been to do this!' and visits her in her cell. When the husband, who has never ceased to mourn for her, hears what she has become, he bursts into tears, and some servant or old nurse, seeing this, bustles off to the nunnery with tales of the husband's despair, and 'Oh Madam, what a shame, what a shame!' Then the nun, forgetting where and what she is, raises her hand to her head to straighten her hair, and finds that it has been shorn away. In helpless misery she sinks to the floor, and do what she will, the tears begin to flow. Now all is lost; for since she cannot at every moment be praying for strength, there creeps into her mind the sinful thought that she did ill to become a nun and so often does she commit this sin that even Buddha must think her wickeder now than she was before she took her vows; and she feels certain that these terrible thoughts are leading her soul to the blackest Hell. But if the *karma* of their past lives should chance to be strongly weighted against a parting, she will be found and captured before she has taken her final vows. In such a case their life will be beyond endurance unless she be fully determined, come good or ill, this time to close her eyes to all that goes amiss.

"Again there are others who must needs be forever mounting guard over their own and their husband's affections. Such a one, if she sees in him not a fault indeed but even the slightest inclination to stray, makes a foolish scene, declaring with indignation that she will have no more to do with him.

"But even if a man's fancy should chance indeed to have gone somewhat astray, yet his earlier affection may still be strong and in the end will return to its old haunts. Now by her tantrums she has made a rift that cannot be joined. Whereas she who when some small wrong calls for silent rebuke, shows by a glance that she is not unaware; but when some large offence demands admonishment knows how to hint without severity, will end by standing in her master's affections better than ever she stood before. For often the sight of our own forbearance will give our neighbour strength to rule his mutinous affections.

"But she whose tolerance and forgiveness know no bounds, though this may seem to proceed from the beauty and amiability of her disposition, is in fact displaying the shallowness of her feeling: 'The unmoored boat must needs drift with the stream.' Are you not of this mind?"

To no Chujo nodded. "Some," he said, "have imagined that by arousing a baseless suspicion in the mind of the beloved we can revive a waning devotion. But this experiment is very dangerous. Those who recommend it are confident that so long as resentment is groundless one need only suffer it in silence and all will soon be well. I have observed however that this is by no means the case.

"But when all is said and done, there can be no greater virtue in woman than this: that she should with gentleness and forbearance meet every wrong whatsoever that falls to her share." He thought as he said this of his own sister, Princess Aoi; but was disappointed and piqued to discover that Genji, whose comments he awaited, was fast asleep.

Uma no Kami was an expert in such discussions and now stood preening his feathers. To no Chujo was disposed to hear what more he had to say and was now at pains to humour and encourage him.

"It is with women," said Uma no Kami, "as it is with the works of craftsmen. The wood-carver can fashion whatever he will. Yet his products are but toys of the moment, to be glanced at in jest, not fashioned according to any precept or law. When times change, the carver too will change his style and make new trifles to hit the fancy of the passing day. But there is another kind of artist, who sets more soberly about his work, striving to give real beauty to the things which men actually use and to give to them the shapes which tradition has ordained. This maker of real things must not for a moment be confused with the carver of idle toys.

"In the Painters' Workshop too there are many excellent artists chosen for their proficiency in ink-drawing; and indeed they are all so clever it is hard to set one above the other. But all of them are at work on subjects intended to impress and surprise. One paints the Mountain of Horai; another a raging sea-monster riding a storm; another, ferocious animals from the Land beyond the sea, or faces of imaginary demons. Letting their fancy run wildly riot they have no thought of beauty, but only of how best they may astonish the behold-er's eye. And though nothing in their pictures is real, all is probable. But ordinary hills and rivers, just as they are, houses such as you may see anywhere, with all their real beauty and harmony of form—quietly to draw such scenes as this, or to show what lies behind some intimate hedge that is folded away far from the world, and thick trees upon some unheroic hill, and all this with befitting care for composition, propor-tion, and the like—such works demand the highest master's utmost skill and must needs draw the common craftsman into a thousand blunders. So too in handwriting, we see some who aimlessly prolong their cursive strokes this way or that, and hope their flourishes will be mistaken for genius. But true penmanship preserves in every letter its balance and form, and though at first some letters may seem but half-formed, yet when we compare them with the copy-books we find that there is nothing at all amiss.

"So it is in these trifling matters. And how much the more in judging of the human heart should we distrust all fashion-able airs and graces, all amiss.

"So it is in these trifling matters. And how much the more in judging of the human heart should we distrust all fashion-able airs and graces, all tricks and smartness, learnt only to please the outward gaze! This I first understood some while ago, and if you will have patience with me I will tell you the story."

So saying, he came and sat a little closer to them, and Genji woke up. To no Chujo, in rapt attention, was sitting with his cheek propped upon his hand. Uma no Kami's whole speech that night was indeed very much like a chaplain's sermon about the ways of the world, and was rather absurd. But upon such occasions as this we are easily led on into discussing our own ideas and most private secrets without the least reserve.

"It happened when I was young, and in an even more humble position than I am today," Uma no Kami continued. "I was in love with a girl who (like the drudging, faithful wife of whom I spoke a little while ago) was not a full-sail beauty; and I in my youthful vanity thought she was all very well for the moment, but would never do for the wife of so fine a fellow as I. She made an excellent companion in times when I was at a loose end; but she was of a disposition so violently jealous, that I could have put up with a little less devotion if only she had been somewhat less fiercely ardent and exacting.

"Thus I kept thinking, vexed by her unrelenting suspicions. But then I would remember her ceaseless devotion to the interests of one who was after all a person of no account, and full of remorse I made sure that with a little patience on my part she would one day learn to school her jealousy.

"It was her habit to minister to my smallest wants even before I was myself aware of them; whatever she felt was lacking in her she strove to acquire, and where she knew that in some quality of mind she still fell behind my desires, she was at pains never to show her deficiency in such a way as might vex me. Thus in one way or another she was always busy in forwarding my affairs, and she hoped that if all down to the last dewdrop (as they say) were conducted as I should wish, this would be set down to her credit and help to balance the defects in her person which meek and obliging as she might be could not (she fondly imagined) fail to offend me; and at this time she even hid herself from strangers lest their poor opinion of her looks should put me out of countenance.

"I meanwhile, becoming used to her homely looks, was well content with her character, save for this one article of

jealousy; and here she showed no amendment. Then I began
to think to myself, 'Surely, since she seems so anxious to
please, so timid, there must be some way of giving her a
fright which will teach her a lesson, so that for a while at
least we may have a respite from this accursed business.' And
though I knew it would cost me dear, I determined to make a
pretence of giving her up, thinking that since she was so fond
of me this would be the best way to teach her a lesson. Accordingly I behaved with the greatest coldness to her, and she
as usual began her jealous fit and behaved with such folly
that in the end I said to her, 'If you want to be rid for ever
of one who loves you dearly, you are going the right way
about it by all these endless poutings over nothing at all. But
if you want to go on with me, you must give up suspecting
some deep intrigue each time you fancy that I am treating
you unkindly. Do this, and you may be sure I shall continue
to love you dearly. It may well be that as time goes on, I
shall rise a little higher in the world and then . . .'

"I thought I had managed matters very cleverly, though
perhaps in the heat of the moment I might have spoken
somewhat too roughly. She smiled faintly and answered that
if it were only a matter of bearing for a while with my failures and disappointments, that did not trouble her at all, and
she would gladly wait till I became a person of consequence.
'But it is a hard task,' she said, 'to go on year after year enduring your coldness and waiting the time when you will at
last learn to behave to me with some decency; and therefore I
agree with you that the time has come when we had better go
each his own way.' Then in a fit of wild and uncontrollable
jealousy she began to pour upon me a torrent of bitter
reproaches, and with a woman's savagery she suddenly seized
my little finger and bit deep into it. The unexpected pain was
difficult to bear, but composing myself I said tragically, 'Now
you have put this mark upon me I shall get on worse than
ever in polite society; as for promotion, I shall be considered
a disgrace to the meanest public office and unable to cut a
genteel figure in any capacity, I shall be obliged to withdraw
myself completely from the world. You and I at any rate
shall certainly not meet again,' and bending my injured finger
as I turned to go, I recited the verse 'As on bent hand I count
the times that we have met, it is not one finger only that
bears witness to my pain.' And she, all of a sudden bursting

into tears . . . 'If still in your heart only you look for pains to count, then were our hands best employed in parting.' After a few more words I left her, not for a moment thinking that all was over.

"Days went by, and no news. I began to be restless. One night when I had been at the Palace for the rehearsal of the Festival music, heavy sleet was falling; and I stood at the spot where those of us who came from the Palace had dispersed, unable to make up my mind which way to go. For in no direction had I anything which could properly be called a home. I might of course take a room in the Palace precincts; but I shivered to think of the cheerless grandeur that would surround me. Suddenly I began to wonder what she was thinking, how she was looking; and brushing the snow off my shoulders, I set out for her house. I own I felt uneasy; but I thought that after so long a time her anger must surely have somewhat abated. Inside the room a lamp showed dimly, turned to the wall. Some undergarments were hung out upon a large, warmly-quilted couch, the bed-hangings were drawn up, and I made sure that she was for some reason actually expecting me. I was priding myself on having made so lucky a hit, when suddenly, 'Not at home!'; and on questioning the maid I learnt that she had but that very night gone to her parents home, leaving only a few necessary servants behind. The fact that she had till now sent no poem or conciliatory message seemed to show some hardening of heart, and had already disquieted me. Now I began to fear that her accursed suspiciousness and jealousy had but been a stratagem to make me grow weary of her, and though I could recall no further proof of this I fell into great despair. And to show her that, though we no longer met, I still thought of her and planned for her, I got her some stuff for a dress, choosing a most delightful and unusual shade of colour, and a material that I knew she would be glad to have. 'For after all,' I thought, 'she cannot want to put me altogether out of her head.' When I informed her of this purchase she did not rebuff me nor make any attempt to hide from me, but to all my questions she answered quietly and composedly, without any sign that she was ashamed of herself.

"At last she told me that if I went on as before, she could never forgive me; but if I would promise to live more quietly she would take me back again. Seeing that she still hankered after me I determined to school her a little further yet, and said that I could make no conditions and must be free to live as I chose. So the tug of war went on; but it seems that it hurt her far more than I knew, for in a little while she fell into a decline and died, leaving me aghast at the upshot of my wanton game. And now I felt that, whatever faults she might have had, her devotion alone would have made her a fit wife for me. I remembered how both in trivial talk and in consideration of important matters she had never once shown herself at a loss, how in the dyeing of brocades she rivalled the Goddess of Tatsuta who tints the autumn leaves, and how in needlework and the like she was not less skilful than Tanabata, the Weaving-lady of the sky."

Here he stopped, greatly distressed at the recollection of the lady's many talents and virtues.

"The Weaving-lady and the Herd boy," said To no Chujo, "enjoy a love that is eternal. Had she but resembled the Divine Sempstress in this, you would not, I think, have minded her being a little less skilful with her needle. I wonder that with this rare creature in mind you pronounce the world to be so blank a place."

"Listen," replied Uma no Kami. "About the same time there was another lady whom I used to visit. She was of higher birth than the first; her skill in poetry, cursive writing, and lute-playing, her readiness of hand and tongue were all marked enough to show that she was not a woman of trivial nature; and this indeed was allowed by those who knew her. To add to this she was not ill-looking and sometimes, when I needed a rest from my unhappy persecutress, I used to visit her secretly. In the end I found that I had fallen completely in love with her. After the death of the other I was in great distress. But it was no use brooding over the past and I began to visit my new lady more and more often. I soon came to the conclusion that she was frivolous and I had no confidence that I should have liked what went on when I was not there to see. I now visited her only at long intervals and at last decided that she had another lover.

"It was during the Godless Month, on a beautiful moonlight night. As I was leaving the Palace I met a certain young courtier, who, when I told him that I was driving out to spend the night at the Dainagon's, said that my way was his and joined me. The road passed my lady's house and here it was that he alighted, saying that he had an engagement which he should have been very sorry not to fulfil. The wall was half in ruins and through its gaps I saw the shadowy waters of the lake. It would not have been easy (for even the moon-beams seemed to loiter here!) to hasten past so lovely a place, and when he left his coach I too left mine.

"At once this man (whom I now knew to be that other lover whose existence I had guessed) went and sat unconcern-edly on the bamboo skirting of the portico and began to gaze at the moon. The chrysanthemums were just in full bloom, the bright fallen leaves were tumbling and tussling in the wind. It was indeed a scene of wonderful beauty that met our eyes. Presently he took a flute out of the folds of his dress and began to play upon it. Then putting the flute aside, he began to murmur, 'Sweet is the shade' and other catches. Soon a pleasant-sounding native zithern began to tune up somewhere within the house and an ingenious accompaniment was fitted to his careless warblings. Her zithern was tuned to the autumn-mode, and she played with so much tenderness and feeling that though the music came from behind closed shutters it sounded quite modern and passionate, and well ac-corded with the soft beauty of the moonlight. The courtier was ravished, and as he stepped forward to place himself right under her window he turned to me and remarked in a self-satisfied way that among the fallen leaves no other foot-step had left its mark. Then plucking a chrysanthemum, he sang:

> Strange that the music of your lute,
> These matchless flowers and all the beauty of the night,
> Have lured no other feet to linger at your door!

and then, beseeching her pardon for his halting verses, he begged her to play again while one was still near who longed so passionately to hear her. When he had paid her many other compliments, the lady answered in an affected voice with the verse:

> Would that I had some song that might detain
> The flute that blends its note
> With the low rustling of the autumn leaves.

and after these blandishments, still unsuspecting, she took up
the thirteen-stringed lute, and tuning it to the *Banjiki* mode
she clattered at the strings with all the frenzy that fashion
now demands. It was a fine performance no doubt, but I cannot say that it made a very agreeable impression upon me.

"A man may amuse himself well enough by trifling from
time to time with some lady at the Court; will get what
pleasure he can out of it while he is with her and not trouble
his head about what goes on when he is not there. This lady
too I only saw from time to time, but such was her situation
that I had once fondly imagined myself the only occupant of
her thoughts. However that night's work dissolved the last
shred of my confidence, and I never saw her again.

"These two experiences, falling to my lot while I was still
so young, early deprived me of any hope from women. And
since that time my view of them has but grown the blacker.
No doubt to you at your age they seem very entrancing, these
'dewdrops on the grass that fall if they are touched,' these
'glittering hailstones that melt if gathered in the hand.' But
when you are a little older you will think as I do. Take my
advice in this at least; beware of caressing manners and soft,
entangling ways. For if you are so rash as to let them lead
you astray, you will soon find yourselves cutting a very silly
figure in the world."

To no Chujo as usual nodded his assent, and Genji's smile
seemed such as to show that he too accepted Uma no Kami's
advice. "Your two stories were certainly very dismal," he
said, laughing. And here To no Chujo interposed: "I will tell
you a story about myself. There was a lady whose acquaintance I was obliged to make with great secrecy. But her
beauty well rewarded my pains, and though I had no thought
of making her my wife, I grew so fond of her that I soon
found I could not put her out of my head and she seemed to
have complete confidence in me. Such confidence indeed that
when from time to time I was obliged to behave in such a
way as might well have aroused her resentment, she seemed
not to notice that anything was amiss, and even when I
neglected her for many weeks, she treated me as though I
were still coming every day. In the end indeed I found this
readiness to receive me whenever and however I came very
painful, and determined for the future to merit her strange
confidence.

"Her parents were dead and this was perhaps why, since I was all she had in the world, she treated me with such loving meekness, despite the many wrongs I did her. I must own that my resolution did not last long, and I was soon neglecting her worse than before. During this time (I did not hear of it till afterwards) someone who had discovered our friendship began to send her veiled messages which cruelly frightened and distressed her. Knowing nothing of the trouble she was in, although I often thought of her I neither came nor wrote to her for a long while. Just when she was in her worst despair a child was born, and at last in her distress she plucked a blossom of the flower that is called 'Child of my Heart' and sent it to me."

And here To no Chujo's eyes filled with tears.

"Well," said Genji, "and did she write a message to go with it?" "Oh nothing very out-of-the-ordinary," said To no Chujo. "She wrote: 'Though tattered be the hillman's hedge, deign sometimes to look with kindness upon the Child-flower that grows so sweetly there.' This brought me to her side. As usual she did not reproach me, but she looked sad enough, and when I considered the dreary desolation of this home where every object wore an aspect no less depressing than the wailing voices of the crickets in the grass, she seemed to me like some unhappy princess in an ancient story, and wishing her to feel that it was for the mother's sake and not the child's that I had come, I answered with a poem in which I called the Child-flower by its other name, 'Bed-flower,' and she replied with a poem that darkly hinted at the cruel tempest which had attended this Bed-flower's birth. She spoke lightly and did not seem to be downright angry with me; and when a few tears fell she was at great pains to hide them, and seemed more distressed at the thought that I might imagine her to be unhappy than actually resentful of my conduct towards her. So I went away with an easy mind and it was some while before I came again. When at last I returned she had utterly disappeared, and if she is alive she must be living a wretched vagrant life. If while I still loved her she had but shown some outward sign of her resentment, she would not have ended thus as an outcast and wanderer; for I should never have dared to leave her so long neglected, and might in the end have acknowledged her and made her mine for ever.

The child too was a sweet creature, and I have spent much time in searching for them, but still without success.

"It is, I fear, as sorrowful a tale as that which Uma no Kami has told you. I, unfaithful, thought that I was not missed; and she, still loved, was in no better case than one whose love is not returned. I indeed am fast forgetting her; but she, it may be, cannot put me out of her mind and I fear there may be nights when thoughts that she would gladly banish burn fiercely in her breast; for now I fancy she must be living a comfortless and unprotected life."

"When all is said and done," said Uma no Kami, "my friend, though I pine for her now that she is gone, was a sad plague to me while I had her, and we must own that such a one will in the end be sure to make us wish ourselves well rid of her. The zithern-player had much talent to her credit, but was a great deal too light-headed. And your diffident lady, To no Chujo, seems to me to be a very suspicious case. The world appears to be so constructed that we shall in the end be always at a loss to make a reasoned choice; despite all our picking, sifting and comparing we shall never succeed in finding this in all ways and to all lengths adorable and impeccable female."

"I can only suggest the Goddess Kichijo,"[4] said To no Chujo, "and I fear that intimacy with so holy and majestic a being might prove to be impracticable."

At this they all laughed and To no Chujo continued: "But now it is Shikibu's turn and he is sure to give us something entertaining. Come Shikibu, keep the ball rolling!" "Nothing of interest ever happens to humble folk like myself," said Shikibu; but To no Chujo scolded him for keeping them waiting and after reflecting for a while which anecdote would best suit the company, he began: "While I was still a student at the University, I came across a woman who was truly a prodigy of intelligence. One of Uma no Kami's demands she certainly fulfilled, for it was possible to discuss with her to advantage both public matters and the proper handling of one's private affairs. But not only was her mind capable of grappling with any problems of this kind; she was also so learned that ordinary scholars found themselves, to their humiliation, quite unable to hold their own against her.

[4] Goddess of Beauty.

"I was taking lessons from her father, who was a Professor. I had heard that he had several daughters, and some accidental circumstance made it necessary for me to exchange a word or two with one of them who turned out to be the learned prodigy of whom I have spoken. The father, hearing that we had been seen together, came up to me with a winecup in his hand and made an allusion to the poem of The Two Wives.[5] Unfortunately I did not feel the least inclination towards the lady. However I was very civil to her; upon which she began to take an affectionate interest in me and lost no opportunity of displaying her talents by giving me the most elaborate advice how best I might advance my position in the world. She sent me marvellous letters written in a very far-fetched epistolary style and entirely in Chinese characters; in return for which I felt bound to visit her, and by making her my teacher I managed to learn how to write Chinese poems. They were wretched, knock-kneed affairs, but I am still grateful to her for it. She was not however at all the sort of woman whom I should have cared to have as a wife, for though there may be certain disadvantages in marrying a complete dolt, it is even worse to marry a blue-stocking. Still less do princes like you and Genji require so huge a stock of intellect and erudition for your support! Let her but be one to whom the *karma* of our past lives draws us in natural sympathy, what matter if now and again her ignorance distresses us? Come to that, even men seem to me to get along very well without much learning."

Here he stopped, but Genji and the rest, wishing to hear the end of the story, cried out that for their part they found her a most interesting woman. Shikibu protested that he did not wish to go on with the story, but at last after much coaxing, pulling a comical wry face he continued: "I had not seen her for a long time. When at last some accident took me to the house, she did not receive me with her usual informality but spoke to me from behind a tiresome screen. Ha, Ha, thought I foolishly, she is sulking; now is the time to have a scene and break with her. I might have known that she was not so little of a philosopher as to sulk about trifles; she

[5] A poem by Po Chü-i pointing out the advantages of marrying a poor wife.

prided herself on knowing the ways of the world and my inconstancy did not in the least disturb her.

"She told me (speaking without the slightest tremor) that having had a bad cold for some weeks she had taken a strong garlic-cordial, which had made her breath smell rather unpleasant and that for this reason she could not come very close to me. But if I had any matter of special importance to discuss with her she was quite prepared to give me her attention. All this she had expressed with solemn literary perfection. I could think of no suitable reply, and with an 'at your service' I rose to go. Then, feeling that the interview had not been quite a success, she added, raising her voice, 'Please come again when my breath has lost its smell.' I could not pretend I had not heard. I had however no intention of prolonging my visit, particularly as the odour was now becoming definitely unpleasant, and looking cross I recited the acrostic, 'On this night marked by the strange behaviour of the spider, how foolish to bid me come back tomorrow,'[6] and calling over my shoulder, 'There is no excuse for you!' I ran out of the room. But she, following me, 'If night by night and every night we met, in daytime too I should grow bold to meet you face to face.' Here in the second sentence she had cleverly concealed the meaning, 'If I had had any reason to expect you, I should not have eaten garlic.' "

"What a revolting story!" cried the young princes, and then, laughing, "He must have invented it." Such a woman is quite incredible; it must have been some sort of ogress. You have shocked us, Shikibu!" and they looked at him with disapproval. "You must try to tell us a better story than that." "I do not see how any story could be better," said Shikibu, and left the room.

"There is a tendency among men as well as women," said Uma no Kami, "so soon as they have acquired a little knowledge of some kind, to want to display it to the best advantage. To have mastered all the difficulties in the Three Histories and Five Classics is no road to amiability. But even a woman cannot afford to lack all knowledge of public and private affairs. Her best way will be without regular study to

---

[6] There is a reference to an old poem which says: 'I know that tonight my lover will come to me. The spider's antics prove it clearly.' Omens were drawn from the behaviour of spiders.

pick up a little here and a little there, merely by keeping her eyes and ears open. Then, if she has her wits at all about her, she will soon find that she has amassed a surprising store of information. Let her be content with this and not insist upon cramming her letters with Chinese characters which do not at all accord with her feminine style of composition, and will make the recipient exclaim in despair, 'If only she could contrive to be a little less mannish!' And many of these characters, to which she intended the colloquial pronunciation to be given, are certain to be read as Chinese, and this will give the whole composition an even more pedantic sound than it deserves. Even among our ladies of rank and fashion there are many of this sort, and there are others who, wishing to master the art of verse-making, in the end allow it to master them, and, slaves to poetry, cannot resist the temptation, however urgent the business they are about or however inappropriate the time, to make use of some happy allusion which has occurred to them, but must needs fly to their desks and work it up into a poem. On festival days such a woman is very troublesome. For example on the morning of the Iris Festival, when everyone is busy making ready to go to the temple, she will worry them by stringing together all the old tags about the 'matchless root';[7] or on the 9th day of the 9th month, when everyone is busy thinking out some difficult Chinese poem to fit the rhymes which have been prescribed, she begins making metaphors about the 'dew on the chrysanthemums,' thus diverting our attention from the far more important business which is in hand. At another time we might have found these compositions quite delightful; but by thrusting them upon our notice at inconvenient moments, when we cannot give them proper attention, she makes them seem worse than they really are. For in all matters we shall best commend ourselves if we study men's faces to read in them the 'Why so?' or the 'As you will' and do not, regardless of times and circumstances, demand an interest and sympathy that they have not leisure to give.

"Sometimes indeed a woman should even pretend to know less than she knows, or say only a part of what she would like to say . . ."

---

[7] The irises used for the Tango festival (5th day of 5th month) had to have nine flowers growing on a root.

All this while Genji, though he had sometimes joined in the conversation, had in his heart of hearts been thinking of one person only, and the more he thought the less could he find a single trace of those shortcomings and excesses which, so his friends had declared, were common to all women. "There is no one like her," he thought, and his heart was very full. The conversation indeed had not brought them to a definite conclusion, but it had led to many curious anecdotes and reflections. So they passed the night, and at last, for a wonder, the weather had improved. After this long residence at the Palace Genji knew he would be expected at the Great Hall and set out at once. There was in Princess Aoi's air and dress a dignified precision which had something in it even of stiffness; and in the very act of reflecting that she, above all women, was the type of that single-hearted and devoted wife whom (as his friends had said last night) no sensible man would lightly offend, he found himself oppressed by the very perfection of her beauty, which seemed only to make all intimacy with her the more impossible. . . .

—Translated by Arthur Waley

KAMAKURA PERIOD

1185–1333

It might not be too wild a generalization to say that the Kamakura period developed as the antithesis of the Heian. While the Heian was steeped in peace and tranquility, the Kamakura was ruled by a military government and embroiled in constant feudal warfare. The gracious—although sometimes petty—imperial court life of Kyoto gave way to bloody battles between the mighty Taira and Minamoto clans, which eventually led to the establishment of a military regime centered in Kamakura, while emperors continued on in Kyoto as no more than puppet figures. Where the Heian was entranced by all that was beautiful and refined ("utterly effeminate," a Western historian called it), the Kamakura became brash and masculine.

This is not to say that all esthetic norms of the previous period were violated over night. To the contrary, they exercised considerable softening influence, with the result that even the accounts of war and destruction were marked by a gentle sense of regret for the impermanency of life and the limited careers of the mighty.

Nevertheless, the Heian setting that had provided a modicum of dignity, respect for human rights, and literary latitude for women was changed to one that emphasized those values based on practical affairs and military power. Diaries and the poetry of courtship, in which women were preeminent, were superseded by heroic tales of battle and by the Buddhist-motivated Nō dramas in which spirits of the war dead returned to recount their sufferings and to seek release through expiation of their sins. Male actors took the roles of sorrowing women or women who returned from the next world possessed of evil spirits that must be expunged by highly formalized ritual.

Gradually the literary genre in which women had become supreme gave way to other art forms—especially the Nō dramas, which were composed for and attended by high-ranking warriors, and, in later eras, the Bunraku puppet theater and Kabuki, the latter originated by a woman dancer of the sixteenth century but later taken over by male writers and all-male casts of actors. The Heian dominance of women writers in Japanese prose fiction was over.

The Confessions of Lady Nijo

These somewhat disjointed but disarmingly frank memoirs of a lady of the imperial court of thirteenth-century Japan came to light only as recently at 1940 and, due to World War II, remained unpublished until 1950. Since their publication and subsequent translation into English, these jottings covering a thirty-six year span (1271–1306) have played a leading role in extending the literary heritage of Japanese women diarists who were preeminent during the Heian period.

The writer's true name is unknown. According to court custom of early Japan in which ladies were designated by a tree or shrub or the locale of residence, this lady was called by the name of the street on which she lived. Nijō—or "second avenue"—would indicate her position of special preference.

We now know that Lady Nijō was first brought into the court at the age of four, following the death of her mother, to be raised as a foster child of GoFukakusa, son of the Emperor GoSaga. When fourteen, with her father's consent, she became her benefactor's mistress. (Almost identical is the story of Murasaki and Prince Genji in *The Tale of Genji*.)

As is evident from the diary, Lady Nijō's relationship to the imperial heir, however, did not preclude her enjoyment of other liaisons.

———————

The diary opens in the year 1271, the year in which Lady Nijō was taken as a lover by GoFukakusa, then retired as emperor at age twenty-nine. Completely unprepared for the change in her palace status, the fourteen-year-old foster child becomes a concubine in a flood of tears and misery, which with time and continued intimacy gradually gives way to acceptance and ultimately affection. She sees as rivals, then, the Empress Higashi-Nijō ("east second avenue"), GoFukakusa's official consort (who was also his aunt and eleven years his elder), and the other ladies whom she herself must often escort to him.

The first selection given here details the disappointing birth of a girl to the Empress consort, Lady Nijō's chief rival.

(1271–72)

In the eighth month of the same year Empress Higashi-Nijō went into confinement in the Corner Mansion. She was somewhat advanced in years and had suffered complications in her earlier deliveries, so there was widespread fear for her condition. Priests performed every possible esoteric rite for her benefit, offering prayers to the Seven Healing Buddhas, the Five Great Guardian Kings, Fugen Bodhisattva, Kongō Dōji, and Aizen-ō. The altar for the Guardian King Gundari was customarily provided by my family's province of Owari; but to show special deference on this occasion, my father also arranged for the prayers to Kongō Dōji. The high priest of the Jōjū Temple served as exorcist.

Shortly after the twentieth there was great excitement over the report that Her Highness was going into labor. We expected the baby to come at any moment, but after two or three days had passed with no results, we grew alarmed and sent word of her condition to His Majesty. When he arrived and saw how weak she was, he ordered the exorcist closer, until he was only separated from Her Highness by a portable curtain. GoFukakusa then called over the abbot of the Ninna Temple from where he was conducting the rites to Aizen-ō and asked him to come inside the curtain to discuss what could be done in view of her apparently hopeless condition.

The abbot said, "The Buddhas and Bodhisattvas have promised that even predetermined fate can be changed. You need not fear for her." He then began his invocations while the exorcist hung a picture of Fudō[1]—it was, I think, the same image that Shōkū had prayed to—before Her Highness and chanted, "He who serves Fudō will have the virtues of a Buddha; he who utters a single secret incantation will have Fudō's protection forever." The abbot fingered his rosary and prayed, "Long ago in my youth my nights were filled with prayer and meditation, and now, in my maturity, my days are spent in strict ascetic practices. Am I then to receive no divine sympathy or aid?"

At signs that the child was about to be born, the prayers grew so fervent they seemed to rise like billows of smoke. The court ladies handed unlined gowns and raw silk gowns under the blinds to the attendants, who presented them to the courtiers. Then imperial guards passed them to the priests reciting the sutras. At the foot of the stairs sat the nobles, hoping the child would be a boy. The masters of divination had set up offeratory tables in the garden and were repeating the purification rite a thousand times. Courtiers passed the purified articles to the ladies, who thrust their sleeves under the blinds to receive them. At the same time royal attendants and junior imperial guards were bringing out the offeratory horses for His Majesty to inspect before they were distributed to the twenty-one shrines. No woman could hope for a more auspicious set of circumstances.

One of the head priests was ordered to chant the *Sutra of the Healing Buddha* with the assistance of three other priests chosen for their fine voices. He had just reached the part that says, "Those who see it are glad," when the baby was born. Amid the clamor of congratulations a rice kettle was rolled down the north side of the roof to indicate it was a girl. Though His Majesty was disappointed, he saw to it that the exorcists received the customary number of gifts.

Cloistered Emperor GoSaga made a great fuss over his new grandchild, even though she was a girl, and the festivities on the fifth and seventh nights after her birth were unusually fine. . . .

---

[1] Fudō: a popular Buddhist deity, reincarnation of the God of Wisdom and a queller of evil spirits.

In contrast, a few months later, Lady Nijō presents GoFukakusa with a son.

(1273–74)

Toward evening on the tenth day of the second month there were signs that my labor was beginning. It was not an auspicious time. GoFukakusa was troubled, and I had worries of my own, although Takaaki[2] had been taking good care of me, and GoFukakusa had already instructed the abbot of the Ninna Temple to perform a service to Aizen-ō, the God of Love, in the main hall. Prayers were also offered to Fugen Bodhisattva at Narutaki, and the high priest of the Bishamon Temple conducted a service to the Healing Buddha. These were all formal services conducted in the main halls of the temples. In my own quarters the high priest Shingen performed an informal service to Shokannon, the goddess of mercy, and the high priest Dōchō, who had just returned from a mountain retreat, came to pay his respects and told me how well he could recall my father's great concern for my welfare.

After midnight I went into painful heavy labor. My aunt, Lady Kyōgoku, who had come as GoFukakusa's representative, merely added to the confusion. Takachika[3] was also present; but tears came to my eyes when I thought of how matters would have been handled if my father were alive. Leaning back against someone, I dozed off and dreamed that my father, looking as he always had, was standing directly behind me with a worried air. It was not long after this that the birth of an imperial prince was announced. I was amazed that the baby had been delivered safely, and I now began to worry about the results of my misconduct and felt, as though for the first time, the full force of my acts. Without any fanfare GoFukakusa sent a sword to his son, and Takaaki distributed unpretentious gifts to all the exorcists.

I longed for the past. I longed to be back at Father's house in Kawasaki. Such thoughts filled my mind as I watched Takaaki hurry off to present clothes to the wet nurse while bowstrings were twanged to ward off evil spirits. From this point on a seemingly endless round of ceremonies took place,

---

[2] Lady Nijō's uncle and confidant.
[3] Lady Nijō's maternal grandfather.

and the entire year passed quickly, as though it were but a dream. . . .

In the first month of her eighteenth year the Lady Nijō writes of a New Year ceremony in which women are beaten about the loins to assist in their bearing male children.

On the day of the Full-Moon Gruel Ceremony, events occurred that were almost more than we women could bear: Not only did His Majesty beat us severely, but he then summoned his attendants and had them strike us too. This annoyed me, and so I connived with Lady Genki to retaliate on the eighteenth by beating His Majesty in return. On that morning, while GoFukakusa was finishing his breakfast, we assembled the ladies in the tray room and assigned each of them to a station. The ladies Shindainagon and Gonchūnagon were placed at the door to the imperial bathing room; Bettō and Kugo remained outside; Chūnagon went to His Majesty's living room; and Mashimizu was stationed in the corridor. Lady Genki and I stood chatting in one of the end rooms.

"His Majesty is certain to come in here, isn't he?" she asked nervously. Then, just as we had expected, he entered the room, dressed informally in wide-legged trousers. His Majesty was blissfully unaware of what was about to happen.

"What's this? There doesn't seem to be anyone in my room. Is anybody here?" At this moment Lady Genki seized him. "Oh, that hurts. Is nobody here? Someone help!" he called, but no one came.

Morotada was immediately outside the room and made an effort to come to GoFukakusa's aid, but Mashimizu, who was standing guard in the corridor, told him that we were busy and that he would not be allowed in. Seeing that she was armed with a stick, he turned and fled.

While this was going on I beat His Majesty so soundly that he apologized profusely and made a solemn vow: "Never again will I order others to strike you."

I was still congratulating myself on our success when, later in the day, the nobles arrived at GoFukakusa's quarters to be in attendance for the evening meal. He spoke to them at once: "This year I am thirty-three, but judging from today's misfortune it might well be an inauspicious year.[4] Something

---

[4] Generally the twenty-fifth and forty-second would be unlucky, not the thirty-third.

terrible has happened to me. I accumulated such great virtue in former lives that I was reborn to be master of all things, and yet someone has dared to beat me with a stick. I can't imagine such a thing has ever happened before. Why is it none of you noticed what was going on? Were you all in it together?" Being scolded in those terms, each man attempted to make excuses for himself.

Morotada, Michiyori, Takaaki, Sanekane, and Morochika were all of the same opinion: "The offense of striking Your Majesty, even though it was perpetrated by a court lady, cannot be dismissed lightly. In former times not even persons hostile to the court and emperor would have committed such an outrageous act. We would not even dream of stepping on Your Majesty's shadow. The actual striking of Your Majesty with a stick is a gross violation of decency and cannot be ignored."

As usual, Takaaki felt the need to distinguish himself by speaking out. "What is the name of the guilty court lady?" he asked. "When we have this information we shall be able to decide together on a condign punishment."

"I don't think the lady ought to be punished singly. Shouldn't her relatives share the burden of responsibility?" His Majesty asked.

"They should indeed," was the reply. "All her near relations should be punished." On this everyone was agreed.

"The person who actually struck me was the daughter of Masatada, the granddaughter of Takachika, and the niece of Lord Takaaki. It is my understanding that you, Takaaki, have been acting as her foster father, and I would assume from this that it is only fair to call her your daughter. This affair being the work of Lady Nijō, shouldn't you be held more responsible than anyone else?" When GoFukakusa made this pronouncement, the nobles in attendance roared with laughter.

Someone said, "It would be too much of a nuisance to banish a court lady at the beginning of the year, and accusing all of her relatives would be even more tiresome. Why not take advantage of precedent and demand immediate reparations?"

In the midst of the clamor I spoke up. "I never looked for this to happen. On the fifteenth of this month His Majesty

not only belabored us severely himself but called in nobles
and courtiers to assist him. Deplorable as it was, there
seemed to be nothing an insignificant person like myself
could do about it—until, that is, Lady Genki suggested that I
join her in an attempt at revenge. I agreed to help, and I
struck His Majesty. But I should not be the only one found
guilty."

"What you say may indeed be true," I was told, "but the
person who actually wielded the stick against His Majesty is
by far the guiltiest." They decided on reparations.

Takaaki went to report what had happened to Lord Takachika, his father. "What a stupid trick!" Takachika said.
"We had better make amends immediately. It won't do to
delay." He urged Takaaki to expedite the preparations.

On the twentieth Takachika came to the palace bringing
elaborate gifts: a court robe, ten light green small-sleeved
gowns, and a sword for GoFukakusa; a sword each for
Morotada and five other ranking nobles; and one hundred
sheaves of fine mulberry paper for the court ladies. Takaaki
arrived on the twenty-first with more ordinary gifts. He
presented GoFukakusa with a miniature *koto* and a tiny
biwa[5] fashioned out of purple brocade, and with a lapis la-
zuli *sake* cup in a silver box. For the nobles he brought horses
and oxen, and for the court ladies, ten baskets made from
dyed silk each containing balls of silk thread made to
resemble melons. . . .

*After the palace New Year's festivities of 1284, Lady Nijō
suffers months of despondency following the secret birth of a
"love child." In the autumn months of that year there is an
unexpected turn of events.*

In early autumn I received a letter from my grandfather,
Lord Takachika, which said: "Prepare to leave the palace
permanently. I'll send for you tonight." Unable to comprehend this, I took it to His Majesty and asked him to explain,
only to be turned away without a reply.

Next I went to Lady Genki (I think she was called Lady
Sammi at that time) and told her of my bewilderment. "I
can't understand what is happening. I received this letter and

---

[5] *Koto*: a harp-like instrument, but played in a horizontal position;
biwa: similar to the mandolin.

asked His Majesty about it, but he wouldn't answer me," I said. She replied that she did not know either.

It appeared I would have to leave. As I made ready for my departure, I recalled coming to the palace for the first time in the ninth month of the year I was four. Ever since that time I had felt a certain uneasiness about being away from the palace even briefly, so I could not accept the fact that today was really the end. I stared at even the trees and grasses in the garden until tears blurred my vision.

I was told that Akebono[6] had arrived and asked where I was. Beside myself with anxiety, I went out to see him, my tear-spotted sleeves showing evidence of my weeping.

He wanted to know what the matter was, and for a silent moment I thought, "Even consolation brings pain." Then I handed him the letter I had received that morning. All I said was, "This is what makes me sad." I admitted him to my room and burst into tears. He too was at a loss to explain it, for it seemed no one could understand this business.

Several of the older court ladies came around to offer their sympathy, but being ignorant of the truth behind the situation I could only weep. That evening I was embarrassed to appear before His Majesty, knowing that it had to be his will that I leave; yet I had no idea what lay ahead, and I longed to see him once again, perhaps for the last time. I was trembling when I entered his quarters, where several nobles were chatting together. My costume was a red formal jacket worn over a raw silk gown with a design of vines and grasses embroidered on it in green thread.

GoFukakusa glanced at me. "Are you leaving this evening?" he asked. I stood there, unable to frame a reply, and he continued, "Perhaps I'll receive word of you through some mountain hermit. The green vines must be unhappy."[7] As he mumbled this he stood up and left, probably to go to Empress Higashi-Nijō's apartments.

Curiously, I felt no bitterness at his abrupt departure, yet I did not fully comprehend what had brought it about. Our relationship was of many years' standing, and he had frequently assured me that his personal feelings would never cause us to be separated. I felt an impulse to vanish from this

---

[6] Akebono was a high court official and one of Lady Nijō's lovers.
[7] A reference to the design on her gown.

world at once; but in vain, for a carriage awaited me. On the one hand I wanted nothing more than to run away and hide myself, but on the other, I was curious to learn what had happened. So I proceeded to Lord Takachika's mansion in the Second Ward.

Takachika greeted me himself. He said, "Old age has come upon me like an incurable disease, and lately my health has become so bad that I have little hope of surviving long. Yet still I have to worry about you. Your father is not alive and Takaaki is no longer here to care for you. All the worry has fallen on my shoulders, and now because of this letter from Empress Higashi-Nijō, I have been forced to withdraw you from the palace."

He held out the letter for me to read: "I am displeased by her persistent involvement with His Majesty and her slights to me. You will recall her to your house at once and keep her there. Her mother is dead so you will have to make plans for her." The entire letter was written in the empress's own hand.

It would have been impossible for me to remain at the palace under such circumstances, and once I was completely away from it I experienced a sense of relief. Yet as I lay awake through the gradually lengthening nights listening to the sounds of wooden mallets beating silk, it seemed that they were echoing near my pillow to inquire after me. And sometimes I imagined that the wild geese winging through the cloudy sky had chosen the ivy around my worry-filled house to shed their tears on.

The days and nights passed slowly until the year drew to its close. Since I could play no part in any of the activities ushering the old year out and the new year in, I decided to fulfill my long-standing desire to make a one-thousand-day retreat at the Gion Shrine. Before, there had always been too many hindrances, but now, on the second day of the eleventh month (the first day of the hare), I set off, going first to the Hachiman Shrine to see the *kagura* dances. I remembered the poet who had written "I never cease to give my heart to the gods," and I composed this poem:

> Depend on the gods, I hang
> My hopes on them—a sash
> Of mulberry bark—in vain;
> I loathe my useless self.

After a seven-day retreat at the Hachiman Shrine I went on to
Gion. With no further reason to remain in the world, I now
prayed to be led from this human realm through the gates of
enlightenment. . . .

*The memoirs are dropped abruptly at the end of 1285 and not
resumed until four years later. Presumably, life in isolated retirement from the court offered little to write about. But early
in 1289, Lady Nijō begins a new life of quiet adventure, following the only acceptable recourse by which a highborn woman
might explore the world about her—to go on pilgrimage from
one Buddhist shrine to another as an itinerant "nun," ostensibly renouncing the world of the flesh, of the misguided
senses.*

Toward the end of the second month I set out from the
capital at moonrise. I had given up my home completely, yet
my thoughts quite naturally lingered on the possibility of return, and I felt that the moon reflected in my fallen tears was
also weeping. How weak-willed I was! These thoughts occupied my mind all the way to Ōsaka Pass, the place where the
poet Semimaru once lived and composed the poem that ends,
"One cannot live forever in a palace or a hut." No trace of
his home remained. I gazed at my reflection in the famous
clear spring at the pass and saw a pathetic image of myself
attired down to the tips of my walking shoes in this unfamiliar traveling nun's habit. As I paused to rest, my glance was
caught by a cherry tree so heavy with blossoms that I could
hardly take my eyes from it. Nearby four or five well-dressed
local people on horseback were also resting. Did they share
my feelings?

Its blossoms detaining travelers
The cherry tree guards the pass
On Ōsaka Mountain.

I composed this poem as I continued on to the way station
known as Mirror Lodge, where at dusk I saw prostitutes seeking companions for the night and realized that this too
formed part of life. Next morning, awakened by a bell at
dawn, I set out once more. . . .

I had left the capital late in the second month intending to push myself hard on my journeys, yet I was so unused to traveling that my progress was slow. Now the third month had already begun. A bright moon rose early, flooding the night sky just as it did in the capital, and once again His Majesty's image floated through my mind. Within the sacred precincts of the Atsuta Shrine cherry trees bloomed in rich profusion. For whom were they putting on this brilliant display?

> Blossoms glow against spring sky
> Near Narumi Lagoon,
> How long now before
> Petals scatter among pines.

I wrote this on a slip of paper and tied it to the branch of a cryptomeria tree in front of the shrine.

For a week I remained in prayer at the shrine before resuming my travels. . . .

Late that month I arrived at the island of E no Shima, a fascinating place that is not easy to describe. It is separated from the mainland by a stretch of sea, and has many grottoes, in one of which I found shelter with a pious mountain ascetic who had been practicing austerities for many years. Senju Grotto, as it was called, was a humble yet charming dwelling, with fog for a fence and bamboo trees for screens. The ascetic made me feel welcome and presented me with some shells of the area, whereupon I opened the basket my companion[8] carried, took out a fan from the capital, and offered it to him.

"Living here as I do, I never hear news from the capital," he said. "Certainly things like this aren't brought to me by the wind. Tonight I feel as though I've met a friend from the distant past." My own feelings quite agreed.

It was quiet with no one around and no special event taking place, yet I could not sleep a wink that night. I lay upon my mattress of moss brooding on the great distance I had traveled and the cloak of worries that covered me, and I wept

---

[8] According to custom, Lady Nijō would have had a servant as traveling companion.

quietly into my sleeve. Then I decided to go outside and look around. The horizon was lost in a haze that might have been clouds, waves, or mist; but the night sky high above was clear, and the brilliant moon hung motionless. I felt as though I had actually journeyed two thousand *li*. From the hills behind the grotto I heard the heart-rending cries of monkeys and felt an anguish so intense it seemed new. I had undertaken this solitary journey with only my thoughts and my grief in hopes that it would dry my tears. How distressing to have come so far and yet to have the worries of the world still cling to me.

> A roof of cedar branches,
> Pine pillars, bambo blinds,
> If only these could screen me
> From this world of sorrow.

Toward the middle of the second month [1290], I decided to set out for Zenkō Temple. The Usui Pass and the Maroki Bridge on the Kiso plank road were dangerous even to set foot on. I had hoped to pause along the way and visit famous places, but I fell in with a group of travelers and allowed myself to be swept along without stopping. Later, when the other travelers were ready to leave Zenkō Temple, I explained that I was bound by a pledge and would remain there in retreat for a time. They were concerned about my staying on alone, but I was firm: "Who can accompany me on that final journey through the afterworld? I entered this life alone; I shall leave it alone. People who meet must part; things that are born must die. No matter how beautiful the plum blossoms, in the end they return to the ground. No matter how many tints the autumn leaves reveal, once the wind rises they do not last long." I remained there alone.

The temple was not in a scenic area, but it was noted for its famous image of Amida Buddha, whose power I had such faith in that I devoted much of my time to reciting invocations to it. In the area there lived a man from Takaoka known as the Iwami lay priest, who was said to be a most hospitable person. Some ascetics and nuns I had become acquainted with told me about the poetry and music parties at his house, and invited me to attend one with them. I went and discovered an impressive house superior to anything else in this countrified place. It was comforting to have people to talk with, and I remained there until autumn.

Early in the eighth month I decided I had lingered long enough. I wanted to go back to Musashino to view the autumn scenery, and so I headed for the temple of Asakusa, which intrigued me because of its eleven-faced Kannon renowned for its miraculous efficacy. To get there I had to pass through vast fields so densely covered with bush clover, *ominaeshi*, reeds, and pampas grass that no other plants were able to grow in them. The height of the grasses was such that a man on horseback could pass through unseen. For three days I pressed on through the fields without reaching my destination. Traveling accommodations could be found on small side roads, but otherwise there was only the plain stretching far into the distance behind and before me. . . .

The moon, having risen from the fields of grass, climbed higher as the night deepened, and the dew on the tips of the grasses sparkled like jewels.

> Once I viewed it from the palace,
> The moon which on this night
> Forces memories to return.

My eyes filled with tears.

> Gazing at the brilliant moon
> As it sails through cloudless skies
> Could I forget his face?

It was reckless to remain in the open fields, so at daybreak I returned to my lodgings.

Later, when as nearly as I could tell I was in the vicinity of the Sumida River, I came to a large bridge similar to those at Kiyomizu and Gion in the capital. Crossing the bridge, I met two well-dressed men and inquired of them, "Where is the Sumida River? Isn't it in this area?"

"This is the Sumida River," they replied, "and you are on the Suda Bridge. Once there was no bridge here, but crossing by ferry became such a nuisance that this bridge was built. The proper name for the river is Sumida, though in the local dialect this is called the Suda River Bridge. A long time ago

on the far side of the river there was a village named Miyo-
shino (which means good plain), where the rice harvest was
always barren. The governor of the province believed the
name of the village was responsible. After the name was
changed to Yoshida (good rice paddies), the harvests were
large and fruitful."

I recalled how Narihira[9] had put a question to a capital
bird here, but I did not see any birds at all. . . .

(1291)

In the second month of the following year I visited the
Iwashimizu Hachiman Shrine on my way back to the capital.
It was a long journey from Nara to Iwashimizu, and the sun
was setting when I arrived and began to climb the Inohana
trail leading to the inner garden. Among the pilgrims on the
road was a dwarf from Iwami province. Talk centered on his
deformity; no one could imagine what kind of karma might
have caused it. I noticed in passing that the residence facing
the riding ground was open. That was where members of the
imperial family stayed when visiting the shrine, but it was also
open when the supervising priest was in residence. No one
along the road had mentioned an imperial visit, and that was
the farthest thing from my mind as we passed by. I was
climbing up to the shrine itself when a man who seemed to be
an imperial messenger approached and told me to go to the
residence facing the riding ground. I asked him, "Who is staying there? Do you really know who I am? Certainly the message cannot be meant for me. Are you sure it is not for that
dwarf?"

"No, I'm quite certain there's been no mistake. The summons is for you. Retired Emperor GoFukakusa has been here
since yesterday."

I was dumbfounded. In all these months I had never forgotten him, but when I committed myself to a new way of
life and took my leave from Lady Kyōgoku's apartments, I
thought I would never see him again in this world. Besides, I
had no idea anyone could recognize me now, dressed in
these humble clothes that had been through frost and snow
and hail. Indeed, I wondered who had spotted me. It was unlikely to have been His Majesty, but perhaps one of the ladies

---

[9] Narihira was hero of the ninth-century *Tales of Ise.*

thought she recognized me and was even now wondering if she had made a mistake. I stood there in bewilderment until a junior imperial guardsman came to hurry me along. There was no opportunity to flee as they led me to an entrance on the north side of the building.

"Come inside where you won't be so conspicuous. Come on." It was His Majesty's voice, unchanged, speaking directly from the past. I did not know what he wanted, and my heart was so agitated that I was unable to move at all. "Hurry up, hurry up!" he urged. Hesitantly, I entered.

"I recognized you easily," he said. "You must realize that even though many months have passed, I have never forgotten you." He began talking of events past and present and of his weariness with this constantly changing world. We stayed up the entire night, until all too soon the sky began to brighten. "I must complete the religious retreat I have begun," he said. "We can have a more leisurely meeting another time." Before leaving he took off the three small-sleeved gowns he was wearing next to his skin and presented them to me. "Don't let anyone know of these keepsakes, yet keep them with you always." At that I forgot completely the past, the future, and the darkness of worlds yet to come. My heart filled with an inexpressible agony as the dawn brightened inexorably. His Majesty murmured goodbye, and I gazed fondly after him as he retired to an inner room. His presence lingered in the fragrance of his scent still clinging to my black robes. The gowns he had given me were so conspicuous they would certainly attract attention. I would have to wear them under my own dark robes, awkward though that was.

> To wear your gowns—
> Love tokens from the distant past,
> Now tears stain dark sleeves.

It seemed a dream within a dream as I departed with his image futilely contained in the tears on my sleeves. We had at least met this once, but I doubted that the opportunity for another quiet tryst would ever come. My wretched appearance must have shocked His Majesty; perhaps he even regretted having called me. To remain here brazenly as though awaiting another summons would have been much too indelicate. And so I prepared to set out for the capital, suppressing my emotions by lecturing my heart.

Before actually leaving, however, I wanted to observe for one last time—now as an outsider—His Majesty make the rounds of the shrine. Fearing that I might attract his attention in my nun's habit, I decided to put on the gowns he had given me over my own robes. Then I mingled with a group of court ladies to watch. Garbed now in priestly robes, His Majesty looked utterly different from how he had appeared in the past, and the change affected me deeply. When he began to ascend the steps to the shrine, Middle Counselor Suketaka, who was at that time still only an imperial adviser and chamberlain, took His Majesty's arm and helped him up. Last night His Majesty had remarked that our similar attire made him feel nostalgic, and he had recalled events going back as far as my childhood. His words still echoed in my ears, and his image shimmered in my tears as I descended the holy mountain. Even after I had turned north toward the capital, I felt as though part of me had remained behind on the mountain. . . .

After spending a week in quiet retreat at the inner shrine [of Atsuta], I inquired about the possibilities of a trip to Futami Beach, wanting to visit that place that had so attracted the goddess.[10] A priest named Munenobu offered to be my guide, and we set off together. We viewed the beach where pilgrims purify themselves, the strand of pine behind it, and a rock said to have been split in two by lightning, and then proceeded down the beach to the Sabi no Myōjin Shrine, where we boarded a boat for a tour of the island of Tateshi, Gozen, and Tōru. . . .

A sacred mirror made by a god to reflect the image of the sun goddess was enshrined at Koasakuma. It is said that it was once stolen and dropped into deep water. When it was recovered and presented at the shrine, the goddess spoke through an oracle: "I have vowed to save all living things—even the fishes in the boundless sea." Then, by its own power, the mirror vanished from the shrine and reappeared on the top of a

---

[10] The goddess Yamatohme was so enchanted by the beauty of Futami Beach that she returned for another look.

rock, beside which grew a lone cherry tree. At high tide the
mirror lodged in the top of the tree; at low tide it remained
on the rock. This illustration of the vow of universal salvation
filled me with great hope and made me decide to remain
quietly in this vicinity for several more days. . . .

Somehow word of my visit to the shore reached GoFukakusa's palace, most likely through a serving girl named Terut-
suki, who was related to someone at the shrine headquarters.
When an unexpected letter came, I presumed it was from a
lady I knew at the palace, yet I felt a strange sensation upon
opening it. "Now that you are making friends with the moon
at Futami, I suppose you've forgotten me completely. I'd like
to talk with you again, as we did so unexpectedly that night."
The letter transmitted His Majesty's sentiments at some
length. Unable to trust my own feelings, I sent this poem in
reply:

> Though I live elsewhere,
> Could I ever forget
> The clear moon shining down
> On that familiar palace?

There was no purpose in my staying longer, so I returned
to the outer shrine for a brief visit before heading back to Atsuta to finish my sutra copying. . . ."[11]

*The next diary entry (which may have been in the following
year, or perhaps in 1293) begins dramatically in midthought:
"I knew I would remember until my death that unexpected
meeting with His Majesty at the Iwashimizu Shrine." It goes
on to relate how the writer succumbs to the supplications of
GoFukakusa ("my love-filled, guilt-ridden heart acquiesced")
and joins him at Fushimi palace for a brief night, after which
she is once more wracked by the sorrow of parting.*

Daybreak approached, and I prepared to leave, tears
streaming down my face. His image lay deep within my
heart. GoFukakusa said, "I hope that we can meet again on
another moonlit night in this lifetime, but you persist in placing your hopes for our meeting only after the far distant

---

[11] The copying of sacred texts was a favorite method of gaining merit.

dawn of salvation. What kind of vows are you cherishing? A man is more or less free to travel eastward or even to China, but there are so many hindrances for a traveling woman that I understand it to be impossible. Who have you pledged yourself to as a companion in your renunciation of this world? I still cannot believe it is possible for you to travel alone. What about Iinuma, from whom, as you wrote, you parted over a 'river of tears,' or the man at Kasuga and his hedge of chrysanthemums, or Tsunayoshi and that 'joyous autumn day'? These were surely more than frivolous exchanges. You must have made some deep and lasting pledges. And there must certainly have been others too with whom you have traveled." His Majesty kept at me with questions and remarks of this sort.

At last I replied, "Ever since I left the mist-shrouded palace to wander perplexed in frost-covered places, I have understood the scriptural passage: 'The restless world of unenlightened men is like a burning house,' for I have known no rest even for a single night. The sutras also say, 'Examine your present state to discover your past karma.' I am well aware of the wretchedness of my condition. Bonds that are once severed cannot be retied. I have certainly not met good fortune in this life, even though my Minamoto lineage puts me under the protection of the god Hachiman. When I traveled east for the first time, I went directly to the Tsurugaoka Shrine just to worship him. In this life I think constantly of salvation, petitioning the gods to dissolve my sins that I may be reborn in paradise. . . .

"Sometimes I stay at cloisters; other times I mix with common men. When I find a place where people are sympathetic and compose poetry, I stay for several days, and of course there is no dearth of people who enjoy starting rumors, whether in the capital or in the countryside. I have heard that sometimes, against her better judgment, a nun will get involved with an ascetic or mendicant she happens to meet, but I have never fallen into such a relationship. I spend my idle nights in solitude. If only I had such a relationship even in the capital. If only I had someone to share my bed, it might help ward off the mountain winds on cold and frosty nights. But there is no such person; no one awaits me, and I pass idle days under the blossoms. In the autumn, when leaves turn, the insect voices, weakening as the frost deepens, reflect my own unhappy fate as I spend night after night in travelers' lodgings."

His Majesty continued to press me: "On pilgrimages to holy places I'm sure you keep your vows in purity, but here in the capital, where you have no vows to keep, what is to prevent you from renewing an old friendship?"

"I have not even reached the age of forty yet, and I have no idea what the future holds—though I doubt that I shall have a very long life—but now, as of this very moment, I assure you I have no such relationships, either old or new. If I am lying, may all the works in which I've placed my hope for salvation—the two thousand days of reading the *Lotus Sutra*, the considerable time I have spent copying sutras in my own hand—may all these become but burdens in hell; may all my hopes come to naught; may I never live to see the dawn of Miroku's salvation, but instead remain forever damned to hell."

I could not tell the effect of what I had said, for he remained quiet for a time before replying. Then he said, "The feelings of a person in love are never logical. It is true that after you lost your mother and then your father, I willingly accepted the responsibility of raising you, but things did not go as I had intended, and I felt that our relationship was, after all, only a shallow one. All this time has passed without my realizing how much you cared for me. The Bodhisattva Hachiman first made this known to me when we met on his sacred mountain." As His Majesty spoke, the setting moon slipped behind the ridge of the mountains to the west, and the rays of the rising sun lit up the eastern sky.

I left quickly, feeling the need to be discreet in my nun's garb. As I returned to my lodgings, I wondered if His Majesty's parting words, "We must meet again soon," might not be a promise I would carry with me beyond death. . . .

After a nine-year break in the writing, the memoirs reopen in 1302 with Lady Nijō's admission that she is fulfilling a long-time dream of taking a sea voyage. By then an experienced traveler and a middle-aged woman (forty-four), she sets out to "retrace the travels of Emperor Takakura." One stop provides a unique experience.

On the small island of Taika, not far offshore from the bustling mainland port of Tomo, there was a row of small huts belonging to women who had fled from lives in prostitution. Born into households whose business meant they were fated to be constantly reborn into the six realms, they had been mired deep in the toils of illusion. They would perfume their gowns in hopes of alluring men, and comb their dark hair, wondering on whose pillows it would become disheveled. When night fell they would await lovers, and when day broke, grieve over the separation. I admired them for having renounced that way of life and come here to live in seclusion.

When I inquired about the religious practices they observed and the reasons behind their conversions, one of the nuns spoke up, "I am the leader of the women on this island. Formerly I made my livelihood by assembling girls and selling their charms. We would attempt to lure travelers, rejoicing if they stopped, disconsolate if they rowed on by. We would vow eternal love to complete strangers and encourage drunkenness beneath the blossoms. I was over fifty when some karmic effect suddenly enabled me to shake off the sleep of illusion, give up my old life, and come to this island, where each morning I climb the mountain and gather flowers to offer to the Buddhas of the past, present, and future." Her words filled me with longing.

In a couple of days, when the ship was ready to embark again, the former prostitutes bade me farewell and asked how long before I would be returning to the capital. At their question, it suddenly occurred to me that I might never return there.

> How many days and nights?
> One cannot determine life
> From this dawn to the next.

In 1304, at the age of forty-six, Lady Nijō settles on the outskirts of Kyoto where she can keep in touch with the life of the court, of which she is no longer a part. Here, with a sense of compassion, she learns of the lingering illness and death of her old rival, the Empress Higashi-Nijō. And here she shares in the sorrow that follows the death of GoFukakusa a few months later. In 1306 the "confessions" conclude:

After GoFukakusa's death I had felt as though there were

no one with whom I could share my feelings. Then last year on the eighth day of the third month I held a service in memory of Hitomaro, and on the exact same day of this year I met Empress Yūgi. Amazingly, the jewellike image I had seen in my dream became real.[12] Now I am anxious about the outcome of my long-cherished desire, and I worry lest the faith I have kept these many years prove fruitless. When I attempted to live in lonely seclusion, I felt dissatisfied and set out on pilgrimages modeled after those of Saigyō, whom I have always admired and wanted to emulate. That all my dreams might not prove empty, I have been writing this useless account—though I doubt it will long survive me.

—*Translated by Karen Brazell*

[12] Here Lady Nijō refers to a dream she had had a year or two earlier in which the Empress Yugi had appeared and told her that the reason for her father's lameness in life was caused by a tumor of the hip and not by any moral unworthiness. This lifted a great weight from Lady Nijō's heart.

MODERN PERIOD

1868 to the present

During the centuries between the Kamakura and the modern periods, both men and women participated in the development of the brief poetic forms of *tanka* (31 syllables) and *haiku* (17 syllables), and there were further developments in the short story and the novel. But it was in the dramatic form that most of the new and major literary experiences occurred.

The favorite art forms of the Kamakura period were directed toward the theater. Highly stylized and slow-moving Nō dramas, in which narrative was chanted against an orchestral background, presented other-worldly representations of heroic feats of the past. The dance-dramas became religious experiences for totally male audiences and performed by all-male casts. Nō became the darling of the samurai who felt themselves cleansed and liberated for further battle exploits after a period at the theater. Women were usually represented as mourning wives who sought by their chants and suffering to release their warrior husbands from the sufferings of hell, or restless spirits wandering in an unexpiated condition through the world of the living, or witches possessed by the fox spirit, endangering both the living and the dead by the evil forces they might let loose in the world.

Bunraku, an enchanting form of puppet theater which reached its apogee in the Tokugawa period (1600–1868), provided a very different form of theatrical experience. The most noted dramatist of the time was Chikamatsu Monzaemon (1653–1725), often called the "Shakespeare of

Japan." One of Chikamatsu's favorite themes was that of love suicide in which star-crossed lovers commit suicide together because their relationship cannot be sanctified by marriage. The theme can be seen as an early expression against the strictures of arranged marriage. Women were presented much more favorably in the puppet theater than in the Nō, with many of them active protagonists.

Arising simultaneously with Bunraku was the Kabuki, Japan's most popular and prolific drama. Okuni of Isumo, a Shinto priestess, is generally recognized as the originator of the Kabuki form. According to tradition, Okuni, in a moment of religious exuberance, went beyond the temple with her dances and performed them with some abandon in a dry riverbed in Kyoto. Spectators sitting on the river bank were so entranced that Okuni continued her performances. Eventually, an all-women's theatrical art developed. It survived for some time as such until a blue-stocking shogun saw it as lascivious and issued an edict against it. The performances were then taken over by young men who performed both male and female roles. This, too, became suspect as encouraging homosexuality, and eventually male Kabuki emerged. Kabuki continues in that tradition to this day.

The Muramachi period (1337–1600) was also known as the period of the Warring States. Nō drama continued to rise in popularity, reaching its heights in the plays of Seami, known as the "master of Nō." Certain literary voices, however, were raised in opposition to the increasing militarism. Poet Yoshida Kenko (1283–1350), who had served as a court official, became a Buddhist priest seeking a life apart from the turmoil of his duty. His "Essays in Idleness" echo to some extent the "Pillow Book" of Sei Shōnagon, contemporary of Lady Murasaki in the Heian court.

An anonymously written romance of the period is a semi-historical reflection of life in the court circles of the Emperors Gotoba (1180–1239) and Godaigo (1288–1339), rulers who made last-ditch stands against the rising tides of conflict.[1]

This also was the era in which the first Europeans visited Japan: Portuguese merchants landed on the island of Kyushu in 1542, and never again would Japan be able to seal herself off from the rest of the world as thoroughly as she had done intermittently during earlier periods.

The Modern period in Japan may be measured from the Meiji Restoration (1868), when the nation was wrenched into the mainstream of international life by means of truly revolutionary documents issued by the Emperor Meiji—a Charter Oath and Constitution—that were obviously influenced by Western concepts. A formerly oligarchical government totally bound first by aristocracy and later by the military, now was to be dedicated to administration by "all classes, high and low." The "common people" as well as officials were to be permitted to "pursue their own callings." And the foundations of the divinely ordained imperial rule were to be based on "knowledge [from] throughout the world."

Literature reflected the changes that were taking place both in modes of expression and in subject matter. And in literature there is often a jarring meeting of old and new, as some of the following selections will indicate. Several are excerpts from novels, a form that was launched by Lady Murasaki centuries before it evolved in the West. But the well-constructed short stories are products of Western influence in form, though in content they continued to be distinctively Japanese —from the shopping experience related in "Aguri" to the devoted wife's suicide in "Patriotism."

A writer in *The East*, a bi-monthly journal from Japan, recently observed that "the end of the [second world] war was a turning point in Japanese society as women gained power and men lost it on an unprecedented scale" and predicted that "the modern Murasaki Shikibu will soon arrive." This may be, but the evidence is that it has not yet happened. At least insofar as English translations are concerned, published male writers far outnumber female. Nevertheless, two out of the five stories presented here were written by women, and all the selections give valid insights into the hopes, dreams, disappointments, and struggles of the women of today's Japan.

Enchantress

Enchi Fumiko

Enchi Fumiko (1905–) came of a literary family, her father being a noted scholar of Japanese languages. After a
largely unsuccessful period of writing plays and novels prior
to World War II, Enchi Fumiko experienced a rebirth in the
feminist tradition. Leaving her marriage behind her, she determined to take on writing as a career, cutting herself free
from domination by her husband and by her father's fame.
As a consequence, her story "Hungry Days" received the
Women's Writer's Prize for 1952 and her novel *Woman on a
Slope* won the Noma Literary Prize in 1957. The Women's
Writer's Prize came to her again in 1966 for *The Tale of Na-
mamiko*. "Enchantress" focuses on a theme that has prevailed
in her later work—woman's struggle against the debilitating
inroads of age.

Near the foot of a gentle hill, the road bent in a sweeping
curve then embracing to the right a high, well-wooded embankment, proceeded upward at an easy incline to the high
ground above. Along its other side ran a fence, now wooden,
now concrete, behind which the ground swept down in another, steeper slope, so that the second floors of the houses
beneath the ledge thus formed were barely on a level with the
road. It was as though the sloping road formed a boundary
to what was, for central Tokyo, a comparatively large hilly
area, hemming it off from the dwellings on the lower ground
below. In the remote past, the whole had doubtless formed
one single, sloping side of a small plateau; then a path had
spread across its flank like a sash, and a continuous stream

of men and horses had trodden it down till it became a kind of natural cutting.

The brick wall that shored up the foot of the high bank to a height of over six feet had been built at the beginning of the Meiji Period, when the great group of temples that once occupied the hill had met their ruin and the place had acquired the Western-sounding name of "park." Now, a greenish patina of moss spread in patches over the space between the brick rectangles, stained a dull pink by damp, that formed its surface, and the creepers twined hither and thither. Above it, the sloping ground had kept its shape unexpectedly well, thanks to the dense profusion of vegetation that grew there—a great zelkova tree, its gnarled roots exposed above the insecure-looking red earth of the bank, and an anonymous crowd of shrubs with leaves of every shape and size.

Chigako, who had lived nearby in her childhood, had been familiar with the hill from her earliest days, and after the war she had bought and settled in an old house in the hollow which happened to be empty. By now, she had spent ten years tucked away at the foot of the slope. The gate of the house was on the side farthest from the hill and she lived with her back, as it were, turned to it; however one might lean back to look up at the great zelkova tree on top of the bank, which needed two men's arms to span it, it hid even its topmost branches from the small garden in the hollow. Yet in autumn it would scatter like rain dead leaves which, brush as she might, would continue to pile up in drifts till she grew annoyed with the tree. It was only about a year previously, when she had had the little sweep of ground that went up toward the hill levelled, and built on it an extra room, that she had come to feel any appreciable familiarity with the hill. At the same time, she had had an exit made in the fence facing the hill, but until then the only way in and out of the house had been the side gate that looked down toward the town below.

It was through this gate that her husband, Kanzaki Keisaku, had come home six months after the war's end, repatriated alive only by exceptional luck from the country where he had been working. It was through this same gate that their two daughters—then little girls, but grown up almost before she could realize it—had gone off with their husbands, one to Kyushu and one to America. Whatever happened to the younger girl, who had married first, she had been sure that the older, Kiriko, would live with them even after her marriage, and it was partly with this in mind that she had built herself an extra room. However, just when the room was at last ready, Kiriko left the house without ceremony to accompany her new husband, a doctor, who was going to take a post in a private hospital in California. The daughters, one might have suspected, were only too eager to sever their ties with this depressing house, where they had so long been constrained to live and breathe in the atmosphere of disharmony that surrounded their parents.

They were on the train after seeing their daughter and her husband off on a cargo ship at Yokohama when Chigako, turning to Keisaku at her side, suddenly spoke in a half-whisper.

"I feel as if Kiriko were never coming back to Japan," she said, and felt after she had said it that some small part of the mental barriers that she had so long put up against her husband had broken down. Keisaku, who was a little deaf, had difficulty in catching what she said amidst the sounds of the train. He perceived, even so, the unaccustomed familiarity in his wife's attitude, and turned his steely-grey head toward her.

"Oh no," he said. "Four years or so will soon go."

Having digested what Chigako had said, Keisaku shook his head vigorously and placed his hands on the black umbrella wedged between his knees to adjust its position. His reply had referred to the terms of Kiriko's husband's contract with the hospital in America, not—as Chigako's remark had done—to the spiritual void their daughter's absence would create. Whenever Keisaku and Chigako talked, some small misunderstanding of this kind inevitably arose in every remark. This never troubled Keisaku, but it gave Chigako the same feeling of impatience as when two foreigners ill-versed in each other's languages try to converse. She would try frantically every way of making the conversation go at a better pace, but in practice the misunderstandings only grew worse. Today, however, she herself lacked the heart to try. She was troubled with an idea—that perhaps Kiriko, who throughout her childhood had been witness to the hard, unsentimental way her mother had treated Keisaku, might herself lack the ability to create, in life in a distant land with a new husband, the beauty that comes from the tender, sentimental and humble things.

Just before they reached Tokyo Station, Keisaku put away in his pocket the weekly magazine he had had open before him. His spectacles went with it.

"I'm dropping in at the Mitsukoshi department store now," he said. "Why don't you come?"

"Why Mitsukoshi?"

"It's the exhibition of Chinese ceramics. Tomorrow's the first day—had you forgotten?"

His tone seemed to reproach the dubious look on Chigako's face; his gaze suggested a teacher waiting for a forgetful pupil to remember the right answer.

"Of course, you're displaying something yourself, aren't you?" she said. "The red-and-blue, gourd-shaped Ming vase—the one Arnold, the Occupation man, wanted."

"They're supposed to be putting it in a good place, but it's too risky leaving it to the store people, so I'm going to have a look today before it starts. How about it—why don't you come with me?"

"No thanks." She replied abruptly and turned away.

The vase of which Keisaku was so proud involved an unpleasant memory for her. Though it was a secret shared only by husband and wife, it had separated Chigako even more decisively from Keisaku, with whom she had already found any conversational contact impossible. And the thought that neither Kiriko nor her sister Shinako in Kyushu had any idea of it had made the secret which she managed alone in her own heart still more of a lonely burden.

Keisaku had been in a bank dealing in loans to the colonies, and had spent close on twenty years going around China and the countries of Southeast Asia. Chigako had accompanied him for the first ten years, but after that she had remained steadfastly in Tokyo, ostensibly to attend to the children's education. It was at this period that she had once more taken up the study of English.

Keisaku disliked pastimes such as chess or mahjong, and neither smoked nor drank, but he had had an interest in curios ever since his youth. His family had been poor, and he had only got into the university by passing the official examinations. During his student days, however, he had worked as a tutor at an art-dealer's house and the chances this gave him of seeing old things, combined with an uncanny natural instinct, soon made him able to distinguish infallibly between the genuine and the fake if they were set together before him.

"Kanzaki," the dealer would say to him, "if you only worked steadily at this business for ten years, you could be a first-rate antique dealer. It's less boring than working in an office, you know . . ."

Such official praise pleased Keisaku, and since he was by nature good at lone studies, believing that there was nothing one could not do in one's spare time, he did everything to develop his taste while he was in the house, taking the owner and his assistant as his masters. While he was in China, too, he economized in his daily life to the point of neglecting his social duties to his colleagues, so that he could spend the greater part of his salary on collecting pictures, scrolls and pots. One reason for the lack of harmony between himself and Chigako was that, though he kept an eye on every detail of his wife's housekeeping, he would spend money quite oblivious of the family's needs when curio-collecting was concerned. After the war, however, when his income dwindled during the severe inflation, his antiques, which he had sent home from abroad in the early days of the war, proved a great source of strength in keeping the Kanzaki family from starvation.

Keisaku became a kind of clandestine antique dealer for a succession of Americans who came to Japan. An Italian broker named Domino—out to make money by preying on the would-be connoisseurs who preferred something more fancy than the routine souvenir fans and dolls—acted as go-between and brought Americans of all types to the house.

He would urge Chigako to come out and entertain them. Since all savings were frozen at the time, and cash hard to come by, she could hardly afford to refuse. So she would entertain her guests, regaling them with beef *sukiyaki* in a room that was often, on account of the frequent power failures, pitch-black except for candles. She was beautiful, familiar with life abroad, and her English was good, yet the idea that her own motive was to sell made it impossible for her to turn on charm at will, and she was teased as "the lady who never smiles."

Selling was not the only unpleasantness for Chigako. Keisaku was loath to sell the genuine pieces which he personally treasured, and she hated to watch as he and Domino worked together to foist on their self-styled connoisseurs, at high prices, scrolls and pots which he had picked up for a song.

Often Chigako would accuse Keisaku of fraud, making no attempt to conceal from him the contempt she felt. In practice, however, they could never have managed to live and send their two daughters to school without the money thus earned. On one occasion, there was a complaint about an imitation piece which Keisaku had sold, and they barely escaped a raid by the military police. No sooner had the affair been hushed up than a request came from an American field officer named Arnold who wished to buy Keisaku's treasured Ming vase. The price offered was, of course, considerable, but Keisaku was deeply attached to the piece with its fresh cobalt and red hues and was unwilling to part with it.

It happened that just at that time their second daughter Shinako, who was ill, required injections of a certain expensive drug. The Colonel Arnold who wanted the vase was the man who had pacified the military police for them. If they sold it, moreover, they would have no need to worry about Shinako's medical expenses for some time to come, so Chigako repeatedly urged Keisaku to resign himself to its loss. In a relationship, however, that was not harmonious at the best of times, her attempts to make Keisaku do something he did not want only stirred up more bad feelings. Suspicious lest Chigako should carry off the vase without his knowledge, Keisaku took it to be kept in a safe at the bank.

The wrangling was still continuing when, one day, Domino suddenly appeared at the house.

"Madame too much the lady," he declared. "No good handling guests, gentleman gets bad temper, me sorry. I got some work you do for me instead—earn lots, lots of money." And he peered into each of their faces in turn, wrinkling the base of his red, beaky nose and giving a cunning laugh. Keisaku stood by in sullen silence.

The work Domino wanted Chigako to do was the translation into English of a pornographic book. Her name would be kept strictly secret. There were many readers in America who were interested in knowing the details of the sex-life of newly-weds in Japan, but old-fashioned books of jokes and cartoons were no good to fill the demand, so a writer and illustrator had already been lined up who would portray modern marriage just as it was. All Chigako had to do was translate the Japanese she was given into easily understandable English. Keisaku was silent, letting Domino do all the talking, but his very silence showed his secret approval.

Chigako had disliked her husband for so unashamedly selling fakes at high prices, but it was with a more complex feeling of distaste that she hated him for trying to force her into such work. Keisaku seemed to assume quite brazenly that, since he was not actually forcing her into prostitution, all was well, but the matter that he took so lightly was almost intolerable for Chigako. It seemed to her, too, that she detected in Domino's lecherous eyes a sadistic delight in forcing this secret publishing work on the Kanzakis.

In the end, however, she undertook the work. Rather than force Keisaku to sell the vase he so begrudged for the sake of Shinako's health, pride made her prefer to keep her shame clamped down within herself. Surreptitiously, as though it were some secret document, Keisaku brought the bundle of script, penned in a round hand, from Domino's house and handed it over to her. She began her work, now thumbing through the dictionary, now writing, shutting herself up from her daughter's eyes in the room upstairs with the key, where Keisaku kept his antiques and where she otherwise never set foot.

The book bore the title "Honeymoon." It began with illustrated explanations of the meeting preliminary to an arranged marriage, the dowry and other such matters, and described how, at the wedding ceremony, the bride in her traditional marriage kimono and the bridegroom in morning dress exchanged *sake* cups before the altar. Then, after the wedding feast, the pair boarded the honeymoon train amidst the blessings of friends and relatives. Their destination, apparently, was a well-known hot-spring resort not far from Tokyo. There, in the folds of the green-clad mountains, the cherry blossom was blooming in profusion and Mount Fuji was visible in the distance. Finally, there followed a description in the frankest terms of how the bashful and inexperienced girl, after a leisurely bath at the hot-spring hotel, in a tub fresh with the fragrance of wood, spent her first night as a bride. Chigako had no interest in pornographic pictures and books; even in the first days of their marriage, when Keisaku had shown her his private store of pictures she had, far from enjoying them, ended by shutting the book unread, thus affording her husband simultaneously both disappointment and a sense of relief at his wife's lack of the lecherous instinct.

The forthright descriptions of sexual intercourse that had merely disgusted her then would now, as she did the translation, make her lay aside her pen from time to time and sit wrapped in a kind of ecstatic daydream. In real life, she had never known the moments of happiness that a woman could supposedly find through a man, yet her whole being now thrilled at the suggestion that they could be found through an intercourse of the flesh.

The translation, it seemed, sold unexpectedly well, and Chigako found herself blessed with a large amount of secretly acquired money. Shinako was able to recuperate from her illness at her leisure, and it was possible to fob off the American officer politely enough without parting with the vase that Keisaku had hung on to for so long. More than that, as an indirect result (it seemed to Chigako) of the connections she had made here, she was approached by the agent of an American publishing company with an offer for translations of Japanese classical works. Though the income was not so great as from the book on marriage, she was delighted, in that it enabled her to make her own living without relying on Keisaku.

As soon as the confusion of postwar days had settled down to a certain extent, Keisaku similarly gave up his more shameless business dealings with Domino. Even so, he still continued to dispose of the second-rate antiques that he had on hand and would occasionally go off on business trips to the provinces. To all appearances, he had everything he needed himself to live; but once it became possible for Chigako to manage on her own, the financial bonds linking them became far more tenuous. Though she lived in the same house, Chigako had even less idea of the extent of Keisaku's savings than she had of the number of the curios that he loved so much.

That evening Keisaku came home before dinner. He was in good spirits and carried a bottle of foreign wine done up in the wrapping paper of some department store. He had, he explained, got some good Italian vermouth cheap at a special sale of imported goods. Fetching two long-stemmed wine glasses from upstairs, he set them on the dining room table.

"How about a drink in one of these cut-glass Dutch glasses I got in Java?" he said. "We haven't used them for ages."

Hardly able to refuse, Chigako took a reluctant sip or two at the bitter-sweet liquid. As she did so, the wretchedness in which her heart was steeped seemed, little by little, to ferment and to pervade her whole body with its vapors. On an occasion such as tonight, a more loving couple than they would have been imagining to themselves the dreams of their young daughter and her husband as they rocked on the waves: would have sat engrossed in the music of the duet that they themselves had jointly composed. In Keisaku's expression as he held the glass of vermouth before him, Chigako detected the signs of a growing familiarity. Here, she realized, was one of the changes made possible in the house by Kiriko's disappearance, and a strange agitation filled her breast. Just as she was ignorant of the contents of his purse, so Chigako had not the slightest idea what Keisaku—who slept in the upstairs room with the lock, alone with his chilly vases and scrolls—did about his sexual needs. Even in later years, when she was sleeping in the downstairs room with her daughters, now fully-fledged women themselves, the thought would sometimes come to her on waking in the depths of the night, and she would lie staring with wide-open eyes into the darkness. Yet the fact that they had lived together for twenty or thirty years and had borne two children between them was, in truth, useless when it came to recalling her husband's perfectly undistinguished sexual habits. Keisaku, on his side too, had almost certainly retained no particular physical memories of Chigako. All was a void now—vast, colorless and insubstantial as a cloud.

It was years, too, since they had sat together drinking like this, husband and wife alone together in one room. This itself made Chigako uneasy, as though she were in a haunted house. Yet worse was to come.

"I say," said Keisaku suddenly, "your hair's got awfully thin at the front, hasn't it? I'd been thinking your face looked longer and narrower, but I only noticed a while ago when we were standing on the pier."

It was the same Keisaku who, when Chigako had first had her hair cut short, had driven his young wife to despair by not noticing for two months. More than that, during recent years when they had virtually lived apart, he had remained completely indifferent to his wife's appearance. False teeth might change the shape of her mouth, she might put on and take off the spectacles lengthening vision now demanded, yet he never noticed.

Taken off her guard by Keisaku's remark, Chigako automatically put her hand to her hairline, then, without changing her position, twisted round to take the hand mirror off the little low dressing table behind her.

"Are you sure?" she said.

"Oh, you can't tell by this artificial light," he replied. "But have a good look in the morning in the sunlight. There's a bit in one of Sōseki's novels about a husband who complains because his wife's getting bald. Well, I got a bit of a shock myself today. Have to get some hair tonic or something, I thought."

Chigako knitted her eyebrows fiercely at her reflection in the mirror. "Don't be silly," she said.

The next day, after Keisaku had left, Chigako went to the mirror and closely scrutinized her hair once more. He was right: the short, curly hair at the front had got noticeably scantier, and the hair at the sides seemed thinner. Up till now, she had been secretly proud of the fact that she had few grey hairs for her age. Thinning hair, however, was for a woman the harbinger of an aging far more cruel than greyness, which could always be dyed away. Chigako had sometimes gazed in wonder at the faces of old women seen on the train or in the streets, with their too-black hair plastered over their foreheads like pieces of sticky rag. She herself then, she suddenly realized, was destined to cut the same weird figure and a wave of unbearable wretchedness swept over her. How, when, could her hair have fallen out like this?

In her youth, her hair had annoyed her by its very abundance, and compliments on it had invariably left her unmoved. Her eyebrows had been thick, and her luxuriant eyelashes had given her eyes a blurred, languorous look. When permanent waves had come into fashion, she had had her locks shorn without regret, and watched the black clippings falling on each side of her face like great, soft, drops with a feeling not of humiliation but of lightheartedness, as though a tree whose branches had grown too crowded were at last being pruned. Two or three times—she now remembered—Kiriko had remarked that her hair was getting thin, but it had not troubled her. "It's more becoming when you get older for it not to be too thick," she had said.

No one, however, until Keisaku the previous night, had told her that her looks had changed. Before last night, Keisaku had never subjected his wife's appearance to the close scrutiny that he gave, for instance, to his antiques. What, then, could have prompted him to bring up the subject out of the blue? Could it be that, as he stood on the pier watching his daughter disappear into the distance, that face he had known for close on thirty years had suddenly changed and become unfamiliar in his eyes?

As Chigako sat idly studying her face in the mirror, a sense of panic, of being driven from behind, began to steal over her. She called her part-time help and told her to take the little dressing table to the annex she had had built onto the house. Surely, the woman protested, it was more convenient where it was? But Chigako would not listen. Kiriko had gone now, and she didn't want the living room cluttered up with it any more.

The annex had two rooms, one medium-sized and one small, and was propped up against the narrow sweep of land that ran from the verandah of the main building to the slope above. While Kiriko had been with them, Chigako had used it almost exclusively for working in. Now that their daughter had gone, however, the living room and its anteroom in the main house had become a yawning void, and she must shift the focus of her life to the annex with all speed if she and Keisaku were not to become unpleasantly entangled with each other.

As she feared, Keisaku came home that evening with a bottle of American hair tonic which he had bought.

"What's happened to the mirror?" he asked, looking with a disgruntled expression at the oblong, greenish patch on the straw mat that marked its former site. "I thought it was just right here, as I could use it myself too."

"Well, we'll put it in the bathroom, then," she replied. "Like that, you can use it any time."

She gave in without thinking here, but she had no intention of using the tonic Keisaku had bought for her thinning hairline. Her one motive was uneasiness—uneasiness lest her husband, so long a stranger, should begin to worm his way back into her life now that their daughter was gone. Kiriko had been invaluable—a solid, flesh-and-blood barrier between them. Now she had vanished, and the gap she had left must, whatever happened, be filled with something else.

For this purpose, the separation made possible by the house's peculiar construction not only more or less served the required purpose but was unlikely to excite outside comment. In building the annex, Chigako had not of course foreseen things in such detail as this, but it struck her now that to build herself a new room with her accumulated earnings had been, in effect, a very clever way of achieving a quasi-separation from her husband.

The annex was not completely cut off from the rest of the house, being joined to it by a flight of four or five steps. The minimum personal contact that this represented would doubtless remain between Chigako and Keisaku till the day one or the other of them died. Complete isolation would be awkward if either of them were ill, and both wished to avoid anything that looked strange in the eyes of others. There was a tacit pledge between them that, to this extent at least, the claims of duty and vigilance would be observed.

Seeing that Chigako deliberately withdrew before his advances, Keisaku gave up the vague attempts at a rapprochement that he had seemed to make since Kiriko's departure, and the conjugal life of the Kanzakis returned to its old tenor. The days passed, cheerless and serene. Before breakfast and after dinner, they would exchange a few remarks without achieving any rapport. For the rest, each remained oblivious of the other, he in his upstairs room with his antiques, she in her annex facing the hill.

It was not until after she had firmly established this wall between her husband's and her own lives that Chigako really got to know the hill before the house.

From the time that Keisaku first spotted her thinning hair—from the time, that is, that she shifted her stronghold to the annex—Chigako began noticeably to devote herself to her hair style and her make-up. It seemed strange to her now that she had never before been aware of growing old. Perhaps the youth ever welling from her young daughters had, in some subtle way, lured their mother into a false sense of security?

Soon, hormone creams, dark lipsticks and a succession of other such articles took their place on the dressing table alongside the hair tonic. Seating herself before them, Chigako would apply herself assiduously to the task of restoring her youth. For what purpose she was making up, for what purpose she wished to be young again she herself did not know. She only knew, vaguely, that unless she made herself up as she was doing now she would reproach herself all in vain later.

When she looked at herself closely, she found that her eyebrows and eyelashes—once so depressingly thick—had likewise become thin, and that an unwonted, cold serenity had spread across her brow. It was, she recognized with loathing, the face of middle age. She pencilled in new eyebrows, smeared oily cream all over the skin, and painted her lips a deep red. As she did so, a different, younger face came floating up from beneath her old face. The exaggeration, the unnaturalness of it alternately titillated and appalled her as she worked, yet the force that dragged her on was too strong to be halted by any movement of self-contempt. Then, a creaking of teeth within her mouth—a pitiless grating from the plastic inserted between her jaws—would seem to tear away the face in the mirror.

On afternoons when she had finished her translation work for the moment, Chigako would apply herself thus to her solitary, aimless toilet. When it was finished, she would emerge through the little gateway into the sloping road outside. When the middle school at the top of the slope came out, the road was filled with a dusty medley of boys' footsteps and voices, but at other times, particularly at noon and at sunset, the loneliness seemed to belie her position in the heart of the city. At such times, bicycles and pedestrians would vanish as if by magic, leaving nothing but the brick walls of the gardens tracing a decorous curve in the whitish concrete surface of the road. In the midst of such loneliness, Chigako would let her mind run where it would. Standing in the middle of the road, she would gaze at the green of the grass and the shrubs that grew in profusion, as by a mountain path, on the high banks; or would rest her eyes on the point where the gentle slopes of the hill, curving like the sleeve of a kimono, vanished out of sight.

Close on forty years ago, when Chigako had been a little girl from the town at the foot of the slope, she had often run up and down it playing with her friends. At that time, the broad main road had not yet been opened up, so that the horses and vehicles crossing the hill all came slowly climbing up this slope. Often, a funeral procession would pass by on its way to the funeral hall near the graveyard at the edge of the park. Sometimes there were white pigeons fluttering in their tall cages on their way to be released by the grave, and sometimes, from within the sliding doors of the gold-embossed, unpainted wooden palanquins that swayed silently past, she would glimpse the many-layered white silk sleeves of the dead man's robe. Occasionally the great white funeral wreaths of artificial flowers would rock by on men's shoulders, or strings of rickshaws pass bearing women with the traditional hair styles of mourning.

There were other memories, too, that bound her to the hill—the fearful curses of a pack-horse driver under the scorching skies of summer, trying against all nature to force his high-laden beast up the hill—and crazily flaying its bony buttocks with his whip; and the white foam that flecked the horse's mouth as, borne down by overwork, it sank to its knees. Only as it was dying had the yoke finally been removed from its back. It was, it seemed to her, the first time she had actually seen hell in this life.

As she stood on the deserted slope, memories such as these would come vividly back to life in her mind. The gravel road of those days had changed to concrete, and the narrow stone-flagged ditch that ran beside the brick wall had given way to underground drains. Yet despite such minor changes, the brick wall, faded to a rusty pink, and the wild profusion of trees and shrubs on the bank above were much as they had been in the past. As she stood there idly, attracted by this changelessness, Chigako often had the illusion that she could go back and forth between past and present as freely as she could go up and down this hill. And the thought was infinitely sweet to her in her efforts, however vain, to bar off the approach of old age and infirmity.

Her room, halfway up between the main part of the house and the road, also taught her a surprising number of things once she began sleeping there alone. Getting out and putting away the heavy quilts at night was too much for her strength, so she kept a sofa-bed in the room. Besides sleeping on it at night, she would lie down on it at all hours, even of the day, if she grew tired from working at her desk. The bed was against the wall facing the hill, so that when she slept on it she was lying right up against the flank of the slope, about three feet below the road. The idea induced a strange peace in Chigako, as though she were sleeping in a coffin.

The sound of the shoes and wooden sandals of passers-by on the hill would make a dry clatter just above her ear, while car horns and voices seemed to come from much higher up. The different planes prevented any feeling that people were walking on her head, and when the rain was pouring down the sound of water running from the road down the little spur of land stood out above all other noises. To lie perfectly still on her side listening to the worldly sounds that floated down from the surface of the road diagonally above gave her a far more vivid picture of the people as they went about and talked, and moved her more, than if she had been up and watching them. Late every night someone, probably a student from the music school at the top of the hill, would walk down the road alone, practising over and over again at the top of his voice one line of the same German *lied*. The young man could never have dreamt the effect his young voice had on the ears of the middle-aged woman lying hidden down on the flank of the slope; yet Chigako, as she heard his youthfully taut, resonant tones, would imagine to herself the muscles swelling at the sturdy throat, the dark amber, glistening swell of the chest, and the tears would gather in her eyes before she was aware of them. A dark despair would settle on her as she thought of herself, too feeble now even to get out and put away the bed. Whatever contact she were to have with the man who lay upstairs amid his chilly antiques, what new hope now could ever be conceived of it? She fretted over her thinning hair, she could not read without glasses, and when she took out her false teeth her mouth was a gaping void. Spectacles, false teeth, false locks made of other people's hair—all kinds of things foreign to her own flesh which she donned like armor in her hungry craving to appear young, to be beautiful. What kind of creature was she?

It was a dank, chilly afternoon in the rainy season. As usual, Chigako was out on the hill drinking in the silence of the deserted road. A few pale hydrangea flowers peered out, half buried, from amidst the green of the shrubs on the bank. The layer of clouds gathered in the sky was thickening and soon the rain, which had let up for a while, would start falling. Chigako liked the rain at this season as it fell, softly blurring the white light.

The first drop or two landed on her forehead, but she remained idly standing, looking down the hill, as though she enjoyed the dampness of the rain. Suddenly a man appeared round the bend. He was dressed in grey and carried a briefcase in one hand, an umbrella in the other. She soon recognized Tōno Shigeyuki, on his way to visit her. Lecturer on the Japanese classics at one of the new universities set up after the war, for the past four or five years he had been helping Chigako in her English translations of the Japanese classics. Thanks to her encounters with this young man, she had acquired quite a familiarity with the women writers of the Heian Period. And, half due to the influence of these writers who lived a thousand years ago, Chigako had come of late to dream up stories of her own as she lay on her coffin-like bed.

He had come quite far up the hill before he looked up and recognized Chigako standing at the top. He nodded slightly, but did not quicken his pace, continuing upwards in the same leisurely, melancholy fashion as before. Impatient, she went in before him, and was lighting the gas when she heard the front door shutting.

Tōno's voice came through to her. "What were you doing standing out there?" he called.

"Waiting for a lover," she called back.

Tōno neither laughed nor attempted to cap her joke, but climbed wearily up to the study and sat himself on the sofa on which Chigako was accustomed to lie.

He lit a cigarette. His back was bent and his shoulders rounded, every line of his body suggesting extreme exhaustion. He had been—Tōno himself always explained—a prisoner in Soviet hands for two or three years after the war, and this had frozen his youth away. Though he was only thirty-three or four, he had been sent to do war-work in Manchuria during his high-school days. Captured and de-

tained there, he found on his return that his classmates were
already working, and he was far behind them in graduating
from the university. Thanks to his reputation as an intellec-
tual, he had been given political education in communism
while in the Soviet Union, and on his return to Japan he had
frequently been unsuccessfully approached by Communists
and the like. It was not that he had ideological objections, but
that, search as he might, he could not find in himself the particular kind of enthusiasm—call it the hotheadedness or the
progressiveness—needed to take part in any political movement. Instead, he had taken up the Japanese classics—inspired, he said, by the vague hope that to bury himself in
something in the past might somehow make life tolerable. In
speaking to another, his eyes always seemed out of focus, as
though his real interlocutor were far away in space behind
the other person's back. With a frighteningly serious expression, he would hold forth on Heian literature. Quite suddenly, and with exactly the same face, he would brazenly
recite someone else's verse and claim it was his own, or
would tell of a plain and somewhat lame girl he had known
at university, refashioning her quite arbitrarily into the
world's most ravishing beauty.

After catching him out once or twice with this kind of lie,
Chigako ceased to swallow whole everything he said; yet,
even so, his accounts of life in prison camp and his richly lyr-
ical tales of his amorous exploits served as a stimulus in her
monotonous life which gave him a value outside that of a
mere translator's assistant.

"How's the translation of the *Tale of Ise* going?" Tōno
asked. "Have you got on with it since last time?"

"Yes, I've got past the part we did together and I'm doing
Chapter LXIII—the one about the old woman in love."

Tōno took an annotated version from his bag and opened
it at the place in question.

"Ah, I remember," he said. "She wants a lover, but can't
find one, so she mentions it to her three sons. The first two
won't answer, but the youngest says 'the right man will turn
up soon,' which pleases her no end. The Oedipus complex
didn't worry him, did it!" He gave a melancholy, old man's
laugh.

"Yes, I more or less got that part," Chigako said. "Then
the hero comes along and sleeps with the old woman, doesn't

he? Then he recites a poem about hair. The word before 'hair,' though, I don't understand. It must have more nuance other than just 'white.' "

As she spoke, she suddenly remembered the hair round her own forehead—short and fine, with a look as though it were starved of pigment. She put her hand up to it.

"Perhaps it was this kind of hair?"

"Don't be silly." He gave a wry smile. "You're still young."

"Oh no, people in the past got older much quicker than now, you know. The old woman in the story was about my age, you mark my words!" She gave a shrill little laugh, a laugh that had an odd ring of youth and coquetry.

"Talking of old people's hair reminds me," she continued. "Tell me, when you kiss your wife, isn't it strange?"

"Uh?" For once, Tōno's far-away eyes came into focus and he stared at Chigako dumbfounded. In all the four or five years they had known each other, Chigako had never once referred to such physical matters, and her question was as alarming as though someone had let off a pistol at him.

"Why?" he asked.

"Well, you've no teeth, have you?"

As a result of Tōno's detention in the Soviet Union, almost all his teeth had fallen out or become useless through cold and malnutrition, and at the time he first knew Chigako he had not as yet got false teeth. Probably, she had suspected, he would never be able to get married, but he had in fact done so some six months previously.

"I had false teeth myself last year, you know. So I sometimes wonder. . . . It's all right for women with hair like me, but isn't it a bit wretched for a bride if her husband's got his mouth stuffed with plastic?"

"Not at all," he replied, without smiling. "At least, I've never asked her, but. . . ."

Now she had broached the subject she felt wretched and ashamed at her unaccustomed lack of reserve. But as she lay on her bed, she would often run her tongue round the artificial palate of plastic in her mouth, and would imagine how it would feel to a tongue other than her own. And at such times a strong curiosity would seize her.

"Are your wife's teeth all right?" she asked.

"You know, I've never actually inspected the inside of her

mouth, so. . . . Apparently she used to eat a lot of sweet things when she was small, and she's always getting toothache. It seems she's got pyorrhea, so she may have to have all false teeth before she's very old, too."

"Not growing grey together, but losing one's teeth together . . . Wretched, isn't it?"

In fact, Chigako was thinking not so much of Tōno's wife as of an ironical discovery she had made concerning her own and Keisaku's teeth recently. Keisaku was ten years her senior, and for long had been having his teeth treated in all kinds of ways in an effort to keep them. Three or four years ago, however, they had finally got past repair, and he had replaced the lot with false teeth. As if to catch up with him, Chigako had had all her own out also, though quite a number were still left, so as to eradicate the pyorrhea that had troubled her for many years.

For some while the alien objects in her mouth troubled her, and she could taste absolutely nothing. When this period passed, however, she gradually acquired the ability to sort out what food was suitable and would automatically avoid tough and crisp things however much she liked them. This was partly due to embarrassment, since whenever she struggled to eat something hard there came from inside her mouth an unaccustomed clacking, like the contact of mahjong pieces with each other. However, it was also because, whenever she sat opposite Keisaku at the mealtable now that their daughters had left, she was almost ridiculously aware of the clatter of his teeth, which she had never noticed before. Their taste in food, hitherto different, similarly began to grow more alike, since they both had to select things that would match the same conditions. What surprised Chigako still more was that when she was alone at table with Keisaku she could click-clack her teeth without any embarrassment whatsoever on foods that she would not have touched when eating with others. Here they were, then, she thought—two separate old people cooped up together to wear away each other's egos in the same house, pecking away at the same kind of foods and pursing their old mouths, ill-fitted with the same kind of false teeth. And the hatefulness of growing old together would prey on her till she all but moaned aloud.

"Really, you know, if a couple's teeth were in completely

different condition they wouldn't be able to eat the same things together, would they?" she continued.

"You do say peculiar things," he replied. "You've changed lately—sometimes you give me a shock."

"How?"

"How? Well, you never used to say things like just now, did you?"

"Do I offend you?"

"It's not a question of offending. . . . It frightens me. It comes so unexpectedly, like a flash of lightning."

"You know, to tell the truth, I've got tired of translating lately."

"Don't say that! You're threatening to do me out of my side job." His tone and the yawn that went with it belied the anxiety he felt.

"But it's half your own fault. You talk so familiarly about those women writers of the Heian Period, as if they were aunts or sisters or something, that I believe their spirits have taken possession of me."

"You're just bored because Kiriko's not here now."

"You're right. Those women writers at court in the old days, too, they must have been so utterly bored as they squatted quite still inside their curtains. I'm sure they had plenty of time to think of all kinds of things—sometimes real things and sometimes things that people's imagination had thought up. When I lie on that sofa where you're sitting now, my body's so still it's as if I were in a coffin, but so many things and so many people come so vividly into my mind I don't know what to do. . . . My body's as limp as an old cat's, but my brain is so agile it makes me uneasy."

"You should do both that and the translation together. If you give up this work now, I shan't have anything to give my wife to spend."

"That's all I *can* do, at any rate. Who on earth would ever buy the kind of complaining nonsense I write?"

From the day on which she first, quite unpremeditatedly, spoke to Tōno on such subjects, something indefinable that had been set rigid within Chigako began to melt. She would often go out onto the hill now, and her make-up was thicker even than before. Sometimes she would stand with her umbrella up in the rain. In the opaque, frosted glass-like light of the rainy season, her made-up face seemed to blur into a strange, ageless youthfulness. Yet the click of the teeth beneath the pitiful camouflage and the colorlessness of the short hair where the dye had worn off constantly appalled her with their reminder of reality. She could not bear to contemplate the natural decline whereby this twilight grey would gradually deepen till, inexorably, it turned to night. The fact that her teeth and nothing else had achieved a reconciliation with Keisaku was enough to darken the twilight still further.

After drifting aimlessly up and down the slope, Chigako would open an exercise book on her desk and continue a kind of romance she was writing. In the story, the music student who went down the hill practising *lieder* late every night fell in love with a young married woman living on the hill, and every night would go in from the road entrance and visit her surreptitiously in her room. To help him in his poverty, the woman sold all kinds of possessions of her own, and in the end took her husband's treasured Ming vase out onto the hill in the middle of the night, meaning to give it to her lover. He embraced her, the box fell from his hands, and the vase broke clean in two. As she described the young people's love for each other, Chigako would sometimes recall scenes from the honeymoon book she had translated four or five years before. By portraying a woman's feelings in introducing another man into the house unbeknown to her husband, she who had never herself done any such thing could enjoy in the story a kind of revenge on Keisaku. The breaking of the vase, of course, was itself a formalization of this revenge. After committing to paper this mixture of wanton fantasy interwoven with reality, she would stay quite still listening for sounds from the hill, the smile of the enchantress still playing around her eyes.

It was a night of wild rain. On her ears as she lay in bed there fell the impetuous rushing of a small waterfall, spilling from the road above down the drop by the side of her room. The rain beat down fiercely till it seemed to pierce through roof, ceiling and down into her very breast. She lay, fascinated by the sound of the rain, imagining the scene as the lovers embraced after breaking the vase. So doing, she must have fallen asleep, for when the shrill pealing of the door-bell awoke her the night was already advanced and the sound of

the rain had ceased. The clock at her bedside said nearly one.
The bell on the hill side of the house was inside the porch
gate where it was not easily noticeable, and letters and telegrams, moreover, were normally delivered at the main entrance. A burglar, she reflected, would hardly ring the bell;
even so, she hesitated nervously at her doorway. Again there
came a persistent ringing from the bell. Keisaku, his face
heavy from sleep, came up the steps to the annex.

"What is it?" he asked. "Is it someone at the door?"

"I wonder who it can be. At this time of night. . . ."

"Well, we can't just leave them. . . . damn them!" And he
stepped down into the hallway and undid the sliding door. He
went out and up a few stone steps at the top of which, as if
blocking the way, stood the fence. As he went to the gate and
peered out, the bell stopped ringing and there was a rustling
sound. Through the crack, he could see two white things
wriggling against each other. Noisily, he flung the gate open.

At once, there came a shrill female cry and something human that had been leaning pressed against the gateway detached itself.

"Who is it?" Keisaku shouted. His voice, filled with fury,
was that of an old man.

The white mass twisted, then split in two and was off, running down towards the bottom of the hill. A woman's white
blouse and a man's open-neck shirt were visible bobbing up
and down in the light of the street lamps. Keisaku turned to
Chigako, who had come out after him.

"Little bastards. Hugging and kissing in a place like this!"
His voice proclaimed his irritation. "They were pressed up
against this post where the bell is without realizing it. They
didn't know it was ringing, because you can only hear it in
the house."

"Well!" Chigako gazed after the two white forms running
down the hill as if it were all still part of a dream. The
fanciful events she had been imagining before going to sleep
imposed themselves perplexingly on the present reality. The
two forms, almost falling in their haste to get away, were
clinging tightly together again by the time they disappeared
round the bend.

From the foot of the hill came the shrill yelping of a dog.

With vacant faces, as if their wits had forsaken them,
Keisaku and Chigako stood in their nightwear in the middle

of the road that still glistened wet with rain. They looked at each other. A smile with a strangeness no words could describe hovered over both pairs of pursy, toothless lips.

—*Translated by John Bester*

Late Chrysanthemum

Hayashi Fumiko

Hayashi Fumiko (1904–1951) was a child of poverty who knew struggle and hard work her entire life. A bleak bonus from her peddler father's nomadic life was an acquaintance with many areas of the country. From her first work, a novel in journal form issued in 1930 under the title *Journal of a Vagabond*, all her writings would have autobiographical undertones, dealing with poverty and generally strong and resourceful women in the face of adversity. "Late Chrysanthemum" is considered one of her finest works and received the Women's Prize for Literature in 1948.

"I'll be round this evening, about five," the voice on the telephone had said. Well, it certainly was a surprise, after a whole year of silence. But then, one never knew. . . . Kin looked at her watch; there were still some two hours to go before five. First and foremost, then, a bath: she gave the maid instructions to prepare an early meal, and hurried off to the bathroom. She must look younger than ever, younger than when they had last said good-bye; one suggestion of her age, and all was up. So thinking, she allowed herself a leisurely soak.

Back from the bath, she got out some ice from the icebox, crushed it finely, wrapped it in a double layer of gauze and spent ten minutes with it before the mirror, massaging her face all over. Her face grew red and numb. Somewhere at her woman's breast there gnawed the realisation of her fifty-six years but, determined that her years of experience should help her to cover up mere age, she took out her long-treasured jar of imported cream and smeared it over her cold face. In the mirror an elderly woman's face, with a deathly, bluish pallor, stared wide-eyed back at her.

For a moment as she worked she was seized with a sudden disgust for her own face; across her mind floated a vision of the bewitching beauty that had been hers, that beauty once celebrated on the picture postcards of the day. She pulled up her clothes, and gazed intently at her thighs. Their former ripe plumpness was gone, and a network of tiny blue veins stood out over the skin. And, yet, she was not skinny—that was one thing to be thankful for—and her thighs when closed still met each other firmly and squarely. Whenever she had a bath, she would seat herself on her heels in formal fashion, knees together, and pour water into the hollow of her thighs. The water remained, forming a pool in the groove between her legs. At this, she would feel a comforting sense of relief, and her age no longer seemed to matter so much. She could still attract a man: while that was true, Kin felt, life still had some meaning. She spread her thighs apart, and furtively, almost as though shy of herself, stroked the skin on the inner side. It was smooth and soft, as doeskin becomes after long treatment with oil.

Kin had once read a novel by the eighteenth-century writer Saikaku, an account of a journey through Japan. In it were described, among the attractions of Ise at the time, two beautiful girls who played the samisen, one named Osugi and the other Tama. Around them as they played were stretched ropes of vivid scarlet, and people would play a kind of game, throwing money through the ropes in an attempt to hit the girls' faces. This scene, with the two girls inside the red ropes, came to Kin's mind with the beauty of some old colour print. Beauty like that was for her, she felt, long since a thing of the past.

In her youth she had been consumed with the lust for money, blind to all else. But now she was getting old; she had lived, moreover, through the fearful ravages of war, and life without men seemed somehow blank and forlorn. Her beauty, too, had altered by imperceptible degrees with age, and the advance of the years had wrought a change in its very character. The older she became, the more careful she was to avoid the gaudy in her dress. She despised the strange wiles resorted to by some women over fifty who ought to know better—the necklace above the sunken breasts, the check skirt in a red more suitable for an undergarment, the too-full white satin blouse, the broad-brimmed hat hiding the wrinkled forehead. Equally did she dislike the woman in Japanese dress who affected a little scarlet peeping out around the neck in the manner of prostitutes.

Kin had never once worn Western dress. Her kimono was of a dark blue silk, freshened with a neckband of purest white crepe. Her sash was of pale cream silk with raised flecks of white; the belt beneath it was pale blue, but she never, as some did, let it show above her sash in front. Her bosom she made to look full and round, her hips narrow; next to her skin, a girdle drawn as tightly as possible, and at her buttocks a pad lightly stuffed with silk-wadding. Her hair had always been lighter than average and, taken with her fair complexion, never suggested a woman of over fifty. Perhaps because her height made her wear her kimono rather short, the hemline at the bottom was always neat and trim, and had an air of freshness.

Before a meeting with a man, Kin would always dress, as today, with a restraint which betrayed years of experience. Then, seated before the mirror, she would gulp down a cup of cold rice wine, never forgetting afterwards to clean her teeth to remove the smell. The merest sip of alcohol, she found, did things for her physically which no cosmetics could ever do. The slight intoxication it produced gave a flush to the cheekbones and the right misty look to the eyes. Her face, smoothed over with face lotion and cream, took on a fresh glow as if new life had been breathed into it. The best-quality lipstick, and that in a dark shade, was the only touch of red she allowed herself. Not once in her life had she painted her nails, and she had even less intention of doing so now that she was old: on an old woman's hands it only contrived to look grasping, undignified and quite incongruous. She confined herself, therefore, to patting lotion into the back of her hands, keeping her nails almost morbidly short and polishing them with a piece of cloth. The colours that peeped out from

inside the sleeve of her under-kimono were all pastel shades.
Her perfume—a sweetish brand—she rubbed on her shoulders and her plump arms; nothing would induce her to put it
behind her ears.

Kin refused to forget her femininity. Death itself was pref-
erable to the blowsiness of the average old woman. There was
a poem—composed, they said, by some famous woman of
the past—

Never could human form
Aspire, I know,
To beauty ripe as that now bends
This rose. Yet, somewhere here,
I see myself.

A life bereft of men was too dreadful to bear thinking of:
Kin gazed into the pale pink petals of the roses Itaya had
brought her, their splendour conjuring images from her past.
Times had changed since those far-off days; her own tastes,
the things that gave her pleasure—these too, little by little,
had changed; and yet she was glad. Sometimes, when she
slept alone, she would wake in the night and amuse herself
by secretly counting over on her fingers the number of men
in her life since she had been a girl. There was that one, and
that one, and him, and oh yes, I'd forgotten him! But perhaps
he came before? Or was it after, now . . .? And as she reeled
them off the memories whirled up in her breast and clutched
at her throat. Some of them made the tears flow when she
remembered how they had parted, so she preferred to think
only of the first meetings. "There was once a man . . ." She
always remembered the beginning of the old romance. Her
own mind was piled high with men who, as in the story, had
"once been," and for this reason, perhaps, it gave her
pleasure on her nights alone to drowse in bed over the men
of the past.

The call from Tabe had come as a surprise to Kin, like a
rare and expensive present out of the blue. He was coming,
of course, for old times' sake—coming, as it were, to inspect
the burnt-out ruins of love, in the sentimental hope of finding some relic from the past. But she would not let it be
enough, this standing and sighing among the weeds and
rubble. Nor must any suggestion of the wretchedness of age

or poverty be allowed to intrude. Her manner towards him
must above all be dignified, the atmosphere that of a discreet
tête-à-tête. When he left, he must carry away with him an in-
delible impression of the unchanging beauty of the woman
who had been his.

At last her toilet was successfully completed and Kin, like
an actress waiting for her cue, stood before the mirror anxiously surveying the result for possible omissions. She went
into the living room. The evening meal was already on the
table and, seating herself opposite the maid, she ate the frugal
meal of thin *miso* soup and substitute rice with pickles. The
meal finished, she broke an egg and swallowed the yolk.

Kin had never been in the habit of giving her men visitors
a meal. She had not the slightest wish to be the kind of
woman who prepared meals carefully and laid them proudly
before a man in the hope of winning his heart with her cooking. Domesticity had no appeal for her. What need had she,
who had not the faintest intention of getting married, to put
on a show of domesticity for men? Such was her nature, yet
the men who came to Kin brought with them presents of every kind. She found nothing strange in this. Kin would have
nothing to do with a man without money; nothing held less
charm for her. The man who made love in an unbrushed suit,
the man who did nothing about the missing buttons on his
underwear—such men were damned at once in Kin's eyes.
Love in itself, she felt, should be like the creation of a succession of works of art.

When she was a girl, people had claimed that she bore a
likeness to the famous geisha Manryū. She had once seen
Manryū after her marriage. Her beauty was as dazzling as
ever; it had produced an unforgettable impression on Kin,
who realised then that the one thing indispensable to a
woman who wished to keep her beauty indefinitely was
money.

Kin had first become a geisha when she was nineteen; her
beauty alone had won her acceptance, for she had little training in the necessary arts of the trade. Soon after she started,
she had been summoned to entertain a Frenchman—no longer young—who happened to be in Japan in the course of a
sightseeing tour of Asia. He took a fancy to her, dubbing her
a Japanese Marguerite Gautier, and at one period, indeed,
Kin had seen herself as a kind of Dame aux Camélias.

Though he had proved surprisingly inadequate as a lover, something about him had made him stay in Kin's mind ever after. His name had been Michel, and judging from his age at the time he doubtless already lay at rest somewhere in the north of France. On his return home, he had sent Kin a present—a bracelet studded with opals and tiny diamonds. During the war, even when things were at their worst, she had resolutely refused to part with this particular possession, whatever else had to go.

All the men whose mistress Kin had been had ended by making names for themselves in their own particular fields, but she had lost touch with most of them during the war and did not even know their whereabouts. Some people claimed that Kin had acquired in her time no small amount of property. True or not, she resisted any temptation to follow in the footsteps of other former geisha and start a tea-house or a restaurant of her own. She was not, in fact, as rich as rumour had it; her only property consisted of the house—spared in the war—in which she lived, and a villa by the sea in Atami. The villa she got rid of, seizing the opportunity afforded by the postwar housing shortage.

She did no work, living entirely from day to day. She had a maid, Okinu, who had been found for her by her foster-sister. Okinu was deaf and dumb. The outsider would have been surprised at the austerity of the life Kin led. For her, neither the cinema nor the theatre held any attractions, nor did she care for pointless outings. She shrank from the light of day, for it exposed her age to the gaze of all and sundry. No costly clothes, she knew, were of any avail beneath the pitiless glare of the sun.

She asked no more than to live the life of the kept woman, and she had a passion for reading novels. Occasionally, people would suggest that she adopt a daughter to comfort her in her old age. To Kin's mind, however, the thought of old age and all it entailed was repugnant. All her life, moreover, she had never been used to attachments of such a kind.

Hers, indeed, was a special case. She had no parents; all that she knew of her origins was that she had been born in Akita Prefecture, in a village called Osagawa. When she was about five, a Tokyo family had adopted her. She had taken their name, and lived with them as their daughter. Her adoptive father had been a civil engineer, and one year his business had taken him to work in Manchuria. He never returned; letters ceased to arrive from him while Kin was still in primary school, and no more was heard of him from that time on. His wife Ritsu was, fortunately, no mean business woman. She dabbled in shares, and built houses which she let. As a result, the family acquired, even in the well-to-do area in which they lived, the reputation of being quite wealthy.

About the time that Kin reached nineteen, a man called Torigoe started to frequent her home, and from that time on the fortunes of the family began almost imperceptibly to decline. Then Kin's foster-mother Ritsu took to drink, and would storm and rage in her cups. Before long Kin led a new life of hardship. The climax came when Torigoe, whose habit it was to flirt with Kin, one day became violent and assaulted her. Kin, past caring what happened, fled the house and eventually took refuge in a tea-house in Akasaka, where she was taken on as a geisha. She made her debut under the name of Kinya, and in no time her photo was appearing in popular story books and on the picture-postcards which were the rage at the time.

Though all these things, for Kin, were now part of the dim and distant past she still found it difficult to accept herself as a woman on the wrong side of fifty. At times the years weighed heavily on her, but she was also smitten occasionally by a sense of the shortness of her youth. On the death of her foster-mother, the dwindled remains of the family fortune had gone to a daughter, Sumiko, born after Kin's adoption. Kin was freed thus from all further sense of obligation to the family.

She had first met Tabe about the time of the outbreak of the Pacific War, during a period when Sumiko and her husband were running a boardinghouse for students in Totsuka. She had broken with her patron of the past three years, and was now living a life of leisure in a room she had rented in the house. Tabe was one of the students she saw from time to time in the living room. She struck up an acquaintance with him, and though he was young enough to be her son their friendship had developed before they realised it into a full-blown clandestine affair. Kin's beauty was still that of a woman of a mere thirty-seven or so rather than the fifty she really was, and there was enchantment in her thick black brows. On graduating, Tabe was whisked into the army as a sub-lieutenant. His unit, however, instead of going straight to the front, was stationed for a while in Hiroshima, and twice Kin went there to see him.

On each occasion, no sooner was she installed in her hotel than the uniformed Tabe put in his appearance. She shrank from the odour of leather that clung to his body, but spent the two nights with him at the hotel nevertheless. She had come far to see him and her utter weariness left her like a scrap of paper tossed in the storm of his masculinity; as she confessed later, she had felt as if her end were near. She went to Hiroshima twice, but refused to go again despite repeated telegrams from Tabe. In 1942 he was sent to Burma, and came back demobilized in May of the year following the war's end. He at once came up to Tokyo and called on Kin in her house at Numabukuro. He had aged terribly, and his front teeth were missing; seeing him Kin felt let down, her dreams shattered.

Tabe came originally from Hiroshima, but with the aid of his eldest brother he started an automobile company and within the year was back in Tokyo. He came to see Kin, who scarcely recognised him, so grand was his appearance now, and announced that he was soon to take a wife. Since then more than a year had passed, during which time she had not even seen him.

Kin had bought her present house in Numabukuro, complete with telephone, for a mere song during the worst of the air raids, and had evacuated herself thither from Totsuka. The two houses were little more than a stone's throw apart, but while Sumiko's house had been burnt down Kin's had come through unscathed. Sumiko and her family took shelter in Kin's house, but when the war ended she promptly turned them out again. By now, however, Sumiko actually seemed to feel grateful to Kin for this, for she had had to build a new house on the site of the old without further ado; this was just after the war, and, as things had turned out, she had managed it more cheaply then than she could have done at any time since.

Kin now sold the villa at Atami. With the proceeds she bought old and dilapidated houses, had them refurnished, and sold them again at three or four times the original price. Where money matters were concerned, she was never known to lose her head. Money, long years of experience had taught her, brought its own returns, growing steadily like a snowball provided only one kept one's wits about one. She took to lending money also, preferring low rates of interest with reliable securities to higher rates without them. Since the war, she had lost her faith in banks, and kept her money circulating as far as possible, not being so foolish as to keep it stored in the house as a peasant might do. To carry out these transactions, she employed Sumiko's husband Hiroyoshi. It was also part of her knowledge that people would work to one's heart's content so long as one paid them a percentage of the profits by way of commission.

She lived alone with her maid. Though the four-roomed house looked lonely from the outside, yet Kin was by no means lonely. Nor, thanks to her dislike of going out, was it at all inconvenient that the two should live alone. Where burglars were concerned, Kin had more trust in firmly-fastened doors than in any watchdog, and no house could have been better locked at night than hers. Whatever men came to the house she had no fear of gossip, for the maid was deaf and dumb.

Despite all this, there were times when she visualised herself meeting some horrible death. Even she was not immune to that disquieting feeling of suspense that hangs over a perfectly silent house, and she invariably kept the radio turned on from morning to night.

Kin's affair of the moment was with a man called Itaya, who grew flowers at a place just outside Tokyo; they had met through his brother, the man who had bought Kin's villa in Atami. During the war, Itaya had started a trading company in Hanoi, but had been repatriated when peace came and had launched into horticulture with capital supplied by his brother. Though only forty or thereabouts, he was almost completely bald, which made him look old for his age. He had visited Kin two or three times on business connected with the villa, and these visits had somehow or other become regular weekly affairs.

From that time on, Kin's house was gay with the flowers he brought her. Today was no exception: into a vase in the alcove had been thrust a mass of yellow roses. Somehow, they reminded her of the beauty of a mature woman, and their scent brought back the past in all its poignancy. Now that Tabe had telephoned, she realised that his youth gave him an appeal that Itaya did not possess. She had suffered at Hiroshima, true, but then he had been a soldier, and the very violence of his youth seemed now in retrospect only natural, somehow touching and a memory to be treasured. For some reason, she thought, it was always the most tempestuous times that made one feel most nostalgic later.

It was well past five when Tabe arrived.

From within the bundle he carried he produced whisky, ham, cheese and other things, then plumped himself down by the charcoal brazier. He had lost every trace of his former youthfulness, and his grey check jacket and dark green trousers were typical of the mechanical engineer of today at his leisure.

"Beautiful as ever, I see," Tabe said once they had settled down.

"Really? Thank you for saying so. But I've had my day, you know," Kin replied.

"Not a bit of it. You've still got more of what it takes than my wife."

"She's young, I expect?" Kin asked.

"Oh, she may be young, but she's only a country girl."

Kin took a cigarette from Tabe's silver case. He lit it for her. The maid brought whisky glasses and a plate on which slices of the ham and cheese had been arranged. Tabe looked at the maid with a leer.

"Nice girl you've got there," he said.

"Mm. But she's deaf and dumb."

"Is she, now?" Tabe raised his eyebrows and fixed the maid with a look of new interest; she bowed her head deferentially. Kin, her attention drawn for the first time to the maid's youthfulness, suddenly found it irritating.

"You get on well together, I suppose?" Kin asked. Tabe recalled himself with a start and puffed out a cloud of smoke.

"We've got a kid due next month," he replied.

Her face registering due surprise at this announcement, Kin got up and fetched the whisky. She gave a glass to Tabe, who drained it at a gulp and poured out a glass for Kin in her turn.

"How I envy your life here," he continued.

"Why, for goodness sake?"

"Well, however rough the going is outside you seem to stay

the same as ever. . . . I can't make it out. Of course, though, when a woman's got all you have she's sure to have a good patron. Lucky devils, women."

"Are you getting at me? I've never done anything to you to make you say that kind of thing, have I?"

"Don't get angry, now. You didn't understand me." His tone was pacifying. "I just meant that you were lucky. You made me feel what a hard time men have, having to work. A man just can't afford to take it easy these days. Either you do someone else down or he does you down. Take me, for instance—life's a sort of continual gamble for me, you know."

"But business is good, isn't it?" Kin asked.

"That's what you think! You feel you're walking on a tightrope all the time. Money's so tight it hurts."

Kin sipped at her whisky without replying. A cricket chirped dismally in the wall. Tabe drank a second glass of whisky and suddenly, without warning, reached out across the brazier and seized Kin's hand roughly in his. The softness of her ringless hand was insubstantial as a silk handkerchief. Kin remained still, scarcely breathing. Her hand, which rested in his with deliberate passivity, was terribly cold and limp.

Through the drunken fumes in Tabe's mind came crowding and whirling a host of pictures from the past. There she still sat, her remembered beauty untouched. He felt a sense of wonder: time rolled by relentlessly, one gained experience bit by bit, one had one's ups, one had one's downs—and all the time this woman from one's past sat there as large as life, changeless and unchanging. He peered intently at Kin's eyes. Yes, even the little wrinkles around them were as they had always been. Her face, too, retained its firmness of outline. He wished he knew more about the way she lived. For all he knew, the social upheavals of the past years had left her untouched. There she still sat and smiled, secure among her possessions—the chest of drawers, the brazier, the magnificence of the roses heaped in the vase. Tabe did not know her real age, but she must have passed fifty by now. Into his mind there came a picture of his wife at work in their apartment home, already tired and haggard though barely twenty-five.

Kin opened the drawer in the brazier and took out a slender pipe of beaten silver. Thrusting in the end of her cigarette, she lit it. Something in the way Tabe's knees twitched nervously from time to time made her feel uneasy. Could it be that he was in financial straits? She scrutinized his face carefully. No longer, now, could she feel the all-absorbing love she had felt in Hiroshima. Now that they were actually together again, the long silence seemed to have created a barrier between them, a barrier which made Kin feel impatient and desolate at once. Somehow, the old emotions refused to be kindled. Was it, she wondered, overfamiliarity with him physically that had robbed him of all his old appeal for her? Why, she thought with something approaching panic, why, when everything in the setting was right, did the heart remain so cold?

Tabe spoke. "I suppose you couldn't find someone willing to lend me about four hundred thousand, could you?"

Kin started. "Money? Four hundred thousand's an awful lot, isn't it?"

"It is, but I've just got to get it somehow. Now. No idea of anybody?"

"None at all. But why talk to me about such things, when you know I don't even have any income to begin with?"

"That's as may be. Look here, I'd give you a very good rate of interest. How about it?"

"It's no good, I tell you! Whatever you say."

A cold chill crept over Kin, and the even tenor of her relationship with Itaya seemed suddenly eminently desirable. Despair in her heart, she reached for the kettle that had begun to sing on the brazier and filled the teapot.

"Couldn't twenty thousand be managed somehow? I'd be eternally grateful. . . ."

"I don't understand you at all. Why talk to me about money when you know very well I don't have any. . . . I could do with it myself, I can tell you. Did you come to talk about money then, and not to see me?"

"No, I came to see you, of course. Well, I admit it, I did think at the same time that you being the one person I could talk to about anything. . . ."

"Why not speak to your brother about it?" Kin asked.

"He's no good in this case."

Kin was silent. Another year or two, she thought, and she would be old. She could see now that for all its intensity that love of theirs had passed, and left them both untouched. Perhaps, then, it had not been love at all, but only the relation-

ship of two animals drawn together by lust. A fragile tie
between man and woman, to be blown away like a dead leaf
in the winds of time, leaving Tabe and herself sitting here
now, bound only by a trivial bond of acquaintance. A cold
ache filled Kin's breast. She picked up her tea and started to
drink.

"Mind if I stay the night?" Tabe asked with a leer. His
voice had dropped and its tone was casual. Kin looked up
from her tea in feigned surprise.

"Yes, I do. You shouldn't poke fun at me like that at my
age." She smiled, deliberately emphasizing as she did so the
crow's-feet round her eyes. Her false teeth flashed brilliantly
white.

"Don't be so horribly cold and hard," Tabe said. "I'll stop
talking about money. Must have got carried away, thinking I
was talking to the same old Kin I used to know. But . . .
that's all done with now, isn't it?" He paused. "You have the
devil's own luck, don't you? Come through smiling whatever
happens. Don't know how you do it. None of these young
girls nowadays could do it. I say, go in for dancing at all?"

"What do you take me for! And you?"

"A bit," he replied.

"Aha, I expect there's someone special you take, isn't
there? Is that what you want the money for, then?"

"Don't be a fool. Do you think I earn enough to waste it
on keeping a woman?"

"I don't know about that, but look at the way you're got
up. You couldn't put up a show like that without quite a
profitable job."

"This is only so much show. Look in the pockets and what
do you find—nothing! Everybody has their ups and downs,
but things lately have been getting just a bit too fast and furious."

Kin was laughing quietly to herself, her eyes riveted on
Tabe's shock of black hair. It still showed little sign of thinning, and it came forward over his forehead. He had lost the
youthful freshness she had found so charming in his student
days, but something in the line of his cheek had the mature
appeal of middle age and, while his bearing lacked refinement, he still retained a certain brute strength. Kin
poured Tabe a cup of tea, her eye on him the while in the
way one animal scents another in the distance.

"They say money's going to be devaluated soon," she said, half in joke. "Is it true?"

"Oh, so you've got enough to get worried, have you?" Tabe enquired.

"How you do jump to conclusions! You certainly have changed, haven't you! I just asked because I'd heard rumours and was interested."

"I don't know, but I shouldn't think Japan could afford to do anything like that just now. At any rate, people who don't have any money don't have to worry, do they?"

"That's true," Kin replied, and with a cheerful air poured Tabe another whisky.

"How I'd like to go to Hakone or somewhere else quiet," he said. "I think it would do me good to do nothing but sleep and sleep for two or three days in a place like that."

"Tired?"

"Yes. All this worry about money, you know."

"But it suits you to be worried about money. It's not a woman's worry, at least."

The smug correctness of Kin's manner irritated Tabe intensely, but at the same time her likeness to a rather refined piece of antique ware amused him. To spend a night with her, he thought, would only be like giving alms to a beggar. His eyes strayed to Kin's chin: the firm line of the jawbone betrayed the strength of will that lay behind it. Suddenly, a vision of the dumb maid—of her freshness and her youth—seemed to impose itself before his eyes; she was not beautiful, the maid, but she was young, and youth was like a breath of fresh air to a connoisseur of women such as Tabe. Probably, he thought, if this were his first meeting with Kin, he would not have this sense of fretful impatience. The tiredness in Kin's face had come nearer the surface now, and she suddenly seemed old in his eyes.

As if sensing his feeling, Kin got up abruptly and went into the next room. Going to the dressing-table, she picked up a syringe full of hormone and jabbed it into her arm, then, while she was scrubbing at the place with a piece of cotton wool, peered at herself in the mirror. She picked up a powder-puff and dabbed at her nose with it. A wave of mortification swept over her at the pointlessness of such a meeting between a man and woman who were physically dead to each other, and the unbidden tears stood for moment in her eyes.

If it had been Itaya, she could have wept on his lap, wheedled him even. But the Tabe who now sat by the fire in there—she had no idea what she felt for him. One moment she wished to see him gone, the next she had the desperate feeling that he must not go till she had moved him to some further recognition of her. There had been many other women in Tabe's life since they had parted. . . .

She went to the toilet; on her way back, she peeped into the maid's room. Kinu was absorbed in practising her dress-making, cutting patterns out of newspaper. Her large buttocks were planted firmly on the mat, her body crouched over the scissors she was plying. The nape of her neck beneath the tightly-bound hair gleamed white in the light, and her whole body had a striking buxomness.

Kin left her working and went back to the brazier. Tabe was sprawled asleep on the floor. She turned on the radio. Music blared out with a startling volume. Tabe sat up with a start and raised the whisky glass to his lips again.

"Remember the time we went to that hotel at Shibamata together?" he asked. "There was a terrific downpour and the rain came in, and we ate the eels by themselves because there wasn't any rice."

"So we did. Food was terribly scarce then, wasn't it. Before you went in the army, that was. Do you remember, there was a red lily in the alcove and the two of us knocked the vase over?"

"So we did, didn't we." Kin's face seemed suddenly to fill out, and her expression became younger.

"How about going again some day?" Tabe asked.

"That's a nice idea, but, you know, I'm too lazy these days. And I expect you can get anything you like to eat there now—it wouldn't seem the same."

Fearful lest the sentimental mood that had overtaken her a while back should disappear, she tried gently to coax back the past once more. In vain though, for it was not Tabe but another man who came at her summons. On one later occasion, just after the war, she had gone to Shibamata with a man called Yamazaki. He had died only a day or two ago, after a stomach operation. They had gone to the hotel on the banks of the Edo River one muggy day the previous summer, and the atmosphere of that dusky room came back to her vividly now . . . the clanking of the motor pump drawing water outside, the incessant song of the cicadas and the silver flashing from the wheels of the cicadas and the silver flashing from the wheels of the bicycles pacing along the embankment. It had been her second meeting with Yamazaki, whose youthful naivety where women were concerned seemed, to Kin, almost sacred. There had been plenty to eat, and now that the war was over the wearied world had seemed strangely quiet, as if one were living in a vacuum. They had come back to Tokyo in the evening, and the bus by which they had returned to the station had run along a wide road once built for army use.

"Come across anybody who took your fancy since I last saw you?" Tabe asked.

"Me?"

"Yes."

"Took my fancy? There isn't anybody but you."

"Liar!"

"Why? It's true! Who's likely to be interested in me any longer?"

"I don't trust you!"

"You don't?. . . . Well at any rate, I'm going to blossom out and enjoy life from now on. I'm alive like anybody else."

"Got a long time to go yet, eh?"

"That's right. I shall go on and on, till I get too old and decrepit for anything."

"And just as fickle as ever?"

"My God, how you've changed! You used to be such a decent boy. What's happened to you, to make you say such nasty things? You were so nice, once."

Tabe took the silver pipe from Kin and tried a puff at it. A jet of thick bitter liquid struck his tongue. He took out a handkerchief and spat into it.

"It's blocked, it needs cleaning." Kin took it from him with a smile and shook it with short, vigorous movements onto a piece of paper.

Tabe was mystified by the way Kin lived, by the way the cruel world outside had, it appeared, left life in this house completely untouched. One would think she could manage two or three thousand somehow, judging from her present circumstances. Her body no longer awoke any response in him, but he sensed beneath the surface of her daily life an abundance which seemed to Tabe to offer a straw at which he might clutch. Back from the wars, he had gone into business more for the fun of it than anything else; the capital his brother had given him had vanished in less than six months. He was having an affair with another woman outside his marriage, and she was to have a child by him shortly. He had remembered Kin again, and had visited her just on the chance that she might be able to help. Kin's old simplicity, however, had been replaced by a dismaying degree of worldly wisdom. She remained utterly unmoved, even at meeting Tabe again after so long. The stiffness of her posture, the correctness of her manner kept him helplessly at a distance.

He took her hand again and gave it a tentative squeeze, but Kin showed no sign of response. Perhaps he had hoped she would come round the brazier to his side; instead, she carried on cleaning the pipe with her free hand.

Exposure to the years had engraved a complex and different pattern of emotions on both their hearts. They had gradually grown older, he in his way, she in hers, and the old fondness was gone beyond recall. Plunged in a sense of disillusion, they took silent stock of each other as they were now. They were weary with a host of different emotions. Nothing could be less like the storybook meeting with its charming fictions than this reality. It would all, without doubt, have been made much prettier in a novel—the truth about life was too subtle. To reject each other—this had been the only purpose of their coming together today.

The idea of killing Kin drifted through Tabe's head. Yet—and the idea seemed somehow strange—to kill even this woman would be murder. Why should it be wrong to kill a woman or two who meant nothing to anybody? Even as he thought this, he realized what it would mean. It was fantastic. This old woman's existence was as unimportant as that of the lowest insect, and yet she must be allowed to go on living her placid life in this house. The two chests of drawers must be crammed with all the clothes she had made herself in the past fifty years. That bracelet from a Frenchman she had shown him once—she must have that and other jewels too somewhere or other. The house must be hers, too. She was a lone woman, with a maid who was deaf and dumb: to kill her should be easy enough.

His fancy led him on and on. And yet, at the same time, the memory of his student days when she had been all to him, the memory of their secret meetings, came back with a painful freshness and vividness. He was drunk. Perhaps this was why the past and present seemed to become blurred, and the image of Kin as she sat before him seemed to take possession of his body. He did not desire her now, but their past together pressed heavily on his heart.

Kin got up. Going to a cupboard, she got out a photograph of Tabe taken when he was a student and brought it to show him. Tabe stared at it in surprise.

"Good Lord, fancy your keeping a thing like that!" he exclaimed.

"I found it at Sumiko's, and got her to let me have it. Taken before I knew you, wasn't it? You know, you were a proper young gentleman when this was taken. Look at that kimono you were wearing—don't you think it suited you? Here—you have it, I'm sure your wife would like to see it." She paused. "You know, you were so nice-looking in those days—not the kind of man you'd think could say such unpleasant things."

"So I was really like this once, was I?" he asked, studying the photograph.

"You were. I should know. If only you'd gone on in the same way, you'd really have been something, you know."

"By which you mean that I didn't go on in the same way, I suppose?" he asked.

"Yes I do."

"Well, no wonder, what with you, and all those years of war."

"Don't try to get out of it! Things like that have nothing to do with it. You've just got coarser somehow . . . awfully so."

"I have, have I? Coarser, eh? But aren't all people the same?"

"What about me?" Kin replied. "Haven't I kept this photograph by me all these years? Doesn't that show people can sometimes keep their finer feelings?"

"I suppose it just gave you something to look back on. You didn't give me one of you, did you?"

"A photo? Of me?"

"Yes."

"Photographs give me the creeps." She reflected. "But didn't I send you one of me as a geisha, though—while you were in the army over there?"

"Believe you did, but it must have got lost somewhere, I . . ."

"There, that shows you!"

Still the brazier remained between them, an apparently impenetrable barrier. By now Tabe was quite drunk, but Kin's first glass remained hardly touched before her. Tabe picked up his tea and drained the now cold liquid at a gulp. The photograph of himself he laid to one side with an apparent complete lack of interest.

"How are you for trains?" Kin asked.

"Trains? I can't possibly go home. You wouldn't turn me out drunk like this, would you?"

"Yes, I would. Out, like that." She gestured with her hands. "There are no men in this house, and I don't want the neighbours talking."

"The neighbours? Come off it. Since when have you started worrying about things like that?"

"Well, I do worry."

"Got a gentleman friend coming, have you?"

"Oh, what a beastly mind you've got! Oh, really. . . .! I hate you when you say things like that!"

"Go on, hate me then. But if I don't get the money, I just can't go home for a day or two. Thought you might put me up here for. . . ."

Kin, chin cupped in hands, gazed with fixed, wide-open eyes at Tabe's bluish lips. So this was how it all ended, that love one swore would last for ever. . . . Silently, she took in every detail of the man slumped before her. Gone, quite gone, was the romantic excitement they had once felt. No trace now of the young man's bashfulness he had once had. . . .

For a moment she was tempted to offer him a bribe to go and leave her in peace, yet something forbade her giving a single penny to this man now sprawled so drunkenly before her. Far rather would she give it to some man of the unsophisticated type; nothing disgusted her so much as a man like Tabe with no self-respect. She was attracted by a lack of sophistication in men—she had found it time and again among those who had fallen victim to her charms—and even found something noble in it. Her only interest lay in choosing the right men for herself. She despised Tabe in her heart for the way he had let himself go to seed. Why should he have come back from the wars when others had not? But then, Fate was like that. . . . She had done her duty by Tabe in going to Hiroshima after him, and she should have had the sense to ring down the curtain on their relationship at that time.

"Why are you staring at a man like that?"

"I thought it was you who'd been staring at me. What were you thinking—looking so pleased with yourself?"

"Just looking and thinking how you never seemed to change. Beautiful as ever."

"Really? Me too. I was thinking what a fine man you'd turned out."

"Coincidence, eh," Tabe said. It was on the tip of his tongue to say that he had been toying with the idea of murder, but he checked himself in time.

"You're lucky, you know," Kin said. "You've got the prime of life still to come."

"What about you? You've got a long time to go yet, surely," Tabe replied.

"Me? I've had my day. I shall just go on gradually withering. I'm thinking of going to live in the country in two or three years' time."

"Then you didn't mean it when you talked about going on as fickle as ever till you were old and decrepit?"

"I said no such thing! I'm a woman living on her memories. That's all. . . . Can't we be good friends?"

"You're only running away from the question. Why don't you stop talking like a schoolgirl? Memories can take care of themselves."

"I wonder. . . . You know, it was you who brought up our trip to Shibamata."

Tabe had started twitching his knees again. He must get money. Money. . . . Kin must lend it to him somehow. Even fifty thousand would be better than nothing.

"So you really can't manage it? Not even if I put up the business as a security?" He appealed to her.

"What, are you on about money again? It's no good, I tell you, whatever you say I don't have a penny, and I don't know anybody who does. I'd like to borrow some myself, let alone lend it to other people."

"Don't worry about that. If only things go well with me, I'll see you're more than provided for. You're not the kind of person I'd be likely to forget. . . ."

"Oh, stop that flattery! I've had enough of it. I thought you promised not to mention money again?"

A chill wind like that of autumn nights seemed suddenly to howl through the room and into Tabe's heart. He grasped the tongs on the brazier. A spasm of violent rage darkened his face. Drawn irresistibly by the image that floated sphinx-like before his eyes, he tightened his grip on the tongs. A thunderous roaring pulsed in his veins. Go on, go on, it seemed to say. Kin's eyes, riveted on his hand, were vaguely apprehensive. The feeling that somewhere, sometime, this had all happened before mingled with the reality in her mind.

"You're drunk, you know. Why not stay the night?" she said.

Why not stay the night. The tongs fell from Tabe's hand. He pulled himself tipsily to his feet and staggered off in the direction of the toilet. Watching him go, Kin suddenly sensed what had been in his mind, and felt a stir of contempt. The war had done something to people, she thought.

She took the philopon from the cupboard and hastily swallowed a tablet. She looked at the whisky bottle; it was still one-third full. He should drink it all, sleep the sleep of the dead drunk and the next morning she would show him the door. Sleep was not for her that night. Picking up the photograph of the young Tabe, she fed it to the blue flames that leapt from the charcoal in the brazier. Smoke rose in clouds, and a smell of burning filled the room. Kinu the maid peeped in through the sliding doors that Tabe had left partly open. With a smile, Kin signed to her to put out quilts for the night in the guest room. To cover up the smell of burning paper, she laid a thin slice of cheese on the fire.

"Hey, what are you burning?" It was Tabe, back from the toilet. He peered through the sliding doors, his hands on the maid's ample shoulders.

"Thought I'd toast some cheese to see what it tasted like, but I went and dropped it out of the tongs."

A column of black smoke rose up through the white, and the bright disc of the lamp-shade was now a moon floating in the clouds. A smell of burnt fat assailed the nostrils. Coughing and spluttering, Kin got up and hurried round the room flinging open the sliding doors.

—*Translated by John Bester*

Otomi's Virginity

Akutagawa Ryonosuke

Akutagawa Ryunosuke (1892–1927) was a master of the modern short story as well as of the short *haiku* poetry form. In his stories he seems to use the *haiku* method of implication as much as direct explication, as is evident in "Otomi's Virginity." From a reading of this one story we recognize the influence of some of his favorite Western mentors: Poe, Baudelaire, Strindberg. Author of over a hundred short stories and many essays, Akutagawa produced only one novel. He committed suicide by taking veronal at the age of thirty-five.

In this quixotic story of a beggar, an impoverished servant girl, and her mistress's cat, atmosphere becomes a major actor in the drama. Otomi's mixed emotions and motivations as she belligerently protects both her virginity and the cat against the beggar's aggression strangely blends humor with the dark forces of nature. The epilog twenty years later lends a touch of irony.

————

At a little past noon, May 14, 1868, in the city of Edo, a notice was posted, reading: "At dawn tomorrow the Imperial Army will attack the 'Shogitai' entrenched in Toei Hill. Civilians living in the vicinity of Ueno should take refuge anywhere they can."

Inside the house evacuated by Masabei Kogaya, a grocer, at Mi-chome, Shitaya-machi, a tortoise-shell colored cat was crouching in front of a large sea-shell in the corner of the kitchen. The house was so tightly shuttered that even in broad daylight it was dark and quiet inside. The only sound was the pattering of the rain that had been falling for days. From time to time a heavy downfall poured upon the roof and each time the sound grew louder, the cat raised her amber eyes—eyes that gave off an ominous phosphorescent glow in the room so dark that even the stove was not discernible. Finding that no change occurred except in the pattering of the rain, the cat stayed still, but narrowed her eyes thread-thin.

Repeating this action again and again, she must have fallen asleep, for soon she stopped opening her eyes at all. The rain continued to fall heavily and to cease, alternately. Three o'clock . . . Four o'clock . . . The time gradually passed into dusk amidst the sound of the rain.

When five o'clock came, the cat suddenly rounded her eyes and pin-pointed them, as if something had frightened her. The rain had subsided, and nothing was audible but the cries of sedan-carriers running down the street. After several seconds of silence, the kitchen suddenly became dimly lighted. Then into view, object by object, came the kitchen-stove, the sparkling of the water in a lidless jar, the kitchen shrine, and the rope for opening the skylight. Looking all the more uneasy, the cat slowly raised her large body and glared at the outer door, which had just been opened.

The person who opened the door at that moment—not only the outer door, but also the inner, paper door—was a beggar as wet as a drowned rat. Stretching his neck, which was wrapped in an old towel, he listened stealthily and attentively for any possible noise in the quiet house. After making sure that there was not a soul within, he went into the kitchen, his new straw raincoat bright with rain. Flattening her ears, the cat recoiled a few steps. Paying no attention to the cat for the moment, the beggar slid the paper door closed behind him and slowly unwrapped the towel from around his neck. His uncut hair was extremely long, and he had a couple of adhesive paper bandages on his face. Although he was very dirty, he had rather regular features.

"Pussy, pussy," he said in a low tone, wiping his hair and face, which were dripping with rain. The cat pricked up her ears as though she recognized his voice. But staying where she was, she fixed suspicious eyes upon him at intervals. Meanwhile, the beggar took off his raincoat, sat down on the floor in front of the cat, and crossed his legs, which were so muddy that the color of his shins was hardly visible.

"How do you do, pussy?" he asked, laughing to himself and stroking the cat on the head. "Seeing nobody's here, I'd say they've left you in the lurch." For a second the cat seemed about to poise on tiptoe for flight, but she did not spring away. On the contrary, she remained sitting, but gradually began to narrow her eyes. When he stopped stroking the cat, the beggar took an oiled pistol out of his pocket and started examining its trigger in the twilight. The beggar, handling his pistol in the kitchen of the deserted house in an atmosphere of threatening war—this certainly was an unusual and curious sight! Yet, with her eyes narrowed and her back humped, the cat remained sitting as indifferently as though she knew all secrets.

"Hey, pussy," the beggar said to the cat; "tomorrow showers of bullets will fall in this neighborhood. If you're hit, you'll die. So no matter how great a tumult breaks out, don't stir out of the house, and lie hidden under the floor.

"We've been pals. But this will be the last I'll see of you," he said to the cat from time to time, while examining his pistol. "Tomorrow may be an evil day for both you and me. Tomorrow I may die, too. Even if I get off unhurt, I won't hunt around rubbish heaps any more, and you'll be mighty happy, won't you?"

In the meantime the sound of the rain was louder. The clouds were close enough to obscure the roof tiles. The twilight which had hung over the kitchen grew darker and fainter than ever. The beggar, without raising his face, started to load his pistol which he had finished examining.

"Will you miss me when I'm gone?" he went on. "No, cats forget three years' kindness, they say, so I guess you can't be trusted, either.—Well, that doesn't matter. But when I'm gone, too. . . ."

The beggar suddenly was silent, for he heard someone stepping up to the outside of the outer door. He thought someone stepped up to the outer door simultaneously with his putting away his pistol, and just as he looked back, the backdoor was thrust open. Quicker than thought, he assumed the posture of defense, and soon the beggar and the intruder were looking straight at each other.

The instant the incomer caught sight of the beggar, she

gave an outcry of sudden surprise. She was a barefooted young woman, holding a paper umbrella in her hand. She had an almost impulsive desire to dash back into the rain, but at last regaining her courage after her first astonishment, she tried to look into the beggar's face through the little bit of light in the kitchen.

In blank amazement, the beggar watched her closely, raising one knee under his *yukata* [unlined kimono]. His look showed that he was no longer on his guard. For a while the two silently looked at each other face to face.

"You're Shinko, aren't you?" she asked the beggar, recovering some of her composure.

"Oh, pardon me," the beggar said with a grin, and bobbed his head a couple of times towards her. "The heavy shower just drove me into your house in your absence. I haven't turned house-breaker, I assure you."

"I'm really surprised. Even if you are not a house-breaker, you carry your impudence too far," she cried out in vexation, swishing water off her umbrella. "Now get out of here. I'm coming in."

"Yes, I'll go, even without your ordering me to. Haven't you taken refuge yet, miss?"

"Yes, I have. Why not? But what does it matter?"

"Then you left something, I guess. Now come right in here. You're exposed to the rain out there."

As if still exasperated, without giving any reply to his remark, she sat down on the kitchen floor. Stretching her dirty feet, she began ladling water over them. Then the beggar, who sat crossed-legged with full composure, stared fixedly at her, stroking his shaggy-bearded chin. She was a buxom country brunette with pimples on her nose. She wore a plain homespun garment and a cotton sash, as befitting a young maid. Her lively features and attractive figure had an irresistible charm.

"Since you have come back in this confusion, you must have left something very important," he went on asking. "What did you leave? Eh? Miss . . . Otomi-san?"

"Mind your own business. First of all, get out at once, I tell you."

Otomi's answer was blunt. Looking up into his face, she started questioning him with a serious look, as if she had thought of something.

"Shinko," she said, "do you know where our pussy is?"

"Pussy? She was here just now," he said, looking around. "Oh, dear! Where could she have gone?"

The cat had crept up to the shelf unnoticed and was crouching between an earthenware mortar and an iron pot. Otomi caught sight of the cat at the same moment as Shinko. Instantly Otomi threw away her dipper, and stood up on the floor as though she had forgotten the beggar's presence. And with a bright smile, she called the cat on the shelf. Shinko shifted his curious eyes from the cat to Otomi.

"Is it the cat that you left, miss?"

"Why shouldn't it be a cat? Pussy, pussy, now come down."

Shinko suddenly burst out laughing. His laughter called forth an eerie echo amidst the resounding noise of the rain. Otomi, quite surprised, shouted at Shinko out of her renewed vexation, with her cheeks all flushed.

"What makes you laugh? The mistress is upset about having left her cat behind. Worried about the life of the cat, she has been crying all the while. Out of pity for her I've come back all the way in the rain . . ."

"All right. I won't laugh any more." Still continuing to laugh, Shinko interrupted Otomi's remark. "I won't laugh any more. But just think of it. When war may break out tomorrow, a mere cat or two—it is funny, whatever one thinks about it. With all deference to your presence, let me take the liberty of telling you the mistress here is the most unreasonable and selfish woman I've ever heard of. First of all, to look for her pussy . . ."

"Shut up!" Otomi exclaimed with a threatening look, "I don't like to hear you slander my mistress."

As might be expected, the beggar was not frightened by her threatening countenance. On the contrary he had been fixing a rude look upon her person. Her figure at that moment was really savage beauty itself. Her rain-wet *yukata* and petticoat were stuck fast to her skin and her bare soft virginal body was transparent. Shinko, with his eyes fixed upon her, continued to talk laughingly.

"Above anything else, you can tell it by her sending you here to look for the pussy. Now every family in the vicinity of Ueno has already taken refuge. The people's houses are as deserted as uninhabited fields. No wolves may possibly come out, but there's no knowing what terrible danger you may meet with."

"Don't worry unnecessarily, and catch the cat quickly. I don't expect war will break out. How could there be any danger?"

"Don't talk nonsense. If there's no danger in a young girl's walking alone, there can be no danger whatever," Shinko gradually began talking in a vein half-serious and half-jocular. "Coming to the point, we're only two of us here. If I should have a funny desire, what would you do, miss?"

There was not a shadow of fear in Otomi's eyes, but her cheeks were flushed with more blood than ever.

"What, Shinko?—Do you mean to threaten me?" Otomi shouted, taking a step up to his side, as though she were threatening him.

"Threaten?" he retorted. "Lots of titled people are rotten and ill-mannered. Moreover, I'm a beggar. I may do more than threaten. If I really got a funny desire, . . ."

Before he had finished, he was knocked heavily on the head. Before he was aware of it, Otomi was brandishing her umbrella in front of him.

"Don't talk fresh!" Again she struck him on the head with her umbrella with all her might. He tried to dodge the blows but at that instant her umbrella hit him hard on his shoulder which was covered only with a hemp garment. Aroused, the cat, kicking down an iron kettle, sprang upon the shelf where the family kitchen shrine was placed. At the same time the pine branch and the oil lamp on the shelf fell down on Shinko. Before he could spring to his feet, he was repeatedly slugged with Otomi's umbrella.

"Damn you! Damn you!" she cried and continued to brandish her umbrella. Finally, he succeeded in snatching the umbrella from her.

No sooner had he thrown off the umbrella than he furiously sprang upon her. For a while the two grappled with each other on the small wooden floor. Amidst this scuffle the shower, gathering in strength, battered the roof. As the sound of the rain became louder, the dusk deepened moment by moment. Beaten and scratched, the beggar furiously strove to overpower and hold her down by his physical strength. The instant he seized hold of her after repeated failures, he dashed toward the entrance like a shot.

"You damned bitch!" he glared at her fiercely with the sliding screen as his shield.

With her hair already disheveled, Otomi sat down flat on the floor, grasping a razor in her hand with the blade down. Presumably she had brought it in her sash. Her grim look and strange maidenly charm was like that of the cat with her back rounded on the shelf of the shrine. Remaining silent for a few seconds, they studied each other's eyes. Then wearing an affected grin, Shinko took the pistol out of his pocket.

"Now struggle as you will," he said, deliberately aiming the muzzle of his pistol at her chest. Although she looked at him regretfully, she did not open her mouth. Noting her silence, he directed the muzzle higher as if he had thought of something. In front of the muzzle gleamed the amber-colored eyes of the cat.

"All right, Otomi-san?" he asked in a voice pregnant with a smile as if to tease her.

"If I fire this pistol, the cat'll drop headlong dead." He was on the point of pulling the trigger. "It'll be the same with you. Agreed?"

"Don't!" Otomi suddenly cried out. "Shinko, don't fire!"

Shinko shifted his eyes towards her, with his pistol still aimed at the tortoise-shell cat.

"Of course, I guess you'll be sorry."

"It's a pity to shoot her. For mercy's sake, don't." Now a complete change came over Otomi. Her eyes showed her concern. Through her slightly trembling lips showed a row of fine teeth. With a look of half-derision and half-wonder, the beggar lowered the muzzle. This brought a look of relief over the girl's face.

"Well, I'll spare the cat. In place of it . . ." he triumphantly declared. "In place of it I'll just take you."

Otomi turned her eyes away. For that instant her inmost heart seemed to seethe in a turmoil of various feelings: hatred, anger, disgust, and grief. Keeping a careful watch over these expressions, he walked sidewise behind her back, and threw open the paper sliding-doors (*shoji*) of the living room, which was still darker than the kitchen. In this room, the chest of drawers and the oblong charcoal brazier loomed up distinctly. The empty room clear of anything else imparted a vivid impression of the evacuation. Standing behind Otomi, he dropped his eyes to her neck which looked slightly moist with perspiration. She may have sensed it. Twisting her body, she looked up into his face. The lively color, just as before, was already back in her face. However, as if he were very confused, giving a queer blink, he turned his pistol again at the cat.

"Don't! I tell you, don't!" Trying to stop him, she dropped the razor which she had held in her hand.

"If I mustn't, go over there," he said with a faint smile.

"Oh, you're nasty," she grumbled in vexation. But getting up, she hurriedly went into the living room in the manner of an indelicate woman. He looked somewhat astonished at her complete resignation to her fate. The noise of the rain had already greatly subsided by that time. Moreover, the breaks in the clouds might have been lit by the glow of the setting sun. The kitchen, which had been gloomy, gradually grew lighter. Standing in the kitchen, he listened carefully to the sound of rustling in the living room, her untying of her cotton sash, and presumably her lying down on the mat. After that the living room became deadly still.

After some apparent hesitation, he set foot in the dimly lit living room. In the middle of the room he found her lying still on her back, her face covered with her sleeves. The moment he saw her, he scurried back to the kitchen. His face had a strange, indescribable expression, which looked like disgust or shame. The minute he was back in the kitchen, he started laughing, with his back still turned toward the living room.

"I've been teasing you, Otomi-san," he cried out. "I've been teasing. Now come out here, please."

Some minutes later Otomi, with the cat in her bosom and her umbrella in her hand, was talking cheerfully with Shinko, who was sitting on a small thin mat.

"Miss!" he asked, without daring to look her in the face as if he were still embarrassed, "I have something I'd like to ask you."

"What is it?"

"Well, nothing particularly serious," he quibbled. "But you see, it's a matter of vital importance in a woman's life to give herself to a man. You Otomi-san . . . in exchange for the cat's life. Anyway that was too reckless of you, Otomi-san, wasn't it?" He held his tongue for a minute. Otomi, with a smile beaming all over her face, gave no answer, only caressed the cat in her bosom.

"Do you love the cat so much?"

"Yes, I do love the cat," she answered vaguely.

"Well, you've got a fine reputation in the neighborhood for your faithful service to your master. Were you afraid that you'd be terribly sorry for your mistress if the cat were killed?"

"Well, I love pussy, and to be sure my mistress is important to me, but I . . ." Inclining her head slightly on one side, she behaved as though she were looking far away. "Well, how should I put it? I somehow felt I must act like that. That's all."

Several minutes later, left alone, Shinko was squatting absent-mindedly in the kitchen, with his hands on his knees under his old hempen garment. Amidst a sprinkling of rain, evening dusk had been gradually closing in around where he was. The rope of the skylight, the water-jar by the sink, sank out of sight one by one, when the sporadic templebells of Ueno, pent up by the rain clouds, began pealing their heavy gongs. As if surprised at the sound, he looked about his surroundings enveloped in dead silence. Then groping his way to the sink, he filled a dipper with water.

"Shinsaburo Shigemitsu, surnamed Muragami, son of the old House of Minamoto as I am, I've suffered a blow today." So grumbling, he enjoyed his fill of water.

The 26th of March, 1889, saw Otomi and her husband walking with their three children on the boulevard of Ueno.

That was the very day when the opening ceremony of the third national exposition was held at Takenodai, Ueno. And, the cherry-blossoms around the entrance to Ueno Park were mostly all out. So the boulevard of Ueno was hustling and bustling with immense crowds of people. From the direction of Ueno there were constant streams of coaches and *jinrikisha* [man-pulled carts] coming on their way home from the opening ceremony. Among the passengers of these vehicles were prominent people, such as Masana Maeda, Ukichi Taguchi, Eiichi Shibusawa, Shinji Tsuji, Kakuzo Okakura, and Masao Gejo.

His eldest son holding onto his sleeve, Otomi's husband was carrying his five-year-old second son in his arms, and

dodging his way through the congestion of the pedestrian and
vehicular traffic; from time to time he anxiously looked back
at Otomi leading her daughter by the hand. Otomi threw him
a radiant smile each time. Of course the lapse of the inter-
vening twenty years had brought her a certain maturity. But
her eyes were just as clear and bright as in her former years.
Around 1870 she had married her present husband, nephew
to Furukawaya Seibei. He kept a small watch store first in
Yokohama and now on Ginza Street, Tokyo.

Otomi happened to look up, and saw Shinko sitting leisurely in a two-horse carriage which happened to be passing
by. She was particularly attracted to his breast which appeared to be buried under various badges of honor—many
large and small decorations, gold-laced stripes, and peacock
feathers. Nevertheless, it was beyond doubt that this ruddy
gray-bearded face looking at her was that of the former beggar. She slackened her pace in spite of herself. But strangely
enough, she was not surprised. Somehow she had known that
he was no mere beggar. She might have observed this by his
countenance, language, or the pistol he carried. She fixed her
gaze intently on his face. Whether intentionally or acciden-
tally he was also closely watching hers. At that instant her
memory of twenty years ago was awakened with painful dis-
tinctness. On that far-away day she had imprudently resigned
herself to giving herself up to him to save the cat's life. What
was her motive then? She could not tell. In such a situation
he could not persuade himself even to touch the body which
she had surrendered to him. What was his motive then? She
could not tell that either. Although she could not tell, that
was all too natural to her. Crossing his carriage, she felt her
mind relieved of all her cares.

When the carriage had passed by, Otomi's husband looked
over at her through the dense throng of people. Looking back
at him cheerfully and happily, Otomi smiled as though nothing had happened.

—Translated by Kuwata Masakazu

Aguri

Tanizaki Junichiro

Tanizaki Junichiro (1886–1965) is noted chiefly for his depiction of the conflict between tradition and new values in twentieth-century Japan and for his insight into the female psyche. Most of his novels focus on women characters and many are written from their point of view, men usually being depicted as weaker than the women with whom they are associated. *The Makioka Sisters* (1944, English translation 1957), in his longest novel. Donald Keene, a translator and authority on Japanese literature, calls it "an elegy for the passing of the traditional Japan."

"Aguri" emphasizes the East-West conflict in a direct yet surrealistic way, using macabre elements that echo Edgar Allan Poe, one of Tanizaki's earliest influences.

"Getting a bit thinner, aren't you? Is anything wrong? You're not looking well these days. . . ."

That was what his friend T. had said in passing when they happened to meet him along the Ginza a little while ago. It reminded Okada that he had spent last night with Aguri too, and he felt more fatigued than ever. Of course T. could scarcely have been teasing him about *that*—his relations with Aguri were too well known, there was nothing unusual about being seen strolling on the Ginza in downtown Tokyo with her. But to Okada, with his taut-stretched nerves and his vanity, T.'s remark was disturbing. Everyone he met said he was "getting thinner"—he had worried about it himself for over a year. In the last six months you could amost see the change from one day to the next, as his fine rich flesh slowly melted away. He'd got into the habit of furtively examining his body in the mirror whenever he took a bath, to see how emaciated it was becoming, but by now he was afraid to look. In the past (until a year or two ago, at least) people said he had a feminine sort of figure. He had rather prided himself on it. "The way I'm built makes you think of a woman, doesn't it?" he used to say archly to his friends at the bathhouse. "Don't get any funny ideas!" But now . . .

It was from the waist down that his body had seemed most feminine. He remembered often standing before a mirror entranced by his own reflection, running his hand lovingly over his plump white buttocks, as well rounded as a young girl's. His thighs and calves were almost *too* bulging, but it had delighted him to see how fat they looked—the legs of a chophouse waitress—alongside Aguri's slim ones. She was only fourteen then, and her legs were as slender and straight as those of any Western girl: stretched out beside his in the bath, they looked more beautiful than ever, which pleased him as much as it did Aguri. She was a tomboy, and used to push him over on his back and sit on him, or walk over him, or trample on his thighs as if she were flattening a lump of dough. . . . But now what miserable skinny legs he had! His knees and ankles had been nicely dimpled, but for some time now the bones had stuck out pathetically, you could see them moving under the skin. The exposed blood vessels looked like earthworms. His buttocks were flattening out too: when he sat on something hard it felt as if a pair of boards had been clapped together. Yet it was only lately that his ribs began to show: one by one they had come into sharp relief, from the bottom up, till now you could see the whole skeleton of his chest so distinctly that it made a somewhat grim anatomy lesson. He was such a heavy eater that his little round belly had seemed safe enough, but even *that* was gradually shriveling—at this rate, you'd soon be able to make out his inner organs! Next to his legs, he had prided himself on his smooth "feminine" arms; at the slightest excuse he rolled up his sleeves to show them off. Women admired and envied them, and he used to joke with his girl friends about it. Now, even to the fondest eye, they didn't look at all feminine—or masculine either for that matter. They weren't so much human arms as two sticks of wood. Two pencils hanging down beside his body. All the little hollows between one bone and the next were deepening, the flesh dwindling away. How much longer can I go on losing weight like this? he asked himself. It's amazing that I can still get around at all, when I'm so horribly emaciated! He felt grateful to be alive, but also a little terrified. . . .

These thoughts were so unnerving that Okada had a sudden attack of giddiness. There was a heavy, numbing sensation in the back of his head; he felt as if his knees were shaking and his legs buckling under him, as if he were being knocked over backward. No doubt the state of his nerves had something to do with it, but he knew very well that it came from long overindulgence, sexual and otherwise—as did his diabetes, which caused some of his symptoms. There was no use feeling sorry now, but he *did* regret having to pay for it so soon, and pay, moreover, by the deterioration of his good looks, his proudest possession. I'm still in my thirties, he thought. I don't see why my health has to fail so badly. . . . He wanted to cry and stamp his feet in rage.

"Wait a minute—look at that ring! An aquamarine, isn't it? I wonder how it would look on me."

Aguri had stopped short and tugged at his sleeve; she was peering into a Ginza show window. As she spoke she waved the back of her hand under Okada's nose, flexing and extending her fingers. Her long slender fingers—so soft they seemed made only for pleasure—gleamed in the bright May afternoon sunlight with an especially seductive charm. Once in Nanking he had looked at a singsong girl's fingers resting gracefully on the table like the petals of some exquisite hothouse flower, and thought there could be no more delicate beauty than a Chinese woman's hands. But Aguri's hands were only a little larger, only a little more like those of an ordinary human being. If the singsong girl's hands were hothouse flowers, hers were fresh young wildflowers: the fact that they were not so artificial only made them more appealing. How pretty a bouquet of flowers with petals like these would be. . . .

"What do you think? Would it look nice?" She poised her fingertips on the railing in front of the window, pressed them back in the half-moon curve of a dancer's gesture, and stared at them as if she had lost all interest in the ring.

Okada mumbled something in reply but forgot it immediately. He was staring at her hands too, at the beautiful hands he knew so well. . . . Several years had passed since he began playing with those delicious morsels of flesh: squeezing them in his palms like clay, putting them inside his clothes like a pocket warmer, or in his mouth, under his arm, under his chin. But while he was steadily aging, her mysterious hands looked younger every year. When Aguri was only fourteen they seemed yellow and dry, with tiny wrinkles, but now at seventeen the skin was white and smooth, and yet even on the coldest day so sleek you'd think the oil would cloud the gold band of her ring. Childish little hands, as tender as a baby's and as voluptuous as a whore's—how fresh and youthful they were, always restlessly seeking pleasure! . . . But why had his health failed like this? Just to look at her hands made him think of all they had provoked him to, all that went on in those secret rooms where they met; and his head ached from the potent stimulus. . . . As he kept his eyes fixed on them, he began to think of the rest of her body. Here in broad daylight on the crowded Ginza he saw her naked shoulders . . . her breasts . . . her belly . . . buttocks . . . legs . . . one by one all the parts of her body came floating up before his eyes with frightening clarity in queer, undulating shapes. And he felt crushed under the solid weight of her hundred and fifteen or twenty pounds. . . . For a moment Okada thought he was going to faint—his head was reeling, he seemed on the verge of falling. . . . Idiot! Suddenly he drove away his fantasies, steadied his tottering legs. . . .

"Well, are we going shopping?"

"All right."

They began walking toward Shimbashi Station. . . . Now they were off to Yokahama.

Today Aguri must be happy, he thought, I'll be buying her a whole new outfit. You'll find the right things for yourself in the foreign shops of Yokahama, he had told her; in Arthur Bond's and Lane Crawford, and that Indian jeweler, and the Chinese dressmaker. . . . You're the exotic type of beauty; Japanese kimonos cost more than they're worth, and they're not becoming to you. Notice the Western and the Chinese ladies: they know how to set off their faces and figures to advantage, and without spending too much money at it. You ought to do the same from now on. . . . And so Aguri had been looking forward to today. As she walks along, breathing a little heavily in the early-summer heat, her white skin damp with sweat under the heavy flannel kimono that hampers her long, youthful limbs, she imagines herself shedding these "unbecoming" clothes, fixing jewels on her ears, hanging a necklace around her throat, slipping into a near-transparent blouse of rustling silk or cambric, swaying elegantly on tiptoes in fragile high-heeled shoes. . . . She sees herself looking like the Western ladies who pass them on the street. Whenever one of them comes along Aguri studies her from head to toe, following her with her eyes and badgering him with questions about how he likes that hat, or that necklace, or whatever.

But Okada shared her preoccupation. All the smart young foreign ladies made him think of an Aguri transfigured by Western clothes. . . . I'd like to buy that for you, he thought; and this too. . . . Yet why couldn't he be a little more cheerful? Later on they would play their enchanting game together. It was a clear day with a refreshing breeze, a fine May afternoon for any kind of outing . . . for dressing her up in airy new garments, grooming her like a beloved pet, and then taking her on the train in search of a delightful hiding place. Somewhere with a balcony overlooking the blue sea, or a room at a hot-spring resort where the young leaves of the forest glisten beyond glass doors, or else a gloomy, out-of-the-way hotel in the foreign quarter. And there the game would begin, the enchanting game that he was always dreaming of, that gave him his only reason for living. . . . Then she would stretch herself out like a leopard. A leopard in necklace and earrings. A leopard brought up as a house pet, knowing exactly how to please its master, but one whose occasional flashes of ferocity made its master cringe. Frisking, scratching, striking, pouncing on him—finally ripping and tearing him to shreds, and trying to suck the marrow out of his bones. . . . A deadly game! The mere thought of it had an ecstatic lure for him. He found himself trembling with excitement. Once again his head was swimming, he thought he was going to faint. . . . He wondered if he might be dying, now at last, aged thirty-four, collapsing here on the street. . . .

"Oh, are you dead? How tiresome!" Aguri glances absentmindedly at the corpse lying at her feet. The two-o'clock sun beats down on it, casting dark shadows in the hollows of its sunken cheeks. . . . If he *had* to die he might have waited half a day longer, till we finished our shopping. . . . Aguri clicks her tongue in annoyance. I don't want to get mixed up in this if I can help it, she thinks, but I suppose I can't just leave him here. And there are hundreds of yen in his pocket. The money was *mine*—he might at least have willed it to me before he died. The poor fool was so crazy about me he couldn't possibly resent it if I take the money and buy anything I please, or flirt with any man I please. He knew I was fickle—he even seemed to enjoy it, sometimes. . . . As she makes excuses to herself Aguri extracts the money from his pocket. If he tries to haunt me I won't be afraid of *him*—he'll listen to me whether he's alive or dead. I'll have my way. . . .

"Look, Mr. Ghost! I bought this wonderful ring with your money. I bought this beautiful lace-trimmed skirt. And see!" (She pulls up her skirt to show her legs.) "See these legs you're so fond of, these gorgeous legs? I bought a pair of white silk stockings, and pink garters too—all with your money! Don't you think I have good taste? Don't you think I look angelic? Although you're dead I'm wearing the right clothes for me, just the way you wanted, and I'm having a marvelous time! I'm so happy, really happy! You must be happy too, for having given me all this. Your dreams have come true in me, now that I'm so beautiful, so full of life! Well, Mr. Ghost, my poor love-struck Mr. Ghost who can't rest in peace—how about a smile?"

Then I'll hug that cold corpse as hard as I can, hug it till his bones crack, and he screams: "Stop! I can't bear any more!" If he doesn't give in, I'll find a way to seduce him. I'll love him till his withered skin is torn to shreds, till his last drop of blood is squeezed out, till his dry bones fall apart. Then even a ghost ought to feel satisfied. . . .

"What's the matter? Is something on your mind?"

"Uh-h . . ." Okada began mumbling under his breath.

They looked as if they were having a pleasant walk together—it ought to have been extremely pleasant—and yet he couldn't share her gaiety. One sad thought after another welled up, and he felt exhausted even before they began their game. It's only nerves he had told himself; nothing serious, I'll get over it as soon as I go outside. That was how he had talked himself into coming, but he'd been wrong. It wasn't nerves alone: his arms and legs were so tired they were ready to drop off, and his joints creaked as he walked. Sometimes being tired was a mild, rather enjoyable sensation, but when it got this bad it might be a dangerous symptom. At this very moment, all unknown to him, wasn't his system being invaded by some grave disease? Wasn't he staggering along letting the disease take its own course till it overwhelmed him? Better to collapse right away than be so ghastly tired! He'd like to sink down into a soft bed. Maybe his health had demanded it long ago. Any doctor would be alarmed and say: "Why in heaven's name are you out walking in *your* condition? You belong in bed—it's no wonder you're dizzy!"

The thought left Okada feeling more exhausted than ever; walking became an even greater effort. On the Ginza sidewalk—that dry, stony surface he so much enjoyed striding over when he was well—every step sent a shock of pain vibrating up from his heel to the top of his head. First of all, his feet were cramped by these tan box-calf shoes that compressed them in a narrow mold. Western clothes were intended for healthy, robust men: to anyone in a weakened condition they were quite insupportable. Around the waist, over the shoulders, under the arms, around the neck—every part of the body was pressed and squeezed by clasps and buttons and rubber and leather, layer over layer, as if you were strapped to a cross. And of course you had to put on stockings before the shoes, stretching them carefully up on your legs by garters. Then you put on a shirt, and then trousers, cinching them in with a buckle at the back till they cut into your waist and hanging them from your shoulders with suspenders. Your neck was choked in a close-fitting collar, over which you fastened a nooselike necktie, and stuck a pin in it. If a man is well filled out, the tighter you squeeze him, the more vigorous and bursting with vitality he seems; but a man who is only skin and bones can't stand that. The thought that he was wearing such appalling garments made Okada gasp for breath, made his arms and legs even wearier. It was only because these Western clothes held him together that he was able to keep on walking at all—but to think of stiffening a limp, helpless body, shackling it hand and foot, and driving it ahead with shouts of "Keep going! Don't you dare collapse!" It was enough to make a man want to cry. . . .

Suddenly Okada imagined his self-control giving way, imagined himself breaking down and sobbing. . . . This sprucely dressed middle-aged gentleman who was strolling along the Ginza until a moment ago, apparently out to enjoy the fine weather with the young lady at his side, a gentleman who looks as if he might be the young lady's uncle—all at once screws up his face into a dreadful shape and begins to bawl like a child! He stops there in the street and pesters her to carry him. "*Please,* Aguri! I can't go another step! Carry me piggyback!"

"What's wrong with you?" says Aguri sharply, glaring at him like a stern auntie. "Stop acting like that! Everybody's looking at you!" . . . Probably she doesn't notice that he has gone mad: it's not unusual for her to see him in tears. This is the first time it's happened on the street, but when they're alone together he always cries like this. . . . How silly of him! she must be thinking. There's nothing for him to cry about in public—if he wants to cry I'll let him cry his heart out later! "Shh! Be quiet! You're embarrassing me!"

But Okada won't stop crying. At last he begins to kick and struggle, tearing off his necktie and collar and throwing them down. And then, dog-tired, panting for breath, he falls flat on the pavement. "I can't walk any more. . . . I'm sick. . . ," he mutters, half delirious. "Get me out of these clothes and put me in something soft! Make a bed for me here, I don't care if it *is* in the street!"

Aguri is at her wit's end, so embarrassed her face is as red as fire. There is no escape—a huge crowd of people has swarmed around them under the blazing sun. A policeman turns up. . . . He questions Aguri in front of everyone. ("Who do you suppose she is?" people begin whispering to one another. "Some rich man's daughter?" "No, I don't think so." "An actress?") "What's the matter there?" the policeman asks Okada, not unkindly. He regards him as a lunatic. "How about getting up now, instead of sleeping in a place like this?"

"I won't! I won't! I'm sick, I tell you! How can I ever get up?" Still sobbing weakly, Okada shakes his head. . . .

He could see the spectacle vividly before his eyes. He felt as if he were actually sobbing. . . .

"Papa . . ." A faint voice is calling—a sweet little voice, not Aguri's. It is the voice of a chubby four-year-old girl in a printed muslin kimono, who beckons to him with her tiny hand. Behind her stands a woman whose hair is done up in a

chignon; she looks like the child's mother. . . . "Teruko!
Teruko! Here I am! . . . Ah, Osaki! Are you there too?"
And then he sees his own mother, who died several years
ago. She is gesturing eagerly and trying hard to tell him
something, but she is too far away, a veil of mist hangs between them. . . . Yet he realizes that tears of loneliness and
sorrow are streaming down her cheeks. . . .

I'm going to stop thinking sad thoughts like that, Okada
told himself; thoughts about Mother, about Osaki and the
child, about death. . . . Why did they weigh so heavily on
him? No doubt because of his poor health. Two or three
years ago when he was well they wouldn't have seemed so
overpowering, but now they combined with physical exhaustion to thicken and clog all his veins. And when he was sexually excited the clogging became more and more
oppressive. . . . As he walked along in the bright May sun-
shine he felt himself isolated from the world around him: his
sight was dimmed, his hearing faded, his mind turned darkly,
obstinately in upon itself.

"If you have enough money left," Aguri was saying, "how
about buying me a wrist watch?" They had just come to
Shimbashi Station; perhaps she thought of it when she saw
the big clock.

"They have good watches in Shanghai. I should have
bought you one when I was there."

For a moment Okada's fancies flew off to China. . . . At
Soochow, aboard a beautiful pleasure boat, being poled along
a serene canal toward the soaring Tiger Hill Pagoda . . . Inside the boat two young lovers sit blissfully side by side like
turtledoves. . . . He and Aguri transformed into a Chinese
gentleman and a singsong girl. . . .

Was he in love with Aguri? If anyone asked, of course he
would answer "Yes." But at the thought of Aguri his mind
became a pitch-dark room hung with black velvet curtains—a
room like a conjurer's stage set—in the center of which stood
the marble statue of a nude woman. Was that really Aguri?
Surely the Aguri he loved was the living, breathing counterpart of that marble figure. This girl walking beside him now
through the foreign shopping quarter of Yokohama—he
could see the lines of her body through the loose flannel
clothing that enveloped it, could picture to himself the statue
of the "woman" under her kimono. He recalled each elegant

trace of the chisel. Today he would adorn the statue with jewels and silks. He would strip off that shapeless, unbecoming kimono, reveal that naked "woman" for an instant, and then dress her in Western clothes: he would accentuate every curve and hollow, give her body a brilliant surface and lively flowing lines; he would fashion swelling contours, make her wrists, ankles, neck, all strikingly slender and graceful. Really, shopping to enchance the beauty of the woman you love ought to be like a dream come true.

A dream . . . There was indeed something dreamlike about walking along this quiet, almost deserted street lined with massive Western-style buildings, looking into show windows here and there. It wasn't garish, like the Ginza; even in daytime a hush lay over it. Could anyone be alive in these silent buildings, with their thick gray walls where the window glass glittered like fish eyes, reflecting the blue sky? It seemed more like a museum gallery than a street. And the merchandise displayed behind the glass on both sides was bright and colorful, with the fascinating, mysterious luster of a garden at the bottom of the sea.

A curio-shop sign in English caught his eye: ALL KINDS OF JAPANESE FINE ARTS: PAINTINGS, PORCELAINS, BRONZE STATUES. . . . And one that must have been for a Chinese tailor: MAN CHANG DRESS MAKER FOR LADIES AND GENTLEMEN. . . . And also: JAMES BERGMAN JEWELLERY . . . RINGS, EARRINGS, NECKLACES . . . E & B CO. FOREIGN DRY GOODS AND GROCERIES . . . LADY'S UNDERWEARS . . . DRAPERIES, TAPESTRIES, EMBROIDERIES. . . . Somehow the very ring of these words in his ear had the heavy, solemn beauty of the sound of a piano. . . . Only an hour by streetcar from Tokyo, yet you felt as if you had arrived at some far-off place. And you hesitated to go inside these shops when you saw how lifeless they looked, their doors firmly shut. In these show windows—perhaps because they were meant for foreigners—goods were set out on display in a cold, formal arrangement well behind the glass, quite unlike the ingratiating clutter of the windows along the Ginza. There seemed to be no clerks or shopboys at work; all kinds of luxuries were on display, but these dimly lit rooms were as gloomy as a Buddhist shrine. . . . Still, that made the goods within seem all the more curiously enticing.

Okada and Aguri went up and down the street several

times: past a shoeshop, a milliner's shop, a jeweler, a furrier, a textile merchant. . . . If he handed over a little of his money, any of the things in these shops would cling fast to her white skin, coil around her lithe, graceful arms and legs, become a part of her. . . . European women's clothes weren't "things to wear"—they were a second layer of skin. They weren't merely wrapped over and around the body but dyed into its very surface like a kind of tattooed decoration. When he looked again, all the goods in the show windows seemed to be so many layers of Aguri's skin, flecked with color, with drops of blood. She ought to choose what she likes and make it part of herself. If you buy jade earrings, he wanted to tell her, think of yourself with beautiful green pendants growing from your earlobes. If you put on that squirrel coat, the one in the furrier's window, think of yourself as an animal with a velvety sleek coat of hair. If you buy the celadon-colored stockings hanging over there, the moment you pull them on, your legs will have a silken skin, warmed by your own coursing blood. If you slip into patent-leather shoes, the soft flesh of your heels will turn into glittering lacquer. My darling Aguri! All these were molded to the statue of woman which is you: blue, purple, crimson skins—all were formed to your body. It's *you* they are selling there, your outer skin is waiting to come to life. Why, when you have such superb things of your own, do you wrap yourself up in clothes like that baggy, shapeless kimono?

"Yes, sir. For the young lady? . . . Just what does she have in mind?"

A Japanese clerk had emerged out of the dark back room of the shop and was eyeing Aguri suspiciously. They had gone into a modest little dress shop because it seemed least forbidding: not a very attractive one, to be sure, but there were glass-covered cases along both sides of the narrow room, and the cases were full of dresses. Blouses and skirts— women's breasts and hips—dangled overhead. There were low glass cases in the middle of the room, too, displaying petticoats, chemises, hosiery, corsets, and all manner of little lacy things. Nothing but cool, slippery, soft fabrics, literally softer than a woman's skin: delicately crinkled silk crepe, glossy white silk, fine satin. When Aguri realized that she would soon be clothed in these fabrics, like a mannequin, she seemed ashamed at being eyed by the clerk and shrank back shyly, losing all her usual vivaciousness. But her eyes were sparkling as if to say: "I want this, and that, and that. . . ."

"I don't really know what I'd like. . . ." She seemed puzzled and embarrassed. "What do *you* think?" she whispered to Okada, hiding behind him to avoid the clerk's gaze.

"Let me see now," the clerk spoke up briskly. "I imagine any of these would look good on you." He spread out a white linen-like dress for her inspection. "How about this one? Just hold it up to yourself and look at it—you'll find a mirror over there."

Aguri went before the mirror and tucked the white garment under her chin, letting it hang down loosely. Eyes upturned, she stared at it with the glum look of a fretful child.

"How do you like it?" Okada asked.

"Mmm. Not bad."

"It doesn't seem to be linen, though. What's the material?"

"That's cotton voile, sir. It's a fresh, crisp kind of fabric, very pleasant to the touch."

"And the price?"

"Let's see. . . . Now this one . . ." The clerk turned toward the back room and called in a startlingly loud voice: "Say, how much is this cotton voile—forty-five yen?"

"It'll have to be altered," Okada said. "Can you do it today?"

"Today? Are you sailing tomorrow?"

"No, but we *are* rather in a hurry."

"Hey, how about it?" The clerk turned and shouted toward the back room again. "He says he wants it today—can you manage it? See if you can, will you?" Though a little rough-spoken, he seemed kind and good-natured. "We'll start right now, but it'll take at least two hours."

"That will be fine. We still need to buy shoes and a hat and the rest, and she'll want to change into her new things here. But what is she supposed to wear underneath? It's the first time she's ever had Western clothes."

"Don't worry, we have all those too—here's what you start with." He slipped a silk brassière out of a glass case. "Then you put this on over it, and then step into this and this, below. They come in a different style too, but there's no opening, so you have to take it off if you want to go to the toilet. That's why Westerners hold their water as long as they can. Now, this kind is more convenient: it has a button here, you see? Just unbutton it and you'll have no trouble! . . . The chemise is eight yen, the petticoat is about six yen—they're cheap compared with kimonos, but see what beautiful white silk they're made of! Please step over here and I'll take your measurements.

Through the flannel cloth the dimensions of the hidden form were measured; around her legs, under her arms, the leather tape was wound to investigate the bulk and shape of her body.

"How much is this woman worth?" Was that what the clerk was calculating? It seemed to Okada that he was having a price set on Aguri, that he was putting her on sale in a slave market.

About six o'clock that evening they came back to the dress shop with their other purchases: shoes, a hat, a pearl neck-lace, a pair of amethyst earrings. . . .

"Well, come in! Did you find some nice things?" The clerk greeted them in a breezy, familiar tone. "It's all ready! The fitting room is over here—just go in and change your clothes!"

Okada followed Aguri behind the screen, gently holding over one arm the soft, snowy garments. They came to a full-length mirror, and Aguri, still looking glum, slowly began to undo her sash. . . .

The statue of the woman in Okada's mind stood naked be-fore him. The fine silk snagged on his fingers as he helped ap-ply it to her skin, going round and round the white figure, tying ribbons, fastening buttons and hooks. . . . Suddenly Aguri's face lit up with a radiant smile. Okada felt his head begin to swim. . . .

—*Translated by Kuwata Masakazu*

Patriotism

Mishima Yukio

Mishima Yukio (1925–1970) is the pen name adopted by Kimitake Hiraoka at the beginning of his comparatively brief but prolific literary career.

Son of a high government official, Mishima attended the Peer's School and then studied law at Tokyo University. His first published work—*The Flowering Grove*—appeared in 1944, the year he entered the university. Following graduation and after less than a year in the Finance Ministry, Mishima withdrew in disillusionment and turned to writing as a full-time career. In short order he produced works in every literary form. At the time of his death in 1970, he had produced 20 novels, 33 plays, 80 stories, and hundreds of articles and essays, as well as a number of film scripts and travel books. He received the first of a number of national literary prizes in 1954 when he was only twenty-nine. Some half-dozen others followed.

Widely traveled and widely published in the West, Mishima's works have been translated into some fifteen foreign languages, and a number of his dramas have been performed in countries other than Japan. On several occasions Mishima performed roles in his own plays, both on stage and in the films.

Although at ease in other countries, East and West, Mishima was steeped in the culture of old Japan and was concerned about its rapid erosion following World War II and the Allied Occupation, a thesis which is central to his novel *The Temple of the Golden Pavilion*. There, his protagonist, a young acolyte in training for the priesthood, becomes so obsessed with the encroaching threats to the sacred beauty of one of Japan's holiest and most beautiful Buddhist shrines that he himself destroys the temple before it can become desecrated by outside forces. The book's theme was based on fact, for the fourteenth-century Golden Pagoda of Kyoto *was* burned in 1950 by a fanatic priest-in-training.

In his later years Mishima organized a right-wing coterie of young men into a para-military "Shield Society" through which he hoped to restore the samurai traditions to what he had come to view as a weakened and effete Japan. His private army numbered some hundred young men who wore expensive uniforms of Mishima's design. In 1970, at the age of forty-five, embittered by the lack of self-effacing dedication on the part of his men, he committed *seppuku*—ritualistic disembowelment—in the national Self-Defense offices in full view of the staff and with the aid of one of his men, who then followed Mishima in death. The reader will note real-life parallels, then, in the situation and controlled passion of the story that follows.

A number of Mishima's works depict women as strong-willed and assertive, whether as partners of their men or when acting alone. In his unusual drama *Madame de Sade*, for instance, the dramatist provides for a cast solely of women who reflect on and respond to the actions of the Marquis de Sade. In the novels *Thirst for Love, After the Banquet, The Sailor Who Fell from Grace with the Sea,* and *The Sound of Waves* women are central to the situations and largely motivate actions and outcomes.

1

On the twenty-eighth of February, 1936 (on the third day, that is, of the 26 February Incident[1]), Lieutenant Takeyama Shinji of the Konoe Transport Battalion—profoundly disturbed by the knowledge that his closest colleagues had been with the mutineers from the beginning, and indignant at the

[1] 26 February Incident: In the early hours of 26 February 1936, detachments from the First Division, about 1,500 men in all, attacked the homes of the Prime Minister and other public figures and occupied several public buildings near the Palace. They set up a kind of occupied zone in central Tokyo. The mutineers gave themselves up after four days. One captain shot himself, the rest were tried by secret court martial.

imminent prospect of Imperial troops attacking Imperial troops—took his officer's sword and ceremonially disembowelled himself in the eight-mat[2] room of his private residence in the sixth block of Aoba-chō, in Yotsuya Ward. His wife, Reiko, followed him, stabbing herself to death. The lieutenant's farewell note consisted of one sentence: "Long live the Imperial Forces." His wife's, after apologies for her unfilial conduct in thus preceding her parents to the grave, concluded: "The day which, for a soldier's wife, had to come, has come . . ." The last moments of this heroic and dedicated couple were such as to make the gods themselves weep. The lieutenant's age, it should be noted, was thirty-one, his wife's twenty-three; and it was not half a year since the celebration of their marriage.

Those who saw the bride and bridegroom in the commemorative photograph—perhaps no less than those actually present at the lieutenant's wedding—had exclaimed in wonder at the bearing of this handsome couple. The lieutenant, majestic in military uniform, stood protectively beside his bride, his right hand resting upon his sword, his officer's cap held at his left side. His expression was severe, and his dark brows and wide-gazing eyes well conveyed the clear integrity of youth. For the beauty of the bride in her white over-robe no comparisons were adequate. In the eyes, round beneath soft brows, in the slender, finely shaped nose, and in the full lips, there was both sensuousness and refinement. One hand, emerging shyly from a sleeve of the over-robe, held a fan, and the tips of the fingers, clustering delicately, were like the bud of a moonflower.

After the suicide, people would take out this photograph and examine it, and sadly reflect that too often there was a curse on these seemingly flawless unions. Perhaps it was no more than imagination, but looking at the picture after the tragedy it almost seemed as if the two young people before the gold-lacquered screen were gazing, each with equal clarity, at the deaths which lay before them.

Thanks to the good offices of their go-between, Lieutenant-General Ozeki, they had been able to set themselves

---

[2] Eight-mat room: The floor area of a room in a traditional house is calculated in terms of the number of reed mats, six by three feet, used to cover it.

up in a new home at Aoba-chō in Yotsuya. "New home" is
perhaps misleading. It was an old three-room rented house
backing on to a small garden. As neither the six- nor the
four-and-a-half-mat room downstairs was favoured by the
sun, they used the upstairs eight-mat room as both bedroom
and guest room. There was no maid, so Reiko was left alone
to guard the house in her husband's absence.

The honeymoon trip was dispensed with on the grounds
that these were times of national emergency. The two of
them had spent the first night of their marriage at this house.
Before going to bed, Shinji, sitting erect on the floor with his
sword laid before him, had bestowed upon his wife a sol-
dierly lecture. A woman who had become the wife of a soldier should know and resolutely accept that her husband's
death might come at any moment. It could be tomorrow. It
could be the day after. But, no matter when it came—he
asked—was she steadfast in her resolve to accept it? Reiko
rose to her feet, pulled open a drawer of the cabinet, and
took out what was the most prized of her new possessions,
the dagger her mother had given her. Returning to her place,
she laid the dagger without a word on the mat before her,
just as her husband had laid his sword. A silent understanding was achieved at once, and the lieutenant never again
sought to test his wife's resolve.

In the first few months of her marriage Reiko's beauty
grew daily more radiant, shining serene like the moon after
rain.

As both were possessed of young, vigorous bodies, their
relationship was passionate. Nor was this merely a matter of
the night. On more than one occasion, returning home
straight from manoeuvres, and begrudging even the time it
took to remove his mud-splashed uniform, the lieutenant had
pushed his wife to the floor almost as soon as he had entered
the house. Reiko was equally ardent in her response. For a
little more or a little less than a month, from the first night of
their marriage Reiko knew happiness, and the lieutenant,
seeing this, was happy too.

Reiko's body was white and pure, and her swelling breasts
conveyed a firm and chaste refusal; but, upon consent, those
breasts were lavish with their intimate, welcoming warmth.
Even in bed these two were frighteningly and awesomely seri-

ous. In the very midst of wild, intoxicating passions, their
hearts were sober and serious.

By day the lieutenant would think of his wife in the brief
rest periods between training; and all day long, at home,
Reiko would recall the image of her husband. Even when
apart, however, they had only to look at the wedding photograph for their happiness to be once more confirmed. Reiko
felt not the slightest surprise that a man who had been a
complete stranger until a few months ago should now have
become the sun about which her whole world revolved.

All these things had a moral basis, and were in accordance
with the Education Rescript's[3] injunction that "husband and
wife should be harmonious." Not once did Reiko contradict
her husband, nor did the lieutenant ever find reason to scold
his wife. On the god shelf below the stairway, alongside the
tablet from the Great Ise Shrine[4], were set photographs of
their Imperial Majesties, and regularly every morning, before
leaving for duty, the lieutenant would stand with his wife at
this hallowed place and together they would bow their heads
low. The offering water was renewed each morning, and the
sacred sprig of *sasaki* was always green and fresh. Their lives
were lived beneath the solemn protection of the gods and
were filled with an intense happiness which set every fibre in
their bodies trembling.

2

Although Lord Privy Seal Saitō's house was in their neighbourhood, neither of them heard any noise of gunfire on the
morning of 26 February. It was a bugle, sounding muster in
the dim, snowy dawn, when the ten-minute tragedy had already ended, which first disrupted the lieutenant's slumbers.
Leaping at once from his bed, and without speaking a word,
the lieutenant donned his uniform, buckled on the sword held
ready for him by his wife, and hurried swiftly out into the

---

[3] Education Rescript: Promulgated by the Emperor Meiji in 1890, the
Education Rescript appealed to Japanese schoolchildren and young
people to honour filial piety, obedience and benevolence, and to offer
their lives "courageously to the state" should any emergency arise.

[4] Most sacred shrine of Shinto, dedicated to the Sun Goddess, Japan's
remotest ancestor.

snow-covered streets of the still darkened morning. He did
not return until the evening of the twenty-eighth.

Later, from the radio news, Reiko learned the full extent
of this sudden eruption of violence. Her life throughout the
subsequent two days was lived alone, in complete tranquillity,
and behind locked doors.

In the lieutenant's face, as he hurried silently out into the
snowy morning, Reiko had read the determination to die. If
her husband did not return, her own decision was made: she
too would die. Quietly she attended to the disposition of her
personal possessions. She chose her sets of visiting kimonos as
keepsakes for friends of her schooldays, and she wrote a
name and address on the stiff paper wrapping in which each
was folded. Constantly admonished by her husband never to
think of the morrow, Reiko had not even kept a diary and
was now denied the pleasure of assiduously rereading her
record of the happiness of the past few months and con-
signing each page to the fire as she did so. Ranged across the
top of the radio were a small china dog, a rabbit, a squirrel,
a bear, and a fox. There were also a small vase and a water
pitcher. These comprised Reiko's one and only collection. But
it would hardly do, she imagined, to give such things as keepsakes. Nor again would it be quite proper to ask specifically
for them to be included in the coffin. It seemed to Reiko, as
these thoughts passed through her mind, that the expressions
on the small animals' faces grew even more lost and forlorn.

Reiko took the squirrel in her hand and looked at it. And
then, her thoughts turning to a realm far beyond these child-
like affections, she gazed up into the distance at the great
sunlike principle which her husband embodied. She was
ready, and happy, to be hurtled along to her destruction in
that gleaming sun chariot—but now, for these few moments
of solitude, she allowed herself to luxuriate in this innocent
attachment to trifles. The time when she had genuinely loved
these things, however, was long past. Now she merely loved
the memory of having once loved them, and their place in
her heart had been filled by more intense passions, by a more
frenzied happiness . . . For Reiko had never, even to herself,
thought of those soaring joys of the flesh as a mere pleasure.
The February cold, and the icy touch of the china squirrel,
had numbed Reiko's slender fingers; yet, even so, in her lower
limbs, beneath the ordered repetition of the pattern which

crossed the skirt of her trim *meisen* kimono, she could feel
now, as she thought of the lieutenant's powerful arms reaching out towards her, a hot moistness of the flesh which defied
the snows.

She was not in the least afraid of the death hovering in her
mind. Waiting alone at home, Reiko firmly believed that everything her husband was feeling or thinking now, his anguish and distress, was leading her—just as surely as the
power in his flesh—to a welcome death. She felt as if her
body could melt away with ease and be transformed to the
merest fraction of her husband's thought.

Listening to the frequent announcements on the radio, she
heard the names of several of her husband's colleagues mentioned among those of the insurgents. This was news of
death. She followed the developments closely, wondering anxiously, as the situation became daily more irrevocable, why
no Imperial ordinance was sent down, and watching what
had at first been taken as a movement to restore the nation's
honour came gradually to be branded with the infamous
name of mutiny. There was no communication from the regiment. At any moment, it seemed, fighting might commence in
the city streets, where the remains of the snow still lay.

Towards sunset on the twenty-eighth Reiko was startled by
a furious pounding on the front door. She hurried downstairs.
As she pulled with fumbling fingers at the bolt, the shape
dimly outlined beyond the frosted-glass panel made no sound,
but she knew it was her husband. Reiko had never known the
bolt on the sliding door to be so stiff. Still it resisted. The
door just would not open.

In a moment, almost before she knew she had succeeded,
the lieutenant was standing before her on the cement floor inside the porch, muffled in a khaki greatcoat, his top boots
heavy with slush from the street. Closing the door behind
him, he returned the bolt once more to its socket. With what
significance, Reiko did not understand.

"Welcome home."

Reiko bowed deeply, but her husband made no response.
As he had already unfastened his sword and was about to remove his greatcoat, Reiko moved round behind to assist. The
coat, which was cold and damp and had lost the odour of
horse dung it normally exuded when exposed to the sun,
weighed heavily upon her arm. Draping it across a hanger,

and cradling the sword and leather belt in her sleeves, she
waited while her husband removed his top boots and then followed behind him into the "living-room." This was the six-
mat room downstairs.

Seen in the clear light from the lamp, her husband's face,
covered with a heavy growth of bristle, was almost unrecog-
nizably wasted and thin. The cheeks were hollow, their lustre
and resilience gone. In his normal good spirits he would have
changed into old clothes as soon as he was home and have
pressed her to get supper at once, but now he sat before the
table still in his uniform, his head drooping dejectedly. Reiko
refrained from asking whether she should prepare the supper.

After an interval the lieutenant spoke.

"I knew nothing. They hadn't asked me to join. Perhaps
out of consideration, because I was newly married. Kanō,
and Homma too, and Yamaguchi."

Reiko recalled momentarily the faces of high-spirited
young officers, friends of her husband, who had come to the
house occasionally as guests. .

"There may be an Imperial ordinance sent down tomorrow. They'll be posted as rebels, I imagine. I shall be in command of a unit with orders to attack them . . . I can't do it.
It's impossible to do a thing like that."

He spoke again.

"They've taken me off guard duty, and I have permission
to return home for one night. Tomorrow morning, without
question, I must leave to join the attack. I can't do it, Reiko."

Reiko sat erect with lowered eyes. She understood clearly
that her husband had spoken of his death. The lieutenant
was resolved. Each word, being rooted in death, emerged
sharply and with powerful significance against this dark, im-
movable background. Although the lieutenant was speaking
of his dilemma, already there was no room in his mind for
vacillation.

However, there was a clarity, like the clarity of a stream
fed from melting snows, in the silence which rested between
them. Sitting in his own home after the long two-day ordeal
and looking across at the face of his beautiful wife, the lieutenant was for the first time experiencing true peace of mind.
For he had at once known, though she said nothing, that his
wife divined the resolve which lay beneath his words.

"Well, then . . ." The lieutenant's eyes opened wide.

Despite his exhaustion they were strong and clear, and now for the first time they looked straight into the eyes of his wife. "Tonight I shall cut my stomach."

Reiko did not flinch.

Her round eyes showed tension, as taut as the clang of a bell.

"I am ready," she said. "I ask permission to accompany you."

The lieutenant felt almost mesmerized by the strength in those eyes. His words flowed swiftly and easily, like the utterances of a man in delirium, and it was beyond his understanding how permission in a matter of such weight could be expressed so casually.

"Good. We'll go together. But I want you as a witness, first, for my own suicide. Agreed?"

When this was said a sudden release of abundant happiness welled up in both their hearts. Reiko was deeply affected by the greatness of her husband's trust in her. It was vital for the lieutenant, whatever else might happen, that there should be no irregularity in his death. For that reason there had to be a witness. The fact that he had chosen his wife for this was the first mark of his trust. The second, and even greater mark, was that though he had pledged that they should die together he did not intend to kill his wife first—he had deferred her death to a time when he would no longer be there to verify it. If the lieutenant had been a suspicious husband, he would doubtless, as in the usual suicide pact, have chosen to kill his wife first.

When Reiko said, "I ask permission to accompany you," the lieutenant felt these words to be the final fruit of the education which he had himself given his wife, starting on the first night of their marriage, and which had schooled her, when the moment came, to say what had to be said without a shadow of hesitation. This flattered the lieutenant's opinion of himself as a self-reliant man. He was not so romantic or conceited as to imagine that the words were spoken spontaneously, out of love for her husband.

With happiness welling almost too abundantly in their hearts, they could not help smiling at each other. Reiko felt as if she had returned to her wedding night.

Before her eyes was neither pain nor death. She seemed to

see only a free and limitless expanse opening out into vast distances.

"The water is hot. Will you take your bath now?"

"Ah yes, of course."

"And supper . . . ?"

The words were delivered in such level, domestic tones that the lieutenant came near to thinking, for the fraction of a second, that everything had been a hallucination.

"I don't think we'll need supper. But perhaps you could warm some *sake*?"

"As you wish."

As Reiko rose and took a *tanzen* gown from the cabinet for after the bath, she purposely directed her husband's attention to the opened drawer. The lieutenant rose, crossed to the cabinet, and looked inside. From the ordered array of paper wrappings he read, one by one, the addresses of the keepsakes. There was no grief in the lieutenant's response to this demonstration of heroic resolve. His heart was filled with tenderness. Like a husband who is proudly shown the childish purchases of a young wife, the lieutenant, overwhelmed by affection, lovingly embraced his wife from behind and implanted a kiss upon her neck.

Reiko felt the roughness of the lieutenant's unshaven skin against her neck. This sensation, more than being just a thing of this world, was for Reiko almost the world itself, but now—with the feeling that it was soon to be lost for ever—it had freshness beyond all her experience. Each moment had its own vital strength, and the senses in every corner of her body were reawakened. Accepting her husband's caresses from behind, Reiko raised herself on the tips of her toes, letting the vitality seep through her entire body.

"First the bath, and then, after some *sake* . . . lay out the bedding upstairs, will you?"

The lieutenant whispered the words into his wife's ear. Reiko silently nodded.

Flinging off his uniform, the lieutenant went to the bath. To faint background noises of slopping water Reiko tended the charcoal brazier in the living-room and began the preparations for warming the *sake*.

Taking the *tanzen*, a sash, and some underclothes, she went to the bathroom to ask how the water was. In the midst of a coiling cloud of steam the lieutenant was sitting cross-legged on the floor, shaving, and she could dimly discern the rippling movements of the muscles on his damp, powerful back as they responded to the movement of his arms.

There was nothing to suggest a time of any special significance. Reiko, going busily about her tasks, was preparing side dishes from odds and ends in stock. Her hands did not tremble. If anything, she managed even more efficiently and smoothly than usual. From time to time, it is true, there was a strange throbbing deep within her breast. Like distant lightning, it had a moment of sharp intensity and then vanished without trace. Apart from that, nothing was in any way out of the ordinary.

The lieutenant, shaving in the bathroom, felt his warmed body miraculously healed at last of the desperate tiredness of the days of indecision and filled—in spite of the death which lay ahead—with pleasurable anticipation. The sound of his wife going about her work came to him faintly. A healthy physical craving, submerged for two days, reasserted itself.

The lieutenant was confident there had been no impurity in the joy they had experienced when resolving upon death. They had both sensed at that moment—though not, of course, in any clear and conscious way—that those permissible pleasures which they shared in private were once more beneath the protection of Righteousness and Divine Power, and of a complete and unassailable morality. On looking into each other's eyes and discovering there an honourable death, they had felt themselves safe once more behind steel walls which none could destroy, encased in an impenetrable armour of Beauty and Truth. Thus, so far from seeing any inconsistency or conflict between the surges of his flesh and the sincerity of his patriotism, the lieutenant was even able to regard the two as parts of the same thing.

Thrusting his face close to the dark, cracked, misted wall-mirror, the lieutenant shaved himself with great care. This would be his death face. There must be no unsightly blemishes. The clean-shaven face gleamed once more with a youthful lustre, seeming to brighten the darkness of the mirror. There was a certain elegance, he even felt, in the association of death with this radiantly healthy face.

Just as it looked now, this would become his death face! Already, in fact, it had half departed from the lieutenant's personal possession and had become the bust above a dead soldier's memorial. As an experiment he closed his eyes tight. Everything was wrapped in blackness, and he was no longer a living, seeing creature.

Returning from the bath, the traces of the shave glowing faintly blue beneath his smooth cheeks, he seated himself beside the now well-kindled charcoal brazier. Busy though Reiko was, he noticed, she had found time lightly to touch up her face. Her cheeks were gay and her lips moist. There was no shadow of sadness to be seen. Truly, the lieutenant felt, as he saw this mark of his young wife's passionate nature, he had chosen the wife he ought to have chosen.

As soon as the lieutenant had drained his *sake* cup he offered it to Reiko. Reiko had never before tasted *sake*, but she accepted without hesitation and sipped timidly.

"Come here," the lieutenant said.

Reiko moved to her husband's side and was embraced as she leaned backward across his lap. Her breast was in violent commotion, as if sadness, joy, and the potent *sake* were mingling and reacting within her. The lieutenant looked down into his wife's face. It was the last face he would see in this world, the last face he would see of his wife. The lieutenant scrutinized the face minutely, with the eyes of a traveller bidding farewell to splendid vistas which he will never revisit. It was a face he could not tire of looking at—the features regular yet not cold, the lips tightly closed with a soft strength. The lieutenant kissed those lips, unthinkingly. And suddenly, though there was not the slightest distortion of the face into the unsightliness of sobbing, he noticed that tears were welling slowly from beneath the long lashes of the closed eyes and brimming over into a glistening stream.

When, a little later, the lieutenant urged that they should move to the upstairs bedroom, his wife replied that she would follow after taking a bath. Climbing the stairs alone to the bedroom, where the air was already warmed by the gas heater, the lieutenant lay down on the bedding with arms outstretched and legs apart. Even the time at which he lay waiting for his wife to join him was no later and no earlier than usual.

He folded his hands beneath his head and gazed at the dark boards of the ceiling in the dimness beyond the range of the standard lamp. Was it death he was now waiting for? Or a wild ecstasy of the senses? The two seemed to overlap, almost as if the object of this bodily desire was death itself. But, however that might be, it was certain that never before had the lieutenant tasted such total freedom.

There was the sound of a car outside the window. He could hear the screech of its tyres skidding in the snow piled at the side of the street. The sound of its horn re-echoed from nearby walls . . . Listening to these noises he had the feeling that this house rose like a solitary island in the ocean of a society going as restlessly about its business as ever. All around, vastly and untidily, stretched the country for which he grieved. He was to give his life for it. But would that great country, with which he was prepared to remonstrate to the extent of destroying himself, take the slightest heed of his death? He did not know; and it did not matter. His was a battlefield without glory, a battlefield where none could display deeds of valour: it was the front line of the spirit.

Reiko's footsteps sounded on the stairway. The steep stairs in this old house creaked badly. There were fond memories in that creaking, and many a time, while waiting in bed, the lieutenant had listened to its welcome sound. At the thought that he would hear it no more he listened with intense concentration, striving for every corner of every moment of this precious time to be filled with the sound of those soft footfalls on the creaking stairway. The moments seemed transformed to jewels, sparkling with inner light.

Reiko wore a Nagoya sash about the waist of her *yukata*, but as the lieutenant reached towards it, its redness sobered by the dimness of the light, Reiko's hand moved to his assistance and the sash fell away, slithering swiftly to the floor. As she stood before him, still in her *yukata*, the lieutenant inserted his hands through the side slits beneath each sleeve, intending to embrace her as she was; but at the touch of his finger-tips upon the warm, naked flesh, and as the armpits closed gently about his hands, his whole body was suddenly aflame.

In a few moments the two lay naked before the glowing gas heater.

Neither spoke the thought, but their hearts, their bodies, and their pounding breasts blazed with the knowledge that this was the very last time. It was as if the words "The Last Time" were spelled out, in invisible brushstrokes, across every inch of their bodies.

The lieutenant drew his wife close and kissed her vehemently. As their tongues explored each other's mouths, reaching out into the smooth, moist interior, they felt as if the still unknown agonies of death had tempered their senses to the keenness of red-hot steel. The agonies they could not yet feel, the distant pains of death, had refined their awareness of pleasure.

"This is the last time I shall see your body," said the lieutenant. "Let me look at it closely." And, tilting the shade on the lampstand to one side, he directed the rays along the full length of Reiko's outstretched form.

Reiko lay still with her eyes closed. The light from the low lamp clearly revealed the majestic sweep of her white flesh. The lieutenant, not without a touch of egocentricity, rejoiced that he would never see this beauty crumble in death.

At his leisure, the lieutenant allowed the unforgettable spectacle to engrave itself upon his mind. With one hand he fondled the hair, with the other he softly stroked the magnificent face, implanting kisses here and there where his eyes lingered. The quiet coldness of the high, tapering forehead, the closed eyes with their long lashes beneath faintly etched brows, the set of the finely shaped nose, the gleam of teeth glimpsed between full, regular lips, the soft cheeks and the small, wise chin . . . these things conjured up in the lieutenant's mind the vision of a truly radiant death face, and again and again he pressed his lips tight against the white throat—where Reiko's own hand was soon to strike—and the throat reddened faintly beneath his kisses. Returning to the mouth he laid his lips against it with the gentlest of pressures, and moved them rhythmically over Reiko's with the light rolling motion of a small boat. If he closed his eyes, the world became a rocking cradle.

Wherever the lieutenant's eyes moved his lips faithfully followed. The high, swelling breasts, surmounted by nipples like the buds of a wild cherry, hardened as the lieutenant's lips closed about them. The arms flowed smoothly downward from each side of the breast, tapering towards the wrists, yet losing nothing of their roundness or symmetry, and at their tips were those delicate fingers which had held the fan at the wedding ceremony. One by one, as the lieutenant kissed them, the fingers withdrew behind their neighbour as if in shame . . . The natural hollow curving between the bosom and the stomach carried in its lines a suggestion not only of softness but of resilient strength, and while it gave forewarning of the rich curves spreading outward from here to the hips it had, in itself, an appearance only of restraint and proper discipline. The whiteness and richness of the stomach and hips was like milk brimming in a great bowl, and the sharply shadowed dip of the navel could have been the fresh impress of a raindrop, fallen there that very moment. Where the shadows gathered more thickly, hair clustered, gentle and sensitive, and as the agitation mounted in the now no longer passive body there hung over this region a scent like the smouldering of fragrant blossoms, growing steadily more pervasive.

At length, in a tremulous voice, Reiko spoke.

"Show me . . . Let me look too, for the last time."

Never before had he heard from his wife's lips so strong and unequivocal a request. It was as if something which her modesty had wished to keep hidden to the end had suddenly burst its bonds of restraint. The lieutenant obediently lay back and surrendered himself to his wife. Lithely she raised her white, trembling body, and—burning with an innocent desire to return to her husband what he had done for her—placed two white fingers on the lieutenant's eyes, which gazed fixedly up at her, and gently stroked them shut.

Suddenly overwhelmed by tenderness, her cheeks flushed by a dizzying uprush of emotion, Reiko threw her arms about the lieutenant's close-cropped head. The bristly hairs rubbed painfully against her breast, the prominent nose was cold as it dug into her flesh, and his breath was hot. Relaxing her embrace, she gazed down at her husband's masculine face. The severe brows, the closed eyes, the splendid bridge of the nose, the shapely lips drawn firmly together . . . the blue, clean-shaven cheeks reflecting the light and gleaming smoothly. Reiko kissed each of these. She kissed the broad nape of the neck, the strong, erect shoulders, the powerful chest with its twin circles like shields and its russet nipples. In the armpits, deeply shadowed by the ample flesh of the shoulders and chest, a sweet and melancholy odour emanated from the growth of hair, and in the sweetness of this odour was contained, somehow, the essence of young death. The lieutenant's naked skin glowed like a field of barley, and everywhere the muscles showed in sharp relief, converging on the lower ab-

domen about the small, unassuming navel. Gazing at the
youthful, firm stomach, modestly covered by a vigorous
growth of hair, Reiko thought of it as it was soon to be, cruelly cut by the sword, and she laid her head upon it, sobbing
in pity, and bathed it with kisses.

At the touch of his wife's tears upon his stomach the lieutenant felt ready to endure with courage the cruellest agonies
of his suicide.

What ecstasies they experienced after these tender exchanges
may well be imagined. The lieutenant raised himself and
enfolded his wife in a powerful embrace, her body now limp
with exhaustion after her grief and tears. Passionately they
held their faces close, rubbing cheek against cheek. Reiko's
body was trembling. Their breasts, moist with sweat, were
tightly joined, and every inch of the young and beautiful
bodies had become so much one with the other that it seemed
impossible there should ever again be a separation. Reiko
cried out. From the heights they plunged into the abyss, and
from the abyss they took wing and soared once more to dizzying heights. The lieutenant panted like the regimental
standard-bearer on a route march . . . As one cycle ended,
almost immediately a new wave of passion would be gener-
ated, and together—with no trace of fatigue—they would
climb again in a single breathless movement to the very sum-
mit.

3

When the lieutenant at last turned away, it was not from
weariness. For one thing, he was anxious not to undermine
the considerable strength he would need in carrying out his
suicide. For another, he would have been sorry to mar the
sweetness of these last memories by over-indulgence.

Since the lieutenant had clearly desisted, Reiko too, with
her usual compliance, followed his example. The two lay
naked on their backs, with fingers interlaced, staring fixedly
at the dark ceiling. The room was warm from the heater, and
even when the sweat had ceased to pour from their bodies
they felt no cold. Outside, in the hushed night, the sounds of
passing traffic had ceased. Even the noises of the trains and
tramcars around Yotsuya station did not penetrate this far.
After echoing through the region bounded by the moat, they

were lost in the heavily wooded park fronting the broad driveway before Akasaka Palace. It was hard to believe in the tension gripping this whole quarter, where the two factions of the bitterly divided Imperial Army now confronted each other, poised for battle.

Savouring the warmth glowing within themselves, they lay still and recalled the ecstasies they had just known. Each moment of the experience was relived. They remembered the taste of kisses which had never wearied, the touch of naked flesh, episode after episode of dizzying bliss. But already, from the dark boards of the ceiling, the face of death was peering down. These joys had been final, and their bodies would never know them again. Not that joy of this intensity—and the same thought had occurred to them both—was ever likely to be re-experienced, even if they should live on to old age.

The feel of their fingers intertwined—this too would soon be lost. Even the wood-grain patterns they now gazed at on the dark ceiling boards would be taken from them. They could feel death edging in, nearer and nearer. There could be no hesitation now. They must have the courage to reach out to death themselves, and to seize it.

"Well, let's make our preparations," said the lieutenant. The note of determination in the words was unmistakable, but at the same time Reiko had never heard her husband's voice so warm and tender.

After they had risen, a variety of tasks awaited them.

The lieutenant, who had never once before helped with the bedding, now cheerfully slid back the door of the cupboard, lifted the mattress across the room by himself, and stowed it away inside.

Reiko turned off the gas heater and put away the lamp standard. During the lieutenant's absence she had arranged this room carefully, sweeping and dusting it to a fresh cleanness, and now—if one overlooked the rosewood table drawn into one corner—the eight-mat room gave all the appearance of a reception room ready to welcome an important guest.

"We've seen some drinking here, haven't we? With Kanō and Homma and Noguchi . . ."

"Yes, they were great drinkers, all of them."

"We'll be meeting them before long, in the other world.

They'll tease us, I imagine, when they find I've brought you with me."

Descending the stairs, the lieutenant turned to look back into this calm, clean room, now brightly illuminated by the ceiling lamp. There floated across his mind the faces of the young officers who had drunk there, and laughed, and innocently bragged. He had never dreamed then that he would one day cut open his stomach in this room.

In the two rooms downstairs husband and wife busied themselves smoothly and serenely with their respective preparations. The lieutenant went to the toilet, and then to the bathroom to wash. Meanwhile Reiko folded away her husband's padded robe, placed his uniform tunic, his trousers, and a newly cut bleached loincloth in the bathroom, and set out sheets of paper on the living-room table for the farewell notes. Then she removed the lid from the writing-box and began rubbing ink from the ink tablet. She had already decided upon the wording of her own note.

Reiko's fingers pressed hard upon the cold gilt letters of the ink tablet, and the water in the shallow well at once darkened, as if a black cloud had spread across it. She stopped thinking that this repeated action, this pressure from her fingers, this rise and fall of faint sound, was all and solely for death. It was a routine domestic task, a simple paring away of time until death should finally stand before her. But somehow, in the increasingly smooth motion of the tablet rubbing on the stone, and in the scent from the thickening ink, there was unspeakable darkness.

Neat in his uniform, which he now wore next to his skin, the lieutenant emerged from the bathroom. Without a word he seated himself at the table, bolt upright, took a brush in his hand, and stared undecidedly at the paper before him.

Reiko took a white silk kimono with her and entered the bathroom. When she reappeared in the living-room, clad in the white kimono and with her face lightly made up, the farewell note lay completed on the table beneath the lamp. The thick black brushstrokes said simply: "Long Live the Imperial Forces—Army Lieutenant Takeyama Shinji."

While Reiko sat opposite him writing her own note, the lieutenant gazed in silence, intensely serious, at the controlled movement of his wife's pale fingers as they manipulated the brush.

With their respective notes in their hands—the lieutenant's sword strapped to his side, Reiko's small dagger thrust into the sash of her white kimono—the two of them stood before the god shelf and silently prayed. Then they put out all the downstairs lights. As he mounted the stairs the lieutenant turned his head and gazed back at the striking, white-clad figure of his wife, climbing behind him, with lowered eyes, from the darkness beneath.

The farewell notes were laid side by side in the alcove of the upstairs room. They wondered whether they ought not to remove the hanging scroll, but since it had been written by their go-between, Lieutenant-General Ozeki, and consisted, moreover, of two Chinese characters signifying "Sincerity," they left it where it was. Even if it were to become stained with splashes of blood, they felt that the lieutenant-general would understand.

The lieutenant, sitting erect with his back to the alcove, laid his sword on the floor before him.

Reiko sat facing him, a mat's width away. With the rest of her so severely white the touch of rouge on her lips seemed remarkably seductive.

Across the dividing mat they gazed intently into each other's eyes. The lieutenant's sword lay before his knees. Seeing it, Reiko recalled their first night and was overwhelmed with sadness. The lieutenant spoke, in a hoarse voice:

"As I have no second to help me I shall cut deep. It may look unpleasant, but please do not panic. Death of any sort is a fearful thing to watch. You must not be discouraged by what you see. Is that all right?"

"Yes."

Reiko nodded deeply.

Looking at the slender white figure of his wife the lieutenant experienced a bizarre excitement. What he was about to perform was an act in his public capacity as a soldier, something he had never previously shown his wife. It called for a resolution equal to the courage to enter battle; it was a death of no less degree and quality than death in the front line. It was his conduct on the battlefield that he was now to display.

Momentarily the thought led the lieutenant to a strange fantasy. A lonely death on the battlefield, a death beneath the eyes of his beautiful wife . . . in the sensation that he was now to die in these two dimensions, realizing an impossible union of them both, there was sweetness beyond words. This must be the very pinnacle of good fortune, he thought. To have every moment of his death observed by those beautiful eyes—it was like being borne to death on a gentle, fragrant breeze. There was some special favour here. He did not understand precisely what it was, but it was a domain unknown to others: a dispensation granted to no one else had been permitted to himself. In the radiant, bridelike figure of his white-robed wife the lieutenant seemed to see a vision of all those things he had loved and for which he was to lay down his life—the Imperial Household, the Nation, the Army Flag. All these, no less than the wife who sat before him, were presences observing him closely with clear and never-faltering eyes.

Reiko too was gazing intently at her husband, so soon to die, and she thought that never in this world had she seen anything so beautiful. The lieutenant always looked well in uniform, but now, as he contemplated death with severe brows and firmly closed lips, he revealed what was perhaps masculine beauty at its most superb.

"It's time to go," the lieutenant said at last.

Reiko bent her body low to the mat in a deep bow. She could not raise her face. She did not wish to spoil her make-up with tears, but the tears could not be held back.

When at length she looked up she saw hazily through the tears that her husband had wound a white bandage round the blade of his now unsheathed sword, leaving five or six inches of naked steel showing at the point.

Resting the sword in its cloth wrapping on the mat before him, the lieutenant rose from his knees, resettled himself cross-legged, and unfastened the hooks of his uniform collar. His eyes no longer saw his wife. Slowly, one by one, he undid the flat brass buttons. The dusky brown chest was revealed, and then the stomach. He unclasped his belt and undid the buttons of his trousers. The pure whiteness of the thickly coiled loincloth showed itself. The lieutenant pushed the cloth down with both hands, further to ease his stomach, and then reached for the white-bandaged blade of his sword. With his left hand he massaged his abdomen, glancing downward as he did so.

To reassure himself of the sharpness of his sword's cutting edge the lieutenant folded back the left trouser flap, exposing a little of his thigh, and lightly drew the blade across the skin. Blood welled up in the wound at once, and several streaks of red trickled downward, glistening in the strong light.

It was the first time Reiko had ever seen her husband's blood, and she felt a violent throbbing in her chest. She looked at her husband's face. The lieutenant was looking at the blood with calm appraisal. For a moment—though thinking at the same time that it was hollow comfort—Reiko experienced a sense of relief.

The lieutenant's eyes fixed his wife with an intense, hawklike stare. Moving the sword around to his front, he raised himself slightly on his hips and let the upper half of his body lean over the sword point. That he was mustering his whole strength was apparent from the angry tension of the uniform at his shoulders. The lieutenant aimed to strike deep into the left of his stomach. His sharp cry pierced the silence of the room.

Despite the effort he had himself put into the blow, the lieutenant had the impression that someone else had struck the side of his stomach agonizingly with a thick rod of iron. For a second or so his head reeled and he had no idea what had happened. The five or six inches of naked point had vanished completely into his flesh, and the white bandage, gripped in his clenched fist, pressed directly against his stomach.

He returned to consciousness. The blade had certainly pierced the wall of the stomach, he thought. His breathing was difficult, his chest thumped violently, and in some far deep region, which he could hardly believe was a part of himself, a fearful and excruciating pain came welling up as if the ground had split open to disgorge a boiling stream of molten rock. The pain came suddenly nearer, with terrifying speed. The lieutenant bit his lower lip and stifled an instinctive moan.

Was this *seppuku?*—he was thinking. It was a sensation of utter chaos, as if the sky had fallen on his head and the world was reeling drunkenly. His will-power and courage, which had seemed so robust before he made the incision, had now dwindled to something like a single hairlike thread of steel, and he was assailed by the uneasy feeling that he must advance along this thread, clinging to it with desperation. His clenched fist had grown moist. Looking down, he saw that both his hand and the cloth about the blade were drenched in blood. His loincloth too was dyed a deep red. It struck him as incredible that, amidst this terrible agony, things which could be seen could still be seen, and existing things existed still.

The moment the lieutenant thrust the sword into his left side and she saw the deathly pallor fall across his face, like an abruptly lowered curtain, Reiko had to struggle to prevent herself from rushing to his side. Whatever happened, she must watch. She must be a witness. That was the duty her husband had laid upon her. Opposite her, a mat's space away, she could clearly see her husband biting his lip to stifle the pain. The pain was there, with absolute certainty, before her eyes. And Reiko had no means of rescuing him from it.

The sweat glistened on her husband's forehead. The lieutenant closed his eyes, and then opened them again, as if experimenting. The eyes had lost their lustre, and seemed innocent and empty like the eyes of a small animal.

The agony before Reiko's eyes burned as strong as the summer sun, utterly remote from the grief which seemed to be tearing herself apart within. The pain grew steadily in stature, stretching upward. Reiko felt that her husband had already become a man in a separate world, a man whose whole being had been resolved into pain, a prisoner in a cage of pain where no hand could reach out to him. But Reiko felt no pain at all. Her grief was not pain. As she thought about this, Reiko began to feel as if someone had raised a cruel wall of glass high between herself and her husband.

Ever since her marriage her husband's existence had been her own existence, and every breath of his had been a breath drawn by herself. But now, while her husband's existence in pain was a vivid reality, Reiko could find in this grief of hers no certain proof at all of her own existence.

With only his right hand on the sword the lieutenant began to cut sideways across his stomach. But as the blade became entangled with the entrails it was pushed constantly outward by their soft resilience; and the lieutenant realized that it would be necessary, as he cut, to use both hands to keep the point pressed deep into his stomach. He pulled the blade across. It did not cut as easily as he had expected. He directed the strength of his whole body into his right hand and pulled again. There was a cut of three or four inches.

The pain spread slowly outward from the inner depths until the whole stomach reverberated. It was like the wild clanging of a bell. Or like a thousand bells which jangled simultaneously at every breath he breathed and every throb of his pulse, rocking his whole being. The lieutenant could no longer stop himself from moaning. But by now the blade had cut its way through to below the navel, and when he noticed this he felt a sense of satisfaction, and a renewal of courage.

The volume of blood had steadily increased, and now it spurted from the wound as if propelled by the beat of the pulse. The mat before the lieutenant was drenched red with spattered blood, and more blood overflowed on to it from pools which gathered in the folds of the lieutenant's khaki trousers. A spot, like a bird, came flying across to Reiko and settled on the lap of her white silk kimono.

By the time the lieutenant had at last drawn the sword across to the right side of his stomach, the blade was already cutting shallow and had revealed its naked tip, slippery with blood and grease. But, suddenly stricken by a fit of vomiting, the lieutenant cried out hoarsely. The vomiting made the fierce pain fiercer still, and the stomach, which had thus far remained firm and compact, now abruptly heaved, opening wide its wound, and the entrails burst through, as if the wound too were vomiting. Seemingly ignorant of their master's suffering, the entrails gave an impression of robust health and almost disagreeable vitality as they slipped smoothly out and spilled over into the crotch. The lieutenant's head drooped, his shoulders heaved, his eyes opened to narrow slits, and a thin trickle of saliva dribbled from his mouth. The gold markings on his epaulettes caught the light and glinted.

Blood was scattered everywhere. The lieutenant was soaked in it to his knees, and he sat now in a crumpled and listless posture, one hand on the floor. A raw smell filled the room. The lieutenant, his head drooping, retched repeatedly, and the movement showed vividly in his shoulders. The blade of the sword, now pushed back by the entrails and exposed to its tip, was still in the lieutenant's right hand.

It would be difficult to imagine a more heroic sight than that of the lieutenant at this moment, as he mustered his strength and flung back his head. The movement was performed with sudden violence, and the back of his head struck with a sharp crack against the alcove pillar. Reiko had been sitting until now with her face lowered, gazing in fascination at the tide of blood advancing towards her knees, but the sound took her by surprise and she looked up.

The lieutenant's face was not the face of a living man. The eyes were hollow, the skin parched, the once so lustrous cheeks and lips the colour of dried mud. The right hand alone was moving. Laboriously gripping the sword, it hovered shakily in the air like the hand of a marionette and strove to direct the point at the base of the lieutenant's throat. Reiko watched her husband make this last, most heart-rending, futile exertion. Glistening with blood and grease, the point was thrust at the throat again and again. And each time it missed its aim. The strength to guide it was no longer there. The straying point struck the collar and the collar badges. Although its hooks had been unfastened, the stiff military collar had closed together again and was protecting the throat.

Reiko could bear the sight no longer. She tried to go to her husband's help, but she could not stand. She moved through the blood on her knees, and her white skirts grew deep red. Moving to the rear of her husband, she helped no more than by loosening the collar. The quivering blade at last contacted the naked flesh of the throat. At that moment Reiko's impression was that she herself had propelled her husband forward; but that was not the case. It was a movement planned by the lieutenant himself, his last exertion of strength. Abruptly he threw his body at the blade, and the blade pierced his neck, emerging at the nape. There was a tremendous spurt of blood and the lieutenant lay still, cold blue-tinged steel protruding from his neck at the back.

4

Slowly, her socks slippery with blood, Reiko descended the stairway. The upstairs room was now completely still.

Switching on the ground-floor lights, she turned off the gas-jet and the main gas tap and poured water over the smouldering, half-burned charcoal in the brazier. She stood before the upright mirror in the four-and-a-half-mat room and held up her skirts. The bloodstains made it seem as if a bold, vivid pattern was printed across the lower half of her white kimono. When she sat down before the mirror, she was conscious of the dampness and coldness of her husband's blood in the region of her thighs, and she shivered. Then, for a long while, she lingered over her toilet preparations. She applied the rouge generously to her cheeks, and her lips too she painted heavily. This was no longer make-up to please her husband. It was make-up for the world which she would leave behind, and there was a touch of the magnificent and the spectacular in her brushwork. When she rose, the mat before the mirror was wet with blood. Reiko was not concerned about this.

Returning from the toilet, Reiko stood finally on the cement floor of the porchway. When her husband had bolted the door here last night it had been in preparation for death. For a while she stood immersed in the consideration of a simple problem. Should she now leave the bolt drawn? If she were to lock the door, it could be that the neighbours might not notice their suicide for several days. Reiko did not relish the thought of their two corpses putrefying before discovery. After all, it seemed, it would be best to leave it open . . . She released the bolt, and also drew open the frosted-glass door a fraction . . . At once a chill wind blew in. There was no sign of anyone in the midnight streets, and stars glittered ice-cold through the trees in the large house opposite.

Leaving the door as it was, Reiko mounted the stairs. She had walked here and there for some time and her socks were no longer slippery. About half-way up, her nostrils were already assailed by a peculiar smell.

The lieutenant was lying on his face in a sea of blood. The point protruding from his neck seemed to have grown even more prominent than before. Reiko walked heedlessly across the blood. Sitting beside the lieutenant's corpse, she stared intently at the face, which lay on one cheek on the mat. The eyes were opened wide, as if the lieutenant's attention had been attracted by something. She raised the head, folding it in her sleeve, wiped the blood from the lips, and bestowed a last kiss.

Then she rose and took from the cupboard a new white blanket and a waist cord. To prevent any derangement of her skirts, she wrapped the blanket about her waist and bound it there firmly with the cord.

Reiko sat herself on a spot about one foot distant from the lieutenant's body. Drawing the dagger from her sash, she examined its dully gleaming blade intently, and held it to her tongue. The taste of the polished steel was slightly sweet.

Reiko did not linger. When she thought how the pain which had previously opened such a gulf between herself and her dying husband was now to become a part of her own experience, she saw before her only the joy of herself entering a realm her husband had already made his own. In her husband's agonized face there had been something inexplicable which she was seeing for the first time. Now she would solve that riddle. Reiko sensed that at last she too would be able to taste the true bitterness and sweetness of that great moral principle in which her husband believed. What had until now been tasted only faintly through her husband's example she was about to savour directly with her own tongue.

Reiko rested the point of the blade against the base of her throat. She thrust hard. The wound was only shallow. Her head blazed and her hands shook uncontrollably. She gave the blade a strong pull sideways. A warm substance flooded into her mouth, and everything before her eyes reddened, in a vision of spouting blood. She gathered her strength and plunged the point of the blade deep into her throat.

—*Translated by Geoffrey W. Sargent*

SELECTED BIBLIOGRAPHY

The following books in English give further background on the readings in this anthology, especially as they pertain to the life experiences of women of China and Japan. Starred are those from which selections have been taken for *Rice Bowl Women*.

GENERAL

Chipp, Sylvia A., and Green, Justin J., eds. *Asian Women in Transition*. University Park, Penn.: State University Press, 1980.

*Miller, James E. Jr., O'Neal, Robert, and McDonnell, Helen M., eds. *Literature of the Eastern World*. Glenview, Ill.: Scott, Foresman and Company, 1970.

Murphy, Gardner, and Lois B. *Asian Psychology*. New York and London: Basic Books, Inc., 1968.

Shimer, Dorothy Blair. *The Mentor Book of Modern Asian Literature: From the Khyber Pass to Fuji*. New York: The New American Library, 1969.

———. *Voices of Modern Asia: An Anthology of Twentieth-Century Asian Literature*. New York: The New American Library, 1973.

CHINA

Ayscough, Florence Wheelock. *Chinese Women: Yesterday and Today*. New York: Da Capo Press, 1975 (copyright 1937).

*Birch, Cyril, ed. *Anthology of Chinese Literature from Early Times to the 14th Century*. New York: Grove Press, 1965.

*————. *Stories from a Ming Collection: Translations of Short Stories Published in the Seventeenth Century*. Bloomington, Ind.: Indiana University Press, 1959 (UNESCO Series).

Broyelle, Claudie. *Woman's Liberation in China*. Translated from the French by Michèle Cohen and Gary Herman. Atlantic Highlands, N.J.: Humanities Press, 1977.

Chao, Pu-Wei (Yang). *Autobiography of a Chinese Woman*. New York: John Day Co., 1947.

Chen, Yuan Tsung. *The Dragon's Village: An Autobiographical Novel of Revolutionary China*. New York: Pantheon Books, 1980.

Chinese Women in the Great Leap Forward. Peking: Foreign Language Press, 1960.

Chow, Ching Lie. *Journey in Tears: Memory of a Girlhood in China*. Translated from the French by Abby Israel. New York: McGraw-Hill, 1978.

Chung, Hua-min, and Miller, Arthur C. *Madame Mao: A Profile of Chiang Ch'ing*. Kowloon, Hong Kong: Union Research Institute, 1968.

Croll, Elizabeth J. *Women and Socialism in China*. London and Boston: Routledge & K. Paul, 1978.

Gulick, Robert Hans van. *Sexual Life in Ancient China: A Preliminary Survey of Chinese Sex and Society from ca. 1500 B.C. till 1644 A.D.* Leiden: E. J. Brill, 1974.

Hahn, Emily. *China to Me: A Partial Autobiography of Emily Hahn*. Philadelphia, Penn.: Blakiston, 1944.

Han, Suyin (pseud.). *A Mortal Flower: China, Autobiography, History*. New York: G. P. Putnam, 1966.

*Hsiao Hung. *The Field of Life and Death and Tales of Hulan River*. Bloomington, Ind. & London: Indiana University Press, 1979.

*Hsieh Pingying. *Girl Rebel: The Autobiography of Hsieh Pingying*. New York: Da Capo Press, 1975 (copyright 1940).

Hsiung, Shih-i. *The Story of Lady Precious Stream*. North Tarrytown, N.Y.: Ted Hutchinson, 1950.

*Ing, Nancy Cheng, ed. *New Voices: Stories and Poems by Young Chinese Writers*. Taipei, Taiwan: Heritage Press, 1961.

*Jenner, W. J. F., Yang, Gladys, transls. and eds. *Modern Chinese Stories*. London, Oxford, and New York: Oxford University Press, 1972 (copyright 1970).

Kristeva, Julia. *About Chinese Women*, translated from the French by Anita Barrows. New York: Urizen Books, 1977.

Levy, Marion Joseph. *The Family Revolution in Modern China*. New York: Atheneum Publishers, 1968 (copyright 1949).

Ling, Yutang, transl. and ed. *Widow, Nun, and Courtesan: Three Novelettes from China*. Westport, Conn.: Greenwood Press, 1971 (copyright 1951).

Lu Hsun, Selected Stories of. Peking: Foreign Language Press, 1972.

Lucas, Christopher. *The Women of China*. Chicago: University of Chicago Press, 1976 (copyright, Hong Kong, 1965).

*Ma, Yau-Woon, and Lau, Joseph S. M., eds. *Traditional Chinese Stories: Themes and Variations*. New York: Columbia University Press, 1978.

Marriage Law of the People's Republic of China. Peking: Foreign Language Press, 1973.

New Women in New China. Peking: Foreign Language Press, 1972.

Ning Lao T'ai-t'ai. *A Daughter of Han: The Autobiography of a Chinese Working Woman by Ida Pruitt, from the Story Told Her by Ning Lao T'ai-t'ai*. Stanford, Calif.: Stanford University Press, 1967 (copyright 1945).

O'Hara, Albert Richard. *The Position of Woman in Early China, According to the Lieh nü chuan ("Biography of Chinese Women")*. Taipei, Taiwan: Mei Ya Publications, 1971.

*Pa Chin. *Family* (novel). Garden City, N.Y.: Doubleday & Co./Anchor Books, 1972.

Pruitt, Ida. *Old Madam Yin: A Memoir of Peking Life, 1926-1938*. Stanford, Calif.: Stanford University Press, 1979.

Sidel, Ruth. *Women and Child Care in China: A Firsthand Report*. Baltimore, Md.: Penguin Books, 1973 (copyright 1972).

Spence, Jonathan D. *The Death of Woman Wang*. New York: Viking Press, 1978.

Swann, Nancy Lee. *Pan Chao: Foremost Woman Scholar of China, First Century A.D.* New York: Russell & Russell, 1968 (copyright 1932).

*Wang, Elizabeth Te-chen, ed. *Ladies of the Tang* (stories). Taipei, Taiwan: Heritage Press, 1961.

Witke, Roxanne. *Comrade Chiang Ch'ing*. Boston: Little, Brown & Co., 1977.

Wolf, Arthur P., ed. *Studies in Chinese Society.* Stanford, Calif.: Stanford University Press, 1978.

Wolf, Margery. *The House of Lim: A Study of a Chinese Farm Family.* New York: Appleton-Century-Crofts, 1968.

————. *Women and the Family in Rural Taiwan.* Stanford, Calif.: Stanford University Press, 1972.

Wolf, Margery, and Witke, Roxanne, eds. *Women in Chinese Society.* Stanford, Calif.: Stanford University Press, 1975.

Yang, Ch'ing-k'un. *Chinese Communist Society: The Family and the Village.* Cambridge, Mass.: M.I.T. Press, 1965 (copyright 1959).

————. *The Chinese Family in the Communist Revolution.* Cambridge, Mass.: Technology Press, M.I.T., 1959.

Yip, Wai-lin, and Tay, William, eds. *Chinese Women Writers Today.* Baltimore, Md.: University of Maryland School of Law, 1979.

JAPAN

Abe, Kobo. *The Face of Another* (novel). New York: Alfred A. Knopf, 1966.

————. *The Woman in the Dunes* (novel). New York: Alfred A. Knopf, 1964.

*Akutagawa, Ryunosuke. *Japanese Short Stories.* New York: Liveright Publishing Co., 1961.

Ariyoshi, Sanako. *The Doctor's Wife* (novel). Tokyo, New York, and San Francisco: Kodansha International, 1978.

Benedict, Ruth. *The Chrysanthemum and the Sword: Patterns of Japanese Culture.* New York: World Publishing Co., 1972 (copyright 1946).

Confessions of Lady Nijō (memoirs). Garden City, N.Y.: Anchor Press, 1973.

Danley, Robert Lyons. *In the Shade of Spring Leaves: The Life and Writings of Higuchi Ichiyo. A Woman of Letters in Meiji, Japan.* New Haven, Conn.: Yale University Press, 1981.

Hibbett, Howard, ed. *Contemporary Japanese Literature: An Anthology of Fiction, Film, and Other Writing Since 1945.* New York: Alfred A. Knopf, 1977.

Higuchi, Chiyoko. *Her Place in the Sun: Women Who Shaped Japan.* Tokyo: The East Publications, Inc., 1973.

Ihara, Saikaku. *Five Women Who Loved Love* (fiction). Rutland, Vt., and Tokyo: Charles E. Tuttle Co., 1956.

―――. *The Life of an Amorous Woman and Other Writings* (fiction). Norfolk, Conn.: New Directions, 1963.

Japanese University Women: Issues and Views, vols., I. & II. Tokyo: Japanese Association of University Women, 1974.

Kawabata Yasunari. *Beauty and Sadness.* Translated by Howard Hibbett. New York: Alfred A. Knopf, 1975.

―――. *House of the Sleeping Beauties and Other Stories.* Transl. by Howard G. Seidensticker. Tokyo and Palo Alto: Kodansha International Ltd., 1969.

―――. *Snow Country.* Translated by Edward G. Seidensticker. New York: Berkley Publishing Co., 1968 (copyright: Alfred A. Knopf, 1956).

*Keene, Donald, transl. and ed. *Anthology of Japanese Literature.* New York: Grove Press, Inc., 1955.

―――. *The Old Woman, The Wife, and The Archer: Three Modern Japanese Short Novels.* New York: The Viking Press, 1961.

Lebra, Joyce, Paulson, Joy, and Powers, Elizabeth, eds. *Women in Changing Japan.* Boulder, Colo.: Westview Press, 1976.

Lebra, Takie Sugiyama, and Lebra, William P., eds. *Japanese Culture and Behavior: Selected Readings.* Honolulu: East-West Center, 1973.

Mishima, Sumie. *The Broader Way: A Woman's Life in the New Japan.* Westport, Conn.: Greenwood Press, 1971 (copyright 1953).

Mishima, Yukio. *After the Banquet.* Translated by Donald Keene. New York: Berkley Publishing Co., 1971 (copyright: Alfred A. Knopf, 1963).

―――. *Madame de Sade* (play). Translated by Donald Keene. New York: Grove Press, Inc., 1967.

―――. *The Sailor Who Fell from Grace with the Sea.* Translated by John Nathan. New York: Berkley Publishing Co., 1971 (copyright: Alfred A. Knopf, 1965).

―――. *The Sound of Waves.* Translated by Meredith Weatherby. New York: Berkley Publishing Co., 1970 (copyright: Alfred A. Knopf, 1956).

―――. *Thirst for Love.* Translated by Alfred H. Marks. New York: Berkley Publishing Co., 1971 (copyright: Alfred A. Knopf, 1969).

*Mishima, Yukio (pseud.), and Bownas, Geoffrey, eds. *New Writing in Japan.* Harmondsworth, Middlesex, England: Penguin Books, 1972.

*Morris, Ivan, transl. & ed. *As I Crossed a Bridge of Dreams: Recollections of a Woman in Eleventh-Century Japan*. New York: Dial Press, 1971.

————. *Modern Japanese Stories: An Anthology*. Rutland, Vt., and Tokyo: Charles E. Tuttle Co., 1968 (copyright 1962).

*Murasaki, Shikibu. *The Tale of Genji (Genji monogatari)*. Seidensticker, Edward D., transl. New York: Alfred A. Knopf, 1976.

Suematsu, Kencho, transl. Rutland, Vt., and Tokyo: Charles E. Tuttle Co., 1974.

Waley, Arthur, transl. New York: Modern Library, 1960.

Nagai, Kafu. *Geisha in Rivalry* (fiction). Rutland, Vt., and Tokyo: Charles E. Tuttle Co., 1963.

Nakane, Chie. *Japanese Society*. Berkeley and Los Angeles: University of California Press, 1970.

Sei Shonagon, *The Pillow Book of* (memoirs). Translated and edited by Ivan Morris. New York: Columbia University Press, 1967.

Seidensticker, Edward, transl. and ed. *The Gossamer Years: The Diary of a Noblewoman of Japan*. Rutland, Vt., and Tokyo: Charles E. Tuttle Co., 1964.

*Seidensticker, E.G., Bester, Jolen, and Morris, Ivan, transl. and eds. *Modern Japanese Short Stories*. Tokyo: Japan Publications, 1970.

Sugimoto, Etsu (Inagaki). *A Daughter of the Samurai* (fiction). Garden City, N.Y.: Doubleday & Co., 1926.

Takasawa, Keiichi. *Women of Japan*. Tokyo: Tokyo News Service, 1955.

Tale of the Lady Ochikubo, The. Translated and edited by Wilfred Whitehouse and Eizo Yanagisawa. Garden City, N.Y.: Doubleday & Co./Anchor Books, 1971.

*Tanizaki, Junichiro. *Seven Japanese Tales*. New York: Berkley Publishing Corp., 1970 (copyright 1963).

————. *Diary of a Mad Old Man*. Translated by Howard Hibbett. New York: Berkley Publishing Co., 1971 (copyright by Knopf, 1965).

————. *The Key* (novel). New York: Alfred A. Knopf, 1961.

————. *The Makioka Sisters* (novel). New York: Grosset & Dunlap, 1966 (copyright 1957).

Vogel, Ezra F. *Japan's New Middle Class*. Berkeley, Los Angeles, and London: University of California Press, 1963.